OXFORD STUDIES IN AFRICAN AFFAIRS

General Editors

JOHN HARGREAVES *and* GEORGE SHEPPERSON

INTERNATIONAL BOUNDARIES
OF EAST AFRICA

A British Boundary Commission in Africa, 1903

INTERNATIONAL BOUNDARIES OF EAST AFRICA

BY

A. C. McEWEN

OXFORD
AT THE CLARENDON PRESS
1971

Oxford University Press, Ely House, London W. 1

GLASGOW   NEW YORK   TORONTO   MELBOURNE   WELLINGTON
CAPE TOWN   SALISBURY   IBADAN   NAIROBI   DAR ES SALAAM   LUSAKA   ADDIS ABABA
BOMBAY   CALCUTTA   MADRAS   KARACHI   LAHORE   DACCA
KUALA LUMPUR   SINGAPORE   HONG KONG   TOKYO

PRINTED IN GREAT BRITAIN
AT THE UNIVERSITY PRESS, OXFORD
BY VIVIAN RIDLER
PRINTER TO THE UNIVERSITY

PREFACE

THIS book is based on a thesis submitted to the University of East Africa as part of the requirements for the degree of Master of Laws. It represents the results of research undertaken in the three East African capitals and in London. A grateful acknowledgement for their valuable advice on the preparation of the thesis is due to Dr. Ian Brownlie and Mr. S. Picciotto, both former members of the Faculty of Law at The University College, Dar es Salaam.

I have attempted to state the legal position of the East African international boundaries in accordance with the source material available to me on 1 August 1970.

A. C. M.

Ottawa
November 1970

CONTENTS

LIST OF ILLUSTRATIONS

ABBREVIATIONS

A.J.I.L.	*American Journal of International Law*
B.F.S.P.	*British and Foreign State Papers*
B.Y.I.L.	*British Year Book of International Law*
Cd., Cmd., Cmnd.	Command Papers (British)
C.O.	Colonial Office Records, Public Record Office, London
D.L.R.	*Dominion Law Reports*
E.A.L.R.	East Africa Protectorate Law Reports
E.S.R.	*Empire Survey Review*, London
F.O.	Foreign Office Records, Public Record Office, London
F.O.C.P.	Foreign Office Confidential Print, Public Record Office, London
G.N.	Government Notice
Geog. J.	*The Geographical Journal*, London
H.C. Deb.	House of Commons Debates, London
H.L. Deb.	House of Lords Debates, London
Hague *Recueil*	Académie de droit international, *Recueil des cours*
Hertslet	Sir Edward Hertslet, *The Map of Africa by Treaty*, H.M.S.O., London, 3rd edn., 1909. Three volumes and a collection of maps
I.C.J. Rep.	*International Court of Justice Reports*
I.C.L.Q.	*International and Comparative Law Quarterly*
J.M.A.S.	*The Journal of Modern African Studies*, Cambridge
L.N.	Legal Notice
L.N.T.S.	*League of Nations Treaty Series*
Mitt.	*Mitteilungen aus den deutschen Schutzgebieten*, Berlin
O.A.U.	Organization of African Unity.
P.C.I.J.	Permanent Court of International Justice
R.I.A.A.	*Reports of International Arbitral Awards*, United Nations
S.I.	Statutory Instrument
S.R. & O.	Statutory Rules and Orders
T.L.R.	Times Law Reports
U.J.	*The Uganda Journal*, Kampala, Uganda
U.N.T.S.	*United Nations Treaty Series*

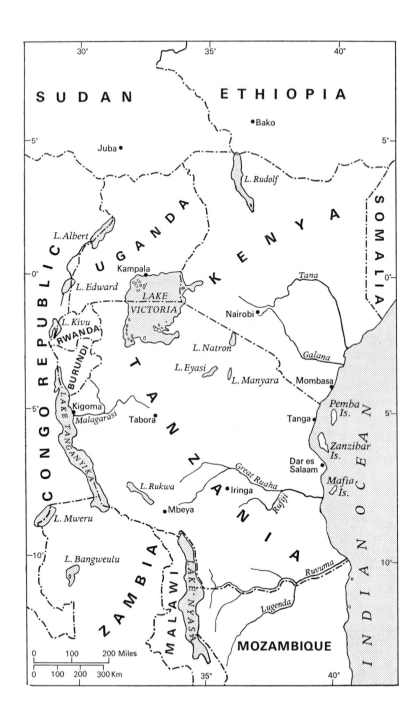

PART ONE

INTRODUCTION

CHAPTER I

Preliminary Remarks

General

LORD CURZON, speaking over sixty years ago, said that boundaries are the razor's edge on which hang suspended the modern issues of war or peace, of life or death to nations, and that just as the protection of the home is the most vital care of the private citizen, so the integrity of her borders is the condition of existence of the State.[1] Boundaries have also been described as the inevitable product of advancing civilization and as human inventions not existing in nature.[2] This form of argument is sometimes used to support the proposition that boundary lines are in themselves an artificial Western concept and that, in Africa particularly, they were unknown to local communities until the advent of European partition in the nineteenth century which demanded precise, unmistakable territorial divisions.

Possibly the question should be looked at in the manner suggested by Fawcett who considers a boundary in terms of a frontier zone the width of which varies in accordance with geographical and sociological circumstances. Thus, he refers to zones of separation and zones of pressure. An example of a zone of separation would be a physical barrier such as a desert or a high mountain range, separating peoples in sparsely inhabited areas, whereas a zone of pressure occurs where favourable living conditions, creating increased population, have brought adjacent communities so closely into contact that the zone itself diminishes and finally becomes a single, widthless line.[3] As a general proposition, this theory has some considerable appeal. Although factual knowledge concerning the territorial limits of African communities in pre-colonial times is often scanty, there are at least a few isolated examples to show that the notion of boundaries as being an entirely foreign concept cannot be unreservedly accepted.

[1] Lord Curzon of Kedleston, *Frontiers*, The Romanes Lecture, Clarendon Press, Oxford, 1907, p. 7.
[2] T. H. Holdich, *Political Frontiers and Boundary Making*, Macmillan, London, 1916, p. 2.
[3] C. B. Fawcett, *Frontiers*, Clarendon Press, Oxford, 1918, pp. 32-3.

Thus, Oldaker describes instances where, in some of the more heavily populated parts of Tanganyika, beating the bounds was required by local custom, and he also cites examples of physical demarcation by the planting of boundary hedges.[1] Even among nomadic peoples, whose tribal limits are seldom if ever static, there is some evidence to show that the extent of pasture land was occasionally demarcated. Lewis cites a Somali practice of cutting marks in the bark of trees in order to indicate the territorial limits of tribal occupation.[2] Such examples are admittedly few in number and inconclusive, but further historical and sociological research would doubtless disclose other instances of tribal boundary demarcation to support a more generalized theory.

Human importance attached to territorial ownership needs little demonstration and, as the value of the land increases, the need for greater precision in determining the extent of the territory becomes more apparent. When land is plentiful, or comparatively worthless in economic terms, less attention need be paid to the establishment of precise boundaries, though in practice this may not be so, and even relatively useless land may be the subject of, or an adjunct to, international disagreement, as may be seen from the Rann of Kutch dispute between India and Pakistan.[3] A colourful analogy is drawn by Kristoff who likens international society in the zonal frontier era to the American West during the period of open-range ranching. There, territorial limits, if any, were ill defined and resented; there was little law and less respect for nominal jurisdiction. Under a boundary regime the international society resembles fenced ranching, each rancher holding a legal title to his land and guarding its limits.[4]

A recent writer,[5] discussing the importance of territory in the animal kingdom, shows that even there the need for boundary determination is sometimes felt. The Arctic wolf pack has a hunting-area of about one hundred square miles, the boundaries of which are fairly precise. As a means of indicating the territorial limits of the pack, and so to provide a warning to possible intruders, the adult

[1] A. A. Oldaker, 'Tribal Customary Land Tenure', *Tanganyika Notes and Records* (1957), at pp. 129, 132.

[2] I. M. Lewis, *Peoples of the Horn of Africa*, International African Institute, London, 1955, p. 43.

[3] For details of the *Rann of Kutch Arbitration* see *International Legal Materials*, vol. vii (1968), pp. 633–705.

[4] W. A. D. Jackson (ed.), *Politics and Geographic Relationships*, Prentice-Hall, 1964, p. 143.

[5] R. Ardrey, *The Territorial Imperative*, Atheneum, New York, 1966.

wolves periodically perambulate the boundaries and demarcate them by squirting urine, the fragrance of which is reinforced by the output of a special scent gland.[1] Another creature, the howling monkey, which lacks the prominent scent glands of the wolf, has adopted a different, and possibly more human, device to establish his territorial claims. Each band of howling monkeys warns its neighbours by emitting piercing cries, the aural reception of which indicates to outsiders the extent of territory claimed by the band. Should two rival groups of these animals meet at some point where territorial limits are vague, then all boundary arguments are settled by discovering which side can out-howl the other.[2]

The Scope of the Work

Part II of this work attempts to bring into relief some of the more important legal and geographical aspects of boundaries, especially as they relate to East Africa. The treatment is not intended to be exhaustive but is offered as a supplement to well-known general works on boundaries, such as those by Adami, Boggs, Jones, and de Lapradelle which, despite their excellence, necessarily give a limited consideration to any particular geographical area. More recently, Dr. Cukwurah has produced a valuable text on the settlement of international boundary disputes though, once again, considerations of space make the treatment somewhat general in scope. Despite the title of the present work, it is hoped that Part II will offer information of value to the general reader whose interest in boundaries is not restricted solely to East Africa. The material offered in Part II is admittedly selective; some topics such as the acquisition of territory and state succession have been sketched in outline only, and further reference on these points should be made to one or more of the many standard texts on international law. The attempted emphasis, however, is on state practice, especially as it concerns, or is likely to concern, East Africa, and it is for this reason that some criticism is offered of traditional juristic views concerning, for example, the effect of avulsion on a boundary river, and the respective authority of written boundary descriptions and maps. Particular stress is given to the boundary resolution of the Organization of African Unity,

---

[1] Ibid., pp. 9–10. Ardrey points out that the wolf is a faithful monogamous creature whose micturition, unlike that of dogs, has no sexual associations.

[2] Ibid., p. 10.

passed in 1964, which has helped to dispel some pre-independence fears of eventual territorial conflict caused by a new fragmentation of Africa. Survey techniques, the composition of mixed boundary commissions and related matters have been only lightly touched upon, not because they are unimportant, but because they must be regarded as peripheral to the main study. Those interested in pursuing these topics will find appropriate references in the bibliography.

Part III forms the main body of this work. It undertakes to show the historical background, legal origin, and present legal status of each of the fifteen international East African boundaries, and to discuss in detail any disputed or problem areas. In each instance, except in the case of the Uganda–Congo boundary, a complete written boundary description is reproduced from appropriate treaties and other sources. Uganda presents a unique situation, since she alone of the three East African countries gives a complete description of her territorial boundaries, in Schedule I to her current (1967) constitution. Obviously this schedule forms an important, and somewhat unusual, official statement as to what Uganda regards as her territorial limits. Close comparison between the schedule and the boundary descriptions contained in the original instruments establishing the various portions of Uganda's boundaries reveals that textual differences are of a comparatively minor nature, and that they stem, for the most part, from clarifying protocols or agreements that were drawn up after the signing of the original boundary instruments. Three examples may be mentioned. First, various protocols, concerning additional demarcation of the Uganda–Congo boundary, which were not included in the Anglo-Belgian agreement of 1915, are, in effect, incorporated in the schedule.[1] Second, the exact location of the Uganda–Sudan boundary, west of the Nile, especially that portion originally described as 'the southern boundary of the Kuku tribe', is now more precisely determined in the schedule.[2] Third, a completely detailed description of the base of the Turkana Escarpment on the Uganda–Kenya boundary, following the demarcation by a joint commission, is given in the schedule by a series of bearings and distances, and references to boundary pillars, thereby precisely indicating the location of a boundary portion that previously had been uncertain.[3] For the sake of convenience, therefore, it was decided to include as an appendix Schedule I in its entirety. The reproduction in Part III of detailed boundary descriptions

---

[1] Below, p. 248.   [2] Below, p. 262.   [3] Below, p. 253.

contained in the instruments by which these boundaries were formally established provides a handy source of reference, though it is recommended that recourse should be had, wherever possible, to original boundary agreement material, such as treaties, protocols, and boundary commission reports. One of the points made in Chapter IV is the frequent absence or inadequacy of maps to illustrate international boundaries. The set of simplified boundary diagrams included in this work has been prepared as a general aid to the reader by depicting the location of each of the boundaries under discussion. As in the case of written descriptions, however, reference to copies of maps attached to original protocols and treaties should be made wherever these are conveniently available.

The object of Part IV is to provide a brief review of the preceding chapters and to underline a few points which are regarded as having particular significance. Some recommendations are offered concerning the removal of certain existing boundary anomalies which, although they may not at present form the subject of actual dispute, could no doubt be adjusted easily and amicably by the interested parties, thereby removing possible causes of boundary friction in the future.

Maritime boundaries, with their associated problems of contiguous zones and continental shelves, are felt to lie outside the proper limits of this work and are not therefore considered in detail. For convenience, however, Appendix B sets out the national declarations concerning the extent of the territorial seas of Tanzania and Kenya, together with those of their respective neighbours, Mozambique and the Somali Republic.

PART TWO

SOME LEGAL ISSUES AFFECTING TITLE TO TERRITORY

CHAPTER II

Some African Territorial Problems

(a) Acquisition of Territory by Treaty, Cession, and Conquest

SIR EDWARD HERTSLET, in the preface to the 1894 edition of his *Map of Africa by Treaty*, says that the object of the work is to facilitate the examination of title deeds of European Powers who, by treaty, conquest, or cession, or under the name of a protectorate, have succeeded in obtaining a footing in the continent.[1] The question as to whether or not the methods used by the imperial powers to partition Africa fall precisely into one or other of the doctrinal moulds from which territorial sovereignty has been traditionally formed is perhaps now of more practical interest than might have been supposed in the late nineteen-fifties and early nineteen-sixties, when the vast majority of colonial territories in Africa stood at the threshold of independence. Indeed, at that time there were grounds for doubting whether African states would continue to accept as binding the principles of international law that were essentially European in origin, especially those relating to territorial acquisition of colonial possessions which, because of their dependent status, were not usually recognized as true subjects of international law.[2] New African states, however, have shown themselves to be less concerned with tracing roots of title in terms of the traditional forms of international law, than with the practical realization that whatever might be the injustices wrought by imperial partition it is better to accept inherited territorial boundaries than to plunge the continent into a readjustment of frontiers that would in effect be a new scramble for Africa. This is borne out by the important boundary resolution passed by the Organization of African Unity in 1964, to which later reference will be made. The traditional modes of territorial acquisition, however, are not entirely irrelevant, since they may still have to be considered when dealing with boundary disputes between individual African states for, it must be emphasized, the acknowledgement by

---

[1] Hertslet, i. vi.
[2] B. V. A. Röling, *International Law in an Expanded World*, pp. 11–13.

O.A.U. members that inherited boundaries should now be respected does not in itself provide a clue as to what those boundaries are, nor can it guarantee the prevention of future disputes concerning the location on the ground of a particular boundary line.

Treaties and Cession

A generally accepted view was that treaties could be concluded only between true subjects of international law, that is, sovereign states. Although the word treaty is often used to describe negotiations between a European power and the ruler of an African community it has been frequently given an ambivalent meaning, since for some purposes it was regarded as an internationally binding agreement, and in other instances it was looked on more in terms of a commercial contract such as might be concluded under private law. A further complicating factor is that the negotiations were often concluded by the local community not with a European state in its sovereign capacity but with agents of a private commercial enterprise which lacked official treaty-making power.[1] Such treaties served a variety of purposes; political, commercial, military protection, anti-slavery, and so on. Representatives of commercial companies often carried standard treaty forms on which they hoped to secure the signature of a local chief that would gain them the desired objective. A first-hand account of how this practice operated in Uganda in the late nineteenth century is given by Thruston:

I had a bundle of printed treaties which I was to make as many people sign as possible. This signing is an amiable farce, which is supposed to impose upon foreign governments, and to be the equivalent of an occupation. . . . A ragged untidy European, who in any civilised country would be in danger of being taken up by the police as a vagrant, lands at a native village, the people run away; he shouts out after them to come back, holding out before them a shilling's worth of beads . . . the so-called interpreter pretends to explain the treaty to the chief. The chief does not understand a word of it, but he looks pleased as he receives another present of beads; a mark is made on a printed treaty by the chief, and another by the interpreter, the vagrant, who professes to be the representative of a great empire, signs his name. . . . The boat sails away, and the new ally and protégé of England or France immediately throws the treaty into the fire.[2]

[1] See, however, Art. 2 of the Royal Charter granted in 1888 to the Imperial British East Africa Company which authorized the negotiation of treaties and cessions with local rulers, subject to the approval of the British Government. Hertslet, i. 348.

[2] A. B. Thruston, *African Incidents*, John Murray, London, 1900, pp. 170–1.

Despite an outward appearance of formality, even when expressed less crudely than in the instance cited above, the prevailing opinion of European signatories was that the 'form of the legal relations created by such contracts is most generally that of suzerain and vassal, or of the so-called colonial protectorate. In substance, it is not an agreement between equals . . .'.[1]

Even when those African rulers, like the Sultan of Zanzibar, who were internationally regarded as the head of a sovereign state with full treaty-making capacity,[2] entered into negotiations with European powers, it was necessary to see whether all the elements of treaty making were present to discover whether a binding agreement had in fact been concluded. Thus, in the *Lamu Arbitration* of 1889, the German claim to the island of Lamu was defeated, in part, by the fact that the verbal agreement by which she alleged to have been granted the island was in an inadequate form. The arbitrator stated that whereas no law prescribed any special form of treaty: 'the adoption of the written form is particularly necessary in dealings with the Governments of but little-civilized nations, which often only attach binding force to promises made in a solemn form or in writing'.[3] He also went on to say that although the good faith of the German negotiator was not impugned, it was impossible to check the exact terms of the verbal agreement since the words of the Sultan 'were spoken in Arabic and gathered and translated by a dragoman, without it being possible to check the accuracy of such translation, and their interpretation was neither confirmed by the Sultan (who died in 1888) nor acknowledged by his successor'.[4] For these and other reasons Germany was unable to sustain her claim to Lamu.

The typical European view as to the international validity of agreements between states and local rulers of territories 'not recognized as members of the community of nations'[5] was expressed in the *Island of Palmas Case* where the arbitrator, Judge Huber, said in 1928 that such contracts:

are not, in the international law sense, treaties or conventions capable of creating rights and obligations such as may, in international law, arise out of treaties. But, on the other hand, contracts of this nature are not wholly void of indirect effects on situations governed by international law; if they

---

[1] *Island of Palmas Case*, 2 R.I.A.A. 829, at p. 858.

[2] The Sultan of Zanzibar, for example, attended the Brussels Slave Trade Conference of 1890 in his capacity as head of state.

[3] *Island of Lamu Award*, Hertslet, iii. 891, at p. 894.

[4] Ibid., p. 895.   [5] 2 R.I.A.A. 858.

do not constitute titles in international law, they are none the less facts of which that law must in certain circumstances take account.[1]

The view of this distinguished arbitrator makes it clear that whether or not an agreement between a European state and a local ruler was an international treaty, properly so called, it could still have evidentiary value. Perhaps it could be referred to as a kind of quasi treaty. In Africa, particularly, European states were anxious to support their claims of 'effective occupation' by reference to paper evidence, however dubious its origin. Examples may be found on the Kenya–Tanzania boundary where the line skirting Mount Kilimanjaro was placed in accordance with the respective treaties made between local chiefs and British and German nationals.[2] The hinterland question involving the disposition of Uganda as a British or a German sphere of influence was solved partly on the basis of treaties alleged to have been made by Stanley.[3] Other examples can be found, such as the treaties concluded between Harry Johnston and the Nyasa chiefs which contributed to the securing of British control around the lake.[4] Legally speaking, the treaties may have been suspect, but their importance was mainly political since they could be used as bargaining counters to provide a more or less harmonious means of settling the rival ambitions of imperial powers. The fact that in many instances the treaties were concluded by individual Europeans acting in a private capacity caused no great problem since their home governments, when it suited them to do so, adopted or ratified the treaties.[5]

Cession of territory in Africa raises questions concerning consideration, capacity, and subject matter. Where cession, rather than a treaty of protection, was involved, consideration was payable but its adequacy, as in private law, was usually immaterial. 'I have known a valuable concession purchased by the present of an old pair of boots', said Lugard.[6] An exaggeration, perhaps, but examples can be found where the consideration was very small. Harry Johnston obtained his Taveta concession, on the slopes of Kilimanjaro, for a quantity of beads, handkerchiefs, and American cloth,[7] and it was this concession which, in part, determined the ultimate location of the boundary

---

[1] 2 *R.I.A.A*, 858.   [2] Below, p. 135.   [3] Below, p. 268.   [4] Below, p. 175.
[5] As, e.g. in the case of Johnston's Kilimanjaro and Stanley's Mufumbiro treaties.
[6] F. D. Lugard, 'Treaty Making in Africa', *Geog. J.* 1 (1893), 53.
[7] Below, p. 135, n. 4.

between Kenya and Tanzania. Another instance concerned the small island of Mussa, on the Somali coast, which was transferred in 1840 by the Sultan of Tajura to the British East India Company for ten bags of rice.[1] Capacity to cede frequently raised difficult problems since it could not always be guaranteed that the European negotiator was in fact dealing with the legitimate ruler of the community or that, even if he was, the ruler had power to dispose of communal territory without the consent of the tribe.[2] Two cases where issues of this kind arose were the Island of Bulama (1870), and the Delagoa Bay (1875) disputes. The first case involved disagreement between Britain and Portugal as to the ownership of the island of Bolama (Bulama), and a portion of the mainland, in what is now Portuguese Guinea. Britain claimed sovereignty by virtue of an alleged cession in 1792 to a British naval officer, Captain Beaver, who established on the hitherto uninhabited island a colony which lasted for about eighteen months. The arbitrator, President Ulysses S. Grant of the United States of America, found *inter alia* that the island was discovered by Portugal in 1446, that long before 1792 Portuguese settlements were established on the coast, and that Bulama was so adjacent to the mainland 'that animals cross at low water'. Apart from these considerations, however, the arbitrator found that the Kings of Niobana and Matchora, who purported to cede the island and the mainland territory to Beaver, had no capacity to do so since they were at that time under the sovereignty of Portugal which had never acquiesced in the alleged transfer.[3] In the *Delagoa Bay Award*, the arbitrator, Marshal McMahon of France, found that certain territories adjoining the Portuguese coastal mainland of Mozambique had been ceded by a treaty made in 1823 between Britain and the chiefs of Tembe and Maputo. He held that the attempted cession was void since it violated the rights of Portugal to whom the chiefs were subject and who had since acknowledged their dependence in the presence of the Portuguese authorities. Moreover, even had the parties been capable of contracting, the failure to undertake certain essential conditions prescribed by the 1823 treaty made the transaction null and void.[4]

[1] Hertslet, i. 408.
[2] For a discussion whether the agreements signed between the Masai tribe and the British Government in 1904 and 1911 were valid treaties, and whether Act of State could be pleaded as a defence to a breach of such agreements see *Ol Le Njogo* v. *A. G.* (The Masai Case), (1913), 5 E.A.L.R. 70.
[3] *Island of Bulama Award*, Hertslet, iii. 988.
[4] *Delagoa Bay Award*, Hertslet, iii. 996.

Although agreement might exist between European states as to the formal completion of a treaty of cession concluded with local rulers, the extent of the territory actually ceded was not always easy to determine. A typical illustration is the *Barotse Boundary Award*,[1] concerning what is now the Zambia–Angola border. By Article 4 of the Anglo-Portuguese treaty of 11 June 1891, the western line of division separating the British from the Portuguese sphere of influence extended to 'the territory of the Barotse Kingdom', and in 1905 the King of Italy, acting as arbitrator, was called upon to determine what was the Barotse western boundary in 1891. In order to do this he examined evidence concerning the extent to which the exercise of authority, payment of tribute, and submission of tribal disputes to the King of Barotse as paramount ruler, had in fact taken place. In the result, however, the arbitrator found that the absence of distinguishing geographical features, imperfect knowledge of the country and 'the notorious instability of the tribes and their frequent intermingling' made a precise interpretation of the treaty impossible, and he decided in favour of an arbitrary boundary.[2]

Conquest

The legal status of African communities, as traditionally defined in the writings of classical Western jurists, has been that of mere objects of international law whose disposition was controllable only by recognized states that alone constituted true international subjects. Nor did it appear to matter whether or not the communities succeeded in ousting the control of the foreign state by force of arms, for this was not regarded as a conquest in the international legal sense:

> Conquest only operates as a cause of loss of sovereignty when there is war between two States and by reason of the defeat of one of them sovereignty over territory passes from the loser to the victorious State. The principle does not apply in a case where a settlement has been established in a distant country and its inhabitants are massacred by the aboriginal population.[3]

In the light of post colonial development it is small wonder that many modern writers tend to discard or challenge views, such as those quoted, which appear much too sweeping in scope. As with other branches of international law, however, the answer is that traditional

---

[1] *Barotse Award*, Hertslet, iii. 1074.   [2] Ibid., p. 1076.
[3] *Eastern Greenland Case*, P.C.I.J., A/B53, p. 47.

doctrine is no longer in itself sufficient. International law, like common law, must be regarded as flexible and evolutionary, and not cast into some pre-determined, immutable mould. Factual situations are more important than a supposed, and artificial, theory.

(b) Spheres of Influence

Many of the territorial agreements made between imperial powers refer to the allocation of 'spheres of influence'. Since the expression occurs in several of the treaties that partitioned East Africa it deserves examination. 'Sphere of influence' is not a term of art. Hall says that no definite meaning has been attached to it and that it implies a moral claim rather than a true right.[1] Holdich explains its practical effect by saying that a sphere of influence involves an agreement between two powers, made over the heads of the nominal rulers of the sphere, to limit and respect each other's prospective interests within a particular geographical area. The state establishing a sphere of influence thereby 'sets up a warning to trespassers'.[2] Another writer has pointed to the positive and the negative aspects of a sphere of influence.[3] On the one hand, the influencing power may be more concerned with excluding outsiders, of which one illustration might be the Monroe Doctrine. On the other hand, it may be anxious to exert its own superior control in the sphere, sometimes through indigenous political agencies and sometimes by its own direct administration. It has also been suggested that in some instances the creation of a sphere of influence might be merely 'alienation in disguise', in an attempt to soothe national susceptibilities.[4] Possibly this latter situation is applicable to territories such as Zanzibar which, unlike many other parts of Africa, was regarded by the European powers as a sovereign state.

The origin of the phrase is uncertain but it appeared in diplomatic language at least as early as 1869 and became a useful description for 'pegging out a potential claim'.[5] Lord Curzon said that a sphere of influence, though a 'less developed form than a Protectorate . . . is more developed than a Sphere of Interest. It implies a stage at which

[1] W. E. Hall, *A Treatise on International Law*, 8th edn. (ed. A. P. Higgins), 1924, para. 38b.

[2] T. H. Holdich, *Political Frontiers and Boundary Making*, pp. 96–7.

[3] G. W. Rutherford, 'Spheres of Influence: An Aspect of Semi-Suzerainty', 20 *A.J.I.L.* 300 (1926).

[4] Ibid., p. 302.   [5] Lord Curzon of Kedleston, *Frontiers*, p. 42.

no exterior Power but one may assert itself in the territory so described . . .'.[1] This attempt to identify a sphere of influence as a particular stage of development appears to be somewhat artificial and should be taken as a general description rather than a rigid classification. A sphere of interest, in its strict sense, may have referred to a trade, rather than a political, arrangement,[2] though it is not at all clear that the distinction was always made in diplomatic documents. Another expression, 'sphere of action', was also sometimes used, possibly as synonymous for 'sphere of influence'. Whether or not any valid theoretical distinctions can be drawn between these various expressions it is quite apparent from the titles of treaties that they were used more or less indiscriminately, and no doubt the draftsmen were inclined to regard them as equivalent terms.[3]

What is clear, however, is that a sphere of influence in Africa was a transitional phase; a kind of amorphous prelude to colonial crystallization. Its international legality could be tested by the reactions of non-contracting states. If they made no objection within a reasonable period of time their acceptance would be presumed. For example, the Congo State did not recognize the north-western limits of the British sphere in East Africa, as laid down in the Anglo-German agreement of 1890,[4] until her own agreement with Britain in 1894.[5] France did not recognize the limits of the spheres established by this latter agreement until 1899.[6]

Very often the treaty creating the sphere of influence contained provisions for the establishment of definite boundaries between the adjacent territorial sovereigns. Thus the Anglo-German agreement of 1890 specifically provided that the limits of the two spheres were subject to rectification by future agreement between the two powers, in accordance with local requirements.[7] Rectification of these limits subsequently occurred on the boundaries separating Tanzania from Malawi[8] and Zambia,[9] Uganda from Rwanda[10] and Tanzania,[11] and Kenya from Tanzania.[12] In other instances, the partitioning power was unable or unwilling to press its claim as far as the theoretical

---

[1] Lord Curzon of Kedleston, *Frontiers*, p. 42.

[2] T. E. Holland, *Lectures on International Law*, 1933, pp. 81–3.

[3] Many examples exist, of which one of each type may be cited. For 'Sphere of Influence' see Hertslet, iii. 948; 'Sphere of Interest' see Hertslet, iii. 925; 'Sphere of Action' see Hertslet, iii. 1014.

[4] Hertslet, iii. 899.   [5] Hertslet, ii. 578.   [6] Hertslet, ii. 796.

[7] Hertslet, iii. 899, Art. VI.   [8] Below, p. 179, n. 1.

[9] Below, p. 218.   [10] Below, pp. 272–3.   [11] Below, p. 280.

[12] Below, p. 144.

limits of its sphere of influence. By her agreement with Italy in 1891, Britain's northern boundary extended as far as the parallel of 6° north latitude, but this was unacceptable to Ethiopia who, taking her cue from the European principle that territorial claims in Africa depended upon effective occupation, succeeded in reducing Britain's claim by forcing her to accept a treaty line considerably further to the south of that defined in the Anglo-Italian agreement.[1] Again, on the Uganda–Congo border, the original western limit of the British sphere of influence was altered as a result of the respective pressures by France and King Leopold II of Belgium.[2] Although, as in the last two examples mentioned, the limits of spheres of influence were frequently described in terms of latitude or longitude, in other instances they were deliberately left fluid. The western portion of the British northern limit as established by the Anglo-German agreement of 1890, along what later became the Uganda–Sudan boundary, extended to 'the confines of Egypt', an extremely vague term since at that time it was impossible to say exactly where Egypt's southern border was, especially since Mahdist forces then occupied a considerable part of her Sudanese territory.[3]

East African experience shows that it would be wrong to regard spheres of influence as mere figments of territorial imagination and aspiration on the part of the colonizing powers. The original limits of the spheres, whether based on vague 'hinterland' doctrines or on so-called 'effective occupation'[4] were in most instances reasonably specific, and subsequently gave rise to more precise boundaries through such consolidating processes as additional boundary agreements, recognition, and acquiescence.

(c) State Succession to Boundaries

Lord McNair, speaking of state succession with respect to boundaries, cites a traditional view that treaty stipulations defining the boundaries of a territory that is later ceded by one of the contracting parties to a third state are of a real nature, and that their burden and benefit run with the territory ceded. In other words, boundary treaties pass from contract to conveyance, and the transaction is unaffected by the fact that the original parties have changed. He expresses

---

[1] Below, p. 105.   [2] Below, pp. 235–6.   [3] Below, p. 257.
[4] The hinterland and effective occupation doctrines are considered below, Ch. XIV, p. 176, and Ch. XX, p. 267.

another view that treaty stipulations defining a boundary form historical matter which, together with other facts, may be resorted to for
the purposes of ascertaining the quantum of a piece of territory, and
that it is unnecessary to consider whether or not the stipulations
survive.[1]

It must be remembered, however, that what have hitherto been
regarded as binding rules of international law are essentially European in origin and it by no means follows that they can or should
receive uncritical acceptance throughout the world community. As
a recent writer asks rhetorically, can Europe which has gambled
away its power and prestige in European wars, demand or even expect
that its law will continue to be universally accepted?[2] Other learned
writers have grappled with the problem of attempting to express a
modern exposition of state succession and their views reinforce the
growing opinion that traditional doctrinal solutions no longer suffice.
In particular, criticism has been offered concerning such questions
as whether a particular treaty can be regarded as real or personal,
and whether some elements of a treaty can survive if they are severed
from the remainder.[3] For reasons already advanced it is no longer
sufficient to point to isolated instances where new European or
European-influenced states have regarded themselves as bound by
pre-succession boundary treaties. What is also relevant is the attitude
displayed by those new states which, especially since World War II,
have emerged from colonial status or similar forms of tutelage. With
respect to these new states the one thing that appears certain is that
they have not as yet accepted universally binding principles regarding
state succession and prefer to deal with individual problems as they
arise. As Zemanek points out, the inter-African and inter-Asian practice concerning succession to treaties *in rem* is still in the making.[4]

Nevertheless, it would be an overstatement to say that the newly
independent African and Asian states reject *in toto* the idea of succession to pre-independence treaties. State practice in this respect is
of the highest significance and may in time lead to more general

[1] McNair, *The Law of Treaties*, Clarendon Press, Oxford, 1961, pp. 656–7.
[2] B. V. A. Röling, *International Law in an Expanded World*, p. 13.
[3] A. P. Lester, 'State Succession to Treaties in the Commonwealth', 12
I.C.L.Q. 475 (1963); 14 *I.C.L.Q.* 262 (1965); K. Zemanek, 'State Succession After
Decolonization', 116 Hague *Recueil* 187 (1965); D. P. O'Connell, *State Succession
in Municipal Law and International Law*, vol. ii, *International Relations*, Cambridge University Press, 1967.
[4] Zemanek, op. cit., p. 242.

conclusions than are at present possible.[1] Speaking with reference to the *Temple Case*,[2] O'Connell stresses the fact that the importance of the decision, so far as the law of state succession is concerned, lies in the implication that the original boundary treaty, made in 1904 when Cambodia was a French colonial territory, continued to bind Thailand and Cambodia after the latter attained independence. At the same time he raises the point that it is not clear whether the assumption of succession to the boundary treaty was based on the personal succession of Cambodia to all French treaties made on her behalf, or whether the 1904 agreement was a dispositive treaty that ran with the territory regardless of the change of sovereignty.[3]

It has also been pointed out that where deviations from the 'rule of automatic succession to dispositive treaties' occur they may be due more to political considerations or to the operation of the *clausula rebus sic stantibus* than to an utter rejection of automatic succession.[4] On the other hand it is equally important to ensure adequate evaluation of all the material that does indicate acceptance of treaties by successor states. Obscure though the theoretical problem may be, some considerable light has been thrown on the practical question of succession to pre-independence boundary treaties in Africa by a resolution passed in 1964 by the Organization of African Unity. This important expression of African attitude must now be examined.

(d) The Organization of African Unity's Resolution Concerning Boundaries

From the foregoing paragraphs relating to state succession it appears fair to say that although the new African states have reserved attitudes concerning the validity of pre-independence treaties, colonial boundary agreements, on the whole, are likely to survive. This conclusion finds support from an important resolution passed by the

[1] For an expression of the official attitudes of some African states towards pre-independence treaties see *The Effect of Independence on Treaties*, Int. Law Assoc., Stevens, London, 1965, pp. 374 et seq. Tanzania's position is stated by E. E. Seaton and S. T. M. Maliti, 'Treaties and Succession of States and Governments in Tanzania', a paper prepared for the African Conference of International Law, Lagos, 14–18 March 1967. Dag Hammarskjöld Foundation (typescript).

[2] *Case Concerning the Temple of Preah Vihear* (*Cambodia v. Thailand*), *Merits*, I.C.J. Rep. 1962, p. 6.

[3] O'Connell, op. cit., p. 147.

[4] Zemanek, op. cit., p. 242.

Organization of African Unity in July 1964,[1] the text of which is as follows:

The Assembly of Heads of State and Government meeting in its First Ordinary Session in Cairo, U.A.R., from 17 to 21 July 1964:

Considering that border problems constitute a grave and permanent factor of dissension,

Conscious of the existence of extra-African manœuvres aimed at dividing African States,

Considering further that the borders of African States, on the day of their independence, constitute a tangible reality,

Recalling the establishment in the course of the Second Ordinary Session of the Council of the Committee of Eleven charged with studying further measures for strengthening African Unity,

Recognizing the imperious necessity of settling, by peaceful means and within a strictly African framework, all disputes between African States,

Recalling further that all Member States have pledged, under Article VI of the Charter of African Unity, to respect scrupulously all principles laid down in paragraph 3 of Article III of the Charter of the Organization of African Unity,[2]

    1. Solemnly reaffirms the strict respect by all Member States of the Organization for the principles laid down in paragraph 3 of Article III of the Charter of the Organization of African Unity;

    2. Solemnly declares that all Member States pledge themselves to respect the borders existing on their achievement of national independence.

The reason why African states have accepted the validity of their inherited boundaries requires examination. It must be stressed at the outset, however, that the resolution, though enjoining the O.A.U. member states to respect each other's boundaries as they existed at the time of independence, is not in itself a solution to boundary problems such as the Kenya-Somali dispute, that existed prior to independence, or to questions concerning the interpretation of boundary agreements themselves.

Why is it that nearly all the new African states wish to retain their old colonial boundaries? It has become trite to say that the original partition of Africa was undertaken in ignorance, even in

    [1] Organization of African Unity, AHG/Res. 17 (I).
    [2] Paragraph 3 of Art. III states, 'respect for the sovereignty and territorial integrity of each State and for its inalienable right to independent existence'.

defiance, of existing tribal boundaries, and that the indigenous inhabitants, even when persuaded to enter into treaty arrangements with the colonizing or protecting powers, had little real say as to the division of their territories. Kwame Nkrumah, the leading advocate of the rearrangement, and eventual removal, of international boundaries in Africa, bitterly pointed out that the only interested parties not represented at the Berlin Conference of 1884–5 were the inhabitants of Africa.[1] Yet it is very doubtful whether even the attendance of African tribal rulers at Berlin would have produced any significantly different results, since they were inevitably destined to be treated as pawns in the imperial game.[2] Even Holdich, himself responsible for a good deal of colonial delimitation and demarcation, remarked: 'In very few instances in the African partition has the will of the inhabitants been really consulted, nor, indeed, would it be of much use to consult it. Between rival claims to govern these dark-skinned people for their own good, advanced by different European nationalities, it might have been difficult to choose. They want none of them.'[3]

Prior to independence, many African political parties advocated an eventual alteration of colonial boundaries to accord more closely with the wishes of local inhabitants. The All-African Peoples Conference, held in Accra in December 1958, adopted a resolution calling for the early abolition and readjustment of existing boundaries. This was seen as a desirable prelude to the formation of regional groupings, based on cultural, linguistic, and religious affinity, that would eventually become an African Commonwealth.[4] The 1958 Accra resolution, however, was passed at a time when very few African countries had attained independence, and a modification of the former attitude was displayed at the inaugural summit conference of the Organization of African Unity, held in Addis Ababa in May

[1] *Official Records, United Nations General Assembly*, 15th Session, 7 March 1961, A/PV. 961, para. 60.

[2] This, admittedly, is a controversial point. See S. Touval, 'Treaties, Borders, and the Partition of Africa', *Journal of African History*, vol. 7, p. 279, where it is argued that, in some instances at least, local conditions and contractual arrangements with African rulers influenced and shaped the pattern of imperial partition. Also some African rulers, such as Menelik II of Ethiopia, were sufficiently powerful to play an active part in controlling the limits of European expansion. On this see below, Ch. VIII.

[3] T. H. Holdich, *Political Frontiers and Boundary Making*, p. 233.

[4] For text of the resolution see C. Legum, *Pan Africanism*, Pall Mall Press, 1965, pp. 247–50.

1963. The vast majority of delegates to this conference emphasized that whatever might be the moral and historical argument for a readjustment of national boundaries, practical attempts to reshape the map of Africa at the present day might well prove disastrous. Thus, the President of the Malagasy Republic pointed out:

> . . . I am not unaware that, when our colonisers set boundaries between territories, they too often ignored the frontiers of race, language and ethics . . . I do not feel that we can question the existence of unities thus created. It is no longer possible, nor desirable, to modify the boundaries of Nations, on the pretext of racial, religious or linguistic criteria. . . . Indeed, should we take race, religion or language as criteria for setting our boundaries, a few States in Africa would be blotted out from the map.[1]

The Ethiopian Prime Minister stated:

> It is in the interest of all Africans now to respect the frontiers drawn on the maps, whether they are good or bad, by the former colonizers. . . .[2]

Similar remarks were made by the President of Mali:

> . . . we must take Africa as it is, and we must renounce any territorial claims, if we do not wish to introduce what we might call black imperialism in Africa . . . African unity demands of each one of us complete respect for the legacy that we have received from the colonial system, that is to say: maintenance of the present frontiers of our respective states. . . . Indeed, if we take certain parts of Africa in the pre-colonial period, history teaches us that there existed a myriad kingdoms and empires . . . which today have transcended, in the case of certain states, tribal and ethnic differences to constitute a nation, a real nation . . . if we desire that our nations should be ethnic entities, speaking the same language and having the same psychology, then we shall find no single veritable nation in Africa.[3]

The above remarks, and similar views expressed by other delegates, though representing the overwhelming opinion of the conference, were not accepted unanimously, two notable exceptions being Morocco and the Somali Republic. When the Assembly of Heads of State and Government met a year later, in 1964, the Somali President was absent, owing to local constitutional problems, but he instructed his representative at the conference to make it clear that the Somali Republic would categorically reject any resolution seeking to declare

---

[1] *Proceedings of the Summit Conference of Independent African States*, Addis Ababa, May 1963, vol. i, section 2, CIAS/GEN/INF/14.
[2] Ibid., CIAS/GEN/INF/43.   [3] Ibid., CIAS/GEN/INF/33.

the sanctity of existing boundaries between states, and that even if such a resolution was adopted by the Assembly the Somali Republic would not consider herself bound by it.[1] The Somali delegate, after attempting unsuccessfully to have the proposed resolution removed from the agenda, emphasized that, in the absence of his country's head of state, the Somali Republic was not taking her full part in the discussions and could not therefore be regarded as being bound by any action that the Assembly might take on the matter of boundaries. It is reported that President Nyerere, the proposer of the resolution, explained to the Somali delegate that the purpose of the resolution was to reaffirm a principle as a guide for the future, and that its adoption would not prejudice any discussions already in progress. In other words, the Somali delegate apparently took this to mean that the resolution referred only to such future boundary disputes as might arise after the adoption of the resolution, and that disputes already existing, such as those between the Somali Republic and her two neighbours, Kenya and Ethiopia, would not fall within the ambit of the resolution.[2] Whether or not the draft resolution was intended to be confined to future disputes only, it is clear that the final wording makes no such distinction and when the resolution was adopted both the Somali Republic and Morocco reserved their position. The Somali Republic's interpretation of the effect of her reservation was that she thereby brought into effective operation her inherent right to refuse to be bound by the provisions of the resolution. A press release issued by the leader of the Somali delegation on 22 July 1964[3] was followed by a note circulated by the Somali Republic on 1 August 1964 to all member states of the O.A.U. stating that the resolution must be regarded by her as being confined to new disputes, since this had been conceded by the proposer of the resolution, even though it did not find that expression in the final text.[4]

The Somali dispute with Kenya is treated in greater detail in a later chapter, where it will be seen that some progress has been achieved towards an eventual settlement, largely owing to the mediation of President Kaunda of Zambia.[5] The Somali attitude that the O.A.U. boundary resolution should be restricted to disputes arising after July 1964 is significant since it is quite possible that this argument

[1] *The Somali Republic and the Organization of African Unity* (published by the Public Relations Section of the Ministry of Foreign Affairs, Mogadiscio), p. 15.
[2] Ibid., pp. 17–18.   [3] Ibid., p. 20.   [4] Ibid., pp. 23–4.
[5] Below, Ch. IX.

might be raised by other member states should they become involved in disputes which, though appearing to be new, are in fact of long standing. For example, the Tanzania-Malawi controversy concerning Lake Nyasa is regarded by some observers as a new dispute, whereas confusion and doubt as to the exact location of the lake boundary arose half a century ago, possibly longer, and even though Tanzania and Malawi have each accepted the O.A.U. boundary resolution, this does not preclude them from examining all the pre-independence evidence to support their respective claims. In fact, the resolution itself would be meaningless unless it is interpreted as a broad principle of accepting inherited boundaries, since it says nothing, for example, of those cases where colonial boundaries are physically non-existent, or incorrectly demarcated, or where boundary documents are impossible to interpret without recourse to arbitration.

A further difficulty in the resolution lies in determining what is meant by the undertaking to respect boundaries as they existed at the time of the member state's 'achievement of national independence'. As Touval points out, under this formula some of the O.A.U. member states, such as Ethiopia, Morocco, and Liberia, could presumably claim territories which had been theirs during their independent existence prior to the colonial partition in the nineteenth century. This, in essence, is the basis of the Moroccan claims.[1]

Although the resolution attempts to stabilize African national boundaries, its language, viewed in isolation, tends to suggest that boundary disputes between O.A.U. member states should never arise. This is obviously an incorrect interpretation since although one of the main objects of the resolution was to prevent boundary conflict and to assuage the fears of smaller states that they might be swallowed up by larger neighbours on the grounds of pre-independence territorial claims, the framers of the resolution were well aware that boundary disagreements already existed between certain African states and that other disputes were likely to spring up from time to time. One must therefore consider what machinery exists within the framework of the O.A.U. to settle boundary disputes. Article XIX of the O.A.U. Charter declares that member states pledge to settle all disputes among themselves by peaceful means, and to this end decide to establish a Commission of Mediation, Conciliation, and Arbitration. Despite the existence of this article, however, it appears

[1] S. Touval, 'The Organization of African Unity and African Borders', *International Organization*, vol. 21 (1967), pp. 102–27, at p. 125.

that the Commission envisaged has yet to play an active part so far as boundaries are concerned, and that such boundary settlement as has been undertaken under O.A.U. auspices has resulted from the efforts of individual mediators, such as President Kaunda in the Kenya-Somali Republic dispute, or from the joint efforts of mediators and an *ad hoc* commission, as in the Algeria-Morocco dispute.[1] Yet in spite of its inherent weaknesses the O.A.U. resolution, together with Article XIX, appears to represent an amicable and honest effort to reduce inherited boundary disputes by peaceful means. It should not be regarded as an automatic acceptance of the theory of state succession but as an attempt to find an African solution to an inherited African problem.

(e) Uti Possidetis

The O.A.U. boundary resolution of July 1964 is sometimes equated with *uti possidetis*, a doctrine that has been sought to be applied to certain Latin American boundary situations. It is submitted, however, that the analogy is both false and misleading in an African context. Historically, the expression *uti possidetis* derives from Roman law, where it formed one of the Praetorian possessory interdicts. In essence, this interdict was a prohibition by the Praetor against interference with the possession of immovable property; its purpose was to decide which of the claimants should be placed in possession and thereby occupy the favoured position of defendant in the *vindicatio*, or action for ownership. In Roman law, therefore, *uti possidetis* was the award of interim possession, as a preliminary to the establishment of ownership.[2] As a modern authority points out, even so obvious a loan from Roman law as the use of *uti possidetis* in Latin American practice is more indicative of the differences between this remedy in Roman law and its application on the inter-state level than of any supposed similarity.[3] Of what, then, do these differences consist?

Uti possidetis, in international law, has hitherto been restricted to boundary cases in Latin America. Following the disintegration of

---

[1] Touval, op. cit.; S. Chime, 'The Organization of African Unity and African Boundaries', in *African Boundary Problems*, ed. Widstrand, Uppsala, 1969.

[2] H. F. Jolowicz, *Historical Introduction to the Study of Roman Law*, 2nd edn., Cambridge University Press, 1952, pp. 273–4; J. B. Moore, '*Uti Possidetis*: Costa Rica–Panama Arbitration, 1911', in *The Collected Papers of John Bassett Moore*, vol. iii, Yale University Press, 1944.

[3] G. Schwarzenberger, *International Law*, vol. i, Stevens, London, 1957, p. 289.

the Spanish and Portuguese colonial empires in South and Central America, the newly independent republics proclaimed a principle of public international law, to which they gave the name of *uti possidetis juris*, the intended effect of which was to stabilize national boundaries in their theoretical positions at the time of independence, the critical dates being, for South America 1810, and for Central America 1821. Thus, although the nominal form of *uti possidetis* was used, its interpretation and application were considerably different from its employment in Roman law. Furthermore, a doctrine which attempts to crystallize, or maintain the *status quo* of, boundaries is little more than an abstract proposition unless there is factual and tangible identification of the boundaries themselves. At the time of independence in Latin America, this was seldom the case. The reason is that, with the exception of the Portuguese colony of Brazil, the new republics had previously formed part of the Spanish empire, of which they constituted all or part of a local administrative unit, such as a vice-royalty, captaincy-general, or *audiencia*. The limits of these administrative divisions, for the most part, were vaguely known and inadequately defined in the legal instruments purporting to establish them. Spanish occupation, even by 1810, was sparse in many areas and much of the territory nominally within Spanish jurisdiction had not even been explored, much less mapped. In these circumstances, the royal decrees, proclamations, and other declarations establishing the limits of Spanish authority frequently conflicted, overlapped, and failed to indicate even approximately accurate boundaries. Thus, in the *Bolivia-Peru Award* of 1909, the Arbitrator, in attempting to establish the relevant portions of a former vice-royalty and *audiencia*, found that neither of the lines claimed by the contesting parties was established by the evidence and that, in reality, the disputed territory was unexplored in 1810 and had remained so up to a recent period.[1]

The fact that not all the Spanish administrative divisions were effectively occupied was clearly recognized by the new republics themselves, and *uti possidetis* was used by them not merely as a title to what they already possessed in fact but as a legal claim to the unoccupied remainder of what, in effect, was regarded by them as a sphere of influence. As expressed by the Swiss Federal Council in the *Colombia-Venezuela Arbitral Award* of 1922:

This general principle offered the advantage of establishing an absolute rule that there was not in law in the old Spanish America any territory

[1] 11 *R.I.A.A.*, 133, at p. 143.

without a master; while there might exist many regions which had never been occupied by the Spaniards and many unexplored or inhabited by non-civilized aborigines, these regions were reputed to belong in law to which-ever of the Republics succeeded to the Spanish Province to which these territories were attached by virtue of the old Royal ordinances of the Spanish Mother Country. These territories, although not occupied in fact were by common consent deemed as occupied in law from the first hour by the new Republic.[1]

The Swiss Federal Council went on to say that, by the adoption of *uti possidetis*, the new republics hoped to eliminate boundary dis-putes, and that a further implication of the doctrine was that it excluded any part of Latin America from being proclaimed *res nullius* and thereby open to colonization by European powers. To this latter extent, the doctrine anticipated the Monroe Doctrine of 1823.[2]

The question of *uti possidetis* was considered at length by a Special Tribunal in the *Guatemala-Honduras Boundary Arbitration* of 1933, when rival interpretations were pressed by the two claimants. Guate-mala contended that the doctrine meant *uti possidetis de facto*, in other words, that the test should be what territory was actually occupied at the critical date of 1821; while Honduras argued that the doctrine meant possession *de jure*. The Tribunal found that an examination of the views of eminent jurists failed to disclose such a consensus of opinion as would establish a definite criterion for the interpretation of *uti possidetis*. It attempted to resolve the question by considering which, if any, of the contesting states had, prior to its independence, exercised administrative control in the disputed area 'with the will of the Spanish monarch', the evidence of which was to be sought in the old royal decrees. In the event, the Tribunal found that the line of *uti possidetis* of 1821 was difficult to establish, owing to the lack of trustworthy information concerning the colonial period:

Much of this territory was unexplored. Other parts which had occasion-ally been visited were but vaguely known. In consequence, not only had boundaries of jurisdiction not been fixed with precision by the Crown, but there were great areas in which there had been no effort to assert any semblance of administrative authority. . . .[3]

Comparison of the post-colonial position in Latin America with the emergence of independent African states shows that boundary

[1] 1 *R.I.A.A.*, 223, at p. 228.
[2] Ibid. The long-standing claim by the Argentine Republic to the Falkland Islands stems from the doctrine of *uti possidetis*.
[3] 2 *R.I.A.A.*, 1307, at p. 1325.

criteria and attitudes, though possibly possessing some similarities, are of an entirely different character. In the first place, the partition of Africa in the nineteenth century was the subject of intense rivalry between six or more powerful European states; whereas in Latin America only two states, Spain and Portugal, were involved, and their respective interests had been settled, in theory at least, by Papal Bull as long ago as 1493.[1] Secondly, it was soon established that a territorial claim in Africa, even to that convenient political amorphism described as a sphere of influence, could not be supported in the absence of effective occupation. Britain's attitude was expressed in 1887 in the following words: 'Great Britain considers that it has now been admitted in principle by all the parties to the Act of Berlin that a claim of sovereignty in Africa can only be maintained by real occupation of the territory claimed . . .'.[2] This requirement of effective occupation was a contributing factor in the delimitation of the British and German colonies in East Africa.[3] By contrast, the Latin American claim of *uti possidetis* was, in large part, an attempt to establish constructive sovereignty over unoccupied territory. Thirdly, many of the boundaries between the colonial territories in Africa were clearly delimited and demarcated, thereby reducing, if not entirely eliminating, the possibility of disputes concerning their exact location.[4] In East Africa, especially, demarcation closely followed delimitation and much was completed soon after the turn of the century. Even where, as in East Africa, adjacent territories were held

---

[1] Later modified by the Treaties of Tordesillas (1494), Madrid (1750) and San Ildefonso (1777).

[2] *Memorandum by Sir E. Hertslet on the Most Important of the Political and Territorial Changes Which Have Taken Place in Central and East Africa Since 1883.* February 1893, F.O.C.P. 6294, p. 55, F.O. 403/192. The words of the Berlin Act itself suggest that the principle was limited in its operation, since the relevant part of the text (Art. 35) applied only to the establishment of authority in coastal regions (Hertslet, ii. 485). Note also the *Guiana Boundary Case*, between Brazil and Britain, where the arbitrator said in 1904 that the 'occupation cannot be held to be carried out except by effective, uninterrupted, and permanent possession being taken in the name of the State, and that a simple affirmation of rights of sovereignty or a manifest intention to render the occupation effective cannot suffice'. 11 *R.I.A.A.*, 11, at p. 21.

[3] It appears that 'effective occupation' was construed somewhat liberally by the partitioning powers and it did not necessarily mean complete occupation. See below, Ch. XX, p. 267.

[4] For a discussion of some current boundary problems in Africa see, e.g., S. Touval, 'Africa's Frontiers', *International Affairs*, vol. 42 (1966), pp. 641–54; I. W. Zartman, 'The Politics of Boundaries in North and West Africa', *J.M.A.S.* 3 (1965), 155.

by the same colonizing power, Britain, the inter-territorial boundaries were, with some minor exceptions, defined in unambiguous terms and clearly demarcated. As a result, most African countries, as they attained independence, inherited stable, well-established boundaries which the vast majority have been willing, even anxious, to accept.[1] It is also necessary to consider the differing motives that led, on the one hand, to the adoption of the doctrine of *uti possidetis* in Latin America, and on the other hand, to the passing of the O.A.U. resolution. As has been shown, *uti possidetis* was regarded as a convenient legal source of boundary pedigree. That it proved unworkable in certain practical cases did not diminish the fact that it provided a legal basis for negotiation, however tenuous, and offered a peaceful means of discussing boundary questions that might otherwise have resulted in greater inter-state conflict than actually occurred. This point is underlined by a learned writer who, while advocating the rejection of *uti possidetis* as a valid principle of international law, recognizes its practical value as a legal argument to the extent that it induces litigation between rival claimants. In his words, 'a long lawsuit is better than a short war'.[2] It must also be stated, in order to avoid creating the impression that undue emphasis is being given here to technical and historical distinctions between *uti possidetis* and the O.A.U. boundary resolution, that each of the two methods of approach has a functionally similar rationale, since both are attempts to provide amicable solutions to inherited boundary problems.

(*f*) *Self-Determination in Relation to National Boundaries*

Prior to the introduction of the United Nations Charter in 1945, the majority juristic view, in the western world at least, was that the principle of self-determination did not form one of the rules of international law.[3] That self-determination was recognized to be one of the 'purposes and principles' of the United Nations is made clear by Article 1 (2) of the Charter which refers, *inter alia*, to the 'principle

---

[1] Internal administrative limits of the former French colonies in Africa were not, however, always clearly defined. See Reyner, *Current Boundary Problems in Africa*, Pittsburgh, 1964, p. 7.

[2] P. de Lapradelle, *La Frontière*, Les Éditions Internationales, Paris, 1928, pp. 86–7.

[3] M. A. Shukri, *The Concept of Self-Determination in the United Nations*, Al Jadidah Press, Damascus, 1965, p. 333; I. Brownlie, *Principles of Public International Law*, Clarendon Press, Oxford, 1966, p. 483.

of equal rights and self-determination of peoples'. This principle, expressed in identical words, also appears in Article 55 of the Charter which calls for the promotion by member states of international economic and social co-operation. Despite the appearance of the principle of self-determination in the Charter, however, there were grave doubts as to whether it represented anything more than a mere exhortation, or whether it possessed a legally binding content. Reservations on this point still appear to linger in the minds of some jurists and governments[1] but the effect of a number of resolutions passed by the United Nations clearly indicates that the great majority of states believe that self-determination has developed into an international right.[2] Important among these resolutions is the Declaration on the Granting of Independence to Colonial Countries and Peoples, passed by the General Assembly on 14 December 1960, as Resolution 1514 (XV), paragraph 2 of which states that 'all peoples have the *right* to self-determination'.[3] The use of the word 'right' to replace the earlier word 'principle' seems to leave little room for doubt that, in the opinion of those member states that supported the resolution, the principle of self-determination should be regarded as an international right. This view is reinforced by the International Covenants on Human Rights, adopted by resolution of the General Assembly on 16 December 1966.[4] Of these covenants, the International Covenant on Economic, Social, and Cultural Rights, and the International Covenant on Civil and Political Rights both proclaim in Article 1, Part I, of their respective texts, that 'all peoples have the right to self-determination', and that the signatories 'shall promote the realization of the right of self-determination, and shall respect that right, in conformity with the provisions of the Charter of the United Nations'. It appears from these covenants that the nature of their subject matter is authoritative evidence, even for non-parties, of the concept of human rights as it appears in the United Nations Charter.[5]

It is insufficient, however, merely to establish that self-determination is now accepted as a binding rule of international law. The reso-

---

[1] See, e.g., D. P. O'Connell, *International Law*, vol. i, Stevens, London, 1965, p. 337.

[2] R. Higgins, *The Development of International Law through the Political Organs of the United Nations*, p. 103.

[3] For text of the resolution, see I. Brownlie, *Basic Documents in International Law*, Clarendon Press, Oxford, 1967, pp. 175–7.

[4] Ibid., pp. 138–74.   [5] Ibid., p. 138.

lutions and covenants referred to combine to show that even those member states which still exercise alien rule in dependent territories are, with some significant exceptions, prepared to concede that the principle expresses a legal obligation. What must also be considered is how far can the process of self-determination be carried? Given a situation where a colonial territory has attained sovereign independence, to what extent can it permit its own disaffected minority groups to invoke a right of self-determination against the territorial integrity of the new state? This question lies at the very heart of African territorial problems and was a major factor in the passing of the resolution by the Organization of African Unity that enjoined all member states to respect colonial boundaries as they stood at the time of national independence.[1]

The 1960 resolution of the General Assembly and the instruments which it adopted in 1966, referred to above, each declare that 'all peoples' have the right to self-determination. What does the expression mean in this context, and are there any necessary limitations on the numbers of inhabitants having ethnic, religious, or other affinities within a particular territorial state before they can fall into the category of 'all peoples'? Obviously some limitation must exist, and a clue is provided by the 1960 resolution, paragraph 6 of which states: 'Any attempt aimed at the partial or total disruption of the national unity and the territorial integrity of a country is incompatible with the purposes and principles of the Charter of the United Nations.' This provision emphasizes the importance attached by the framers of the resolution to territorial integrity. The point is by no means new, for as long ago as 1921 a commission of the League of Nations observed: 'To concede to minorities either of language, or religion, or to any fractions of a population, the right of withdrawing from the community to which they belong because it is their wish or their good pleasure, would be to . . . uphold a theory incompatible with the very idea of the State as a territorial entity.'[2] As has been shown elsewhere,

---

[1] Above, p. 22.

[2] Cited by A. A. Mazrui, *Towards a Pax Africana*, Weidenfeld and Nicolson, 1967, p. 9. The problem was not confined to cases where a minority wished to withdraw, but also extended to instances where local inhabitants did not wish the cession of their territory to another state. When Heligoland was ceded by Britain to Germany in 1890, as part of their African territorial arrangements, the 2,000 inhabitants of the island were not consulted. Said Lord Salisbury in the House of Lords, '. . . a hint was given that we ought to have taken the opinion of the people (of Heligoland) in some form or another . . .', 346 H.L. Deb., 3rd Series, 10 July 1890, cols. 1262–3.

it was this fear that attempts to ignore colonial boundaries, however badly drawn, would permit balkanization purely on tribal or other kindred grounds, that led the vast majority of new African states to reject earlier proposals for a wholesale readjustment of frontiers.[1]

Emerson sums up the position by saying that when 'a people' has come to independence, no residual right of self-determination remains with any group within it or cutting across its frontiers. In other words, self-determination is not a continuing process but has only the function of bringing independence to people under colonial rule. He adds that what is involved is the disparity between the assumption of national solidarity which accompanies the newly independent states and the more polyglot realities of the actual inhabitants.[2]

Whether the problem looms large or small in a particular state is mainly a matter of historical accident. The new African states are not responsible for their ethnic composition and must be excused if they give pre-eminence to stability through strong and unmistakable national boundaries, rather than allow their minority groups to prejudice this national stability by asserting a right of secession. So far as East Africa is concerned, the problem is most acute in Kenya, where the North-Eastern Province, which is part of the former Northern Frontier District, is inhabited mainly by Somalis, the majority of whom have expressed the desire to unite with the Somali Republic. Some writers appear to have assumed that this Somali element was always present in Kenya but, as is shown in a later chapter, the problem can be traced in part to the westward pressure of Somali tribes in areas of Kenya which they had not previously occupied, rather than to an arbitrary territorial division of existing Somali people by the colonial powers.[3] On the other hand, the line between Kenya and Tanzania was drawn by Britain and Germany in 1890 in the full knowledge and complete disregard of the fact that the Masai people living on each side of the arbitrary boundary were thereby severed.[4]

In conclusion it may be said that there is nothing unreasonable in the attitude of the new African states in their earnest desire to preserve inherited boundaries, even though this may run counter to the

---

[1] Above, pp. 23–4.
[2] R. Emerson, *Self-Determination Revisited in the Era of Decolonization*, pp. 28–32.
[3] Below, Ch. IX.   [4] Below, Ch. XI.

wishes of certain minority groups. The problems relating to the rights of minorities are too complex to be discussed in detail here,[1] nor do they properly lie within the compass of this work; but as a corollary to the rule that the majority of people living within a colonial entity have the right to self-determination it is necessary to provide constitutional safeguards to protect the rights of minorities who choose to live within the new state after independence, or to allow them to join their kinsmen in adjoining territories if this arrangement can be made between the respective states.[2] Problems of minority groups may thus require some revision of static legal situations by considerations of what is fair and reasonable in all the surrounding circumstances. The solution is not necessarily confined to cession of territory but should be sought by attempting to find the most satisfactory peaceful change.

(g) *Local Customary Rights in Boundary Zones*

Proof of the existence of local customary rights in cases concerning international boundary disputes is not an empty academic abstraction. Indeed, it may play a vital role in judicial evaluation of the claims advanced by the respective parties. Article 38 (1) (*b*) of the Statute of the International Court of Justice provides that 'international custom, as evidence of a general practice accepted as law' is one of the four elements of international law which shall be applied by the Court in reaching its decisions. This is a mandatory direction regarding applicable law but it does not preclude the Court from examining custom which does not form part of 'a general practice'. The point is underlined in the *Case Concerning the Right of Passage over Indian Territory*, between India and Portugal in 1960, where the Court rejected India's contention that no local custom could be established between only two states.[3] After receiving proof of a

---

[1] For the position in Kenya see Y. P. Ghai, 'Independence and Safeguards in Kenya', *East Africa Law Journal*, vol. 3 (1967), pp. 177–217.

[2] See *Kenya-Somalia Relations*, Government Printer, Nairobi, April 1967, where, at p. 9, the Kenya Minister for Justice and Constitutional Affairs is reported to have said in the Kenya Parliament that those Somalis who have made Kenya their home were welcome to stay, but that 'those who wish to go and live in Somalia, because it is a better place, are free to do so at any time'. He also said, 'what we cannot accept is the Somalis who think they can take away Kenya and carry it to the Somali Republic'. For details of improvements in Kenya-Somali Republic relations see below, Ch. IX.

[3] *Case Concerning Right of Passage over Indian Territory (Merits)*, I.C.J. Rep. 1960, p. 6, at p. 39.

customary practice of passage between the Portuguese enclaves that had existed over a century before the attainment of Indian independence in 1947, the Court found that in view of all the circumstances it was satisfied that the practice was accepted as law by the parties and gave rise to a right and a correlative obligation.[1] That the Court felt itself entitled to decide the case on the basis of particular local facts supporting the existence of a local customary right is made clear by the following passage from the judgement:

> Having arrived at the conclusion that the course of dealings between the British and Indian authorities on the one hand and the Portuguese on the other established a practice, well understood between the Parties, by virtue of which Portugal had acquired a right of passage in respect of private persons, civil officials and goods in general, the Court does not consider it necessary to examine whether general international custom or the general principles of law recognized by civilised nations may lead to the same result.[2]

In the *Fisheries Case*, between Britain and Norway in 1951, where the main issue concerned the legality of Norway's delimitation of base lines from which her maritime zone extended, the International Court of Justice considered the peculiar geographical nature of the coast and found that there were certain fishing grounds that had been exploited by Norwegian fishermen from time immemorial.[3] It refused to confine its assessment of evidence solely to geographical facts concerning Norway's unusually indented coastline but also regarded as important the economic interests of the region which were clearly evidenced by long usage.[4] These local factors which, as in the *Right of Passage Case*, may not appear to fall precisely within the scope of international custom or the general principles of international law, contributed to the establishment of an historic title and led the Court to hold:

> the historical data produced . . . by the Norwegian Government lend some weight to the idea of the survival of traditional rights reserved to the inhabitants of the Kingdom over fishing grounds included in the 1935 delimitation . . . such rights, founded on the vital needs of the population and attested by very ancient and peaceful usage, may legitimately be taken into account. . . .[5]

---

[1] *Case Concerning Right of Passage over Indian Territory (Merits)*, I.C.J. Rep. 1960, p. 6, at p. 40.   [2] Ibid., p. 43.

[3] *Fisheries Case (United Kingdom v. Norway)*, I.C.J. Rep. 1951, p. 116, at p. 127.

[4] Ibid., p. 133.   [5] Ibid., p. 142.

Again, in the *Rann of Kutch Arbitration*, between India and Pakistan in 1968, the tribunal found that in an area constituting about 10 per cent of the disputed territory the inhabitants of Sind in Pakistan had exercised grazing rights for over one hundred years, and since there had been no effective opposition from the Kutch (Indian) side, Pakistan had made out a better and superior title.[1] It is important, however, to consider the Dissenting Opinion of Judge Bebler who pointed out that since 1926 there had in fact been some admittedly ineffective attempts by the Kutch authorities to exert control over the disputed area by imposing a grazing tax and by establishing a police outpost in 1941. His main point, however, is that the grazing of cattle in the Rann: 'being a purely private activity, would not constitute display of State authority. It might constitute the basis of a claim for an international servitude in the neighbour's territory; but Pakistan did not formulate such a claim.'[2]

These three cases where local customary rights have been regarded as significant by virtue of their probative value in determining the location of a boundary, are not submitted here in support of a general proposition that proof of the existence of local custom in boundary zones can override stronger forms of evidence such as clear agreement between the parties. Nor can it be treated in isolation, but may be accompanied by considerations of acquiescence, estoppel, and good faith. The point to be observed is that international courts and tribunals can, and do, consider customary rights as part of the fasciculus of evidence in appropriate situations.

Boundary agreements, either expressly or by implication, sometimes provide that the inhabitants of each side of the line may cross the frontier in order to exercise certain rights or privileges to which they have been long accustomed. Typical provisions of this kind concern fishing, navigation, grazing, and the use of wells. A few East African examples will be given to illustrate these situations, together with a short account of an instance where tribal courts exercised a limited form of trans-frontier jurisdiction.

Fishing and Navigation

In the Ruvuma (Rovuma) River, the thalweg of which forms part of the Tanzania–Mozambique boundary, an Anglo-Portuguese

---

[1] *Rann of Kutch Arbitration*; extracts from the award are given in *International Legal Materials*, vol. 7 (1968), pp. 633–705; see p. 690.   [2] Ibid., p. 702.

agreement, which came into effect in 1938, makes the following provisions relating to the rights of local inhabitants:

(4) Freedom of navigation in the River Rovuma, without distinction of nationality, shall be maintained in accordance with the treaties and conventions in force.

(5) In order to supply their needs the inhabitants of both banks shall have the right over the whole breadth of the river to draw water, to fish and to remove saliferous sand for the purpose of extracting salt therefrom.

(6) The local authorities shall conclude whatever agreements may be necessary in order that the inhabitants on both banks may be granted such facilities as are possible with regard to hunting, fishing and the collection of salt in the neighbourhood of the river, without prejudice to the existing sovereign rights and in such measure as may, in the circumstances, be permissible without inconvenience to the two Administrations concerned.[1]

On the boundary of Tanzania with Rwanda and Burundi, which is formed in large part by the Kagera River and other watercourses, an agreement was made between Britain and Belgium that came into force on 19 May 1938. This agreement is mainly concerned with setting out the terms whereby the adjoining states could divert and use boundary waters for mining, industrial, and other purposes, an overriding condition of which was that the exercise of the rights created by the agreement should not cause the pollution, or impair the navigability, of boundary waters and their tributaries. With regard to the rights of inhabitants on each side of the boundary, Article 9 of the agreement provides that they 'shall be permitted to navigate any river or stream forming the common boundary and take therefrom fish and aquatic plants and water for domestic purposes and for any purposes conforming with their customary rights'.[2] This provision is of interest since it appears to be the only East African instance where the expression 'customary rights' occurs in an international boundary agreement.

Again, on the Kenya–Tanzania boundary, the Anglo-German draft agreement of 1914 contains, *inter alia*, the following article: 'Art. 6. British and German subjects shall have equal rights of fishing in Lake Jipe (Djipe), and, where the boundary is formed by the thalweg of a river, in those reaches of the river through which the boundary passes.'[3] Other international agreements involving boun-

[1] 185 *L.N.T.S.* 205.   [2] 190 *L.N.T.S.* 103.
[3] F.O. 372/523. For a discussion of the validity of this unsigned treaty see below, pp. 144–5.

dary rivers and lakes in East Africa are silent as to the preservation of customary riparian rights but it would seem to be a fair inference that even in such cases proof of customary usage should justify the legality of its continued exercise. Apart from Lake Jipe, on the Kenya–Tanzania boundary, fishing and other rights on lakes are not specifically referred to in the various agreements. Here again, however, subject to the rights of each riparian state to impose customs, conservation, and navigational regulations on its own side of the actual boundary line, there may be a good case for arguing the international legality of customary riparian rights across the frontier where they can be clearly shown to exist. Lake Nyasa presents a particularly difficult problem, since the treaty boundary, by the Anglo-German agreement of 1890, was drawn along the eastern and northern shores of the lake, thereby excluding any part of the waters from German East Africa. As is argued elsewhere, however, right of navigation on the lake was granted to Germany by the agreement, and it cannot be contended that lakeside dwellers on what is now the Tanzania shore have no legal right to navigate and fish the waters in accordance with their customary usage. The question, quite apart from the central issue concerning the precise location of the lake boundary, involves the extent to which the two other lacustrine states, Malawi and Portugal, have the right to exercise control over such matters as large-scale commercial fishing, and the operation of motor vessels, in such manner as to deny or restrict the participation of Tanzanian inhabitants.[1]

Grazing and the Use of Wells

Boundary agreements affecting land occupied by nomadic people often make provision for trans-frontier grazing and watering. Article 7 of the Anglo-German draft agreement of 1914, concerning the Kenya–Tanzania boundary, provides:

The British Government will give instructions that, in the event of the natives of the German side of the boundary desiring to obtain water from the springs at Kigalalwa (latitude south 2° 58′ 33″; longitude east 37° 36′ 35″) and Lesako (latitude south 2° 58′ 15″; longitude east 37° 36′ 40″), the British authorities shall, so far as circumstances permit, place no obstacles in the way of their doing so.

[1] Below, Ch. XIV. Article 1 (3) of the Anglo-Portuguese agreement of 18 November 1954 provides that in '*all the waters*' of Lake Nyasa, 'the methods of fishing which may be employed shall be only those which are agreed upon by the Government of Nyasaland and the Government of Mozambique'. 325 *U.N.T.S.* 307.

Natives crossing the boundary for this purpose shall, while in British territory, be entirely subject to British jurisdiction and regulations as to time, place, and manner of obtaining water which the local authorities may see fit to impose.

As is shown in a later chapter, the Masai inhabitants on each side of this arbitrary boundary frequently crossed it in search of grazing and water for their cattle.[1]

Another example occurred on the Kenya–Somali Republic boundary where, by Article 9 of the Anglo-Italian treaty of 1925, it was provided that if in a certain area specified in the treaty there existed a shortage of pasture for tribes on the Somaliland side, and if during the rainy season the pasturage on the Kenya side exceeded local requirements, then those tribes might be permitted to cross the boundary. The duration of this provision and the prescribed number of tribesmen who at any time might cross the boundary were to be determined by a mixed commission. The western limit of such grazing penetration was precisely defined by this article.[2] In the event, however, the members of the mixed commission did not recommend the retention in the treaty of grazing provisions, since they found in 1927 that in the absence of satisfactory evidence that all the conditions required by Article 9 actually existed, 'there was no case for the concession referred to in that Article'.[3]

Grazing rights were also an important element of the Anglo-Ethiopian treaty of 14 May 1897, which established the boundary between Ethiopia and British Somaliland. By this treaty the subjects of both contracting parties were permitted to cross the international frontier to graze their cattle, provided they obeyed the instructions of the local administration and shared neighbouring wells with each other.[4] In 1960, upon the attainment of independence by the Somali Republic, Ethiopia declared that she would no longer recognize the validity of the 1897 grazing provisions. The Somali Republic, in turn, refused to accept the boundary defined by the Anglo-Ethiopian treaty. Apart from the practical difficulties involved, the question has evoked much academic interest concerning the international legality of severing treaty provisions.[5]

---

[1] F.O. 372/523. See below, pp. 148–9.   [2] 36 *L.N.T.S.* 379.
[3] 145 *L.N.T.S.* 337, at p. 342.
[4] For the text of the treaty see Hertslet, ii. 423.
[5] See, e.g., D. J. L. Brown, 5 *I.C.L.Q.* 245 and 10 *I.C.L.Q.* 167; A. P. Lester, 12 *I.C.L.Q.* 475, at pp. 493–5; D. P. O'Connell, *State Succession in Municipal Law and International Law*, vol. ii, pp. 302–4.

Frontier Tribunals

An illustration of permissive trans-frontier jurisdiction by local tribunals is provided by a situation which existed on the boundaries of Ruanda-Urundi with its three neighbours, Congo, Uganda, and Tanganyika. These tribunals, composed of chiefs of tribes living on opposite sides of the border, settled disputes concerning the ownership of cattle and other livestock that strayed or were carried across the line. They also decided matters relating to customary family law, such as marriage, and the handing over, or restitution, of dowries. Although it was alleged at meetings of the Permanent Mandates Commission that the tribunals did not function as courts in a strict sense, since they had neither an authority granted by the territorial government, nor the power to impose penalties, it appears that their decisions were regarded as binding by customary law, and were invariably heeded by the litigants. Occasionally the tribunals would perform an extraditionary function by returning fugitives to the appropriate administering authority. The system appeared to operate successfully, mainly owing to the fact that the imposition of arbitrary boundaries meant that in many cases the applicable customary law on each side of the frontier, in the particular area concerned, was similar if not identical. During the early years of the mandate the administrative authorities played no part in the function of the tribunals, nor did they attempt to exercise control over them. By 1933, however, it appeared that the tribunals, though still consisting entirely of Africans, were supervised by European officials who at times presided over the hearings, but intervened only where it was felt that a decision of the tribunal was contrary to natural justice and equity. The Belgian representative to the Permanent Mandates Commission reported in 1933 that, so far as he was aware, in only one area, on part of the boundary between Ruanda-Urundi and the Belgian Congo, had the administrative authorities been obliged to modify the tribunal's award, on the sole ground that it had shown partiality in its decision.[1]

---

[1] For details of the frontier tribunals and questions concerning their function, see *Minutes of the Permanent Mandates Commission*, 7th Session, 22 October 1925, pp. 61–2; ibid., 12th Session, 7 November 1927, p. 134; ibid., 24th Session, 30 October 1933, p. 76.

CHAPTER III

Delimitation and Demarcation

IN any discussion concerning the establishment of international boundaries it is important to distinguish the processes of delimitation and demarcation. These two words have been frequently regarded as synonymous and interchangeable, and even today the distinction is not always properly appreciated. Whatever may be the strict etymological similarity between them it is desirable and convenient that the words be used to describe two separate stages of boundary development. Sir Henry McMahon first drew the distinction between delimitation and demarcation as long ago as 1896: ' "Delimitation" I have taken to comprise the determination of a boundary line by treaty or otherwise, and its definition in written, verbal terms; "Demarcation" to comprise the actual laying down of a boundary line on the ground, and its definition by boundary pillars or other similar physical means.'[1] These definitions were accepted by Lord Curzon in 1907: 'Delimitation signifies all the earlier processes for determining a boundary, down to and including its embodiment in a Treaty or Convention. But when the local Commissioners get to work, it is not delimitation but demarcation on which they are engaged.'[2] Thus, by their very nature, delimitation and demarcation are operations of completely different character, though the latter complements and stabilizes the former. They will not normally be performed by the same personnel, but the demarcation commission may, and usually should, be given limited powers of delimitation, by having authority to make minor alterations of the paper boundary to suit local conditions. Delimitation is essentially the work of diplomats and treaty makers who should decide on trustworthy evidence the boundary that will be acceptable to both high contracting parties.[3] Demarcation is a field operation; its purpose is to mark the boundary

---

[1] Sir A. H. McMahon, 'International Boundaries', *Journal of the Royal Society of Arts*, vol. 84 (1935), p. 4. For McMahon's original remarks see *Minutes of Proceedings of the Royal Artillery Institution*, vol. 24 (1897), p. 224.

[2] Lord Curzon, *Frontiers*, p. 51 footnote.

[3] T. H. Holdich, *Political Frontiers and Boundary Making*, p. 179.

on the ground for all to see. It is the crux of all boundary making.[1]

Although modern tribunals tend to interpret the words demarcation and delimitation according to the respective definitions given above,[2] the distinction is not always noted. In the *Temple Case* the task of the Franco-Siamese Delimitation Commission, so far as the disputed portion of the boundary was concerned, was to establish not the theoretical but the practical location of a boundary that had already been delimited by the two states as the watershed. Thus the real function of the mixed commission was to survey on the ground, and subsequently to map, the actual line of the watershed, and this is a process of demarcation, whether or not artificial boundary pillars are used to indicate more clearly the precise course of this geographical feature.[3] The terminological point is perhaps not worth pressing too far, since the distinction is one of convenience rather than etymology but when, as frequently occurs, the expressions Delimitation Commission and Demarcation Commission appear in boundary agreements it is necessary to look behind the formal title to discover exactly what the commission is required and empowered to do. Nor should demarcation itself be regarded merely as a routine process confined to the mechanics of erecting boundary pillars along an established line. This is indicated by the advisory opinion delivered by the Permanent Court of International Justice concerning the *Jaworzina Boundary* in 1923:

... the word *abornement* (marking out) used by the Conference of Ambassadors has not always, in fact, nor necessarily, the narrow technical meaning which the Czechoslovak Government desires to give it. The process of marking out does not merely consist of the actual placing of posts and stones which are to indicate the line separating two neighbouring countries; the expression must be held to include all operations on the ground.[4]

The commission appointed by Britain, France, and Germany in 1886 to determine the extent of the territorial possessions of the Sultan of Zanzibar refers in parts of its report to 'a line of demarcation', but it is quite apparent that although the various areas said to belong to the Sultan may have been actually visited by the

[1] Ibid., p. 208.
[2] e.g. *Award of Her Majesty Queen Elizabeth II for the Arbitration of a Controversy between The Argentine Republic and The Republic of Chile*, H.M.S.O., London, 1966, p. 78.
[3] Below, p. 70.
[4] *Jaworzina Boundary*, P.C.I.J. Series B/8 (1923), at p. 47.

commission members, the arbitrary nature of the lines recommended by them leaves no doubt that delimitation, not physical demarcation, was undertaken, nor is there any evidence to show that, except in those few places where rivers were used, any tangible boundary lines existed.[1] On the other hand, the main task of the mixed commission appointed in 1898 to 'delimit' the Anglo–German boundary between Lakes Nyasa and Tanganyika was physically to mark a boundary line that had already been clearly delimited on paper by the Anglo-German agreement of 1890. In this instance, however, the commission, in accordance with Article 6 of the agreement, was empowered to make minor rectifications to the delimited boundary to meet local requirements and there are one or two places where such rectifications were in fact made.[2]

In some other instances East African demarcation commissions were given power to deviate from the paper boundary when circumstances made it desirable to do so. The Anglo-German agreement of 1910, respecting what is now the Uganda–Rwanda boundary, gave the commission authority to depart from certain of the delimited straight lines in order to make the boundary coincide with natural features, provided these deviations 'shall not, however, exceed 5 kilom. on either side of the straight lines, and neither the total area of British territory nor the total area of German territory shall be altered thereby'.[3] A similar provision was made in the Anglo-Belgian agreement of 1910 concerning the southern portion of the Uganda–Congo boundary, though here the permitted extent of deviation from the delimited straight-line sections was only three kilometres, with the same overriding qualification that the total area of British and Belgian territory was to remain unaffected.[4] In order to satisfy these requirements the respective mixed commissions were obliged to adopt a give-and-take policy which, while placing the demarcated boundary along a line of natural topographical features wherever this was possible, involved the minute, and seemingly absurd, calculation of areas in order to ensure that one state was not gaining extra territory at the expense of the other. E. M. Jack, one of the British commissioners engaged in this demarcation, expressed himself forcibly on the subject some years later:

. . . we were given a very narrow zone on either side of that line. It was not more than 5 kilometres on each side . . . we were told that if we added so

[1] Hertslet, iii. 874.
[2] Below, Ch. XVI.
[3] 107 B.F.S.P. 394, at p. 395.
[4] 107 B.F.S.P. 348.

many square miles to the territory of one Power, we must take it off further down from the territory of another. That seems to me a childish sort of provision to make. On either side of this boundary were many million square miles, and to insist on balancing the plus or minus of a few hundred square miles seems to me the sort of thing you would expect from a Babu clerk.[1]

An even more grotesque situation occurred during the German–Portuguese demarcation of the western portion of the present Tanzania–Mozambique boundary. In order to compensate for the deviation from the theoretical boundary formed by the parallel of latitude of the Ruvuma-Msinje confluence, the commissioners made several exchanges of territory the areas of which were computed to the nearest square metre and balanced exactly.[2] When one considers that the country through which these various boundary lines passed was sparsely inhabited and of no great economic value, it is difficult to comprehend why such pedantic insistence should have been placed by diplomats on boundary adjustment through the exchange of equal areas.

When the delimitation of a boundary is contemplated it is highly desirable that the negotiators should make use of the advice of those who have had practical experience in the laying down of boundaries on the ground. The use of such expert opinion will help to avoid the adoption of absurd boundaries which can be physically established only with the greatest difficulty. Lines of latitude and longitude have often been castigated as arbitrary and unrealistic boundaries, but even more unsatisfactory methods have been adopted, notably those which place boundaries 'parallel to' and at a considerable distance from some irregular feature such as the sea shore, and those, for-tunately few in number, which make use of circular arcs.

The outstanding example in East Africa of a boundary line being placed at a constant distance from an irregular topographical feature is the former coastal strip, constituting part of the mainland terri-tories of the Sultan of Zanzibar, which was described as having 'an

[1] H. St. J. L. Winterbotham, 'The Demarcation of International Boundaries', *Empire Conference of Survey Officers, 1928, Report of Proceedings*, Colonial, No. 41, H.M.S.O., London, 1929, p. 189.

[2] Since the commissioners placed the boundary along the course of the Msinje instead of on the parallel of latitude of the Ruvuma-Msinje confluence, Germany gained 3,857,300 square metres of territory. It was agreed that Portugal should be compensated for her loss by receiving three portions of land on the German side of the parallel, having areas of 652,678, 1,304,880, and 1,899,742 square metres respectively. *Deutsches Kolonialblatt*, vol. 21 (1910), pp. 123-4.

internal depth of 10 sea miles measured from the coast direct into the interior from high-water mark'.[1] The western limit of part of the Sultan's coastal territory formed the boundary between what later became Kenya Colony and the Kenya Protectorate.[2] No proper attempt seems to have been made to demarcate this boundary, but since both components of Kenya were under British administration there may have been no practical need. In 1898 a provisional demarcation of the coastal strip's western limit was carried out but it was specifically stated that 'The boundary which was agreed to was not measured according to any hard and fast rule, but for mutual convenience in order that no changes might be made which could affect localities hitherto recognized as lying either within or without the Zanzibar dominions.'[3] In other words, an approximate line was demarcated, but had the true position of the boundary been required it would have been necessary, failing some additional compromise agreement, to trace on the ground a line lying ten nautical miles from the coast and following its sinuosities for about 200 miles. The physical and computational labour involved in conforming precisely to this requirement would have been enormous and completely unjustified, since the boundary itself was never more than an arbitrary line.

That the unwisdom of attempting to demarcate sinuous boundary lines like that of the Kenya coastal strip was not always unnoticed by diplomats is shown by a memorandum by Lord Lansdowne during the negotiations with King Leopold II of Belgium relating to the proposed delimitation of the Lado Enclave on the Uganda–Congo border:

. . . the frontier line should be drawn along the Jei River rather than that a line should be found to the east of that river, and at a distance of not less than 40 miles from the Nile. To mark out a line of this nature in an unexplored tropical country is a notoriously difficult, expensive and laborious task, and the exact trace to be followed is likely to be a subject of much discussion and argument between the members of the Commission of Delimitation. His Majesty's Government are unable to believe that the tract of country to be gained or lost by either party is of sufficient value to justify the rejection of a plan which provides a distinct frontier easy both to ascertain and observe.[4]

[1] Hertslet, iii. 882.
[2] S.R. and O. 1920/2342 and 1920/2343. For details concerning the transfer of sovereignty of the Coastal Strip, which now forms part of Kenya, see Cmnd. 1701, Cmnd. 1971, and Cmnd. 2161.
[3] Hertslet, i. 384.
[4] Lansdowne to Phipps, 3 June 1902, F.O. 10/776.

Another interesting African boundary situation of a similar, but somewhat more complicated type, is the line separating Gambia from Senegal. By an Anglo-French agreement of 1889, part of this boundary ran on each side of the Gambia River at a distance of ten kilometres from the river bank. The map attached to the agreement shows the course of the Gambia to be extremely tortuous and the delineated boundary on each side of the river is portrayed as a series of intersecting arcs of circles, each having an apparent radius of ten kilometres, the centres of which lie at the middle of the major bends of the river.[1] It is almost inconceivable that such a clumsy boundary description could have been devised.

The use of what are frequently, but inexactly, called astronomical boundaries, that is to say, lines of latitude and longitude, has been very common in Africa. Territorial expansion by European powers during the nineteenth century was not a mere gradual penetration, but a collision between a multitude of rival national interests that demanded clear evidence as to the precise geographical limits of those interests. Since much of the continent was at that time either unmapped or imperfectly mapped, astronomical lines presented themselves as a highly suitable means of delimiting spheres of influence. Diplomats who, 'in the happy irresponsibility of their office-chairs think nothing of intersecting rivers, lakes, and mountains, or of severing communities and tribes',[2] did so largely because they lacked topographical information, the gathering of which was a costly and time-consuming operation for which boundary negotiators were usually not prepared to wait. The tragedy lay not so much in the initial selection of astronomical lines as in their retention when local surveys disclosed the existence of more appropriate boundaries. As has been seen, although some minor efforts were made at boundary rectification, too much emphasis was placed on equal area adjustment, rather than on finding the most suitable line for local circumstances. Even the abandonment on the Congo–Uganda border of the famous 30th meridian in favour of natural features, resulted not so much from the rejection of a meridional boundary *per se* as from the ability of Britain and Germany to force Belgium, in 1910, to grant them the territory they required. Had the true position of the 30th meridian been found, in 1903, to lie

---

[1] Hertslet, ii. 729, and the map facing p. 730. For another example in West Africa where a boundary followed the arcs of various circles, see Hertslet, ii. 849.
[2] Curzon, op. cit., p. 34.

considerably to the west, instead of to the east, of its previously supposed location, it is probable that Britain and Germany would have been far more inclined to accept it as their western limit, without raising the issue of the desirability of using natural topographical features for the boundary.[1]

In featureless and uninhabited country, however, the selection of an astronomical line as a boundary may serve as well as any other, provided the delimitation is not allowed to override the practical problems of the demarcation commission by requiring a too slavish adherence to the theoretical line. Obtaining precise geographical co-ordinates, that is to say, latitude and longitude, is no simple matter, even with modern instruments and techniques, and positional errors in the placing of boundary pillars are inevitable. A treatment of this specialized subject is inappropriate here but, put briefly, it may be said that what is required are the geodetic co-ordinates[2] of the boundary points and that these are usually obtained from computations based on a combination of astronomical and triangulation observations.[3] The technical details of the work of a demarcation commission are normally contained in its final report and, generally speaking, are of interest only to cartographers and to surveyors who are likely to be called upon to restore the lines in the future. But even the final boundary description should make certain technical details clear, such as the origin and source of the co-ordinates, the projection, and the figure of the earth[4] on which the computations are based.

---

[1] Below, p. 272.

[2] Astronomical latitudes and longitudes are positions on the geoid which is the irregular surface of the earth corresponding in shape to mean sea level. Geodetic coordinates are computed on a mathematically regular surface known as the spheroid, or figure of the earth. See below, note 4.

[3] Triangulation, to express it in its simplest form, is a surveying technique in which a base line forming one side of a triangle is measured directly with a steel tape and the interior angles of the triangle are measured directly with a theodolite. The remaining sides of the triangle can thus be computed by trigonometry and then used themselves to provide 'base lines' for the computation of additional connecting triangles by further angular measurement. In this way indirect measurements of distance can be made rapidly over extensive areas, such as international boundary zones. Recent electronic equipment, such as the geodimeter, and the tellurometer, allow direct distance measurement of triangle sides by a process known as trilateration. Quite frequently, triangulation and trilateration are used together. For an example of present-day methods of boundary survey see A. D. Bancroft, 'Modern Techniques Applied to a Boundary Survey in the Mountains of Southern Iran', *The Chartered Surveyor*, May 1962.

[4] The figure of the earth means a mathematical spheroid, closely approximating

Two examples of situations where efforts to demarcate theoretical boundaries caused difficulty are, first, that portion of the boundary between Canada and the United States which is defined by the parallel of 49° north latitude. Because latitude values were independently obtained at various points on the line, and owing also to errors caused by physical conditions, two different lines were cut and demarcated in one area, and, since the reports of the commissions had been lost, there was nothing to tell which line should be accepted.[1] The second instance occurred during the demarcation of a meridional boundary through the Kalahari desert where

years of scientific labour in a most unwholesome climate . . . which cost valuable lives as well as money, was no more useful than would have been attained by a rapid compass traverse and an artificial demarcation with piles of stones. . . . The question whether that boundary were half a mile in error one way or the other, or whether the line was absolutely straight or not, was not worth a discussion involving the expenditure of a £10 note.[2]

The longest meridional boundary in East Africa forms part of the line dividing Kenya from the Somali Republic. This boundary section, which runs along the meridian of 40° 59' 44·34" east longitude for a distance of about 250 miles, was created as a result of the Jubaland transfer from Britain to Italy in 1925. Demarcation was undertaken by means of pillars and stone cairns, many of which were subsequently destroyed and had to be replaced. The apparent exactitude with which this longitude observation was made, that is to say, to the nearest one-hundredth of a second of arc,[3] requires a caution against absolute reliance upon astronomical observations, especially when they have to be made under trying conditions, and this is illustrated by the Anglo-Italian agreement of 1927, paragraph 13 of which states that the mixed commission

. . . having taken into consideration the possible errors inherent in the methods of survey imposed upon themselves by the terrain, involving errors of position and of direction, decided that the boundary, as actually demarcated by themselves by means of a lane cut through the vegetation and supplemented by cement or masonry beacons or by cairns, shall be

the geoid or mean sea level surface of the earth. There have been over 100 separate scientific determinations of the dimensions of the spheroid, but at present none is universally employed, and at least seven major figures are in practical use in various parts of the world.

[1] *Geog. J.* 96 (1940), 288.   [2] Holdich, op. cit., p. 186.

[3] In the latitude of Jubaland, one second of arc (longitude) represents a linear distance, in an east–west direction, of about 101 feet.

E

observed provisionally as an accurate interpretation of the true boundary without prejudice to subsequent correction by mutual agreement of both parties concerned.[1]

This provision is simply the common-sense realization that, despite their most careful technical efforts, the meridian established by the commissioners might be found, on later investigation, to lie slightly to one side or the other of its stated value. In other words, the line as actually demarcated, and not the theoretical meridian, should be regarded as the true boundary.

The main example of a boundary formed by a line of latitude in East Africa is the parallel of 1° south which is the boundary in Lake Victoria between Kenya and Uganda on the north and Tanzania on the south, and also, in theory at least, part of the boundary between Uganda and Tanzania west of the lake. This parallel is one of the few surviving remnants of the Anglo-German agreement of 1890 that partitioned the British from the German sphere of influence and, originally, the boundary was drawn along the parallel westward from the eastern side of Lake Victoria as far as the 30th meridian, which was recognized at that time to be the eastern limit of the Congo State.[2] As a result of the Anglo-German agreement of 1910, the boundary between Uganda and what was then German East Africa ran westward from the western shore of Lake Victoria along the parallel as far as its intersection with the 'second crossing' of the Kagera River, between boundary pillars Nos. 26 and 27.[3] Between the western lake shore and the Kagera crossing, the parallel had been demarcated by an Anglo-German commission in 1902–4 and it is evident from recent maps that the line of demarcated pillars is not exactly on the theoretical parallel but lies approximately one-quarter of a mile to the north of it.[4] The question arises, therefore, does the demarcated boundary, or the true parallel of 1° south represent the actual position of the boundary? It is submitted that the only realistic answer must be that the pillars themselves, if found *in situ*, define the true location of the boundary, despite any positional errors they may have. Two grounds of support for this conclusion can be found. First, the description of this boundary, contained in an Order of the Secre-

---

[1] 145 *L.N.T.S.* 337, at p. 343.
[2] Hertslet, iii. 899.   [3] 107 *B.F.S.P.* 394, at p. 396.
[4] See the 1:50,000 map sheets published by the Government of Tanzania (Series Y742, Sheet 3/2, Edition 1—T.S.D.), and by the Government of Uganda (Series Y732, Sheet 88/111).

tary of State in 1913, provides that from the second crossing of the parallel by the Kagera: 'The boundary then follows the line of boundary pillars already erected along the 1° south as far as the intersection of this line with the western shore of Lake Victoria.'[1] Second, even more conclusive evidence that boundary pillars, and not their theoretical position, are intended to mark the actual boundary line is provided by the Anglo-German agreement of 1914 which, although never signed owing to the outbreak of war, contains a boundary description that appears to have been accepted by the Kenya, Tanzania, and Uganda governments. Article 4 of this agreement states: 'The geographical co-ordinates of the boundary pillars, so far as they are known, have been inserted in the maps annexed to this Agreement. The pillars marking the boundary shall determine the course of the boundary, even in the event of future alteration of their co-ordinates.'[2] A similar provision appears in the unratified Anglo-German agreement of 1906, which the 1914 agreement was intended to supersede. In the 1906 agreement the western boundary terminal was the 30th meridian of east longitude, which was marked by the mixed commission of 1902-4 by boundary pillar No. 1, but the agreement states that 'it is agreed that the 30th meridian east of Greenwich is 9·595″ true west of boundary-pillar No. 1, west of Lake Victoria.'[3] In other words, the pillar was agreed to be about 970 feet east of the true meridian of 30° east longitude.

Sometimes the discrepancy between true and assumed positions of boundary pillars may not be discovered for several years and, in the absence of provisions similar to those cited, it will be necessary to reach a compromise agreement. Thus, the line dividing those portions of New Guinea administered respectively by the Netherlands and Australia was described as the meridian of 141° east longitude. When independent determinations of longitude were made by surveyors from the two states, a discrepancy amounting to 398 metres in position was discovered. It was agreed, however, to halve this difference and a boundary pillar, placed in a position approximately midway between the two observed meridional points, was thereupon declared to mark the boundary, 'whether or not subsequent surveys

---

[1] *The Uganda Official Gazette*, 15 July 1913, p. 287, para. 19.
[2] Agreement Respecting the Boundary Between the British and German Territories in East Africa, From Mount Sabinio to Lake Jipe (1914), F.O. 372/523.
[3] Agreement between Great Britain and Germany determining the Boundary between their respective territories in East Africa (East and West of Lake Victoria), Berlin, 18 July 1906, para. 3, F.O. 367/10.

should indicate that the said monument is in fact situated somewhat to the East or West of the 141st Meridian of East longitude.'[1]

The above instances refer to boundaries formed by meridians and parallels but it is a useful practice to include similar provisions regarding the evidentiary superiority of boundary pillars over theoretical positions in all boundary agreements. One example is provided by the Anglo-German agreement of 1901, regarding the boundary between Lakes Nyasa and Tanganyika, section 3 of which reads: 'Any fresh determination of the geographical positions of the boundary pillars or of other points here mentioned shall make no alteration in the boundary itself.'[2] The 'other points' referred to in this section would include the watershed of the Congo Basin, part of which forms the boundary. Thus, if, as in the *Temple Case*, a fresh determination of the watershed was obtained,[3] its location as established by the original commission would be preferred.

Other boundary agreements often make no mention as to whether boundary marks or their theoretical positions are to prevail in the event of conflict between them. It is submitted, however, that in those situations where a boundary has been demarcated by a properly appointed mixed commission, then the boundary marks, provided they remain *in situ*, must take precedence over a written description which assigns a different position to the boundary. Judicial support for this view is provided by *State of South Australia* v. *State of Victoria*,[4] where the Judicial Committee of the Privy Council held that although the demarcated position of the 141st degree of east longitude that theoretically separated the two states was about $2\frac{1}{4}$ miles in error, the boundary marks themselves must be deemed to define the correct boundary. Lord Moulton, after stressing the difficulties involved in laying down on the earth's surface a line of longitude, especially in the mid nineteenth century when less refined techniques and instruments were available than at the present time, went on to say that the facts of the case showed that the 'two Governments made with all care a sincere effort to represent as closely as was possible the theoretical boundary assigned by the letters patent by a practical line of demarcation',[5] and that in 1847 there had been no intention to depart from the boundary but only a practical attempt to reproduce it on the ground.

[1] 173 *L.N.T.S.* 325.   [2] Hertslet, iii. 925.
[3] Below, pp. 67–8.   [4] A.C. (1914), 283.
[5] Ibid., pp. 309–10.

It seems probable, therefore, that courts and tribunals will, as a general rule, prefer actual demarcated points, whether or not exactly placed in their theoretical positions, to written descriptions that conflict with them.[1] A few qualifications should be mentioned, however. First, it is essential that the demarcation should have been carried out jointly by a mixed commission. Arguments that unilateral demarcation nullified a boundary line were advanced by Ethiopia concerning the Kenya–Ethiopia boundary,[2] and by Thailand in the *Temple Case*.[3] Second, the boundary mark should be unmistakable and proved either to be *in situ* or an exact positional replacement of the original. If they are to serve any practical purpose boundary pillars must be clearly visible to inhabitants on both sides of the line, yet their very prominence may of itself invite destruction by human, animal, or natural agency. Frontier dwellers may hope to acquire extra territory by the surreptitious shifting of boundary marks, animals have been known to uproot pillars[4] or to cause their disintegration by clambering on top of them,[5] and water seeping through minute cracks in the masonry may eventually cause the marks to crumble and disappear. Problems of this kind can be avoided by placing a number of subsidiary marks, inconspicuous to the casual observer by which the main pillars can be restored in their correct position by surveyors when the need arises. Nowadays this is a normal surveying procedure[6] and no modern international demarcation commission worthy of the name would think of placing a boundary mark without referring it to several near-by unobtrusive witness points, consisting, for example, of metal bolts cemented in rock, or concrete surface beacons, depending on the nature of the country.[7]

[1] In other words, the effect of an original mistake in demarcation may be overridden by prescription and consolidation.

[2] Below, p. 108.   [3] Below, p. 58.

[4] Elephants were reported to have pushed over several boundary pillars erected during the 1956–7 redemarcation of the south-eastern portion of the Kenya–Tanzania boundary. See Tanzania Govt. File 2220/19/107.

[5] As was done by goats on the Tanganyika/Ruanda-Urundi boundary pillars. See below, p. 158.

[6] McMahon, op. cit., p. 5, reported that in order 'to baffle those with evil intent', he adopted amongst other precautions the practice of secretly burying a bag or two of charcoal a few feet beneath the pillar so that even if the pillar itself was later removed a 'tell-tale' stain, caused by the effect of moisture on the charcoal, would remain for many years. This procedure, though possibly a little too quaint for modern surveyors, illustrates the general principle of boundary preservation.

[7] A common precaution in demarcation against the wilful or accidental disturbance of boundary marks is known as 'double beaconing'. This consists of

In former days less care was paid to such details. Boundary commissions, working in difficult and at times hostile country, and frequently faced with small budgets and strict time limits, too often carried out rapid triangulation work that was below the desirable mathematical standard, and their boundary marks usually consisted of piles of stones, wooden posts, or other material which later became lost or impossible to identify with certainty. If it is true to say, with Holdich, that demarcation is the crux of boundary making, then it is equally true to say that the crux of demarcation is the intelligent placing of boundary marks in such manner that they can be preserved or restored without giving rise in the future to even the smallest dispute as to their original location.[1]

placing a second mark, two or three feet under the ground surface, which is separate from but exactly vertically beneath the main surface mark.

[1] Provisions for the preservation and restoration of boundary marks are sometimes written into the original agreements. See, e.g., Hertslet, iii. 925. Secs. 4 and 5; 145 *L.N.T.S.* 337, at p. 339. The placing of intermediate 'line beacons' (below, p. 225), the cutting of lanes through vegetation (below, p. 122), and the digging of trenches (below, p. 148), may also be appropriate aids to boundary-line identification.

CHAPTER IV

Evidentiary Value of Maps

IT is scarcely necessary to stress the value of maps as an aid to the interpretation of boundary agreements; indeed, many boundary descriptions are almost unintelligible unless accompanied by a pictorial representation of the lines they purport to establish.[1] While it is true that courts and tribunals concerned with boundary disputes have always recognized the importance of maps as a means of lending support to the arguments of opposing parties, it is also true to say that the judicial approach to the assessment of the cogency of such graphical evidence has undergone some shift over the years. This can be seen from an examination of actual cases, of which a few illustrations will be given. The main reason why modern maps are more likely to be given greater credence than those of former years is, of course, the vast improvement in cartographic skill, especially since the beginning of the present century. In several early boundary disputes courts were presented with maps of doubtful authenticity and origin which, in many instances, were found to bear inaccurate relationship to the geographical conditions they were intended to portray. The improvement in mapping techniques, notably through the application of air photography, means that cartographical material can now be produced rapidly, and usually relatively cheaply, to a technical standard of accuracy that was virtually unattainable in the past. Thus the problem of present-day boundary interpretation is likely to lie less in a scarcity of modern maps of the disputed area than in attempting to reconcile existing textual descriptions with their contemporary maps, and to decide the respective weight that can be reasonably attached to each type of evidence. It may also be found that international boundary descriptions and maps, even when both

[1] *Manica Boundary Arbitration*, between Britain and Portugal, 1897, Hertslet, iii. 1036, where it was said, at p. 1044, 'No geographical map was annexed to the Treaty . . . and in our opinion there is none which can be adopted as a sure and complete proof of the intention of the negotiators of the Treaty. . . . It is an inconvenience much to be regretted, for in the absence of a solid and constant basis for discussion we are obliged to follow minutely the two Parties through the arguments which they brought forward . . .'.

have been prepared by a mixed demarcation commission, later reveal inconsistencies with each other. In such instances, as will be shown, a greater weight has in the past been usually given to the written, rather than the pictorial, description but two recent cases, admittedly of a rather special character, show that, even if it existed formerly, there is no longer a necessary presumption in international law that the text of a boundary description prevails over a contemporaneous, or even a subsequent, map. Apart from cases involving discrepancies between map and text, special difficulties may arise, as where a map forming an integral part of a boundary description is not available, or where two or more extant maps, each alleged to be the original, are in conflict. Some East African examples of these problems will be considered later. Lastly, a brief mention will be made of the scale and quality of maps found in international boundary documents.

A well-known, and frequently cited, opinion as to the validity of maps in international boundary disputes was expressed by the arbitrator in the *Island of Palmas Case*, between the Netherlands and the United States of America, in 1928:

> Among the methods of indirect proof, not of the exercise of sovereignty, but of its existence in law . . . there is the *evidence from maps*. . . . A comparison of the information supplied by the two Parties shows that only with the greatest caution can account be taken of maps in deciding a question of sovereignty. . . . Any maps which do not precisely indicate the political distribution of territories . . . must be rejected forthwith, unless they contribute—supposing that they are accurate—to the location of geographical names. Moreover, indications of such a nature are only of value when there is reason to think that the cartographer has not merely referred to already existing maps—as seems very often to be the case— but that he has based his decision on information carefully collected for the purpose. Above all then, official or semi-official maps seem capable of fulfilling these conditions, and they would be of special interest in cases where they do not assert the sovereignty of the country of which the Government has caused them to be issued.[1]

In the *Palmas Case*, the arbitrator was dealing with maps some of which had been made centuries earlier by Spanish and Dutch cartographers, who to a certain extent copied each other's work. His point concerning the respective merits of official and semi-official maps was also considered by the Judicial Committee of the Privy Council in the *Labrador Boundary Case* of 1927:

> Maps published by private persons must, of course, be received with

---

[1] The *Island of Palmas Case*, 2 *R.I.A.A.* 829, at p. 852.

caution, as such persons depend to a large extent upon information obtained from general and unauthoritative sources; but from a map issued or accepted by a public authority, and especially by an authority connected with one of the governments concerned, an inference may not improperly be drawn. . . . The maps here referred to, even when issued or accepted by departments of the Canadian Government, cannot be treated as admissions binding on that Government; for even if such an admission could be effectively made, the departments concerned are not shown to have had any authority to make it.[1]

These remarks of the Judicial Committee concerning departmental authority to issue maps are of interest in the Tanzania–Malawi boundary dispute concerning Lake Nyasa, where, for a number of years prior to World War II, maps published in both the Nyasaland and the Tanganyika Annual Reports showed a median line lake boundary, which conflicted with the shore line boundary originally established in 1890.[2] In the *Labrador Case*, however, the Judicial Committee went on to say that the publication of maps through a long series of years is of some value as showing the construction put upon boundary descriptions by persons of authority.

As was stated by Hyde, although the unreliability of certain older maps has led arbitrators to accentuate their insufficiency as evidence, tribunals in more recent times have been inclined to attach greater weight, even to early maps, when the object has been to test the pretensions of opposing litigants by reference to a remote past, rather than to a present situation.[3] This was precisely the point in the *Temple Case*, between Cambodia and Thailand, in 1962.[4] Even though the location of the watershed boundary near the temple, as shown on a French map *c.* 1908, was demonstrably incorrect, and the error was detected by Siamese surveyors in 1935, the Thailand Government was precluded from denying the validity of the French map since, firstly, despite its equal participation in the original delimitation commission, it had been content to leave the physical investigation of the watershed and the preparation of boundary maps to French surveyors and, secondly, by long acquiescence it must be regarded as having accepted the map, which clearly showed the temple to lie in Cambodian territory. The International Court of Justice, therefore, was

[1] Re *The Labrador Boundary* (1927), 43 T.L.R. 289, at pp. 298–9.
[2] Below, Ch. XIV.
[3] C. C. Hyde, 'Maps as Evidence in International Boundary Disputes', 27 *A.J.I.L.* 311 (1933), at p. 314.
[4] *Case Concerning the Temple of Preah Vihear (Cambodia v. Thailand) Merits*, I.C.J. Rep. 1962, p. 6.

not so much concerned with the true line of the watershed in the temple area (and even the recent surveys specially undertaken to locate the watershed failed to agree as to its precise position),[1] as in the historical fact that Thailand, by her acquiescence, had accepted a map, whether or not theoretically accurate, which had become 'an integral part'[2] of the treaty. The Court also stressed the 'overriding importance, in the interests of finality', of pronouncing in favour of the line delineated on the French map.[3]

The consensus of the three dissenting opinions in the *Temple Case* was that the disputed map, although published by a reputable French cartographical firm, bore neither date nor signature, and that at best it represented the work of only the French section of the mixed delimitation commission.[4] In view of other considerations, some of which have already been mentioned, the majority of the Court was not convinced by this line of reasoning, but it is essential to point out that the mere production of a map which on its face does not appear to have an official character will usually be insufficient evidence, in itself, to sustain a boundary claim. As was stated by the Permanent Court of International Justice in its advisory opinion on the *Monastery of Saint-Naoum* dispute between Albania and Yugoslavia in 1924:

A map which has been submitted to the Court and which is described as that sent by Yougoslavia to the Conference of Ambassadors . . . contains a frontier line leaving Saint-Naoum outside Albania . . . it must be observed that this line . . . did not necessarily represent the Albanian frontier. Moreover the map in question is unsigned and its authentic character is not established.[5]

In the *Frontier Land Case*, between Belgium and the Netherlands in 1959,[6] disputed plots forming one of several territorial enclaves lying across the frontier zone between the two states, were held by the International Court of Justice to belong to Belgium. The judgement is based, in part, on the fact that a map drawn by a mixed commission and forming part of the Boundary Convention of 1843 between the two states showed 'clearly, and in a manner which could not escape notice, that the disputed plots belonged to Belgium. . . .

---

[1] *Case Concerning the Temple of Preah Vihear (Cambodia v. Thailand) Merits*, I.C.J. Rep. 1962, pp. 98–9, where four alternative watershed lines were indicated.
[2] Ibid., p. 33.   [3] Ibid., p. 35.   [4] Ibid., p. 69.
[5] *Monastery of Saint-Naoum*, P.C.I.J., Series B/9 (1924), at p. 21.
[6] *Case Concerning Sovereignty Over Certain Frontier Land (Belgium/Netherlands)*, I.C.J. Rep. 1959, p. 209.

This map, signed by the members of the respective Commissions, of its very nature must have been the subject of check by both Commissions against original documents and surveys.'[1] Whether or not the map received the checks suggested by the Court is open to question, since in his Dissenting Opinion Judge Armand-Ugon pointed out that the map showed several unallocated plots, whereas the text did not disclose that any plots remained unallocated at the time when the map was made.[2] Judge Moreno Quintana, in his Dissenting Opinion, also raised objection to the map, but on somewhat more general grounds since, citing the views of the arbitrator in the *Island of Palmas Case*, he referred to 'the very relative value . . . which international law attaches to geographical maps'.[3] In the *Frontier Land Case*, however, the Court was faced with discrepancies between minutes signed by the two states in 1841 and 1843; nor could it be satisfied that it was dealing with original minutes and not copies. Amidst an array of documents that contained such an accumulation of errors 'as though some evil genius had presided over the whole affair',[4] the map stood out as a highly cogent piece of evidence that substantially contributed to the finding in favour of Belgium.

Another interesting illustration is provided by the *Rann of Kutch Arbitration* between India and Pakistan in 1968. The tribunal was presented with a vast quantity of maps, published at different periods of time, which were alleged to support the Indian claim. Of these maps it was said: '. . . the maps listed above do depict with a striking uniformity a conterminous boundary lying along the northern edge of the Rann and a few of them were seen and approved by the highest British authorities',[5] and, later, that the maps 'form the third and most convincing ground of India's case . . .'.[6] Nevertheless, the tribunal found that this cartographic evidence was persuasive only, and that it did not provide conclusive support for a positive claim by India to sovereign title over the Rann.[7]

Although, as a recent commentator suggests,[8] the decisions of the International Court of Justice in the *Temple Case* and the *Frontier Land Case* appear to indicate that maps produced in boundary

---

[1] Ibid., pp. 225–6.   [2] Ibid., p. 246.
[3] Ibid., p. 254.   [4] Ibid., p. 231.
[5] *Rann of Kutch Arbitration, International Legal Materials*, vol. 7 (1968), pp. 633–705, at p. 672.
[6] Ibid., p. 683.   [7] Ibid., p. 685.
[8] G. Weissberg, 'Maps as Evidence in International Boundary Disputes: A Reappraisal', 57 *A.J.I.L.* 781 (1963), at p. 801.

disputes may now have a higher evidentiary value than they have been formerly accorded, these two cases should not be taken as an implication that a map will always be preferred when it conflicts with other documentary evidence. As was said in the *Temple Case*, there is no general rule that a map line predominates[1] and, indeed, Judge Moreno Quintana went so far as to say that a 'well-established rule' of international law, exemplified by Article 29 of the Treaty of Versailles, 1919, 'states that, when there is a discrepancy concerning a frontier delimitation between the text of a treaty and maps, it is the text and not the maps which is final'.[2] The problem, it appears, should not be regarded as a theoretical contest between maps and other documentary material, but rather as a practical matter of eliciting the most reliable evidence from all the surrounding circumstances. The advisory opinion delivered by the Permanent Court of International Justice, in the *Jaworzina Boundary Case*, between Czechoslovakia and Poland in 1923, provides an example where harmony of approach was attainable:

It is true that the maps and their tables of explanatory signs cannot be regarded as conclusive proof, independently of the text of the treaties and decisions; but in the present case they confirm in a singularly convincing manner the conclusions drawn from the documents and from a legal analysis of them; and they are certainly not contradicted by any document.[3]

When drawing boundary agreements, states frequently attempt the avoidance of subsequent disputes by specifying whether, in the event of conflict between them, the text or the map shall prevail. East African practice has varied in this respect, for in some instances it is the text, and in other instances the map, which is intended to be conclusive as to the position of the boundary, while there are several agreements which make no particular provision regarding this question.

What seems to be the only East African boundary agreement that clearly favours the text over the map is that signed by Britain and Ethiopia in 1947, relating to the Kenya–Ethiopia boundary, where it is stated: 'that, in the event of any conflict between the boundary line as drawn on the map, and the description of the boundary annexed hereto, the description shall prevail'.[4] On the other hand, there are several instances where the map, not the text, is declared

---

[1] I.C.J. Rep. 1962, p. 6, at p. 65.   [2] Ibid., p. 70.
[3] *Jaworzina Boundary*, P.C.I.J., Series B/8 (1923), at p. 33.
[4] 82 *U.N.T.S.* 191, at p. 194. This agreement was superseded in 1970; see below, Ch. VIII.

to be authoritative, as in the Exchange of Notes between Britain and Belgium in 1926, establishing what is now the Tanzania–Burundi boundary: 'Should the description of the frontier given above not agree exactly with the line shown on the map attached to the present Protocol, it is distinctly understood that the Boundary as shown on the map is authoritative.'[1] This agreement also related to that section of the boundary now separating Tanzania from Rwanda, the line of which is the thalweg of the Kagera River from its confluence with the Mwibu River to the Uganda frontier. Owing to imperfect knowledge concerning the actual geographical course of the Kagera, the 1926 agreement provided for an accurate survey to be made, and this boundary sector was described in detail by an Anglo-Belgian Treaty of 1934.[2] The final boundary description is based on a combination of straight lines between boundary pillars near the edge of the swamp and portions of shore line. Although reference is made to an annexed map, the 1934 treaty fails to specify whether map or text shall prevail. As mentioned elsewhere, the Kagera is a somewhat special riparian boundary, possibly requiring a new agreement,[3] and it seems likely that the map, and the survey records on which it is based, are more authoritative than the text, since the written description itself is insufficient to show the location of the margin of the swamp as it existed when the treaty was ratified.

The description of the frontier between Mounts Sabinio and Nkabwa, on the Uganda–Congo boundary, is referred to in the protocol of the mixed Anglo-Belgian boundary commission of 1911 in words identical to those quoted above in the Tanganyika–Ruanda-Urundi boundary protocol of 1926.[4] Whereas, however, the latter was clearly accepted by an Exchange of Notes, the 1911 protocol forms only part of the entire Uganda–Congo boundary, a complete description of which was not provided until the Anglo-Belgian agreement of 1915, ratified in 1919.[5] This description, though citing the work performed by the mixed commission, and making particular reference to curved lines 'as shown on the map', does not repeat the words of the protocol that the map itself shall prevail over the text. A similar instance occurred on the Uganda–Rwanda boundary, where a protocol signed by the Anglo-German mixed commission, in terms identical to those quoted, repeats the formula that the

---

[1] 54 *L.N.T.S.* 239, at p. 251.
[3] Below, p. 95.
[5] Treaty Series 1920, No. 2, Cmd. 517.

[2] 190 *L.N.T.S.* 95.
[4] 107 *B.F.S.P.* 349, at p. 351.

boundary shown on the map is authoritative.[1] As in the case of the Uganda–Congo frontier, the Anglo-German protocol related to only part of the boundary, and when a final description was drawn in the unratified Anglo-German agreement of 1914,[2] no specific mention was made concerning the respective authority of map and text, though, like the Anglo-Belgian agreement of 1915 for the Uganda–Congo boundary, reference appears in the description to a 'curved line shown on the map'.

Reference to boundary maps presupposes that the particular map in question is available and can be readily identified. It will be found in many instances, however, that even when what are otherwise authoritative boundary descriptions depend in part on such words as 'the line shown on the map', there is a footnote to the effect that the map itself is not reproduced therewith. Omission to reproduce maps which form an integral part of a boundary agreement, without which the written description may be insufficient to indicate the boundary, not only lessens the value of the text by keeping the reader in ignorance as to what information the map reveals, but often provides him with no clue as to the map source. Notable offenders in this respect are *British and Foreign State Papers*,[3] *League of Nations Treaty Series*,[4] and Government Gazettes.[5] In former times map reproduction was a more costly and less convenient process than it is today, and there is some justification for the absence of maps in the older boundary sources mentioned above. But there is no excuse for failing to specify, even in a footnote, by reference to name, number, date, scale, publisher, etc., the map on which the authoritative lines are to be found. Examples where map references have been given in East African boundary descriptions are the Anglo-German agreement of 1890, respecting the boundary between Lakes Nyasa and Tanganyika,[6] the creation by the League of Nations of the line originally separating the British from the Belgian mandated territories,[7] and the German-Portuguese protocol relating to the western portion of the boundary between Mozambique and Tanzania.[8] The current United Nations Treaty Series very often contains a map to illustrate the text of boundary descriptions, though the source of the

---

[1] 107 *B.F.S.P.* 397, at p. 399. [2] Below, p. 274.
[3] 107 *B.F.S.P.* 350, 397. [4] 190 *L.N.T.S.* 98; 145 *L.N.T.S.* 338.
[5] *The Uganda Official Gazette*, 15 July 1913, p. 286.
[6] Hertslet, iii. 899, Art. I (2).
[7] British Mandate for East Africa, Cmd. 1794, Art. I.
[8] *Deutsches Kolonialblatt*, vol. 21 (1910), p. 126, footnote.

map is not always apparent and the quality of its reproduction, in some instances, is extremely poor, one example being the map showing the Kenya–Ethiopia boundary.[1] The above arguments can be legitimately countered by saying that those seeking the most reliable boundary sources should consult original diplomatic material or authoritative official documents such as the British Treaty Series, which usually contains detailed maps explanatory of the text, instead of depending on other references that do not have maps. Nevertheless, access to original documents may not be readily available and it is submitted that copies of authoritative maps, or at the very least, specific map references, should always accompany boundary descriptions.

Failure to be sure of the authenticity and origin of a map which is being used to support a territorial claim is an obvious impediment to the settlement of a boundary dispute. It will be remembered that in the *Temple Case*, it was by no means certain that the French map was an exact representation of the work performed by the mixed delimitation commission, though its ultimate acceptance by the Court turned not on the question of its technical accuracy but on the fact that it had been accepted by Thailand. An interesting situation where two maps, each alleged to be the original, were found to be in serious conflict, occurred at the Brussels Conference of 1910, where Germany argued that a false treaty map, detrimental to her own interest, had been deliberately substituted for the original. In this particular instance, however, the identity of the true map was not really established and, in any event, the result turned on political, rather than cartographical, argument.[2] Another curious instance related to the meridian of 30° east longitude which formed the original treaty line separating the Congolese from the German and British possessions in East Africa. When the exact position of the 30th meridian was established by British and German surveyors in 1903 it was found to lie about twelve miles east of its previously assumed location. To shift the boundary eastward, twelve miles away from the geographical features it was thought to divide, would have resulted in considerable loss of territory for both Britain and Germany and, by a secret agreement signed in 1909, the two states: 'agreed that the interpretation of the treaties relating to the boundaries in question is to be based on the old maps which either were attached to the treaties or were prepared to illustrate them'.[3] In other

[1] 82 *U.N.T.S.*, between pp. 202–3.   [2] Below, p. 244.
[3] Below, p. 272.

words, Britain and Germany not only refused to accept the 'well-established rule' that the text of a description prevails over a map, but they insisted in defining their present territorial limits by reference to old maps which were now clearly shown to be inaccurate. Questions of this kind may still arise, as for example on the Sino–Indian border where the position of the McMahon line and other portions of the boundary depends to some extent on the interpretation and acceptance of old maps.[1]

A further point to make regarding map evidence is that suitable map scales are absolutely essential. While there is no objection, and it is in fact an advantage, to having a single key map showing the entire border region, the line itself should be indicated on a series of map sheets drawn to such scale that the boundary is immediately obvious. If this is not done there is a risk that disputes may arise in boundary sections, indicated so minutely on small-scale maps, that even a trained observer might find interpretation difficult. One of the arguments advanced by the Court in the *Temple Case* was that the French map plainly showed the temple to lie within Cambodian territory, but as was pointed out by Judge Wellington Koo in his Dissenting Opinion, the map was drawn at a scale of 1:200,000 and the mark indicating the temple was 'buried in a tangle of contour lines in a small part of the map. Even if one looks specially for the mark, it is by no means easy to find it.'[2] The same point has been well taken by a recent writer on the China–India border, where he states that boundary discussions took place on maps drawn to a scale of between 1:4,000,000 and 1:5,000,000.[3] When it is appreciated that these scales represent ratios of between 60 and 80 miles to the inch, it is not difficult to understand their inadequacy in boundary interpretation.

Finally, in all the East African examples that have been given above, even in the Anglo-Ethiopian agreement of 1947 that preferred the written description to the map, it appears that the map is to be regarded as an integral part of the agreement. It is perhaps worth pointing out that, for the most part, East African boundary descriptions are based on reliable surveys, performed comparatively recently by mixed commissions of undoubted technical competence, and that should any situations arise where map and text are found to be in conflict they are probably likely to be few and of small territorial extent.

---

[1] A. Lamb, *The China–India Border*, Oxford University Press, London, 1964.
[2] I.C.J. Rep. 1962, p. 6, at p. 84.   [3] Lamb, op. cit., p. 192.

CHAPTER V

Mountain Boundaries

(a) Watershed

MOUNTAINS are frequently used for the delimitation of international boundaries, and historically are among the earliest and most obvious barriers between states.[1] One eminent authority says that of all natural features, a definite line of watershed carried by a conspicuous mountain ridge, or range, is undoubtedly the most lasting, the most unmistakable, and the most efficient as a boundary.[2] Apart from their function as a physical barrier, mountains often form a convenient economic division between neighbouring peoples, though even in such instances it does not necessarily follow that the watershed should be the inevitable boundary line, for other considerations, such as rainfall and pastoral limits, may be of greater significance.[3] Whatever may be their merits from military and economic aspects, however, watershed boundaries have often proved unsatisfactory in international law, partly because the term watershed lacks a unique definition, and partly because the watershed line is not always easy to trace physically on the ground. These two disadvantages must be examined in closer detail.

A recent compilation of geographical terms shows that two broad meanings attach to the word watershed. Firstly, it means a water-parting, the line separating the waters that flow in different directions into different rivers or river basins. This line is sometimes referred to in international documents as the *ligne de partage des eaux*, the *displuviale*, or the *divortium aquarum*, and it is in this sense that the watershed line is usually intended to be interpreted in boundary descriptions. Secondly, it means the whole gathering ground of a river system; that is to say, the catchment basin or the entire

[1] Curzon, op. cit., pp. 17–18.
[2] Holdich, op. cit., p. 147.
[3] F. Kingdon Ward in *Geog. J.* 80 (1932), 465, says of the Tibetan (p. 469): 'His frontier is the verge of the grassland, the fringe of the Pine forest, the 50-inch rainfall contour beyond which no salt is . . . The barrier may be invisible, but it is a far more formidable one to a Tibetan than the Great Himalayan range.'

area contributing to the supply of a river or lake. These two distinct meanings of watershed are said to cause confusion because of the difference between British and American usage. In British practice, watershed means the waterparting, while Americans use it as equivalent to river basin. Through international agencies such as UNESCO and FAO, the American meaning has spread widely in recent years.[1] In this connection, it is noteworthy that a British tribunal in the recent *Argentine–Chile Arbitration* consistently refers to waterparting in its Award, and does not use the expression watershed.[2]

Even if watershed is intended to be defined in the first of the two senses given, that is, as the waterparting, difficulties of interpretation may still remain. It is first necessary to understand that the waterparting of a mountain range does not necessarily coincide with the crest line, that is to say, the line joining the summits of the highest peaks. It often happens that the highest peaks of the range lie to one side of the line of waterparting and form, not part of the line itself, but one of its branches. Failure to appreciate the possibility that, in a given mountain range, the waterparting might not in fact coincide with the crest line, has led to serious problems in international boundary agreements. The classic example is the boundary between the Argentine Republic and Chile, where, by Article 1 of a Treaty signed in 1881, the line dividing the two states was described, in part, as: 'the limit between Chile and the Argentine Republic is the Cordillera of the Andes from the north to latitude 52° south. The frontier-line shall follow the crest of the Cordillera, which divides the waters, and will pass between the sources thereof on either side.'[3] In Article 2 of the same treaty, reference is also made to the *divortium aquarum* of the Andes. The treaty draftsmen evidently regarded the crest line and the waterparting as synonymous terms, yet it soon appeared that although the two lines coincided at certain points, in other places they lay a considerable distance apart. It proved impossible to recon-

---

[1] L. Dudley Stamp (ed.), *A Glossary of Geographical Terms*, Longmans, London, 1961, p. 482.

[2] *Award of Her Majesty Queen Elizabeth II for the Arbitration of a Controversy between The Argentine Republic and The Republic of Chile*, H.M.S.O., London, 1966.

[3] Treaty between Argentine Republic and Chile, Establishing the Neutrality of the Straits of Magellan. This translation is given in 9 *R.I.A.A.* 29, at p. 45. For a reference to other translations, some of which are said to contain important differences, see S. W. Boggs, *International Boundaries*, Columbia University Press, 1940, p. 86, footnote.

cile the treaty terms and a compromise boundary was eventually established in 1902 through submission to arbitration.[1]

In the *Temple Case*, between Cambodia and Thailand, the International Court of Justice held that words used by the treaty makers of 1904 should be strictly interpreted in accordance with their correct geographical meaning: '. . . the Parties provided for a watershed line (*la ligne de partage des eaux*). In so doing, they must be presumed to have realized that such a line would not necessarily, in any particular locality, be the same as the line of the crest or escarpment.'[2] It is very doubtful, however, whether the contracting parties were in fact aware of the geographical difference between a waterparting and a crest, for in Article 1 of the 1904 Treaty, the boundary was described as running along the watershed (*la ligne de partage des eaux*) of the Pnom Dang Rek mountain chain as far as the Pnom Padang chain, whose crest (*la crête*) it then followed.[3] It seems more than possible that, in employing the two different expressions, watershed and crest, in the same article, the draftsmen were using words which they regarded as synonymous, rather than attempting deliberately to create a technical distinction between the geographical determination of each of the two boundary courses.

In the disputed portion of the boundary in the *Temple Case*, however, the Court had no difficulty in deciding that watershed meant, and was intended to mean, waterparting. Thus, Judge Quintana, in his Dissenting Opinion, said: 'The decisive geographical factor in this case is the line of the watershed or *divortium aquarum* between two river basins. A watershed is not an intellectual abstraction; it is the result of the characteristics of the terrain, and it is always a topographical feature—the crest of a mountain, the ridge of an escarpment or the height of a piece of land—which will form a natural watershed.'[4] It is submitted, with respect, that the learned judge made too sweeping a statement when he went on to say: 'Geography is not however a subject which is open to divergent interpretations. It reflects one and the same reality.'[5] The facts of the case itself do not bear out this latter contention. In the critical area surrounding the temple, expert witnesses disagreed as to the precise location of the

---

[1] 9 *R.I.A.A.* 29. Part of the boundary remained in dispute and was finally settled by arbitration in 1966. See above, p. 66, note 2.

[2] *Case Concerning the Temple of Preah Vihear* (*Cambodia* v. *Thailand*), *Merits*, I.C.J. Rep. 1962, p. 6, at p. 15.

[3] Ibid., p. 16.   [4] Ibid., p. 68.

[5] Ibid., p. 69.

waterparting, and although their disagreement, in terms of geographical position, was quite small, it was sufficient to place the temple on either the Cambodian or the Thailand side of the waterparting, depending on which expert opinion was accepted. Furthermore, apart from the two waterparting lines contained in the recommendations of the opposing expert witnesses, cross-examination showed that two other possible alternatives for the precise location of the waterparting could exist, thus making altogether four lines which, although all fairly close together, and in some places coincident, failed to resolve the crucial question of which was the true line.[1]

A further difficulty in interpreting a watershed is that, even though it be accepted as the waterparting and not the crest line, there are still a number of alternative ways by which it can be theoretically defined, quite apart from the problem of establishing its physical location when an exact definition has been decided upon.[2] Adami suggests three possible ways to define this type of boundary, the true topographic watershed, the true watershed, and the apparent topographic watershed. First, the true topographic watershed, which assumes the surface of the ground to be impervious, is formed by the line joining all points on the ground from which water runs in opposite directions into adjacent river basins. Second, the true watershed is the line formed by connecting all points where the water divides, whether on or below the surface of the ground, and flows into adjacent basins. Third, the apparent topographic watershed is similar to the true topographic watershed, but it is formed by the most clearly pronounced line and leaves out minor hydrographic features.[3] It is quite apparent that, in a particular locality, each of these three interpretations could produce significantly different results on the ground, and if a watershed is to be used for the delimitation of an international boundary, it is most important to specify clearly what manner of line is intended.

[1] I.C.J. Rep. 1962, p. 6, at pp. 98–9. The result of the case did not depend on the exact position of the waterparting, for although French surveyors in 1906 had incorrectly located it in the disputed area, subsequent French maps clearly portrayed the temple as lying on the Cambodian side of the international boundary. Thailand, who made no survey of her own until many years later, was held by the Court to have accepted the French maps through acquiescence or preclusion.

[2] For a description of the practical difficulties involved see J. K. Trotter, 'The Science of Frontier Delimitation', *Minutes of Proceedings of the Royal Artillery Institution*, vol. 24, 1897, at pp. 217–18.

[3] V. Adami, *National Frontiers in Relation to International Law* (translated by T. T. Behrens), Oxford University Press, London, 1927, pp. 111–12.

If the boundary is to be interpreted as the true topographic water-shed, practical difficulties may arise when its location on the ground is attempted. Not infrequently the waterparting bifurcates, as when a swamp or a lake lies astride a mountain ridge. In the one instance there may be over a wide area no sensible flow of water to establish the direction of the waterparting, and in the other instance the lake may be contained within an undrained basin the rim of which pro-vides alternative lines of waterparting. Quite apart from the fact that the watershed may be in an area difficult of access and covered by forbidding vegetation,[1] a more serious problem arises when it lies not along a well-defined mountain ridge but in relatively flat country. In such instances, the line of waterparting will by no means be apparent to the inexperienced eye, and even surveyors called on to establish it may find their work to be tedious and costly, with the risk of possible error. A good African example of this type of waterpart-ing is the Nile–Congo divide which forms the boundary between Sudan and the Central African Republic. This boundary was found by the surveyors to be:

. . . a winding line in the flattest of flat forests . . . and the ground between trees is filled by the toughest and most prolific grass imaginable. . . . To find a watershed and to survey it in such flat country is by no means easy. . . . To say definitely which way a stream was flowing when first reached was not always as easy a matter as it sounds, for the water in these Nile and Congo tributaries within a dozen miles or so of the marshes which gave them birth proved usually to be practically stagnant. A stick thrown in would not move, and often careful search up and down the stream for some sign of water movement would reveal nothing.[2]

The true watershed does not appear to be a convenient form of boundary and its use should probably be restricted to cases where the preservation of water rights requires that subterranean rivers and streams have to be considered. It is evident that, if this definition is to be employed, adequate artificial demarcation on the surface of the ground is essential to prevent future dispute as to the exact location of the boundary.

The third type of waterparting, the apparent topographic water-shed, is essentially a compromise and is likely to prove the most

[1] In the *Guatemala–Honduras Boundary Arbitration* it was said, 'The watershed was at that time (during the colonial period) for the most part a tangle of impene-trable forest that defied the explorer, and even more the surveyor . . .' 2 *R.I.A.A.* 1307, at p. 1341.

[2] P. K. Boulnois, 'On the Western Frontier of the Sudan', *Geog. J.* 63 (1924), 465, at pp. 470–2.

useful in actual practice. Boundary agreements adopting this form of delimitation should give the demarcation commission appropriate powers to depart from the theoretical waterparting where circumstances make it desirable to do so. Such powers should enable the boundary commissioners to diverge from the true waterparting in places where the presence of minor streams results in an undesirably winding or crooked line. An additional power to deviate from the precise waterparting should be given where it lies in an anomalous position such as the edge of an overhanging cliff face, where it bifurcates along the margin of a swamp or the rim of an undrained lake basin, or where it cuts through existing limits of cultivation. Power given to demarcation commissions to depart from the watershed line should, generally speaking, be of a fairly minor positional and economic nature, as there might otherwise be claims for exchange of territory that would involve lengthy negotiation and require a further delimitation agreement between the contracting parties.

Ideally, the waterparting line, whichever type is adopted, should be marked by boundary pillars at suitable intervals and, for the avoidance of later dispute, it should be stated in the final agreement that the line as jointly demarcated represents the true boundary, irrespective of whether or not it precisely coincides with the theoretical position. Had this been done in the Franco-Siamese delimitation of 1906 the *Temple Case* need never have arisen. An African illustration of a realistic approach to watershed delimitation and demarcation is given by the Anglo-Belgian agreements of 1927–33, relating to what is now part of the Zambia–Congo boundary. For the Congo–Zambezi watershed section of this boundary it was provided that:

1. The Commissioners shall have authority, generally, to make such minor rectifications and adjustments, to the ideal watershed as are necessary to avoid the troubles which might arise from a literal interpretation of the Treaty.

2. The present position of the boundary pillars shall be accepted where they lie not farther than 200 metres from the ideal watershed. In exceptional circumstances, and in areas of no particular known economic value, errors of position up to 500 metres may be allowed. In adjusting such departures from the ideal watershed to the general run of the boundary, no sharp re-entrants will be formed.

3. Where there are alternative ideal watersheds, including undrained basins, the Commissioners shall agree upon, and demarcate, a compromise line.[1]

[1] 140 *L.N.T.S.* 71, at p. 74.

In the event it was found that a number of compromises and minor deviations were required during the demarcation of the Congo–Zambezi watershed. The general boundary description states:

Except on rare occasions the watershed ridge is of a flat-topped nature showing very little rise or fall for a considerable distance on either side. In the following description the terms 'unmistakable', 'well-defined', and 'ill-defined' afford a relative idea as to the nature of the actual watershed ridge.[1]

An example of a departure from this waterparting for economic reasons was a shifting of part of the boundary where the British railway line inadvertently entered Congolese territory for a distance of about 5¾ kilometres. The commissioners reported that 'owing to the thickly wooded nature of the country, the actual watershed is nowhere obvious and the good faith of the railway engineers who sited the railway must be acknowledged'.[2]

East African examples of watershed boundaries are not numerous. The Tanzania–Zambia boundary follows, in part, 'the waterparting of the geographical Congo Basin'. This line was demarcated in 1898 by a mixed commission which, in accordance with a provision of the Anglo-German delimitation agreement of 1890 that permitted minor boundary rectification to meet local requirements, departed from the waterparting line in two places. This section of the boundary was demarcated by a number of boundary pillars placed on the waterparting itself, and by a few other pillars marking straight-line segments in the two places where divergence from the waterparting was considered desirable. Additional boundary marks were erected in 1934–5 to indicate the waterparting more clearly between the original pillars. These intermediate marks were placed sufficiently close together that the waterparting may quite reasonably be taken as following the straight line between adjacent marks. In addition, about forty beacons, consisting of old iron telegraph poles capped by a metal target, were later placed at certain points on the straight lines connecting adjacent boundary marks, so as to indicate as clearly as possible the actual course of the boundary.[3]

Another instance where a watershed has been used in an East African boundary description is on the border between Kenya and Ethiopia. The 1947 Anglo-Ethiopian agreement described part of the boundary as following 'the watershed between the Gaddaduma

---

[1] 140 *L.N.T.S.* 87, at p. 96.   [2] Ibid., p. 110.
[3] Below, Ch. XVI.

and Adde valleys on the one side, and the valleys of Bor and Dembi on the other'. This agreement was never ratified, mainly owing to disputes concerning the ownership of certain wells, including those at Qadaduma (Gaddaduma). In 1970 Kenya and Ethiopia signed a treaty which, *inter alia*, abrogated the provisions of the Anglo-Ethiopian agreement and established a new boundary.[1] The present description, contained in Schedule I to the treaty, defines the boundary as a series of straight lines drawn between adjacent pillars. In those few places where the line of watershed is followed, its demarcated, and not its theoretical, position forms the true boundary.

From the western end of the Uganda–Rwanda boundary, the line follows the watershed between the highest points of Mounts Sabinio and Mgahinga. The map attached to the Anglo-German protocol of 1911 shows that this line follows the curve of the waterparting and is not simply a straight line joining the respective summits. Again, on the same boundary, between pillars 28 and 29, the line is described as 'a very conspicuous waterparting' and here also the map shows a pronounced curve between the two pillars.[2] Northward from Mount Sabinio the Uganda–Congo boundary, in accordance with the Anglo-Belgian agreement of 1915, follows the watershed in a number of places, and the relevant maps show, in each instance, that the watershed is a topographic and not a mere geometric course between adjacent boundary pillars.[3]

The final, and possibly the most important, illustration of the use of a watershed in an East African delimitation agreement is on the Uganda–Congo boundary which is defined in part by the Congo–Nile watershed. This section of the boundary, originally created by the Anglo-Congolese agreement of 1894, is about 90 miles in length and extends northerly from boundary pillar No. 26 (the western terminal of the old Mahagi Strip) as far as the Sudan tripoint near the source of the Kaia River. So far as is known, this watershed boundary has never been artificially demarcated, but a local expert has described it as 'mutually well known, for it follows for the most part the crest (*sic*) of a gentle treeless undulation, and the absence of monuments has given rise to no difficulty'.[4]

[1] Below, Ch. VIII.
[2] *Report on the Work of the British Section of the Anglo-German-Belgian Commission, 1911,* H.M.S.O. London, 1912.
[3] U.K. Treaty Series, 1920, No. 2, Cmd. 517.
[4] H. B. Thomas and A. E. Spencer, *A History of Uganda Land and Surveys . . .* Govt. Press, Entebbe, 1938, p. 37.

(b) Crest

The distinction between a crest line and a watershed has already been given, and it will be recalled that Adami's definition is that a crest is the general line formed by joining the summits of the main ridge of a chain of mountains. It is probably in this sense that the word crest has been used in East African delimitation agreements, and notable examples exist on the Uganda–Congo,[1] Uganda–Rwanda,[2] Uganda–Sudan,[3] and Kenya–Sudan boundaries.[4] In other parts of the Uganda–Sudan and Kenya–Sudan boundaries, delimitation consists of straight lines joining the summits of named peaks, and this practice was followed in the Uganda–Kenya boundary[5] where the words crest and watershed have been avoided. It is possible that the interpretation of these two words can be assisted by an examination of the availability of topographical information at the time when the delimitation agreement was concluded. The Uganda–Sudan and Kenya–Sudan boundaries were delimited largely on paper, and even though some field investigation took place it was rapid and incomplete. Although this delimitation was intended to be provisional no demarcation commission was subsequently appointed to provide a final, and more precise, description of the line. It seems reasonable in such cases, therefore, that the crest is intended to be a series of straight lines joining the prominent features referred to, rather than as a line which at every point conforms to the sinuosity of the theoretical and, at the time, unsurveyed, watershed. On the other hand, where, as on the Uganda–Congo and Uganda–Rwanda boundaries, careful topographical surveys preceded the final boundary agreement, there is more justification for interpreting the words crest and watershed strictly and separately.

(c) Foothills

The foot of a hill, even to the most uninformed layman, must appear at once to be an unsatisfactory and imprecise boundary mark, since there are no technical rules to define it and its exact geographical position is very much a matter of opinion. Unfortunately the inadequacy of the expression has not prevented its use in international boundary agreements. Holdich, speaking of the Afghanistan–

---

[1] Below, pp. 992–3. [2] Below, pp. 275–6. [3] Below, p. 263.
[4] Below, p. 131. [5] Below, pp. 250–2.

Baluchistan boundary, says: '. . . the boundary . . . was defined as following "the foot of the hills". Here at once was the opening for serious disagreement—and the disagreement promptly arose. What was the "foot of the hills"?'[1] Another example occurred on the Iran–Turkey boundary, of which it was said: 'The crest of a range is not so bad an expression to decide a frontier, but the foot of the hills is a bad one. It is not often that hills end abruptly, they usually indefinitely melt into the plain. . . .'[2]

Some unfortunate examples of the use of this term can be found in East Africa. On the Uganda–Sudan boundary, west of the Nile, the description reads, in part: 'thence in a straight line due west to the bottom of the foothills of the escarpment running north-west from Jebel Elengua; thence following the bottom of the foothills of this escarpment in a north-westerly direction . . .',[3] and east of the Nile, on the same boundary, the description for the Tereteinia transfer from Uganda to Sudan refers to '. . . a straight line to the most south-easterly foothills of Jebel Tereteinia . . .'.[4]

The longest boundary of this type occurs on the Uganda–Kenya boundary where it is described by an Order in Council of 1926 as a line running 'to the base of the Turkana Escarpment; thence the boundary follows the base of that escarpment in a generally north-westerly direction . . .'.[5] In this particular instance, however, it is no longer necessary to seek the theoretical base of the Turkana escarpment for, in 1959–60, a joint Uganda–Kenya demarcation party defined it on the ground throughout its entire length of approximately 200 miles as a series of straight lines marked by 180 boundary pillars.[6]

Another particularly bad example of this type is the eastern terminal of the Kenya–Sudan boundary which is theoretically fixed by a line passing through 'the northernmost point of the northernmost crest of the long spur running north of Mount Lubur'.[7] No one can say with certainty where this precise point lies and it provides a

---

[1] Holdich, op. cit., pp. 193–4.

[2] C. H. D. Ryder, 'The Demarcation of the Turco-Persian Boundary in 1913–1914', *Geog. J.* 66 (1925), 227, at p. 232. The writer went on to say that apart from the technical difficulties of interpreting the boundary agreement, the personnel engaged in the survey suffered personal discomfort through lack of water. When a river was eventually reached its laxative properties caused such distress that the commissioners were only too happy to reach an accelerated settlement so as to leave the area as quickly as possible.

[3] Below, pp. 260–1.   [4] Below, p. 264.   [5] Below, p. 252.
[6] Below, p. 253.   [7] Below, p. 131.

perfect illustration of a boundary situation where an original hasty delimitation based on insufficient topographical information was allowed to remain ambiguous owing to the absence of subsequent investigation and survey by a demarcation team.[1]

[1] For a discussion of other problems regarding this boundary see below, Ch. X.

CHAPTER VI

River Boundaries

(a) The Selection of Rivers as Boundaries

FOR obvious historical reasons rivers have often been regarded as an ideal form of boundary delimitation. In unexplored country especially, the river provided a most convenient, and sometimes the only, means of transportation and communication, and since its geographical location could be traced more or less accurately by early explorers[1] and it could usually be identified by a distinctive name, it frequently formed the only known topographical feature on an otherwise blank map. In such circumstances, it is easy to appreciate that diplomats attempting to draw the limits of territories should regard rivers as eminently suitable boundary material. Two examples will suffice to show the attitudes of nineteenth-century boundary makers. Holdich writes:

> Next to mountain ranges, rivers afford the most tangible line for boundary definition. There is no mistaking the line, there is no waste over artificial constructions in connection with demarcation. . . . There are geographical conditions in many parts of the globe where a river line is the only one possible to afford any prospect of permanence and easy recognition. . . . Where the surrounding country is a waste of trackless forest or wild upland, and where the river is confined to a comparatively narrow channel in a rock-bound bed, it is a God-sent feature for boundary-making, and requires no assistance from man.[2]

and Trotter remarks: 'A river forms, so far as my experience goes, an excellent natural frontier, by far the best from the delimiter's point of view, for it requires no delimitation. A river delimits itself.'[3] Yet the very reasons that made rivers attractive to paper delimitation are an indication of their general unsuitability as boundaries. It has been pointed out that a river basin is commonly inhabited by the same

---

[1] See below, pp. 179–80, for David Livingstone's caustic comments concerning the inaccurate mapping of the Zambezi and Lake Nyasa.
[2] Holdich, op. cit., p. 156.
[3] Trotter, op. cit., p. 209.

peoples or tribes.[1] Such people frequently live on both banks[2] and the river, far from being a line of separation, is itself a major economic factor inducing kindred habitation. As Lord Curzon remarks, the teaching of history is that rivers connect rather than separate, but with the growth of states, strategic considerations have almost invariably been responsible for their conversion into boundaries.[3] It is not to be supposed that those concerned with early delimitation were entirely unaware of the sociological and ethnological nature of boundary rivers but too often they appear to have regarded the boundary line itself as the paramount consideration, and its effect on local population as a merely secondary matter. Thus Trotter, writing in 1897, says that when tribes and races 'have in some instances pushed beyond the natural (river) barriers, it is an easy matter to make them withdraw'.[4]

The shortcomings of original boundary delimitation in Africa are well known and need not be pressed too far, especially in view of the 1964 resolution of the Organization of African Unity stating that inherited colonial boundaries should now be respected.[5] The sociological implications of river boundaries, for example, would no doubt prove to be an interesting and important study, but it is one which lies outside the scope of this work. Instead, it is proposed to examine existing river boundaries from the legal standpoint, with particular regard to difficulties of interpretation in boundary descriptions.

East African boundaries are formed in large part by rivers and smaller watercourses. Important examples are the Ruvuma, Kagera, and (until 1925) the Juba rivers. In nearly every instance where the line is described in a boundary document as following a watercourse, the word thalweg is used or implied, and this technical term requires explanation. Other expressions, such as bank, mouth, and source, also occur and, as will be shown, are not necessarily susceptible of precise interpretation. Some consideration must also be given to the effect on territorial sovereignty when a boundary river changes its course, and to the question of the ownership of islands in the middle of a river.

[1] Boggs, op. cit., pp. 23–5. S. B. Jones, *Boundary-Making*, Columbia Univ. Press, New York, 1945, p. 110.
[2] Such as the Makonde who live on both sides of the Ruvuma River which separates Tanzania from Mozambique.
[3] Curzon, op. cit., pp. 20–1.
[4] Trotter, loc. cit.
[5] Above, Ch. II (d).

(b) Thalweg

'Thalweg' means the line of greatest depth of the main channel of a stream or river. The word is of German origin and its literal meaning is the 'downway' or the track of fastest current followed by a boat going downstream. It is not clear when the expression first appeared in boundary descriptions. According to Westlake, the thalweg was proposed as the dividing line of a river at the Congress of Rastatt in 1797,[1] and Adami says that the term was first used in the Treaty of Luneville, 1801.[2] Another eminent writer, de Lapradelle, claims that the usage is far older, and that the thalweg of the Rhine defined the boundary between Alsace and the German Empire in the Treaty of Munster of 1648.[3]

Although the precise date of its origin is of no more than historical interest, thalweg is now firmly entrenched in international boundary language. Yet its precise interpretation is still not altogether clear and direct judicial authority is scanty. As is pointed out by de Lapradelle, various meanings have been attached to the word, including the line of deepest soundings of a river, the path of the main current which is normally used by downstream traffic, and the axis of the safest and most accessible channel for the largest ships.[4] The possibility of different interpretations of thalweg for a particular river has led a recent commentator to say that the definitions of thalweg fall into two main groups; those in which the thalweg is related to the navigable channel, and those in which it relates simply to the physical line of deepest soundings.[5] As with other geographical terms, however, it is difficult to formulate an exact definition that will meet every possible situation and it seems likely that, in a particular case, many considerations must be taken into account, including, for example, the extent of navigability (itself a term of somewhat uncertain meaning), the volume of traffic, the economic importance of the river, the geological composition and stability of its bed and, above all, whether there is a relevant boundary agreement that provides any clue as to the manner in which thalweg is to be interpreted. As will be seen later, there is a tendency in East African boundary

---

[1] J. Westlake, *International Law*, Part I, Peace, 2nd edn., Cambridge University Press, 1910, p. 144.

[2] Adami, op. cit., p. 17.   [3] de Lapradelle, op. cit., p. 202.

[4] Ibid., pp. 202–4.

[5] E. Lauterpacht, 'River Boundaries: Legal Aspects of the Shatt-al-Arab Frontier', 9 *I.C.L.Q.*, 208 (1960), at p. 222.

descriptions to use thalweg for all rivers and streams, whether navigable or not, whereas the expression applies more properly to navigable watercourses.

In the case of *New Jersey* v. *Delaware*, the United States Supreme Court said in 1934:

> International law today divides the river boundaries between states by the middle of the main channel, when there is one, and not by the geographical centre, halfway between the banks. . . . It applies the same doctrine, now known as the doctrine of the Thalweg, to estuaries and bays in which the dominant sailing channel can be followed to the sea. . . . The underlying rationale of the doctrine of the Thalweg is one of equality and justice.[1]

Again, in the *Grisbadarna Case*, between Norway and Sweden, the Permanent Court of Arbitration equated thalweg with the most important channel, *chenal le plus important*.[2]

Juristic writing usually distinguishes non-navigable from navigable boundary rivers and says that, in the absence of treaty or other stipulations, the rule is that the boundary line in a non-navigable river follows the median line, or *medium filum aquae*, but that, in the case of navigable rivers the boundary runs along the thalweg.[3] An example of the practical application of this doctrine, which derives from the rules of municipal law, appears in Article 30 of the Treaty of Versailles, 1919, which reads:

> In the case of boundaries which are defined by a waterway, the terms 'course' and 'channel' used in the present Treaty, signify: in the case of non-navigable rivers, the median line of the waterway or of its principal arm, and, in the case of navigable rivers, the median line of the principal channel of navigation. . . .[4]

Although 'median line' is used in Article 30 for both navigable and non-navigable waterways, there seems little doubt that the navigable median should be interpreted as the thalweg, and the non-navigable median as the *medium filum aquae*.

Very little thought should suffice to show that the thalweg and the median of a particular river seldom, if ever, coincide. The median, if

---

[1] 291 U.S. 361 (1934), at p. 379.
[2] 11 *R.I.A.A.* 147, at p. 160.
[3] See, e.g., L. Oppenheim, *International Law*, vol. i, 8th edn. (ed. H. Lauterpacht), Longmans, London, 1955, p. 532.
[4] The text is given by H. W. V. Temperley, *A History of the Peace Conference of Paris*, Henry Frowde, Hodder & Stoughton, London, 1920, vol. iii, p. 128.

interpreted as the *medium filum* of the water surface, is frequently difficult to establish with certainty, since in most instances, owing to unequal height and slope of opposite banks, its position will shift as the river rises and falls. If the median line is intended as the boundary, therefore, it is most essential to specify in the boundary agreement some definite water stage, such as low water mark, by which the median shall be established.[1] The thalweg, on the other hand, especially if it is interpreted as the continuous line of deepest sound-ings, is relatively easy to establish physically, and is less susceptible of alteration than the *medium filum aquae*, though even when the expression thalweg is used in boundary descriptions, care should be taken to give it an appropriate geographical definition and to specify what effect any future change in its lateral position shall have on adjacent territorial sovereignties.

Where rivers and streams have been used to separate the countries of East Africa, the boundary in nearly every instance has been described as the thalweg, whether or not the waterway is navigable. This may have been intended as a practical procedure, possibly designed to remove ambiguity and to avoid confusion with the median. There are many examples illustrating the use of the expres-sion. The earliest employment of thalweg in East Africa occurs in the Anglo-Italian protocol of 24 March 1891, setting out the respective spheres of influence of the two states. Here the boundary is described, in part, as 'the mid-channel (thalweg) of the River Juba'.[2] It seems evident from the choice of words that the boundary was intended to follow the main channel and not merely the median line of the water.

In the Anglo-German agreement of 1 July 1890 the boundary description, on what is now the Tanzania–Malawi boundary, runs to the 'northern bank of the mouth of the River Songwe', whence it 'ascends' and 'follows' that river, without specifying whether or not the line continues along the north bank.[3] The Songwe question was soon settled, for by the Anglo-German agreement of 1901, following the work of a mixed demarcation commission undertaken three years earlier, it was provided that in all cases (including the Songwe) 'where a river or stream forms the boundary, the "thalweg" of the same shall form the boundary; if, however, no actual "thalweg" is to

---

[1] For a discussion of median line boundaries and the different ways by which they can be established see Boggs, op. cit., pp. 178–84.

[2] Hertslet, iii. 948. See below, p. 115.

[3] Hertslet, iii. 899, Art. I, para. 2.

be distinguished, it shall be the middle of the bed'.[1] The effect of this provision is that in those places, and there are several, where the Tanzania–Malawi and Tanzania–Zambia boundary is formed by a river or stream, the thalweg, or navigational channel, is the actual boundary line, except where it cannot be distinguished, in which latter case the middle of the bed forms the boundary. 'Middle of the bed' is itself a rather vague term and should probably be taken to mean the *medium filum* at low water mark. An important water feature on the Tanzania–Zambia boundary is the Kalambo Falls, situated on the Kalambo River. Despite the fact that this waterfall, with a height of about 700 feet, is among the highest in Africa, it was not surveyed, or even recorded, by the mixed commission of 1898,[2] and its 'discovery' some years later was the subject of considerable geographical interest, leading to an expedition in 1928 which investigated the Kalambo Falls and obtained their correct location.[3] It is apparent that neither thalweg nor median is really an appropriate term to apply to boundary waterfalls, and, especially in those cases where hydro-electric power can be developed, the desirable solution is probably the preparation of a special agreement for the ownership, control, and use of the waters.

The same Anglo-German agreement of 1890, on what is now the Tanzania–Mozambique boundary, established the line as following the 'course of the River Rovuma'.[4] For many years, uncertainty prevailed as to what was the meaning of 'course'. German opinion inclined to the view that, in this particular instance, it meant either the thalweg or the south (right) bank; in other words, that Germany owned either the whole, or approximately half the width, of the river. The question was settled in 1913 by an agreement between Germany and Portugal which placed the boundary along the thalweg.[5] Amplification of the river's boundary status occurred in 1938, when, by an Anglo-Portuguese agreement that took effect in that year, it was provided that

> Throughout the course of the River Rovuma in those places where there are no islands, the boundary shall follow the thalweg even when the position

---

[1] Hertslet, iii. 925, Sec. 2.

[2] *Geog. J.* 67 (1926), 248, at p. 250, where an original member of the mixed demarcation commission said that during the survey he became aware of the existence of the falls but excused the commission's failure to reach them by saying that 'we were surveying, not exploring, and our time-table had to be adhered to'.

[3] *Geog. J.* 74 (1929), 28.

[4] Hertslet, iii. 899, Art. I, para. 2. [5] Below, p. 212.

of the latter is changed by a natural alteration in the bed of the river.
By thalweg is understood the line of minimum level[1] along the river bed;
   In places in the river where the channel between the islands and the bank
belonging to the other territory does not contain the thalweg of the river,
the boundary shall follow the thalweg of that subsidiary channel until it
meets the thalweg of the River Rovuma.[2]

It will be noted, first, that this provision includes a definition of
thalweg as the line of minimum level along the river bed, in other
words, the continuous line of deepest soundings, and, second, that
it allows a divergence of the boundary into a subsidiary channel where
the main thalweg runs between the bank of a riparian state and islands
over which that state has sovereignty. The remaining part of the
Tanzania–Mozambique boundary is formed, in part, by the rivers
Msinje, Kipingi, and Kiwindi. For these riparian sections the German-Portuguese protocol of 1909 states that the boundary follows the
course of the river.[3] This matter appears never to have been the subject of dispute between the adjoining states and no further definition
of 'course' appeared in either the German-Portuguese agreement of
1913, or the Anglo-Portuguese agreement of 1938. Probably, by
analogy with the Anglo-German agreement of 1901, respecting the
Tanzania–Malawi and Tanzania–Zambia boundaries, the Msinje,
Kipingi, and Kiwindi courses should be taken as the thalweg if it is
distinguishable, and the median if it is not.

   Other examples of the use of thalweg as a boundary are the river
Daua, between Kenya and Ethiopia;[4] the Kirurumu and Chizinga,
between Uganda and Rwanda;[5] the Kachwamba–Kakitumba and
Kagera, between Uganda and Tanzania;[6] the Khor Kayu, Kaia, and
Unyama, between Uganda and Sudan;[7] and the Losoyai and Ruvu,
between Kenya and Tanzania.[8] Many examples also exist on the
Uganda–Congo[9] and Tanzania–Burundi[10] boundaries. Between
Uganda and Kenya, however, the boundary follows[11] the 'course' of

---

[1] i.e. the continuous line formed by connecting those points on the river bed
that have the lowest altitude.
[2] 185 *L.N.T.S.* 205, para. 2.   [3] Below, pp. 215–16.   [4] Below, p. 110.
[5] Below, pp. 275–6.   [6] Below, p. 276.   [7] Below, pp. 260–1.
[8] Below, p. 146.   [9] Below, pp. 292–4.   [10] Below, pp. 159–62.
[11] In the *Manica Boundary Arbitration* of 1897, between Britain and Portugal,
(Hertslet, iii. 1036), concerning part of the Mozambique–Rhodesia boundary,
the arbitrator considered the Portuguese argument (at p. 1059) that to 'follow'
a watercourse means to go downstream, not upstream. He decided (at p. 1064)
that apart from the 'philological point of view', the word follow, in diplomatic
documents, can mean going downstream, as well as upstream. Nevertheless, in

several rivers and streams, such as the Sio, Sango, and Suam-Turkwel. No definition of the word course appears in the boundary description contained in the Order in Council establishing this boundary,[1] but, as in the case of the other boundaries referred to, it may mean the thalweg in those places where it can be distinguished and the median line where it cannot.

The Tanzania–Rwanda boundary, throughout its entire length, was intended to be defined by the thalweg of the Kagera River, but it presents a special problem. By an Exchange of Notes between Britain and Belgium in 1926, the boundary between what is now Tanzania and Rwanda is described as commencing at the confluence of the Mwibu and Kagera rivers and thence running northward 'from this point down the Kagera River to the Uganda Frontier, the two Governments agree that the midstream of this latter River shall be accepted as the Boundary . . .'.[2] It is not clear why the expression midstream should have been used when other riparian portions of the Tanganyika–Ruanda–Urundi boundary were described in the same document as the thalweg. North of the Mwibu-Kagera confluence, however, the Kagera follows, for a considerable distance, a winding and variable course through wide papyrus swamps and it may be that midstream was deliberately chosen as a less exact provisional description, pending the completion of the accurate survey of the Kagera that was provided for by the 1926 agreement.[3] The final description of the boundary northward from the Mwibu–Kagera confluence was established by the Anglo-Belgian treaty of 1934 which, generally speaking, defines the boundary in terms of the Kagera thalweg. Owing to the presence of the swamp, and the meandering course of the river, it was decided to define a portion of the boundary as a combination of stretches of shore-line and straight-line segments between artificial boundary pillars placed on dry land. The advantages of this arrangement were, first, that the boundary was formed in part by the shore of the dry land near the pillars, thereby avoiding the creation of undesirable small enclaves belonging to the state on the other side of the river and, second, that islands in the river were clearly placed on one side or other of the boundary.[4] The Tanzania–Rwanda boundary is therefore a unique riparian limit

order to avoid ambiguity, it may be desirable in some instances to use 'ascend' and 'descend' in boundary watercourse descriptions.

[1] S.R. & O. 1926/1733, below, Ch. XVIII.   [2] 54 *L.N.T.S.* 239, at p. 249.
[3] Below, Ch. XII.   [4] 190 *L.N.T.S.* 95, Art. 2.

in East Africa, with respect to both delimitation and demarcation. Another important aspect of this boundary is the Anglo-Belgian agreement of 1934,[1] concerning water rights affecting diversion of waters, mining and industrial operations, irrigation, fishing and other rights to be enjoyed by inhabitants of the adjacent states. These provisions, it should be noted, apply not only to the Kagera, but to all rivers and streams crossing the Tanzania–Rwanda and Tanzania–Burundi boundaries.

(c) Bank

There is no theoretical reason why one riparian state should not own the entire width of a boundary river, in which event its limits would extend to one of the river banks and, in the absence of special agreement, deprive the adjoining state of access to, and enjoyment of, the water. As was pointed out by Mr. Justice Cardozo in *New Jersey* v. *Delaware*,[2] however, the underlying rationale of the thalweg is one of equality and justice, and in most instances it would be plainly inequitable that one of the riparian states should enjoy the exclusive economic benefits of a boundary river. River bank boundaries are not very common,[3] and the only East African example appears to be of comparatively minor significance. A West African case deserves examination since it demonstrates the need for a clear understanding of what is meant by the word bank.

The eastern end of the Kenya–Tanzania boundary on the Indian Ocean coast is formed, in part, by a line running from the 'eastern mouth' of the Ngobwe Creek along the 'eastern bank' of the creek to its end.[4] This description first appeared in 1893, and apart from an Anglo-German protocol of 1900 which describes this section of the boundary as following the 'left bank of the Ngobwe',[5] it has never been formally altered. During the negotiations leading to the signing of the 1900 protocol, Britain asked Germany to amend the boundary description by shifting the line from the left bank to the course (thalweg), but Germany refused to do so on the grounds that this would mean 'a cession, without good reason, of territory which would be inconsistent with the [Anglo-German] Agreement of 1893'.[6]

---

[1] 190 *L.N.T.S.* 103.   [2] 291 U.S. 361 (1934), at p. 380.
[3] The Shatt-al-Arab, between Iran and Iraq, is one example. See 9 *I.C.L.Q.* 208.
[4] Hertslet, iii. 911.   [5] Ibid., 921, at p. 922.
[6] Ibid., p. 924.

The amount of territory which Germany would have lost by this amendment is trifling, since the creek is small and only about a mile in length, nor does it appear to have so high an economic value that its waters could not reasonably be shared by riparian neighbours. The creek itself, which winds through swampland, has changed its position over the years,[1] and since the surrounding area is relatively lightly populated there appears to have been no dispute or practical difficulty regarding the creek's function as a boundary.

The Ngobwe boundary, it will be noted, was described in 1893 as the eastern bank, and in 1900 as the left bank, of the creek. Although cardinal points[2] frequently provide the most useful references in boundary descriptions they are often unsuitable for rivers and streams, especially when the course of the latter is tortuous. Indeed, one bank of a river may completely box the compass throughout its various changes of direction. Where the bank of a river or stream is to be used as a boundary, therefore, it is more appropriate to use the expressions 'left' and 'right', but it is essential to apply them in the way they would appear to an observer facing downstream, and not necessarily as they appear to an observer facing the map. Cartographic convention shows north at the top of a map sheet, and, in the case of a southward flowing river, it is easy for an uninstructed person looking at the map to assume that the eastern river bank, that is to say, the bank on his own right hand side, is the right bank of the river, whereas it is actually the left bank, because of the southward flow. It would be scarcely necessary to labour this rather elementary point had not an instance arisen when just such a mistaken notion led to the establishment of a river boundary that later proved controversial. By the Franco-Liberian delimitation agreement of 1892,[3] the boundary between Liberia and the Ivory Coast was described as the thalweg of the River Cavally, but a later agreement between the same two states, made in 1907, altered this part of the boundary to the right bank of the river.[4] The effect of this latter description was to place the entire course of the Cavally, between its confluence with the River Nuon and the Atlantic Ocean, under French sovereignty, and although both agreements provided for free navigation to the inhabitants of opposite banks, Liberia, by entering into the 1907 arrangement, relinquished her sovereign rights over half the river. The River Cavally flows southward into the Atlantic and it is said

[1] Ibid., p. 922, and see below, p. 142.
[2] i.e. the points of the compass.
[3] Hertslet, iii. 1134.
[4] Ibid., 1140.

that the Liberian diplomats who negotiated the 1907 agreement were confused into believing that what is in fact the left bank appeared to them as the right, and they therefore unwittingly gave up control of a share of the river.[1]

Again, if bank is to be used as a boundary description a more precise definition of the term is required. If no such definition appears in the original agreement difficulties in interpretation may arise. Where one state owns the entire river, its most advantageous boundary is the high-water mark on the opposite bank, whereas the low-water mark favours the other state.[2] In the absence of any special provisions it seems that the low-water mark is the fairest boundary in such situations.

(d) Mouth

Jones points out the danger of assuming that the mouth of a river has a precise location, since some rivers enter the sea through swamps or by several branches of a delta, and that even when a river has a single embouchure its mouth is an area, rather than a precise geographical determination, which may cause trouble in boundary treaty interpretation.[3] It appears, however, that the doctrine of the thalweg can be applied in most instances to a river mouth or estuary, especially if thalweg is interpreted as the centre of the main channel. It will be recalled that in New Jersey v. Delaware,[4] the Supreme Court described the thalweg as applicable to estuaries and bays in which the dominant sailing channel can be followed to the sea.

The difficulty raised by Jones was taken up in the Case Concerning the Honduras and Nicaragua Arbitral Award, in which Nicaragua 'argued that the mouth of a river is not a fixed point and cannot serve as a common boundary between two states, and that vital questions of navigation rights would be involved in accepting the mouth of the river as the boundary between Honduras and Nicaragua'. The International Court of Justice found that since the operative part of the original Award of 1906 stated that the boundary started from the mouth of the Segovia or Coco River and followed the thalweg

---

[1] I. W. Zartman, 'The Politics of Boundaries in North and West Africa', J.M.A.S. 3 (1965), 155, at p. 172.

[2] L. J. Bouchez, 'The Fixing of Boundaries in International Boundary Rivers', 12 I.C.L.Q. 789 (1963), at p. 791.

[3] Jones, op. cit., p. 130.

[4] 291 U.S. 361 (1934), at p. 379.

upstream, it was obvious that the thalweg constituted the boundary even at the mouth of the river. In the Court's opinion, the determination of the boundary in this section should give rise to no difficulty.[1] Problems of this type do not appear to have arisen in East Africa. In a number of descriptions the boundary line is drawn to the mouth of a river; some examples are the Sio in Lake Victoria, between Uganda and Kenya; the Songwe in Lake Nyasa, between Tanzania and Malawi; and the Semliki in Lake Albert, between Uganda and Congo. All of these, it will be seen, are river mouths in lakes and it is probable that their geographical position could be established without much trouble should the need arise. Different problems occur when a river enters the sea, especially when it passes through swamp or shifting sandbank. The only East African example of this type is the Ruvuma, separating Tanzania from Mozambique, where the river mouth is about two miles wide.[2] The Anglo-Portuguese agreement of 1938 provided that the boundary line should follow the thalweg, described as the line of minimum level along the river bed, even when the position of the thalweg is changed by a natural alteration in the bed of the river.[3] It seems, therefore, that the boundary line at the mouth of the Ruvuma could, if necessary, be established without much difficulty.

(e) Source

Boundary descriptions commonly follow a river or stream to its source, thereby implying that this section of the boundary terminates at a precise, unmistakable point. In practice, however, it is very difficult to trace the exact source of a river, and upstream investigation may end in an indeterminate area such as a swamp, or disclose several alternative sources.[4] Watershed surveys in flat country, referred to

[1] *Case Concerning the Arbitral Award made by the King of Spain on 23 December 1906, Judgment of 18 November 1960.* I.C.J. Rep. 1960, p. 192, at p. 216.

[2] For recent maps, published by the Tanzania Government, showing the Ruvuma mouth see 1:50,000 Series Y742, Sheet Nos. 296/4 and 308/2, Edn. 1-TSD, 1968.

[3] 185 *L.N.T.S.* 205, para. 2.

[4] For example, Art. VI of the Treaty of 12 February 1869 (Hertslet, i. 212) defined part of the northern limit between Basutoland and the Orange Free State as 'the centre of the Caledon River to its source'. An account of the practical difficulties involved in the interpretation of this description is given by C. E. Walton, 'Discovery and Exploration of Basutoland: II, Tracing the Source of the Caledon River', *Lesotho: Basutoland Notes and Records*, vol. 2 (1960), pp. 27–36.

previously, give some idea of the practical difficulties that may be involved.[1] The problem is underlined by Holdich: 'The source of a river is sometimes adopted as a definite geographical point in a boundary agreement, regardless of the fact that every great river in the world must have several sources. To indicate that the source intended is to be the source of the principal affluent, is merely to invite a storm of dispute.'[2] Two distinct difficulties may occur; first, where the river or stream, although consisting of only one, unmistakable, channel, terminates at a point which cannot be precisely determined; and, second, where the watercourse separates into two or more branches, neither or none of which is immediately obvious or identifiable as the main channel.

A solution to the first type of problem can be provided by allowing the demarcation commission to establish an artificial boundary pillar as close as possible to the assumed source and to make this pillar, not the theoretical source, the actual boundary course terminal. East African examples of instances where this procedure has been followed occur on the Uganda–Congo boundary, where pillars were placed to mark the respective sources of the Chako and Lamia rivers.[3] Apart from its value as a physical identification of the agreed source, a pillar placed at the site accepted by the demarcation commission prevents future disagreement as to which point was actually selected. This is particularly valuable where the river or stream has an unknown name, or a variety of local names, some of which may perhaps coincide with those of other streams in the vicinity.[4] Another way of describing the agreed river source is to give its geographical co-ordinates, that is, its latitude and longitude, but as is shown elsewhere, in the absence of physical demarcation this is not always a reliable method.[5] Where, during demarcation, there is likely to be uncertainty as to the future location and interpretation of a river source, there is no adequate substitute for an artificial boundary pillar.

[1] Above, p. 69.   [2] *Geog. J.* 13 (1899), 465, at p. 470.
[3] Below, p. 246.
[4] See below, p. 273, where the mixed commission on the Uganda–Rwanda boundary found that the 'River Vigaga', referred to in the delimitation agreement was difficult to trace since *Vigaga* was simply a local word for river. Another example occurred during the Franco-Liberian demarcation when a river referred to as Fodedugu-ba, which is a local name for a river or stream, was confused with the 'real' Fodedugu-ba elsewhere. See H. H. Johnston, *Liberia*, Hutchinson, London, 1906, vol. i, p. 283.
[5] Above, pp. 48–53.

The *locus classicus* of the second type of problem, that is to say, which of two or more alternative channels is to be followed in order to obtain the correct source of a river, is provided by the *Argentine–Chile Award*.[1] An initial difficulty may be expressed parenthetically by saying that the River Encuentro, whose course the Court had to interpret, was not in fact the boundary river originally contemplated, since it had been confused with the River Salto, several miles to the west. Nevertheless, the Court, in interpreting the boundary agreement, was obliged to face the problem of deciding which of two branches, known respectively as the Eastern Channel and the Southern Channel, formed the main course of the Encuentro. In its award, the Court stated the general principle that where a treaty has laid down that a boundary must follow a river, and that river divides into two or more channels, and nothing is specified as to which channel the boundary shall follow, the boundary must normally follow the major channel.[2] The question to be decided, therefore, was whether the Eastern or the Southern Channel was the main one, and the Court held the three principal criteria applicable to problems of this nature to be the length of the watercourse, the size of its drainage area, and the annual volume of its discharge.[3] A prerequisite to investigations of this kind are accurate large-scale maps of the disputed region which, in the present instance, were not provided by the contesting parties to support the views of their respective expert witnesses, whose conflicting opinions could not therefore adequately be assessed.[4] In the result, the Court decided, on other grounds, that the boundary must be interpreted as following the Eastern Channel of the Encuentro.

(f) Alteration of a River Course

A modern authority, expressing the majority juristic viewpoint, states that where gradual additions to one river bank occur the state controlling that bank is presumed to own the territorial increment.[5] This stems from the Roman law of accretion, whereby land naturally added to the bank of a river accrued to the riparian owner of that

---

[1] *Award of Her Majesty Queen Elizabeth II for the Arbitration of a Controversy between The Argentine Republic and The Republic of Chile*, H.M.S.O., London, 1966.
[2] Ibid., p. 80.   [3] Ibid., p. 82.   [4] Ibid., p. 83.
[5] G. Schwarzenberger, *International Law*, Stevens, London, 1957, vol. i, pp. 294–5.

bank. The rule became accepted as part of international law largely as a result of the teaching of Grotius who wrote: '. . . a river by gradually changing its course changes the boundary also, and whatever the stream adds to either side becomes subject to the jurisdiction of the state to whose territory it is added . . .'.[1] Grotius applies this rule, however, only to gradual and natural accretion. With respect to cases where the bed of a river has been completely changed (*avulsio*) he says: '. . . if a river, abandoning its old course, has burst through in a different channel, it will not be the same as it was before, but a new river, the former river having ceased to be. In such a case the boundary of a country would remain in the middle of the channel which had last existed, just as if the river had dried up.'[2] The effect of these two rules, therefore, is that one state may gain or lose territory depending, respectively, on whether its bank gradually encroaches towards, or recedes from, the opposite riparian state. On the other hand, if the alteration is so sudden and violent that the river changes its course altogether, the boundary between the two states remains in its original position which, in the absence of special agreement, is presumably the thalweg in the case of a navigable river, and the *medium filum aquae* where the river is not navigable.

Despite their hallowed origin, these rules have an artificial air, and although most jurists, and even some states, pay them lip service, there is evidence to suggest that, in particular cases, they will not always be rigidly applied. The former rule seems reasonable enough, since in the absence of any artificial tampering with the watercourse, common sense suggests that a river boundary defined in terms of the thalweg or the *medium filum aquae* should shift from time to time, even though some territorial gains and losses will inevitably occur. Where rivers completely change their course, however, so as to leave the former bed entirely dry, the rationale of the alleged rule that the boundary is unaltered becomes harder to accept. Schwarzenberger suggests that it is based on the fact that once the land formerly occupied by the river becomes exposed, each of the states that was able to exercise some jurisdiction over the river bed and the water above it is now in a much stronger position to exercise such jurisdiction.[3] This may be very true, but its practical implications could be most serious, for if a state finds that, as the result of avulsion, its former

---

[1] Grotius, *De Jure Belli Ac Pacis*, Book II, Ch. 3, xvi (2).
[2] Ibid., xvii (1).
[3] Schwarzenberger, op. cit., p. 295.

access to a boundary river is denied because the waters now lie entirely within the territory of the opposite state, it might suffer considerable economic loss unless some special arrangement as to the continued common user of the river could be negotiated with the riparian neighbour. In the words of Mr. Justice Holmes, 'a river is more than an amenity, it is a treasure'.[1]

An example where two riparian states appear to have adopted the classical rules concerning the change of a river bed occurred in the *Chamizal Arbitration*, between Mexico and the United States in 1911.[2] In this case, however, the parties could not agree as to whether the alteration of the bed of the Rio Grande was due to accretion or avulsion, yet the main issue turned not on this particular point but rather on that of treaty interpretation; nor was the award itself accepted.[3] Although it may be wrong to attach too much significance to the *Chamizal Case* as an international expression of adherence to theoretical riparian boundary rules, there have been several instances, notably in disputes between individual states of the United States of America, where these rules have been accepted as valid in principle.[4] Of greater importance, however, is the growing tendency of riparian nations to enter into treaties which modify, or even abandon, the classical rules where particular situations make it desirable for them to do so. Several examples exist, of which one of the most interesting appears in East Africa, and although the latter is no longer relevant in a practical sense, it does provide a useful illustration of state practice.

By the Anglo-Italian protocol of 24 March 1891 the dividing line on the Indian Ocean coast between the British and Italian spheres of influence commenced at the mouth of the River Juba, the thalweg of which it followed as far as latitude 6° north.[5] The river therefore formed the boundary between the territories later known as Kenya and Italian Somaliland. A sudden alteration of the position of the mouth of the Juba occurred in 1909, the effect of which was to shift the river mouth about one and a half miles to the south.[6] The question

---

[1] *New Jersey* v. *New York*, 283 U.S. 336, at p. 342.
[2] *The Chamizal Case*, 11 *R.I.A.A.* 309, at p. 322.
[3] The dispute has now been settled. See 58 *A.J.I.L.* 336 (1964); *Geog. J.* 131 (1965), 149 and 135 (1969), 150.
[4] See, e.g. *Kansas* v. *Missouri*, 322 U.S. 213 (1943); *Arkansas* v. *Tennessee*, 310 U.S. 563 (1940); *Oklahoma* v. *Texas*, 260 U.S. 606 (1923); *Nebraska* v. *Iowa*, 143 U.S. 359 (1892).
[5] Hertslet, iii. 948.   [6] *Geog. J.* 34, 571; 38, 318.

then arose as to whether the old or the new mouth of the river should form the boundary. If the principle of *avulsio* was adopted, the boundary would remain in the location of the former thalweg, and Italy would have no access to the main entrance to the river. In 1910 the matter was discussed by an Anglo-Italian mixed commission which failed to resolve the issue and referred it to their respective governments.

The geographical circumstances prior to this dispute were that on its southward course, at a point about 300 feet from the shore, the Juba turned abruptly northward and ran parallel to the coast for about two miles before entering the sea. On its right (British) bank, the river thus created a small sandy peninsula between itself and the sea. In 1909 the Juba suddenly cut through this sandy strip, opening a new navigable mouth and leaving the old one dry. Britain argued, in accordance with the classical rule of *avulsio*, that the boundary remained as the thalweg of the old bed, and that she now owned both banks of the river in its new course. Italy, on the other hand, claimed that the correct interpretation of the 1891 protocol was that the boundary followed the thalweg in general, and not the thalweg as fixed at any particular moment. She therefore claimed access to the new river mouth and ownership of the sandy territory to the north of it which, in 1891, was undisputably British. When the issue was referred to the British and Italian governments the latter took the view that the modification of the river was of a minor nature and the boundary should shift with the river, just as it would had the movement been due to gradual accretion. Italian juristic opinion interpreted the words 'mid-channel (thalweg)' that appeared in the 1891 protocol as the mass of liquid in the running water, and not the actual bed of the river. Again, and what is undoubtedly more important, the Italian government produced what they regarded as evidence to show that, in 1891, both contracting parties intended the common use of the river right up to the sea.[1]

The Juba problem was finally settled in 1911,[2] and it was agreed that, in the event of future displacement, the thalweg as it existed from time to time, should continue to mark the boundary between the two states, so as always to leave the left bank in Italian, and the right bank in British, hands. This case is of major significance since it is a clear departure from the supposed rule of *avulsio*, and the matter was settled instead on an equitable basis of sharing boundary

[1] Adami, op. cit., pp. 24–6.   [2] 104 *B.F.S.P.* 158.

waters. The final agreement also provided that the rights of individual owners of land affected by the altered boundary should be respected.

As is shown elsewhere, the Juba case no longer has practical meaning since, as a result of the Jubaland transfer to Italy in 1925, the river is not now an international boundary and lies entirely within the limits of the Somali Republic.[1] The practical solution adopted in this instance, however, indicates that strict acceptance of the technical rule of avulsion will in many cases provide undesirable, even absurd, solutions to boundary river problems. The Juba settlement is not an isolated instance, and two more recent cases may be briefly mentioned.

First, an agreement made in 1932 between Britain and Brazil, respecting the Brazil–Guyana boundary, provides that should a boundary river 'suffer complete dislocation of its course, on account of any sudden natural phenomenon, in such a way as to abandon its bed and to open up another, the boundary line shall continue to be the thalweg of the river'. The agreement also provides that either state affected by loss of territory as a result of the shifting thalweg shall have the right, within four years from the date of the agreement, to force the river back into its abandoned bed. Again, individual proprietary rights are to be respected in the event of alteration to the international riparian boundary, and provision is made for compensation in such cases.[2]

Secondly, an agreement concluded between Britain, India, and Siam on 1 June 1934, respecting part of the River Pakchan boundary between Burma and Thailand, provides that the existing channel of the river, 'wherever it may be, should always be accepted as the boundary'.[3]

These, and other,[4] examples where a sudden change of the thalweg does not alter a riparian boundary cast considerable doubt on the present validity of the doctrine of *avulsio* which, it is submitted, should not be regarded as a universally accepted rule of international law.

(g) Islands in Boundary Rivers

Sovereignty over islands in boundary rivers may be a matter of considerable uncertainty. In principle, the ownership is decided in

---

[1] Below, Ch. IX. [2] 177 *L.N.T.S.* 127, paras. (iv) and (v).
[3] 154 *L.N.T.S.* 373, at p. 378.
[4] For some other examples, see Bouchez, op. cit., p. 802, footnote.

accordance with the relationship of the island to the thalweg or, in appropriate cases, the *medium filum aquae*. As has been seen, however, where a river divides into two or more branches it may be no easy matter to decide which is the principal channel along which the boundary line runs.[1] To provide for such contingencies, riparian states may make special arrangements, either by specifying the sovereignty of a particular island by its name or geographical location, or by creating elaborate provisions relating to the movement of the thalweg. Thus, to take an East African example of the first kind, which once again refers to the Juba, an official boundary description of 1914 proclaiming the limits of Jubaland specifically states that two islands in the river, named Mombasa and Towata islands, are, respectively, a part of Italian Somaliland and the East Africa Protectorate.[2] An example of the second type occurs in the River Ruvuma, dividing Tanzania from Mozambique, where the Anglo-Portuguese agreement of 1938 provides:

All the islands of the Rovuma river situated between the confluence of the River Domoni with the Rovuma river and the mouth of the latter belong to Portugal;
All the islands situated above the said confluence are part of the Tanganyika Territory.
For the purpose of this Agreement there shall be considered as islands only those which emerge when the river is in full flood and which contain land vegetation and rock or firm soil and are not shifting sandbanks.[3]

This agreement makes it clear that the deciding factor as to the sovereignty of an island in the Ruvuma is whether it lies above or below the Domoni confluence (approximately 38° 8′ east longitude), and not its relation to the thalweg of the river.

On the Kagera river between Tanzania and Burundi, the Anglo-Belgian agreement of 1934 established the boundary partly by straight lines drawn between boundary pillars, and partly by the margin of the swamp. Where a pillar was placed on an island, the boundary was drawn along the island shore by the shortest route between the straight lines running from the island pillar to its two adjacent pillars, thereby avoiding the division of an island between the two states and, at the same time, indicating clearly on which side of the boundary a

[1] Above, pp. 88–9.
[2] *The Official Gazette of the East Africa Protectorate*, 8 April 1914, p. 308.
[3] 185 *L.N.T.S.* 205, para. (1).

particular island lay.[1] The Kagera, as has been noted, follows a winding course through wide swampland and it is more than probable that its present course varies considerably from that which it followed in 1934. Even within a few years of their emplacement some of the boundary pillars began to disintegrate or disappear, and it is quite likely that many of them have now been completely lost. A joint Anglo-Belgian triennial inspection of pillars was contemplated but this proposal does not seem to have survived for long, nor to have resulted in the preservation of the pillars. Although it is possible that the theoretical positions of the original pillars could be established from the contemporary survey records, the changeable geographical course of the Kagera suggests that a new demarcation agreement may be desirable.

Apart from the Ruvuma and Kagera, which are special cases, it seems that disputes concerning the ownership of islands in East African rivers are not likely to occur frequently since, in most cases, the thalweg should be capable of fairly easy determination. Should such problems arise, however, they might include questions concerning the ownership of an island when the thalweg shifts from one side of it to the other; when an island belonging to one state becomes, through gradual alluvium, physically attached to the bank of the other state; where natural alluvial action joins together two islands that previously were under separate sovereignty; and where new islands are formed. An interesting treatment of these various problems is provided by the Anglo-Brazilian agreement of 1932,[2] to which previous reference has been made. It must be emphasized that the relevant provisions of this agreement are not necessarily universally acceptable rules of international law, but because they appear to offer a reasonable and practical solution, they may justifiably be quoted *in extenso*:

(ii) Subject to the provisions of paragraph (iii) the sovereignty of islands shall be determined by their situation in relation to the thalweg at the time of demarcation, or to the median line in reaches where it forms the boundary. Islands shall belong to that State on whose side of the boundary they are situated.

(iii) The position of the thalweg cannot be relied upon to remain constant owing to the natural action of the water, e.g., the gradual deposit of alluvium silting up and perhaps even closing channels. The question of the

[1] Below, p. 157.
[2] 177 *L.N.T.S.* 127, at p. 129.

change of sovereignty of islands on account of the movement of the thalweg through such causes shall be determined as follows:

(a) Where, owing to the gradual movement of the thalweg, an island situated at the time of demarcation on one side of it is found, at any subsequent time, to be situated on the opposite side of the thalweg and still remains an island, its sovereignty shall not change, despite the change in the position of the thalweg.

(b) Where, owing to the gradual movement of the thalweg or to the deposit of alluvium or to the other gradual and natural causes, an island situated at the time of demarcation in the territory of one State becomes joined to the territory of the other State its sovereignty shall change.

(c) Where, in virtue of the gradual and natural action of the river, two islands of different sovereignty unite and form one island, the sovereignty of the island resulting from that union shall be determined by its position with relation to the thalweg at that time.

(d) An island shall be deemed to be joined to another island or to the mainland when the level of the bed separating the two shall have risen to a height greater than that of the water at other than flood periods in that part of the river.

(e) Where, owing to the deposit of alluvium, or other gradual and natural causes, a new island is formed attaining a height greater than that of the water at other than flood periods in that part of the river, where previously no land existed, it shall belong to that State on whose side of the thalweg it may be situated, wherever the thalweg may be at the time of the appearance of the island.

(f) Each State shall have the right both to protect its own banks and islands from the gradual and natural action of the river and also to effect works in its own territory to prevent any local deviation of the current of the main stream, or of any branch of the river, from its course at the time, provided in both cases that such works do not themselves cause any deviation elsewhere.

CHAPTER VII

Lake Boundaries

IN this short chapter it is not proposed to enter into exhaustive discussion concerning boundary lakes, since those that concern East Africa are considered in detail elsewhere in this work. Some problems that require emphasis, however, include first, what constitutes a lake; secondly, how should a lake median be interpreted; and thirdly, what is meant by the shore line of a lake?

The first question is not quite so easy to answer as it might appear, since the margins of many lakes merge into surrounding swampland and, owing to seasonal fluctuation of water level, it is frequently difficult to determine where the lake ends and dry land begins. Indeed, some lakes may from time to time dry up altogether and it then becomes difficult to assess their lacustrine character. Thus in 1890, Lord Salisbury, referring to competing territorial claims by Britain and Germany in Botswana (Bechuanaland), said in the House of Lords: 'We have had a fierce controversy over the possession of a lake whose name I am afraid I cannot pronounce correctly—I think it is Lake Ngami . . . and there are great doubts as to whether it is a lake at all, or only a bed of rushes.'[1] Similar difficulties arose with respect to Lakes Chiuta and Chilwa (Shirwa), on what is now the Malawi–Mozambique boundary, both of which lie in swampland and have a water surface which varies in area according to the degree of rainfall and evaporation. Both Chiuta and Chilwa are rare examples of international boundaries formed by the shores of lakes.[2] An artificial boundary line for Lake Chiuta, approximating to the existing lake margin, was established in 1920, though the boundary was later shifted by agreement from the edge of the lake to a line passing through the approximate middle of the water. Lake Chilwa presents a more difficult problem, since the international boundary still passes along its eastern shore which is an indeterminate geographical feature. This lake, which has no outlet, has a reputed area of about 1,000 square miles, but less than half is open water, the remainder being

---

[1] 346 H.L. Deb. 3s. 10 July 1890, col. 1269.
[2] For a discussion of lake shore boundaries, see below, pp. 201–5.

made up of shallow, reed-covered swamp and seasonally inundated grassland. At any given moment, therefore, it might be no easy matter to say exactly what the limits of Lake Chilwa are.[1]

Another interesting example concerns the Rann of Kutch dispute between India and Pakistan, which was settled by arbitration in 1968. During wet years the disputed region of Kutch, which covers an area of about 3,500 square miles, is completely separated from the mainland and, in dry years, it is tenuously connected to the mainland through transitory gains of sea-bottom land in the area that was previously flooded.[2] Pakistan submitted that the Rann should be regarded as a 'marine feature' and since it formed a 'separating entity' lying between India and Pakistan the boundary line should be drawn along the median line, to accord with the principles of equitable distribution. In short, Pakistan argued in favour of a width-less median line through the Rann, the precise location of which should be determined by the Tribunal.[3] Despite the ingenuity of Pakistan's argument, the Tribunal had little hesitation in rejecting it since 'for the purpose of this opinion, it needs only to be observed that the Rann is a unique geographical phenomenon'.[4] In other words, the median line principle was held by the majority of the Tribunal to be inapplicable in such circumstances. Judge Bebler, however, in his Dissenting Opinion, appeared to favour Pakistan's claim for equitable distribution, but although he admitted that the Rann of Kutch is a 'peculiar surface, most akin to a marsh or swamp' he found that no binding rules exist in international law, or existed during the period of British administration, to show how such a surface must be divided between neighbours.[5]

The second question; how the expression 'median line' is to be applied in the case of a lake is a matter of some considerable difficulty, since although several methods have been suggested, none can be said to have received universal acceptance. Small boundary lakes, such as Lakes Jipe and Chala on the Kenya–Tanzania boundary, present little difficulty since, as was done in these instances,[6] it is usually possible to draw a straight line through the approximate centre of the water surface without creating too serious a departure

---

[1] Below, p. 202.

[2] A. Tayyeb, *Pakistan: A Political Geography*, Oxford University Press, 1966, p. 76.

[3] *Rann of Kutch Arbitration*. Extracts from the award are given in *International Legal Materials*, vol. 7 (1968), pp. 633–705. See p. 647.

[4] Ibid., p. 665.   [5] Ibid., p. 695.   [6] Below, Ch. XI.

from the principle of equitable distribution. Even larger lakes, such as Lakes Edward and Albert on the Uganda–Congo border, have been dealt with in this way. In the case of Lake Edward the boundary runs in a straight line across the lake between the respective mouths of the Ishasha and Lubilia-Chako rivers.[1] This arbitrary line gives Uganda and the Congo substantially equal shares of the waters without resorting to a theoretical median. Lake Albert, which is somewhat larger than Lake Edward, is divided by what might be termed an arbitrary mathematical median, for here the boundary consists of a series of straight lines connecting points situated midway between the shores on specified parallels of latitude.[2] As is pointed out elsewhere, such a boundary can be physically established fairly easily if necessary,[3] and its superiority over a theoretical median line, which at every point is exactly midway between opposite shores, appears to be self-evident. Lake Tanganyika, the most important East African example of a lake median,[4] presents, in theory at least, a more complicated situation, though, so far as is known, no serious practical problems have yet arisen concerning the exact location of the median line, even though the southern portion lacks a legal description and is usually shown cartographically as a geometrical curve.[5] The problem is treated more extensively in later chapters[6] but it is worth mentioning here that despite the opinions of learned writers, notably Boggs,[7] as to the best method of interpreting the word median, the mathematical method adopted in Lake Albert appears to be preferable. Lake Victoria, the largest of the East African lakes, is a special case, since no attempt was made there to ensure exact equality of distribution. The limits of Kenya did not extend as far as the lake until 1902, when she received a transfer of territory from Uganda.[8] As between Tanzania on the south side, and Uganda and Kenya on the north, the position was determined by the Anglo-German agreement of 1890 which, although it placed the boundary along the arbitrary parallel of 1° south latitude, did in fact divide the lake more or less equally between the two European powers.

Finally, what is meant by shore and shore line? In tidal waters, the word shore is usually interpreted as being the land lying between the lines of high and low water. As we have seen, however, non-tidal lakes

---

[1] Below, p. 247, and Appendix A, p. 293.
[2] Below, p. 247, and Appendix A, p. 293.
[3] Below, pp. 168–9.   [4] Below, Ch. XIII.   [5] Below, Ch. XVI.
[6] Below, Chs. XIII and XVI.   [7] Boggs, op. cit., pp. 178–84.
[8] Below, Ch. XVIII.

very often have a periodic rise and fall of water level which affects the location of the water's edge. In boundary lakes, the shifting shore line might well produce unequal territorial effects on the riparian states, according to the slope and geological formation of the respective banks. If an interpretation of the word 'shore' becomes necessary during an international boundary dispute it is conceivable that a claimant state will submit an argument based on a definition that will enable it to gain the greatest amount of territory. International agreements establishing lake boundaries in East Africa are all silent as to what constitutes the shore, but it is submitted that in most instances the fairest interpretation would be to regard it as the line of low water. Very often there may be no appreciable variation in lake level, so whether or not high water or low water is specified may be a matter of little practical moment. Lake Nyasa poses a special problem, however, since its water surface fluctuates considerably and causes severe flooding in some places. Despite the fact that this variation is not a recent phenomenon, and was well known during colonial times, no attempt was ever made to say how the word shore should be interpreted in the Anglo-German agreement fixing the boundary between Tanzania and Malawi. Further aspects of this controversial boundary are dealt with later,[1] but enough has been said here to offer a caution against the use of seemingly obvious, yet frequently ambiguous, words like 'shore' in boundary agreements, without defining in clear terms what the contracting parties intend the words to mean.

[1] Below, Ch. XIV.

PART THREE

PARTICULAR BOUNDARIES

CHAPTER VIII

Kenya–Ethiopia

THE legal status of the boundary between Kenya and Ethiopia was for many years a matter of uncertainty. Historically the pattern consisted of dispute followed by international agreement, but each agreement, though producing apparent settlement at the time, proved to be merely the precursor of further dispute. In June 1970, however, after a period of nearly eighty years of negotiation, a solution to this difficult boundary problem was finally provided by the signing of a treaty between Kenya and Ethiopia. Prior to this date, Ethiopia's failure to ratify a 1947 agreement concerning the boundary meant that the quest for legal pedigree led to an examination of the boundary arrangement made in 1907 between Britain and Ethiopia and this, as will be shown, was itself a long-standing bone of contention. An investigation into the manner whereby the boundary was originally purported to be established may lead to a better understanding of the present position.

Under the provisions of paragraph 2 of Article I of the Anglo-German agreement of 1890, the northern limit of the British sphere of influence in East Africa was defined as a line: '. . . commencing on the coast at the north bank of the mouth of the River Juba; thence it ascends that bank of the river and is conterminous with the territory reserved to the influence of Italy in Gallaland and Abyssinia, as far as the confines of Egypt'.[1]

The line dividing the respective British and Italian spheres was described in an Anglo-Italian protocol of 24 March 1891, as follows:

1. The line of demarcation in Eastern Africa between the spheres of influence respectively reserved to Great Britain and Italy shall follow from the sea the mid-channel (thalweg) of the River Juba up to latitude 6° north. . . . The line shall then follow the 6th parallel of north latitude up to the meridian 35° east of Greenwich, which it will follow up to the Blue Nile.

[1] Agreement between the British and German Governments, respecting Africa and Heligoland. Berlin, 1 July 1890. Hertslet, iii. 899.

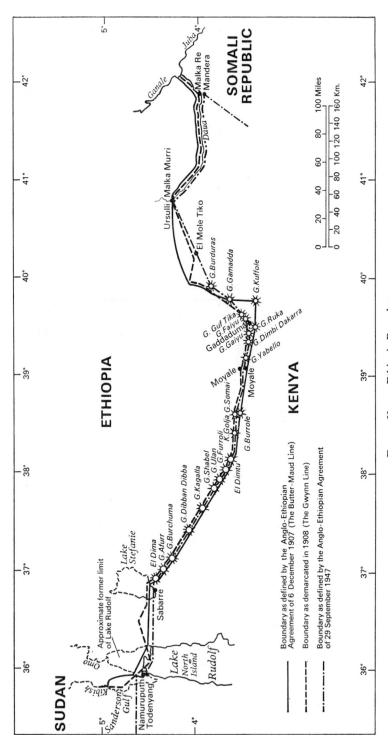

FIG. 1. Kenya–Ethiopia Boundary

Boundary as defined by the Anglo-Ethiopian
Agreement of 6 December 1907 (The Butter-Maud Line)

Boundary as demarcated in 1908 (The Gwynn Line)

Boundary as defined by the Anglo-Ethiopian Agreement
of 29 September 1947

2. If future explorations should hereafter show occasion, the line following the 6th parallel of north latitude and the 35th degree of longitude east of Greenwich, may, by common agreement be amended in its details in accordance with the hydrographic and orographic conditions of the country.[1]

The Emperor Menelik II of Ethiopia refused, however, to recognize the Anglo-German and Anglo-Italian agreements. In a circular letter addressed to the European powers in April 1891[2] he claimed sovereignty over an area which, in the south, included Boran Galla and was bounded by a line extending from the southern end of Lake Rudolf to the Somali border. Menelik's boundary, though not precisely defined, lay about 200 miles to the south of the line described in the Anglo-Italian protocol. Because of her agreement with Italy, and her anticipation that Ethiopia would shortly become an Italian colony, Britain disregarded Menelik's circular.[3]

To support his claim, Menelik pushed southward with his forces and a British report in 1897 stated that effective Ethiopian occupation had now extended far into the British sphere of influence. Since Britain had only a paper claim to the disputed area, and had never established occupation there, it became apparent that the Ethiopian intention was to continue their expansion into territory that had no visible display of sovereignty until they came into contact with the northern British outposts.

In May 1899 Menelik offered to settle the southern boundary with Britain on the basis of his 1891 circular which he now fortified by a claim of effective occupation. British rejection of this offer was followed by two further Ethiopian proposals, made in June 1899 and in 1900,[4] in which the boundary would follow tribal limits along a line lying roughly halfway between the border claimed by Menelik in 1891 and the northern boundary of the British sphere as defined in the Anglo-Italian protocol. Britain, though reluctant to abandon her claim to such a large amount of territory, was unwilling to make attempts to enforce it. Her hope that diplomatic negotiation would

---

[1] Protocol between the British and Italian Governments for the Demarcation of their respective Spheres of Influence in Eastern Africa, from the River Juba to the Blue Nile. Signed at Rome, 24 March 1891. Hertslet, iii. 948.

[2] The text of this circular is given by R. Greenfield: *Ethiopia*, Pall Mall Press, London, 1965, at pp. 464–5.

[3] H. G. Marcus, 'A History of the Negotiations Concerning the Border between Ethiopia and British East Africa, 1897–1914', Boston University Papers on Africa, vol. 2, 1966, pp. 239–65, at p. 240.

[4] Ibid., pp. 246–7.

produce a more acceptable proposal from the Emperor was not realized, and the resulting delay favoured the Ethiopians who were now said to be 'flowing southwards with a fairly rapid aggressive advance'.[1]

In 1902 the British Government arranged for Mr. A. Butter, a private citizen, to undertake at his own expense an expedition into the disputed border region and to place the results of his work at the government's disposal. The expedition was made with Ethiopia's consent and its object was to supply Harrington, the British Agent and Consul-General in Ethiopia, with sufficient information to enable him to discuss the boundary with Menelik, with a view to its subsequent definition by treaty.[2] Butter was requested to recommend a line that followed natural features and tribal limits, taking into account Menelik's previous proposals. By arrangement with the Foreign Office, Captain Maud, a military surveyor, was attached to the expedition to take charge of the survey operations. He was required to survey the locations of the Ethiopian posts, the extreme limits of their permanent occupation, and the areas into which their raiding parties penetrated.[3]

Maud's survey showed the Ethiopians to be 'in effective occupation far south of the line accepted in principle by the Emperor Menelik in 1898'.[4] Following the return of the expedition in 1903, similar but separate boundary proposals were submitted by Butter and Maud.[5] Butter recommended a boundary that followed physical features and separated the Galla from the non-Galla population. Maud proposed that Ethiopia should receive all the territory of which she was then in occupation, and that areas which her tribes had raided but not occupied permanently should remain British.[6]

Early in 1903, Italy, fearing that the results of the Butter expedition might lead to an Anglo–Ethiopian boundary settlement that would prejudice Italian interests, sought and received assurance from Britain that she would obtain the concurrence of the Italian Government

---

[1] J. P. Barber, 'The Moving Frontier of British Imperialism in Northern Uganda, 1898–1919', 29 *U.J.* 27 (1965), at p. 30.

[2] P. Maud, 'Exploration in the Southern Borderland of Abyssinia', *Geog. J.* 23 (1904), 552.

[3] Marcus, op. cit., p. 248.

[4] Gwynn to Foreign Office, 27 July 1909. F.O.C.P. 9666. F.O. 401/13.

[5] *Report by Mr. A. E. Butter on the Survey of the Proposed Frontier Between British East Africa and Abyssinia (with a map).* Africa No. 13 (1904), Cd. 2312.

[6] *Report by Captain Maud, R.E. of Mr. Butter's Expedition,* 4 September 1903. Harrington to Lansdowne, 28 September 1903. F.O.C.P. 8235, F.O. 403/334.

before making any alteration to the boundary as laid down in the Anglo-Italian protocol of 1891.[1] Britain was prepared to negotiate a new boundary with Menelik on the basis of the Butter–Maud proposals which she regarded as a reasonable compromise between the two competing claims. Italy, though not completely satisfied, agreed to a boundary modification in return for British support for her own claim to Lugh on the Juba River.[2]

It was not until 1907 that a decision concerning the disputed boundary was finally reached. By an Anglo-Ethiopian agreement[3] made in December of that year the frontier separating Ethiopia from the British territories to the south was described as a line which

. . . starting from the junction of the River Dawa with the River Ganale, follows the thalweg of the River Dawa to Ursulli, and from that point follows the tribal limits between the Gurré and the Borana to Gebel Kuffolé; from Gebel Kuffolé the line passes through the summits of the following hills: Roka, Churré Moyele, Burrolé, El Dimtu, Furroli, Dugga Kakulla, Burrchuma, Afur. From there the line goes to the creek at the south end of Lake Stefanie, thence due west to Lake Rudolf, thence north-west across Lake Rudolf to the point of the peninsula east of Sanderson Gulf, thence along the west shore of that peninsula to the mouth, or marshes at the mouth of the River Kibish (River Sacchi), thence along the thalweg of this river to latitude 5° 25′ north; from there due west to a point 35° 15′ longitude east of Greenwich, thence the line follows this degree of longitude to its intersection with latitude 5° 40′ north, and runs from there to the intersection of the 6° north latitude with the 35° of longitude east of Greenwich.

The agreement further provided that

The tribes occupying either side of the line shall have the right to use the grazing grounds on the other side as in the past, but during their migrations it is understood that they shall be subject to the jurisdiction of the territorial authority. Free access to the nearest wells is equally accorded to the tribes occupying either side of the line.

Both Governments shall send Commissioners, who shall, in concert, delimit the exact line of the frontier which is above described, and which is

[1] Notes exchanged between the British and Italian Governments relative to the observance of the Protocol of 24 March 1891 in the Settlement of the Frontier between Abyssinia and the East Africa Protectorate. Rome, 29 January, 9 February 1903. Hertslet, iii. 953.

[2] Marcus, p. 252.

[3] Agreement between Great Britain and Ethiopia relative to the Frontiers between British East Africa, Uganda and Ethiopia. Signed at Addis Ababa, 6 December 1907. Hertslet, ii. 445.

marked, pending such delimitation, with a red line upon the accompanying maps.

While they are there they shall settle the frontier of the Borana with the Gurré in concert with the heads of those tribes and in accordance with their customs.

In May 1908 Major C. W. Gwynn was appointed British commissioner for the boundary demarcation. On his arrival at Addis Ababa he found that, owing to the illness of the Emperor Menelik, no steps had been taken, or seemed likely to be taken, towards the appointment of an Ethiopian Commissioner. After a delay of several months Gwynn was instructed to carry out the demarcation without the participation of accredited Ethiopian representatives.[1] It was suggested that Ethiopia might later send her own commissioner to join Gwynn but her continued inaction persuaded local British officials that she would in fact be willing to abide by Gwynn's recommendations.[2] This, as subsequently appeared, was an erroneous assumption.

Gwynn felt that, in the circumstances, he could do no more than show the local tribes the boundary which the British Government would be prepared to accept. Since at that time the most northern British posts were still far from the border region, and most of them had never been officially visited, 'it was not easy to be convincing'. He also considered it 'obviously necessary . . . to ensure that there should be such water points on the British side of the frontier as would enable police work to be carried out effectively in the future', and recommended the rectification of the Butter–Maud line by shifting it northward so as to include a number of wells within Kenya.[3] The justification for this action was that these wells, though lying on the Ethiopian side of the treaty boundary, had been previously claimed for Britain by Zaphiro, the British boundary Inspector, and that this claim had not been disputed by local Ethiopian officials. Moreover, Gwynn regarded the natural features referred to in the 1907 agreement as a mere identification of the line and not as 'hard and fast points to which it was necessary to adhere'.[4]

Ethiopia rejected Gwynn's proposals and refused to accept the boundary until it had been demarcated by a joint commission in accordance with the 1907 agreement. The British argument was that

[1] Sir Charles Gwynn, 'The Frontiers of Abyssinia', *Journal of the Royal African Society* 36 (1937), 150, at p. 159.
[2] Marcus, p. 255.
[3] Gwynn, op. cit., p. 160.
[4] Gwynn to Foreign Office, 27 July 1909, F.O.C.P. 9666. F.O. 401/13.

Ethiopia was at fault by not appointing her own commissioner in time, but the most that the Ethiopian Government would concede was that Britain might continue to hold the wells appropriated by Gwynn until such time as a final settlement could be reached. Diplomatic negotiations concerning the boundary were undertaken during the ensuing years but reached an impasse. Ethiopia, despite the strongest British pressure, recognized only the 'red line' boundary of 1907 and refused to surrender the strategic wells. Meanwhile, Britain took steps to garrison the border with a military force whose initial task, however, was not to attempt administration but to gather information regarding local tribes and their habits.[1] The first garrisons were established at Marsabit and Moyale in 1909, and a further post at Loiyangolani was opened in the following year. The subsequent decision of the British Government to adopt 'a more vigorous policy' in what was then known as the Northern Frontier District and the need to protect the users of near-by wells from dispossession by hostile tribes, led to the opening of further border stations at Wajir, Mandera, and Malka Murri. In 1919, as part of a combined Anglo-Ethiopian patrolling operation against the Tigre, a lawless tribe in southern Ethiopia, British troops occupied Gaddaduma, a frontier post which had until recently been held by an Ethiopian garrison.[2] Gaddaduma, with its twelve wells, possessed a double importance that had been previously noted by Gwynn. Apart from containing a perennial water supply it also lies in a valley which provides an important pass from the upland districts to the north.[3] Local recommendations that Gaddaduma should be permanently occupied were not accepted by the British Government which ordered the evacuation of the garrison in October 1919.[4]

No meaningful attempt to settle the boundary dispute appears to have been made until 1947 when, by an exchange of notes between the British and Ethiopian Governments, a new boundary description was drawn up in substitution of that adopted in 1907.[5] The 1947

[1] H. Moyse-Bartlett, *The King's African Rifles*, Gale & Polden, Aldershot, 1956, p. 212.
[2] Ibid., p. 448.
[3] C. W. Gwynn, 'A Journey in Southern Abyssinia', *Geog. J.* 38 (1911), 113, at p. 121.
[4] Moyse-Bartlett, op. cit., p. 448.
[5] Exchange of Notes Constituting an Agreement Between the Government of the United Kingdom and Northern Ireland and the Government of Ethiopia Amending the Description of the Kenya-Ethiopia Boundary. Addis Ababa, 29 September 1947. 82 *U.N.T.S.* 191.

agreement abrogated the 1907 provisions concerning grazing and watering rights across the boundary. It also provided for the appointment of a mixed commission to demarcate the boundary, in conformity with the new description. The new boundary agreement came into operation on 29 September 1947, but it was agreed that, until the completion of the boundary demarcation, there would be no change in the areas actually administered by either government, or with regard to grazing and watering. The boundary description is contained in an Annex to the agreement and reads as follows:

From Malka Re along the thalweg of the Daua River to a point at Malka Murri to be decided on the spot by the Commissioners in accordance with the details recorded in the minute on the subject written at the meeting of 13th May.

Thence in a straight line to El Mole Tiko, leaving the Hara at El Mole Tiko in Kenya, and the Italian road to the Daua River in Ethiopia.

Thence in a straight line to the summit of G. Burduras so that the Police Post and well at El Roba will be in Ethiopia.

Thence to the summit of G. Gamadda.

Thence to the summit of G. Guf Tika leaving Gagabba in British territory.

Thence to the summit of G. Faiyu.

Thence following the watershed between the Gaddaduma and Adde valleys on the one side, and the valleys of Bor and Dembi on the other, to a point on the hill south of the Hara of Dembi (leaving Gaddaduma and Adde in British territory and Bor and Dembi in Ethiopia).

Thence following the same watershed to the summit of G. Gaiyu.

Thence to the summit of G. Dimbi Dakarra.

Thence to the summit of G. Yabello leaving the wells of Godoma in Ethiopia.

Thence along the valley to the east of the Harbor Police Post.

Thence along the bottom of the valley between the two Moyales to the summit of G. Gaferso.

Thence to the summit of G. Ajali leaving the wells of El Guda in Ethiopia.

Thence to the summit of G. Abo leaving the wells of Waiye in Kenya.

Thence to the summit of G. Somai.

Thence to the summit of G. Uran or to a point near G. Uran so as to leave all the Uran wells in Kenya (but the Golole wells remain in Ethiopia).

Thence to the summit of K. Golja (near Uran).

Thence to the summit of El Dimtu, leaving the wells of Sala, Salole and Dukanle in Ethiopia.

Thence to the summit of G. Furroli.

Thence through the summits of Ulan, Shabel, Dakka Kagalla and Dibban Dibba to the summit of G. Burchuma.

Thence to the summit of G. Afurr.

Thence to the summit of G. El Dima leaving the El Dima wells in Ethiopia.

Thence west along the parallel of approximately 4° 27′ to a point in Lake Rudolf due north of North Island (approximately 36° 3′ longitude) leaving the Kenya Police Posts at Sabarre and Banya (Ilola) in Kenya. Sabarre is approximately longitude 36° 47′.

Thence in a straight line to a point on the Todenyang–Namuruputh road known as Consul's Rock.

Thence along the road to the junction of the Sudan–Kenya boundary, leaving in Ethiopia Namuruputh (together with an adequate area surrounding the Police Post).

Replying to a question in the House of Commons regarding the 1947 agreement, the British Secretary of State for the Colonies stated that there had been no previous satisfactory determination of the Ethiopia–Kenya boundary, and that the line agreed to in 1907 had remained undemarcated. He continued: 'The rectification now agreed upon involves some small, and mutually advantageous, exchanges of territory, arising principally from the need to secure suitable watering places for tribes in British and Ethiopian territory respectively.'[1]

A mixed commission to demarcate the boundary was constituted by an exchange of notes between the two governments in July 1950.[2] The task of the commission included the placing of boundary marks and the preparation of topographical maps of the border region. An accompanying operation was the air photography of a strip about 20 miles wide, extending along the boundary zone from Malka Murri to Lake Rudolf. The work of the commission was to be completed within three years from the date of its commencement, subject to the extension of this period by agreement between the two states. The commission first met on the boundary on 17 March 1951. By two further exchanges of notes in 1954[3] and 1955[4] its operations were extended to 1 April 1956.

The final report of the commission was signed in Addis Ababa on 26 September 1955.[5] Although the boundary established by the 1947 agreement was now completely demarcated, the Ethiopian Government would not ratify the mixed commission's work and the agreement itself remained inoperative.

---

[1] 445 H.C. Deb. 5s., 3 December 1947. Written Answers, col. 78.
[2] Exchange of Notes Constituting an Agreement with regard to the Demarcation of the Boundary Between Ethiopia and Kenya. Addis Ababa, 3 July 1950. 99 *U.N.T.S.* 338, 348.
[3] 191 *U.N.T.S.* 374.
[4] 211 *U.N.T.S.* 406.
[5] *The Times*, London, 27 September 1955.

Discussions concerning the boundary took place between the two governments and continued until September 1963 when Kenya's Acting Prime Minister reported that all outstanding border disputes between Kenya and Ethiopia had now been settled. He also stated that it was intended to send a joint demarcation team to three points on the boundary where it was agreed that changes should be made.[1] Further negotiations between Kenya[2] and Ethiopia led to the signing in June 1970 of a new treaty,[3] Article I of which states that the boundary shall follow the line described in Schedule I. This schedule and thirty accompanying maps are declared to form an integral part of the treaty. In the event of discrepancy between map and text, the boundary description contained in Schedule I shall prevail.[4] For the purpose of clarification, Article V refers by name to certain wells and other important border features, and specifies their territorial location.

Owing to the importance of the River Dawa (Daua) it is agreed that the boundary shall follow the natural changes of the river bed. Should these changes cause the river to deviate more than half a kilometre from its treaty-map position, the two states shall decide on the true location of the river boundary. Provision is also made for the continued enjoyment of the waters by riverain inhabitants, and for their repatriation if future changes in the river boundary deprive them of their previous territorial status.[5]

Schedule II allocates the respective responsibility of each of the two states in specified boundary sectors, with regard to maintenance of pillars and the clearing of vegetation along the boundary line. All previous agreements affecting the boundary are declared to be abrogated.[6]

A separate protocol, forming Annex I to the treaty, grants transfrontier watering and grazing rights to Kenya nationals at Qadaduma (Gaddaduma), and to Ethiopian nationals at Godoma. It remains valid for five years and is renewable for further five-year periods until such time as alternative national watering facilities are made available.

---

[1] *The Times*, London, 28 September 1963.
[2] Kenya became an independent state on 12 December 1963.
[3] Treaty Between the Empire of Ethiopia and the Republic of Kenya Respecting the Boundary Between the Two Countries. Signed at Mombasa, 9 June 1970 (Typescript).
[4] Art. III. See above, p. 60.
[5] Art. VII. See above, Ch. VI (*f*).   [6] Art. XIV.

CHAPTER IX

Kenya–Somali Republic

RELATIONS between Kenya and the Somali Republic are marred by what is usually referred to as a border dispute. In a sense, this is a correct description but it is a mistake to suppose that the present territorial argument rests solely on the validity and interpretation of boundary agreements, though these must of necessity be considered. Nor does the difficulty date from 1963 when Kenya became an independent state, or even from 1960 when the Somali Republic was born. Yet the emergence of these two neighbours as new sovereign states has brought into relief a problem which, though of long standing, had hitherto been contained and subordinated by colonial administration.

Kenya's basic position is that of territorial integrity. Within her inherited boundaries, and almost entirely within a single province, live about 240,000 Somali people, most of whom have expressed the desire to secede from Kenya and join their kinsmen in the Somali Republic. To the Kenya Government, the Somali element represents a minority group, entitled under the law to equal, but not preferential, treatment with the non-Somali majority. If one minority group can be permitted to secede, the argument runs, why not others?[1] And how far could such a policy of permissive fragmentation be allowed without destroying the nation? In common with most other new African countries, Kenya favours the crystallization of national boundaries in the positions they occupied at the time of independence. The reason is not that the new states see historical or ethnological justification for the manner in which their boundaries were drawn during the period of imperial partition, but simply because they view any present attempt to rearrange national boundaries as an invitation to disaster.

The Somali Republic, on the other hand, is not prepared to accept the validity of pre-independence boundary arrangements, and claims a territorial area that includes all the Somali people within a single,

[1] Above, p. 35, n. 2.

ethnically homogeneous state. The total Somali population, which
has been estimated at about four million, is separated into five distinct political divisions. Two of these divisions, British Somaliland
and Somalia (formerly Italian Somaliland) united on 1 July 1960 to

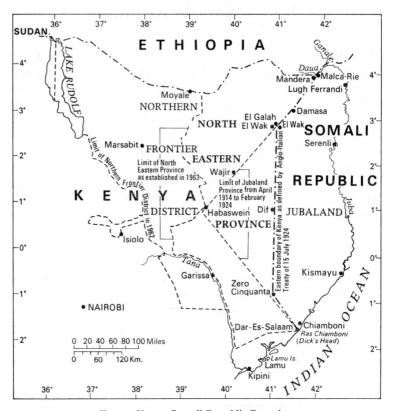

FIG. 2. Kenya–Somali Republic Boundary

form the Somali Republic. The other three divisions are the Haud and
Ogaden regions of Ethiopia, the Territory of the Afars and Issas
(French Somaliland), and the Northern Frontier District of Kenya.
Somali unification is not a vague historical ambition but a firm
political commitment. The present Somali national flag, which was
in existence six years before independence, consists of a five-pointed
star, each point of which represents one of the five political components of the Somali people. Moreover, the constitution of the

Somali Republic states that it 'shall promote, by legal and peaceful means, the union of Somali territories . . .'.[1] An increasing amount of recent literature deals with the political implications of the Somali Republic's claims against her three neighbours.[2] So far as the claim against Kenya is concerned, the territory in dispute is approximately one-half of Kenya's total area and comprises the vast semi-arid region formerly known as the Northern Frontier District. Before considering the substance of this claim it is appropriate to examine in some detail the manner in which the boundary between the two states was originally established.

The line separating the respective British and Italian territories in East Africa was originally defined in an Anglo-Italian protocol of 24 March 1891 as follows:

> The line of demarcation in Eastern Africa between the spheres of influence respectively reserved to Great Britain and Italy shall follow from the sea the mid-channel (thalweg) of the River Juba up to latitude 6° north, Kismayu with its territory on the right bank of the river thus remaining to England. . . .[3]

Although the Juba, a well-defined physical feature, may have seemed to provide a convenient and natural boundary,[4] it did not in 1891 represent a line of ethnic division, since even at that time there were Somalis living on both sides of the river.[5] In Jubaland, the area lying to the west of the river, the Somali population was comparatively small at the time of the formation of the British East Africa Protectorate in 1896, but it later grew considerably as Somali tribes entered from Italian Somaliland and Ethiopia. This Somali migration, which has been described as 'one of the most sustained, and in its effects, far-reaching movements of population in the history of North-East Africa',[6] was not simply the migration of a nomadic people into unoccupied land. Instead, the Somali intrusion involved the displacement of other local tribes who were continually forced back by a

---

[1] Art. VI, sect. 4.
[2] See, e.g., I. M. Lewis, *The Modern History of Somaliland*; J. Drysdale, *The Somali Dispute*; S. Touval, *Somali Nationalism*; A. Castagno, 'The Somali-Kenyan Controversy: Implications for the Future', *J.M.A.S.* 2, 165.
[3] Protocol between the British and Italian governments for the Demarcation of their respective Spheres of Influence in Eastern Africa, from the River Juba to the Blue Nile. Signed at Rome, 24 March 1891. Hertslet, iii. 948.
[4] The suitability of river boundaries is discussed above, pp. 76-7.
[5] Trans-Juba migrations by the Somali appear to have commenced in the mid nineteenth century.
[6] Lewis, op. cit., p. 18.

pressure that continued until the Somali advance was halted by the British civil and military authorities. The Somali expansion was not a concerted movement but consisted rather of a series of independent clan penetrations which were sometimes peaceful and at other times the result of war. The peaceful infiltration arose from a system known as *shegat*, a custom existing among Somali and kindred nomads whereby one tribal group was permitted to attach itself to a stronger or more powerful tribe, and to live with it.[1] The weaker group was called *shegat*, a term which indicated a client-patron relationship, rather than complete dependence. In this manner, for example, many Somalis attached themselves to the Ajuran, a tribe then occupying the Wajir area of Jubaland. As the Somali population grew more numerous, with the further influx of their kinsmen from Ethiopia, the former Somali *shegat* became able to revert to their original independent status, while their indigenous patrons were gradually driven westward into the Northern Frontier District.

It should be remembered that although, by the 1891 Anglo-Italian protocol, the Juba represented the eastern boundary of Britain's East African territories, it was many years after that date before the colonial Government was able to establish effective civil administration in Jubaland. Sir Charles Eliot, Commissioner for the East Africa Protectorate from 1901 to 1904, stated that the occupation of Jubaland was at that time entirely military, and that military officers exercised the necessary powers in the absence of a civil administration.[2] It is also of interest to note the following comment by Eliot, with regard to the idea of a separate Somali administration:

If it were possible to detach the districts inhabited by Somalis, it would be an excellent thing to form them into a separate government, as they are different in population, economic and physical conditions from the other provinces; but, unfortunately, they are too small to form a separate administration, and the adjoining Somali territories are not British.[3]

Ogaden Somalis reached Wajir in 1906 and were later joined by Degodia Somalis from Ethiopia. By 1909 Darod Somalis had advanced as far as the Tana River. In 1912 British civil authority was extended to Wajir, where an administrative officer was stationed, with the object of preventing the Boran and Ajuran from being driven out of the district by the incoming Somalis. An attempt to halt the Somali

[1] Kenya Land Commission, *Evidence*, Nairobi, 1933, vol. ii, p. 1650.
[2] Sir Charles Eliot, *The East Africa Protectorate*, Edward Arnold, London, 1905, p. 37.　　　　　　　　　　　　　　　[3] Ibid., pp. 180–1.

expansion was made when the government divided the wells in the Wajir area and allocated to the Somalis the territory lying to the east of the El Wak–Wajir–Habaswein Road. The area to the west of this road was designated the Boran area, but in fact it also contained two Somali tribes, the Rer Mohamud Libin, and the Gelibleh, who were *shegat* to the Ajuran.[1]

The administrative limits of Jubaland Province were defined by proclamation in 1914.[2] It appears from the boundary description that the north-western limit of Jubaland followed the approximate course of the El Wak–Wajir–Habaswein Road. In other words, it coincided with the line between the Boran and Somali areas.

Administrative problems in Jubaland were aggravated by the outbreak of World War I. Wajir and the territory to the north-west was evacuated by the colonial government in 1916–17, as no troops could be sent to defend it.[3] During this hiatus, Degodia Somalis attacked the Boran who retired to Moyale District, and the two Somali tribes in the Boran area, the Rer Mohamud Libin and the Gelibleh, declared themselves no longer *shegat* and reverted to their independent status.[4]

A secret treaty between France, Russia, Britain, and Italy was signed at London in April 1915.[5] Italy had remained neutral since the outbreak of war in the previous year, and the Treaty of London offered her territorial reward if she would join the other three powers in an alliance against Germany. The inducement offered to Italy with respect to her African ambitions is contained in Article 13 of the treaty:

> In the event of France and Great Britain increasing their colonial territories in Africa at the expense of Germany, those two Powers agree in principle that Italy may claim some equitable compensation, particularly as regards the settlement in her favour of the questions relative to the frontiers of the Italian colonies of Eritrea, Somaliland and Libya and the neighbouring colonies belonging to France and Great Britain.

Since Britain, as a result of World War I, considerably increased her African territories at Germany's expense, Italy,[6] under the terms

[1] Kenya Land Commission, op. cit., pp. 1650–1.
[2] Proclamation No. 2 of 1914. *The Official Gazette of the East Africa Protectorate*, 8 April 1914, p. 308.
[3] H. Moyse-Bartlett, *The King's African Rifles*, Gale & Polden, Aldershot, 1956, p. 447.
[4] Kenya Land Commission, op. cit., p. 1651.
[5] For text of the treaty see H. W. V. Temperley (ed.), op. cit., vol. v, p. 390.
[6] Italy entered the war in May 1915.

of the Treaty of London, was entitled to call for 'equitable compensation'. Although Article 13 of the treaty made no reference to specific boundary adjustments,[1] it was decided that Italy should receive a portion of the Jubaland Province of Kenya.[2] By the terms of an Anglo-Italian treaty, dated 15 July 1924,[3] the territory lying between the Juba River and a new boundary defined by the treaty was ceded to Italy by Britain.[4] Article 1 of this treaty describes the new boundary as follows:

From the confluence of the rivers Ganale and Daua, along the course of the Daua upstream to the southern point of the small southerly bend of the latter river in the vicinity of Malka Ré; thence in a south-westerly direction in a straight line to the centre of the pool of Dumasa; thence in a south-westerly direction in a straight line towards Eilla Kalla (which remains in British territory) to such meridian east of Greenwich as shall leave in Italian territory the well of El Beru; thence along the same meridian southwards until it reaches the boundary between the provinces of Jubaland and Tanaland; thence along that provincial boundary to a point due north of the point on the coast due west of the southernmost of the four islets in the immediate vicinity of Ras Kiambone (Dick's Head); thence due southwards to such point on the coast. Ras Kiambone (Dick's Head) and the four islets above mentioned shall fall within the territory to be transferred to Italy.

In the event, however, of it being found by the Commission referred to in Article 12 that the well of El Beru does not contain water either sufficient or suitable for the maintenance at that point of an Italian frontier post, then the line, as between El Beru and Eilla Kalla, shall be so drawn by the

---

[1] 170 H.C. Deb. 5s., cols. 954–5. Another indication that the Jubaland transfer was not contemplated in 1915 is provided by the Anglo-Italian River Juba agreement of 24 December 1915, which provided, inter alia, for the establishment of a Permanent Mixed Commission to regulate customs transit, conservation, navigation, and irrigation on the river. See The Official Gazette of the East Africa Protectorate, 7 June 1916, p. 461.

[2] The East Africa Protectorate was renamed the Kenya Colony and Protectorate in 1920.

[3] Treaty between Italy and the United Kingdom regulating certain questions concerning the boundaries of their respective territories in East Africa, signed at London, 15 July 1924, and Notes defining a section of the said boundaries, exchanged at Rome, 16 and 26 June 1925. 36 L.N.T.S. 379. For British ratification of the treaty see the Anglo-Italian Treaty (East African Territories) Act, 1925. 15 & 16 Geo. 5, cap. 9.

[4] Britain also acted on behalf of the Sultan of Zanzibar, so far as a portion of his mainland territories was included in the cession. Under Article 4 of the treaty, Italy undertook to pay to the Sultan the annual sum of £1,000, being the proportionate share of the annuity payable by Britain under her 1895 agreement with Zanzibar. See Hertslet, i. 382.

Commission as to include in Italian territory the neighbouring well of El Shama.

From the above description it can be seen that the transfer to Italy did not include the entire Jubaland Province, as established in 1914. In February 1924, however, a few months before the signing of the Anglo-Italian treaty, the western limits of Jubaland Province were redefined so as to conform, in effect, to the proposed new international boundary. Jubaland, as constituted by the new proclamation,[1] consisted of that part of the former province lying to the east of the meridian of 41° east longitude, leaving a triangular remainder to the west of this meridian which now became part of Northern Frontier Province. Under the treaty, therefore, Italy received all the new Jubaland Province, 36,740 square miles in extent,[2] while the triangular portion of approximately 14,000 square miles that had previously formed part of the province, remained in the Northern Frontier Province of Kenya. Since the old western limits of Jubaland had been intended to mark the dividing line between the Boran and Somali areas, it was evident that the new international boundary would create an artificial division between Somali kinsmen on opposite sides of the line. In recognition of this factor, provision was made in the treaty whereby those Somalis living in the territory transferred to Italy were given a limited right of return to British territory. Article 6 reads in part:

The same right is conferred on such a number of Somalis who are separated from their families by the new frontier as the wells and pasturages in the territory defined in the Annex to this article can support, having regard to the present and reasonable future requirements of the tribes or sections of tribes already there, provided that such persons must be individually registered before they are allowed to cross into British territory. The commission referred to in Article 12 shall decide as to the capacity in this respect of the said wells and pasturages and as to the number of the persons who may avail themselves of this right . . .

Annex.

The territory lying within a straight line from the Lorian Swamp to Saddi: a straight line from Saddi to El Beru: the line defined in Article 1 from El Beru to its junction with the Tanaland–Jubaland frontier: and a straight line from the said junction to the Lorian Swamp.

The territory described in the above Annex, into which Somalis from the Italian side might be permitted to cross, corresponds to the

[1] Proclamation No. 54 of 1924. *Kenya Official Gazette*, 29 February 1924, p. 185.   [2] *Kenya Legislative Council Debates*, 1925, vol. ii, p. 388.

triangular remainder of the old Jubaland Province. In other words, the apparent intention was that any Somalis allowed to re-enter Kenya territory under the provisions of Article 6 would be kept from penetrating beyond the western limits of Jubaland as established in 1914.

Article 9 of the treaty is also of interest. It provided that if in the neighbourhood of the boundary sector from El Beru to the Jubaland–Tanaland provincial limit there existed a shortage of pasture for tribes on the Italian side, and if during the rainy season the pasturage on the British side exceeded local requirements, then those tribes might be permitted to cross the boundary. The duration of this provision and the prescribed number of tribesmen who might cross were to be determined by the mixed commission. The maximum westerly extent of the grazing area permitted by this article was defined by the line Goochi–Ribba–El Tulli–Lakola–Toor Guda–Ramaguda.

Ceremonial cession of Jubaland took place at Kismayu on 29 June 1925. The transferred territory, renamed Oltre Giuba, was administered as a separate Italian colony for one year, after which time it became part of Italian Somaliland.[1]

Lieut.-Col. King was appointed in early 1925 as senior British Commissioner of the Jubaland Boundary Commission,[2] a mixed commission whose task was to undertake the demarcation of the new line. The description contained in Article 1 of the 1924 treaty provided that the boundary should follow the meridian of El Beru southward as far as its intersection with the Jubaland–Tanaland provincial boundary.[3] Since the inland terminal of this latter boundary was indefinite, King could obtain only an approximate position of the intersection by scaling from a map, and he recommended that the boundary should be carried along the meridian as far south as 0° 50′ south latitude, a point which, in consequence, became known as Zero Cinquanta. This proposal was accepted by the British and Italian Governments and an amendment to the boundary description was made by notes exchanged in June 1925.[4]

---

[1] L. N. King, 'The Work of the Jubaland Boundary Commission', *Geog. J.* 72 (1928), 420.

[2] There were in fact two commissions, the Jubaland Commission which was authorized by Article 12 of the 1924 treaty, and the Jubaland Boundary Commission which was its subsidiary. King, op. cit., p. 420.

[3] As a result of the 1924 proclamation (note 1, p. 119 above), there was no longer a Tanaland Province when the treaty was signed. The line intended was the boundary between Jubaland Province and Northern Frontier Province.

[4] 36 *L.N.T.S.* 379.

Following the completion of boundary demarcation, an agreement recording the decisions of the mixed commission was signed on 17 December 1927.[1] The following is a summary of some of the more important sections of this agreement dealing with the commission's interpretation of the treaty provisions:

First, with regard to the selection of the boundary itself. At the northern end of the boundary, no 'small southerly bend', as described in Article 1, could be found, and a point about 450 metres upstream from Malca Rie (Malka Re) was chosen as the boundary terminal. Since there was doubt concerning the sufficiency of water at El Beru, it was decided to include the well of El Sciama (El Shama) in Italian territory and to pass the meridional portion of the boundary through a point about 300 metres to the west of this latter well. On the coast, Ras Chiamboni (Ras Kiambone) was found to consist of a headland comprising a series of coral eminences, of which the highest was selected as the terminal of the directional line for the boundary towards the interior. The 'four islets in the immediate vicinity of Ras Kiambone' proved to be six in number, five of which lie to the south of the headland and form a group known collectively as Diua Damasciaca. The parallel of latitude passing through the southern extremity of the most southerly islet of this group was chosen and from this parallel, at a point 15 metres inland from high-water mark, the boundary was made to follow the meridian northward as far as its intersection with the line running from Ras Chiamboni to Zero Cinquanta.

Secondly, with regard to the treaty provisions concerning the trans-frontier movement of population. In accordance with Article 6, the commission decided that, where there were genuine cases of Somalis separated from their families, the right of crossing into British territory should be restricted to not more than 500 persons, excluding children under 10 years of age, and that this right should be exercised within one year from the date of formal confirmation of the 1927 agreement.[2] No grazing concession, as provided by Article 9 of the treaty, was recommended by the commission since it found that the existence of all the conditions required by the article was not proved by the evidence available.

Demarcation of the boundary consisted of twenty-nine principal boundary beacons, supplemented by a number of secondary cairns. Throughout much of its length the boundary was heavily overgrown

[1] 145 *L.N.T.S.* 337.
[2] The agreement was confirmed on 22 November 1933.

with such dense vegetation as camel thorn, 12 feet high, and tropical forest. To make the boundary line more clearly visible the commission proposed the cutting of a lane which, it was hoped, would be kept open by the passage of cattle traffic and might later be suitable as a route for a motor road.[1]

After only a short period following the commission's work, however, it was found that the boundary was inadequately defined on the ground. An agreement made between local commissioners in August 1930 stated that the lanes previously cut through vegetation were no longer traceable, owing to new growth. It was also reported that, of the twenty-nine principal beacons, only four were still in good condition, and that there was almost no sign at all of the secondary cairns. In the view of the local commissioners the poor definition of the boundary was a cause of continual friction between inhabitants of opposite sides of the line, and its uncertain location prevented adequate surveillance by the respective authorities. They recommended the replacement of the missing principal beacons and the construction of a track, 4 metres wide, along the entire boundary line from Malca Rie to the coast, a distance of 681 kilometres.[2]

By an exchange of notes between Britain and Italy in November 1933[3] the recommendations of the local commissioners were approved, except that the width of the proposed track along the boundary was reduced from 4 to 3 metres. It was agreed that each principal beacon in poor condition would be reconstructed on its former site by an iron mark placed in a concrete base, and that the maintenance of the beacons and track would be shared by the two governments, Kenya accepting responsibility for the section from Malca Rie to beacon No. 15, near Dif, and Italian Somaliland the remainder. Provision was made for the future biennial inspection of the boundary and report on its condition.

The notes exchanged in 1933, which constituted a definitive agreement between the two states, confirmed the agreement made by the

[1] King, op. cit., p. 424. See also L. N. King, *Report on the Work of the Jubaland Boundary Commission, 1925–1928*. (Typescript), Cat. No. DT 436, Commonwealth Relations Office Library, Great Smith Street, London.

[2] Agreement Between the Local Commissioners Appointed to Settle Certain Points Connected with the Demarcation of the Boundary Between Kenya and Italian Somaliland. Cmd. 4231.

[3] Exchange of Notes between His Majesty's Government in the United Kingdom and the Italian Government regarding the boundary between Kenya and Italian Somaliland, together with the Agreement adopted by the Boundary Commission and Appendices. London, 22 November 1933. 145 *L.N.T.S.* 337.

mixed commission in 1927, Appendix I of which sets out, in two separate parts, the general and the detailed description of the boundary. The general description reads:

Starting in the north from the Abyssinian frontier at a point in the 'thalweg' of the Uebi Daua about 450 metres upstream from Malca Rie, the boundary passes, in a south-westerly direction, in a straight line through the point where the south bank of the Uebi Daua is intersected by the meridian of longitude 41° 54′ 36″·43 East of Greenwich to a point in the pool of Damasa so chosen as to afford equal watering facilities to both parties in the deepest portion of the pool without transgression of the frontier;

thence in a straight line and still in a south-westerly direction towards the centre of the well of El Ghala (of the El Wak group), which remains British, until this line is intersected by the meridian of longitude 40° 59′ 44″·34 East of Greenwich;

thence due south along this meridian, leaving the well of El Sciama in Italian territory, to its intersection with the parallel of south latitude 0° 50′ 00″·00;

thence in a straight line, in a south-easterly direction, towards the highest point of Ras Chiamboni until this line is intersected by the meridian of longitude which passes through a point at Dar Es Salam 15 metres inland from high water mark and due west of the southern extremity of the southernmost of the group of 5 islets known as Diua Damasciaca;

thence due south along this meridian as far as the point at Dar Es Salam defined above;

thence, in a south-easterly direction, to the limit of territorial waters in a straight line at right angles to the general trend of the coastline at Dar Es Salam, leaving the islets of Diua Damasciaca in Italian territory.

The second part of Appendix I provides a complete description of each section of the boundary, and gives the location of all beacons and cairns placed by the commission during the original demarcation. Appendices II, III, and IV contain respectively the geographical co-ordinates of boundary points, a map of the boundary area, and a gazetteer listing equivalent British and Italian place-name spellings. Despite the reference to geographical co-ordinates, however, paragraph 13 of the 1927 agreement makes it clear that the boundary points as actually demarcated, and not their theoretical position, define the true location of the boundary line.[1]

Thus, by the end of 1933, the legal status of Kenya's new eastern boundary was at last settled by international agreement. During the

---

[1] Above, pp. 49–50.

following years a number of boundary beacons were destroyed or damaged by natural and human agency. The boundary was cleared and redemarcated with new pillars in 1957–8.[1]

The transfer of Jubaland to Italy reduced Kenya's Somali population by an amount which was estimated, 'with great reserve', at 12,000 people.[2] The cession itself was accompanied by local disturbances but the Kenya Government reported that it had 'passed off satisfactorily which . . . is largely due to the impression produced amongst all the tribes by the despatch of a large military force and the confiscation of a very considerable number of cattle'.[3] From the administrative point of view the territorial relinquishment may even have been welcome and 'the loss of this troublesome province was expected to afford some relief to the military commitments of Kenya'.[4] Nevertheless, the new international boundary did little to solve the ethnic problem. Somali tribes still lived to the west of the line and continued to penetrate beyond the western limits of the old Jubaland Province. A further influx of Degodia from Ethiopia occurred in 1923–4 and a proposal to return them had to be abandoned as the necessary troops were required elsewhere.[5]

Following the alteration of internal administrative boundaries, made necessary by the Jubaland transfer, the area of Kenya now occupied by the Somali population formed part of Northern Frontier Province, which later became the Northern Frontier District of Northern Province. This vast district was for many years a separately administered part of Kenya and it was treated as a closed district the entry to which required a special permit. Legislation providing for the closing of the Northern Frontier District to travellers and for the maintenance of order within the district was introduced in 1902 and 1934. This legislation still survives.[6]

At the end of World War II when the fate of Italy's former colonies was being considered, the British Foreign Secretary, Mr. Bevin, unsuccessfully proposed the formation of a trust territory that would

---

[1] *Report on Cartographic Activity in Kenya*. United Nations Regional Cartographic Conference for Africa. E/CN. 14/CART/4, E/CONF. 43/4, p. 4.
[2] 170 H.C. Deb. 5s., col. 954.
[3] Kenya Legislative Council Debates 1925, vol. ii, p. 389.
[4] Moyse-Bartlett, op. cit., p. 456.
[5] Kenya Land Commission, op. cit., p. 1651.
[6] *Laws of Kenya 1962*, The Outlying Districts Act, Cap. 104; The Special Districts (Administration) Act, Cap. 105, as amended by L.N. 459/1963. For provisions relating to the exercise of emergency powers in the area see S.I. 1963/1968, Sec. 19, and Kenya Constitutional Amendment Act, No. 16 of 1966.

include the territories of British and Italian Somaliland, and the Somali areas of Ethiopia.[1] Instead, Italian Somaliland became the United Nations trust territory of Somalia and, in July 1960 joined the newly independent British Somaliland to form the Somali Republic. The incorporation of these two former colonial territories into a single state raised Somali hopes for a complete unification of their people. Somali tribesmen in the Northern Frontier District announced that they would seek self-determination independently of the rest of Kenya, in order to join their kinsmen in the Somali Republic, and optimism ran high. Since Britain, in response to the wishes of the inhabitants of British Somaliland, had been willing to facilitate their union with Somalia, it was argued, how could she ignore a similar demand from her Somali subjects in Kenya?[2] The British Government's view on this matter was expressed in April 1960 when, in reply to a question regarding the establishment of a Greater Somalia that would incorporate neighbouring territories, the Prime Minister, Mr. Macmillan, said: 'Her Majesty's Government do not, and will not, encourage or support any claim affecting the territorial integrity of French Somaliland, Kenya or Ethiopia. This is a matter which could only be considered if that were the wish of the Governments and peoples concerned.'[3]

At the Kenya constitutional conference held in London during February 1962 the delegation from the Northern Frontier District requested that before any further constitutional changes affecting Kenya were made, autonomy should be granted to the district so that it might join the Somali Republic when Kenya attained independence.[4] Other Kenya delegations opposed this request on the grounds that it would endanger Kenya's territorial integrity and encourage tribal separatism. In October 1962 the Northern Frontier District Commission, consisting of two members, was appointed by the British Government to ascertain and report on public opinion in the Northern Frontier District,[5] regarding the future constitutional development of Kenya. The commission, which was purely fact-finding,

[1] 423 H.C. Deb. 5s., cols. 1840-1. Castagno, op. cit., p. 171, states that the proposal was for a British trusteeship over the 'entire Somali region of East Africa', but this is not borne out by Mr. Bevin's own remarks in the House of Commons.

[2] Lewis, *Mod. Hist. of Somaliland*, pp. 184-5.

[3] 621 H.C. Deb. 5s., Written Answers, cols. 104-5.

[4] *Report of the Kenya Constitutional Conference*, Cmnd. 1700, p. 11.

[5] The commission was not concerned with the sub-district of Samburu which, though a part of the Northern Frontier District, was separately administered.

reported that, of the six sub-districts concerned, the majority view in Wajir, Mandera, Isiolo, the eastern part of Moyale, and the northern part of Garissa, supported the Somali, or secessionist, opinion, while in Marsabit, western Moyale, and southern Garissa the prevailing view supported the Kenya, or non-secessionist, opinion.[1] The secessionist view was held not only by the Somali inhabitants, who were estimated by the commission to form 62 per cent of the total population, but also by certain other Moslem tribes.[2]

In March 1963 the British Colonial Secretary announced that a new North Eastern Region of Kenya was to be established, consisting of predominantly Somali areas.[3] The western portion of the Northern Frontier District had already been severed to form part of the Eastern Region, following recommendations by the Regional Boundaries Commission.[4]

At a conference held in Rome during August 1963 between the British Government and that of the Somali Republic, the Somali delegation proposed that the entire Northern Frontier District should be placed under a special administration to be undertaken either jointly by the governments of Kenya and the Somali Republic or by the United Nations. This proposal was rejected and the conference reached no agreement.[5]

The new regional arrangement, which was embodied in Kenya's Independence Constitution of December 1963, meant that the old Northern Frontier District was no longer a single administrative entity. The eastern part of the district, containing the bulk of the Somali population, became the North Eastern Region, while the remainder was divided between the Eastern and Coast Regions. The Constitution provided for the establishment of Regional Assemblies, possessing certain legislative powers, a procedure which, it was anticipated, would safeguard the interests of the Somali inhabitants of the North Eastern Region. The Somali Government did not accept this arrangement and its opposition intensified when the regional system of government was abolished by Kenya in 1965. In a White Paper issued in December 1964, on the eve of Kenya's new constitu-

---

[1] *Report of the Northern Frontier District Commission.* Cmnd. 1900.

[2] The Somali Republic estimated that 86 per cent of the inhabitants of the N.F.D. wished to secede from Kenya to join the Somali Republic. *White Paper on N.F.D.*, Mogadiscio, December 1964, p. 4.

[3] *The Times*, London, 9 March 1963.

[4] *Report of the Regional Boundaries Commission*, Cmnd. 1899.

[5] Drysdale, op. cit., pp. 157–8.

tional amendments, the official view of the Somali Republic was expressed in the following words: '. . . to the extent that it is not co-extensive with the former N.F.D., the Somali Republic has always been equally clear that its own concern lay with the territory formerly known as the N.F.D. and irrespective of any new titles or new definitions of boundaries'.[1]

This statement makes it clear that the Somali Republic's dispute with Kenya involves the former Northern Frontier District itself, and not merely the North Eastern Province.[2]

The relations of the Somali Republic with her neighbours have been summarized by a recent writer: 'As Somalis see it, their frontier dispute is not essentially about land. It is about people—nomadic people at that—for whom there is one frontier only: the furthest limits to their pastures.'[3] This is a circular and somewhat disingenuous argument. Since land is an inseparable element of nomadic life, the Somali problem must be regarded as much from the territorial as from the human point of view. The findings of the Northern Frontier District Commission show that the issue turned on whether or not the inhabitants wished themselves and the land they occupied to be a part of the Somali Republic. Those who supported the secessionist opinion did so on the understanding that they would not be required to move from their present homes.

Pre-independence hopes by many African political parties for an eventual alteration of national boundaries led to the passing of a resolution by the All-African Peoples Conference in Accra, 1958, which was referred to in a previous chapter.[4] As has been seen, this resolution was passed at a time when there were very few independent African states, and its concept received diminishing emphasis with the passage of time. Majority opinion among O.A.U. member states in 1963 and 1964 favoured the retention of inherited colonial boundaries, mainly on practical grounds, and this opinion found expression in the resolution passed by the organization in July 1964.[5] For reasons already discussed, the Somali Republic dissociated

[1] *White Paper on N.F.D.*, p. 5.
[2] The Regions of Kenya were renamed Provinces, with unchanged boundaries, in December 1964. Constitutional Amendment Act, No. 14 of 1965. For boundary descriptions see Schedule 11 of the Kenya Constitution, S.I. 1963/1968.
[3] Drysdale, op. cit., p. 7. This point is emphasized in a recent statement by the Somali Prime Minister, who declared the Somali aim to be self determination, not territorial annexation or expansion. *Somali News*, 11 August 1967.
[4] Ch. II (*d*), above.
[5] For the text of the resolution see above, p. 22.

herself from the O.A.U. resolution and has refused to be bound by it.[1]

The failure of the 1964 conference to produce an accord between Kenya and the Somali Republic led to a period of increased tension between the two states in which the disputed region was the scene of frequent violence and loss of life. A significant improvement in the deteriorating relations occurred at the O.A.U. summit conference held at Kinshasa in September 1967, when Kenya and the Somali Republic agreed to discuss their differences at a meeting to be held under the chairmanship of President Kaunda of Zambia.[2] This meeting took place at Arusha in Tanzania on 28 October 1967 and led to the issue of a joint communiqué in which the two disputants agreed, *inter alia*, to maintain peace and security on both sides of the border, gradually suspend emergency regulations affecting the border areas, refrain from conducting hostile propaganda against each other, resume diplomatic relations, and to appoint a joint working committee to undertake a periodic review of the progress made towards implementing the agreement.[3]

Since the Arusha meeting, there have been several indications that Kenya and the Somali Republic are anxious to bring their dispute to an end. Diplomatic and commercial relations have been restored, emergency regulations eased, and the Somali Republic has expressed the desire to join the East African Community. At present, however, the root problem remains unsolved and it is not yet clear what steps can or will be taken to reconcile the opposing views of ethnic self-determination and territorial integrity.[4]

[1] Above, pp. 24–5.
[2] The text of the Kinshasa Declaration is given in *International Legal Materials*, vol. vi, November 1967, p. 1242.
[3] *The Nationalist*, Dar es Salaam, 30 October 1967.
[4] See Ch. II (*f*), above.

CHAPTER X

Kenya–Sudan

PRIOR to 1926 Kenya had no common boundary with Sudan. In that year The Kenya Colony and Protectorate (Boundaries) Order in Council transferred to Kenya the eastern part of Uganda known as Rudolf Province, the northern limit of which was also part of the Uganda–Sudan boundary. The schedule to this Order in Council describes in detail the new Kenya–Uganda boundary in its entirety, from Tanganyika to Sudan,[1] but in order to obtain the definition of the northern boundary of the transferred territory it is necessary to refer to the manner in which it had been previously established by the governments of Uganda and Sudan.

Expansionist aims of Sir Harry Johnston in the early years of the present century resulted in the extension of the country known as Uganda far to the north of its present limits.[2] The transfer of the Lado Enclave from the Congo to Sudan, in 1910,[3] meant that Sudan acquired a wedge of territory that extended deep into Uganda. The geographical configuration of the southern part of the Lado Enclave, which made it difficult to administer from Sudanese stations but more easily approachable from the Uganda side, contributed to a decision that this portion of the enclave should be transferred from Sudan to Uganda, in exchange for a strip of territory east of the Nile, adjoining Uganda's northern boundary.[4]

In 1912 adjustment of their common boundary was agreed to in principle by the governments of Uganda and Sudan, and a mixed boundary commission left Nimule, then in Uganda, in the following year to investigate the terrain and submit their recommendations. The work of the commission with regard to the western section of the boundary is considered in a later chapter,[5] and it is sufficient to say here that the proposed line was carried eastwards as far as the summit of Jebel Latome (Lonyili). The dry nature of the country and

---

[1] Below, pp. 250–2.   [2] J. P. Barber, op. cit.   [3] Below, Ch. XIX.
[4] R. O. Collins, 'Sudan–Uganda Boundary Rectification and the Sudanese Occupation of Madial, 1914', *U.J.* 26 (1962), 140.
[5] Below, Ch. XIX.

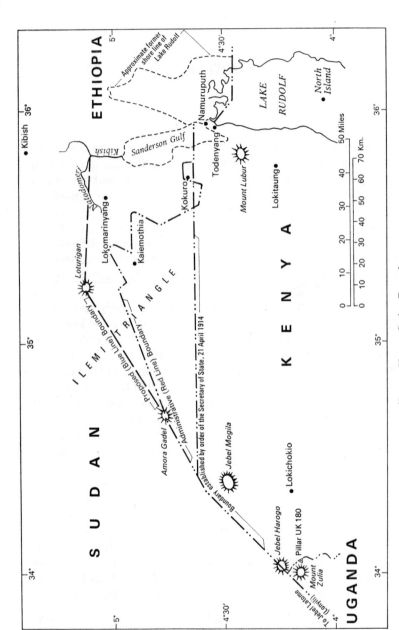

FIG. 3. Kenya–Sudan Boundary

the absence of water for their animals prevented the Uganda commissioners from continuing the journey, and the Sudan members of the party, who were more suitably equipped with camel transport, went on alone.

From the summit of Jebel Latome, the boundary was delimited as a straight line in a north-easterly direction to 'the southernmost point at the bottom of Jebel Harogo', and from thence, still north-easterly, in a straight line to the 'northernmost point of the northernmost crest of the long spur running north-west from Jebel Mogila'.

Recommendations required from the commissioners should have been based on their personal investigation of the entire boundary as far as its eastern extremity at Lake Rudolf. At Jebel Mogila, however, the commission, now consisting only of the Sudan members, abandoned any attempt to advance towards the lake, and simply accepted the remaining portion of the boundary as a straight line. This line was adopted on the assumption, which was later to prove unfounded, that it lay clear of the customary grazing-grounds of the Turkana tribe in Uganda. The failure of the commissioners to conduct a more thorough investigation of this eastern part of the boundary seriously diminished the value of their recommendations. It has, moreover, resulted in an ambiguous legal definition that to this day remains unclarified.

The boundary proposed by the commission was accepted by the two neighbouring governments in January 1914. Formal transfer of territory took place on 21 April 1914, by Order of the Secretary of State, under the provisions of The Uganda Order in Council, 1902. The relevant part of the boundary is described in the Order as follows:

A line beginning at a point, on the shore of the Sanderson Gulf, Lake Rudolf, due east of the northernmost point of the northernmost crest of the long spur running north from Mount Lubur; thence following a straight line to the northernmost point of the northernmost crest of the long spur running north from Mount Lubur; thence following a straight line, or such a line as would leave to Uganda the customary grazing grounds of the Turkhana tribe, to the northernmost point of the northernmost crest of the long spur running north-west from Jebel Mogila; thence following a straight line in a south-westerly direction to the southernmost point at the bottom of Jebel Harogo; thence following a straight line to the summit of Jebel Latome; thence . . .[1]

[1] *The Uganda Official Gazette*, 30 May 1914, p. 256.

The above description invites some comment. First, 'the shore of Sanderson Gulf' apparently refers to the western shore of the gulf situated at the north-western end of Lake Rudolf. The exact point on the shore that defines the eastern extremity of the boundary described in the 1914 Order is theoretically fixed by the line drawn 'due east of the northernmost point of the northernmost crest of the long spur running north from Mount Lubur'. In actual fact, however, examination of the terrain shows that the northernmost point is susceptible of several geographical interpretations, one of which is that it refers to Loruth Hill.[1] The precise location on the ground of this part of the legal boundary cannot therefore be regarded as beyond dispute.[2]

Furthermore, even assuming that this northernmost point has been correctly identified, the description of the boundary then proceeds in terms of two irreconcilable alternatives, by following 'a straight line, or such a line as would leave to Uganda the customary grazing grounds of the Turkhana tribe, to the northernmost point of the northernmost crest of the long spur running north-west from Jebel Mogila'. Even at the time of the delimitation in 1913, the belief that the straight line from Jebel Mogila to Mount Lubur lay to the north of the Turkana grazing-grounds was an incorrect assumption, and one which arose from the failure of the commission to make an actual visit to the site. The result of the description was thus to create a fluid boundary that depended upon the location of the northern limits of grazing-grounds occupied by nomadic people.

Despite these theoretical difficulties in the interpretation of the boundary description, no practical need for the determination on the ground of the Turkana's northern grazing-limits arose until the extension of civil administration to the area which, as a result of its transfer from Uganda in 1926, now formed part of Kenya. During the years 1929-30 proposals were put forward by officials of the Kenya Government for the establishment of the actual grazing-limits, but no official approach was made to the Sudanese authorities, owing

[1] 'Notes on the Red Line Boundary', an anonymous, undated (c. 1964) memorandum supplied to the author by Survey of Kenya, Nairobi.

[2] Sanderson Gulf is now entirely dried up, and even in 1907 the location of its shore line was a matter of some doubt. Gwynn's survey, made in 1908, revealed that much of what had been believed to be water was actually under cultivation and that the surveyor of Butter's 1902 expedition, on which the Anglo-Ethiopian boundary agreement of 1907 was based, was deceived by flood water or mirage into sketching an incorrect shore line. For references to the Butter and Gwynn expeditions see above, Ch. VIII.

partly to the view that these limits, though vaguely described, were suitably flexible. Also, the fact that Kenya had been given a free hand by Sudan in the conduct of military operations across the border led to the feeling that no useful purpose would be served by approaching Sudan for any alteration of the boundary.[1] The part of Sudan in which military authority was then exercised by Kenya is known as the Ilemi Triangle. This roughly triangular shaped piece of territory, about 150 by 200 miles in extent, lies in the south-east corner of Sudan and has been the scene of friction between neighbouring tribes from Kenya, Sudan, and Ethiopia, such as the Turkana, Taposa, and Donyiro. In the extreme south-east corner of the Triangle is the Ilemi Appendix, a finger of Sudanese territory extending to Lake Rudolf, and cut off from the rest of the country by the Lotagippi Swamp.[2]

Agreement concerning the Turkana's customary grazing-grounds was reached in 1931 between the Provincial Commissioner of Kenya's Turkana Province and the District Commissioner of the Eastern District of what was then the Mongalla Province of Sudan. The northern limits of the grazing-area were drawn on a map, and the delineated boundary became known as the Red Line. As a result of discussions mainly concerned with tribal access to essential water-holes, various modifications to the Red Line were proposed during the next few years, the general effect of which was to extend the line further to the north.

At this time when the problem of civil administration lay under discussion, the military authorities were also concerned with the establishment of a strategic line that would reduce the number of avenues through which tribal raids from the Ilemi Triangle could be directed. Nevertheless, the line finally chosen as militarily acceptable was based on the recommendations that had been put forward by the civil administrators before the question of the strategic position had been considered. Evidence that the Red Line, as adopted in 1937, brought no improvement in the strategic situation is provided by reports that tribal raids from the Ilemi Triangle continued, through the same avenues as before.

Demarcation of the Red Line boundary was commenced in 1938. The realization that, from the strategic point of view, the line was still unsatisfactory led the military authorities to attempt a last-minute

---

[1] 'Notes on the Red Line Boundary.'
[2] K. D. D. Henderson, *Sudan Republic*, pp. 15–16.

alteration of its location during the course of the survey. It appears, however, that only slight departures were made from the 1937 line, mainly to accommodate certain areas which the Turkana, with the permission of the Sudan Government, had been allowed to penetrate.[1]

The Red Line, as finally demarcated, failed to prevent the tribal raids, although it did include all the grazing-land that could fairly be claimed by the Turkana to be theirs by custom. This difficult border area still lacks an effective administration and negotiations between the two neighbouring countries concerning a final boundary have yet to be completed. Meanwhile, proposals have been put forward for the adoption of a new line as the international boundary. The Blue Line, as it is called, lies even further north than the Red Line but it has been claimed to offer the strategic advantages that are said to be absent from the latter. It must also be mentioned that Kenya, with the permission of the Sudanese Government, maintains a number of police posts between the Red and the Blue Lines, and that an additional post, at Kibish, lies even to the north of the Blue Line.

Final delimitation must therefore await the solution by the two countries of a complex political problem. Meanwhile, it should be emphasized that neither the Red Line nor the Blue Line can be regarded as necessarily representing the true location of this part of the boundary between Kenya and Sudan, the only legal definition of which remains the ambiguous description contained in the Order of 1914.[2]

[1] 'Notes on the Red Line Boundary.'
[2] Recent maps published by the Kenya Government show the Red Line as the international boundary.

CHAPTER XI

Kenya–Tanzania

SMALL-SCALE maps show the boundary between Kenya and Tanzania to consist mainly of two long, approximately parallel, straight segments, connected by a series of short irregular lines passing round the northern side of Mount Kilimanjaro. From time to time, speculation has arisen concerning the origin of the interesting bend in the boundary that placed Africa's highest mountain in German, and now Tanzanian, hands. A commonly repeated legend is that Kilimanjaro was a gift by Queen Victoria to her grandson Wilhelm, later Emperor Wilhelm II of Germany.[1] Possibly this tale originated, or became widespread, soon after World War I when local European settlers sought to attach the Kilimanjaro region to Kenya. An older, and also discredited, view is that Britain conceded Kilimanjaro to Germany in exchange for the recognition of her own right to Mufumbiro in the south-west corner of Uganda.[2] In truth, however, it appears that the line skirting this mountain with, according to Gladstone, an unrememberable name,[3] was established as the result of compromise between the competing claims of treaties made by Britain and Germany with tribal rulers in the late nineteenth century.[4]

---

[1] For a refutation of this myth see G. W. Hatchell, 'The Boundary Between Tanganyika and Kenya', *Tanganyika Notes and Records*, No. 43, June 1956, p. 41.

[2] Sir E. Hertslet, 'Mfumbiro as a *quid pro quo* for Kilimanjaro', memorandum dated 17 April 1906. F.O. 367/10.

[3] S. Gwynn and G. M. Tuckwell, *Life of Sir Charles Dilke*, J. Murray, London, 1917, vol. ii, pp. 83–4.

[4] In September 1884 H. H. Johnston acquired on his own behalf approximately six square miles at Taveta, in exchange for a quantity of beads, handkerchiefs, and American cloth. He later transferred his rights to the forerunner of the Imperial British East Africa Company (Sir Harry Johnston, *The Kilima–Njaro Expedition*, Kegan Paul, Trench, London, 1886, p. 110). Johnston also made treaties with tribal rulers at Moshi and Taveta who accepted British protection, subject to the Sultan of Zanzibar's waiver of suzerainty (Sir Harry Johnston, *The Story of My Life*, Bobbs-Merrill, Indianapolis, 1923, p. 136). Treaties with the chiefs of Chagga and Taveta were made by the German East African Company in May–July 1885. For details see Hertslet, ii. 685.

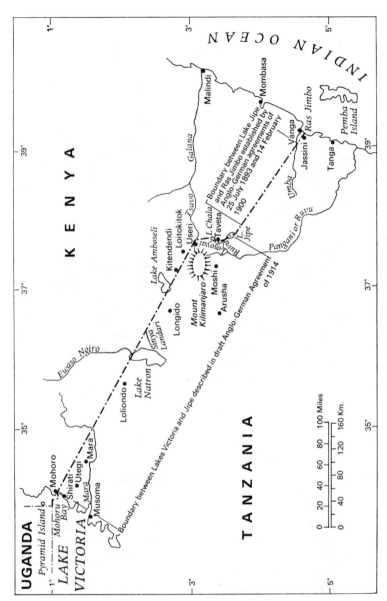

FIG. 4. Kenya–Tanzania Boundary

Despite some later adjustments, the description and location of the present boundary remain substantially unchanged from the initial Anglo–German delimitation. The boundary is well demarcated and no serious differences need arise as to its exact position on the ground. From a strictly legal point of view the description of the western section is not entirely satisfactory since it derives from an international agreement that was never signed. In practice, however, there seems little doubt that both Kenya and Tanzania accept this description as a correct definition of their common boundary.

Britain and Germany delimited their spheres of influence on the East African coast by an agreement made in 1886.[1] The boundary separating the British sphere on the north from the German sphere on the south[2] is described in the agreement as follows:

The line of demarcation starts from the mouth of the River Wanga or Umbe, runs direct to Lake Jipé, passes thence along the eastern side and round the northern side of the lake and crosses the Lumi River;

After which it passes midway between the territories of Taveita and Chagga, skirts the northern base of the Kilimanjaro range, and thence is drawn direct to the point on the eastern side of Lake Victoria Nyanza which is intersected by the 1st degree of south latitude.

No attempt was made in 1886 to delimit the respective spheres west of the eastern shore of Lake Victoria, though each state agreed that it would not encroach beyond the boundary, and later undertook to discourage annexation of the territories lying to the rear of each other's sphere.[3] The struggle for possession of the hinterland ended with the signing of the Anglo-German agreement of 1 July 1890 which, *inter alia*, redefined the limits between the East African

---

[1] Agreement between the British and German Governments, respecting the Sultanate of Zanzibar and the opposite East African Mainland, and their Spheres of Influence. 29 October–1 November 1886. Hertslet, iii. 882.

[2] It should be noted that although the 1886 agreement separated the British from the German spheres, Germany until 1890 retained an interest in certain coastal tracts lying to the north of the delimited line. In 1885 the Sultan of Witu ceded sovereign rights to a German subject over part of his coastal territory which in 1889 became a German protectorate (Hertslet, ii. 688–90). Under their 1890 agreement Germany withdrew this protectorate in favour of Britain (Hertslet, iii. 901). Later in the same year Britain formally declared a protectorate over Witu, adjacent territories and islands, Hertslet, i. 364, and in 1896, these were included in the East Africa Protectorate (Hertslet, i. 383).

[3] Agreement between Great Britain and Germany, respecting the Discouragement of Annexations in Rear of their Spheres of Influence in East Africa. July 1887. Hertslet, iii. 888.

spheres. The relevant portion of the boundary is described by Article I
of this agreement, in terms almost identical to those used in 1886, as

'. . . a line which, commencing on the coast at the north bank of the
mouth of the River Umba (or Wanga), runs direct to Lake Jipé; passes
thence along the eastern side and round the northern side of the lake, and

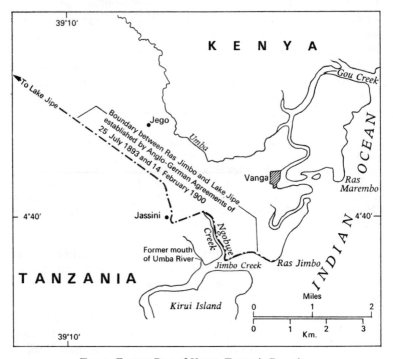

FIG. 5. Eastern Part of Kenya–Tanzania Boundary

crosses the River Lumé; after which it passes midway between the territories of Taveita and Chagga, skirts the northern base of the Kilimanjaro
range, and thence is drawn direct to the point on the eastern side of Lake
Victoria Nyanza which is intersected by the 1st parallel of south latitude;
thence, crossing the lake on that parallel, it follows the parallel to the
frontier of the Congo Free State, where it terminates.'[1]

The eastern extremity of the boundary was defined by the 1886
agreement as 'the mouth of the River Wanga or Umbe', a description

[1] Agreement between the British and German Governments, respecting Africa
and Heligoland. Berlin, 1 July 1890. Art. I. Hertslet, iii. 899.

that produced immediate difficulty of interpretation. No River Wanga existed and the port of Vanga (Wanga) was found to stand not on a river but on a salt water creek about two miles to the north of the mouth of the River Umba (Umbe). Rival British and German claims were complicated by the fact that the coastal concession granted in 1887 by the Sultan of Zanzibar to the British East African Association extended northward from Vanga,[1] whereas the concession granted in 1888 by the Sultan's successor to the German East African Association ran southward from the Umba.[2] These two grants appeared to leave a gap between the Umba and the village of Vanga, yet the British company considered this area to be a part of its own concession, and took possession of it in January 1889.[3] The German company, on the other hand, claimed not only that its territory extended north of the Umba, but that it included Vanga as well. In October 1889 a joint Anglo-German commission was appointed by the British and German governments to delimit the Vanga boundary. The inquiry was completed in less than a month and was understood locally to favour the British claim, though the official report was withheld by both governments. Despite its apparent success, the British company received official instructions in February 1890 to abstain from administering Vanga until such time as the British and German governments decided in which sphere the village lay.[4] Since the point had already been settled by the delimitation commission, these instructions were a little surprising, but the explanation seems to be that this issue was but one of the many bargaining points in the negotiations leading to the Anglo-German agreement of July 1890. No excuse, however, can be offered for the retention in this agreement of the same geographical inconsistency that had appeared in 1886, yet the line is again described as commencing at 'the mouth of the River Umba (or Wanga)', thereby leaving unsettled the question of ownership of the port.

In 1892, British and German commissioners demarcated the exact point where they considered the line from the coast to strike the southern end of Lake Jipe. They could not agree, however, as to

---

[1] Concession granted by the Sultan of Zanzibar to the British East African Association. 24 May 1887. Art. I. Hertslet, i. 339. See also Art. I of the agreement of 9 October 1888. Hertslet, i. 350.

[2] Concession from Sultan of Zanzibar to German East African Association. Zanzibar, 28 April 1888. Art. I. Hertslet, ii. 695.

[3] P. L. McDermott, *British East Africa or IBEA*, 2nd edn., Chapman & Hall, London, 1895, p. 82.   [4] Ibid., p. 85.

whether Vanga lay in the British or the German sphere, nor did they regard the boundary in the Kilimanjaro region as settled.[1] A further agreement was made between Britain and Germany in 1893, settling the points of difference noted in the previous year, and redefining the boundary from the coast to Laitokitok, on the northern slopes of Kilimanjaro:

Section 1. On the coast the line shall start from the high-water mark on Ras Jimbo, and shall run from thence in a straight line to the point where the parallel of 3° 40′ 40″·3 S. (astronomically determined) cuts the eastern bank of Lake Jipé. But on the coast the boundary shall be deflected as follows: It shall run from the Indian Ocean along the northern bank of the Jimbo Creek, making the foreshore in the British sphere, as far as the eastern mouth of the Ngobwe Ndogo. It shall then follow the eastern bank of the Ngobwe Creek to its end, and then run to the point where the above described straight line from Ras Jimbo to Lake Jipé meets the rising ground on which the village of Jasini stands.

Section 2. From the point on Lake Jipé, described in Section 1, the boundary line shall follow the eastern side of Lake Jipé, and round the northern side of the lake crossing the River Lumi, and following the northern bank of the Rufu River (by which is also understood its swamp), as far as the point which is distant 1 English mile east of the German road going from the Marangu station to the coast. From thence it shall run to the summit of Chala Hill in the manner shown in the annexed map. The boundary line shall bisect the Chala Lake. From the north side of the Chala Lake onwards the boundary line shall run parallel to the track, as shown in the annexed map, and 1 English mile west of it as far as the latitude of the so-called Useri Camp. It shall then run at a distance of 1 kilom. south-west of the track shown in the annexed map as going to Laitokitok, as far as the point where it crosses the Ngare Longei (Rongei).[2]

As a result of this agreement the boundary on the coast was shifted southward from the Umba to the mouth of the Jimbo Creek, thereby placing Vanga clearly within the British sphere. Despite the title of the 1893 agreement, the Umba itself is nowhere referred to in the description, though a contemporary map[3] shows the river to flow into

---

[1] Protocols between the British and German Commissioners for the Delimitation of the Anglo–German Boundary in East Equatorial Africa. Signed at Taveta, on 27 October, and at Zanzibar, on 24 December 1892. Hertslet, iii. 909. For a geographical and technical account see C. S. Smith, 'The Anglo-German Boundary in East Equatorial Africa. Proceedings of the British Commission, 1892', *Geog. J.* 4 (1894), 424.

[2] Agreement between Great Britain and Germany respecting Boundaries in East Africa from the Mouth of the Umba River to Lake Jipe and Kilimanjaro. Signed at Berlin, 25 July 1893. Hertslet, iii. 911.   [3] Hertslet, iii. 912.

the Ngobwe Creek whose left bank forms part of the boundary.[1] The Umba crosses the straight line from Ras Jimbo to Lake Jipe at a point about 15 miles from the coast. Below this crossing the river runs north of the boundary in a sweeping curve to the sea, so that an area of approximately 30 square miles of Kenya lies to the south of the river. Controversy arose in 1898 when a German official, believing the boundary to follow the course of the Umba, instead of the theoretical straight line, proceeded to notify villagers living south of the river that they fell within German jurisdiction. Britain protested at this action and also claimed that the border village of Jassini had been improperly annexed by Germany.[2] Since its actual location still remained uncertain it was decided to demarcate the boundary from the coast to Laitokitok, and an Anglo-German agreement, signed in 1900, settled the problem in the following manner:

I. The boundary follows the left bank of the Ngobwe to about the point No. 13 on Mr. Boehler's Map. But inasmuch as since the drawing of the map the Ngobwe has altered its course, the exact point No. 13 has not been taken as a boundary, but a point situated on a branch of the river flowing out of the rice-fields, the situation of which has been determined by means of cross-bearings taken by signal fires from point No. 5 and from point No. 2 of Mr. Boehler's Map. This point has been marked by a tall mangrove-post painted with tar.

II. From this point the boundary follows N. 70 E. (astronomical) in a straight line to point No. 5 (large baobab tree on the high part of the bank). On this line several mangrove-poles have been planted in the rice-fields and in the mangrove forest. The line is cut through the forest.

III. On the high bank the boundary goes from the baobab at No. 5 past a second baobab to a third baobab. Two blocks of cement have been placed in the intervening space, and marks have been cut upon the baobabs.

IV. From the third baobab the boundary turns to the line drawn by Sir Arthur Hardinge and Mr. Meyer. On this connecting-line two blocks of cement have been placed (one in the middle and one at the end). On the former provincial boundary-line one cement block has been placed at the point where a path coming from the house of the D.O.A.G. (German East Africa Company's) Settlement crosses the frontier. The frontier passes a few metres west of point No. 12, strikes point No. 2, and turns to point No. 11 (white ant-hill known as Dr. Stuhlmann's hill). The line from point

[1] One reason for not using the mouth of the Umba to define the boundary is that its exact location is difficult to establish, since the river flows through swamp and has a number of minor outlets. Recent maps show the Umba to enter the sea at Gou Creek, a little to the north of Vanga.

[2] Sir Arthur Hardinge, *A Diplomatist in the East*, Jonathan Cape, London, 1928, pp. 228–30.

No. 5 to point No. 2 has been accurately mapped by Surveyor Lang by tachymetry.

V. The theoretical, astronomical azimuth of the boundary-line (Jimbo-Jipé) has been calculated from point No. 11 at N. 55° 22′ 41″ W. This direction has been accurately determined by the use of Boehler's co-ordinates, and has been indicated by a stone set-up about 100 metres from the ant-hill. The magnetic azimuth of the boundary (in June, 1897, the magnetical variation was 7° 46′ W., the annual decrease 8′–10′) has been taken as N. 48° W.[1]

(sections VI to X omitted)

The 1900 agreement has several points of interest. First, it contains the most recent legal description of this portion of the boundary, for although the line was redemarcated a few years ago no formal amendment to the description has ever been made. Second, it provides a good example of the type of problem encountered at that time when marking a boundary in difficult country. Dense bush restricted the employment of normal surveying techniques and it was necessary in certain places to fire rocket signals, in order to obtain observations for bearing.[2] Third, a curious supplementary boundary description is given with respect to the dense, uninhabited area to the south of the Umba River. Article VIII of the agreement provides that until such time as the line is cut through the forest, the boundary shall be taken as lying at a distance of three-quarters of an hour's caravan march along the path leading southward from Maharani (Gonja), and one hour and twenty minutes along each of the two paths leading southward from Jilibe. No caravan specifications are given.

During the 1900 negotiations a British request for the alteration of the Ngobwe boundary from the left bank to the thalweg of the creek was rejected by the German commissioner who pointed out that he was being asked to cede territory in a manner inconsistent with the 1893 agreement.[3] Germany thus retained both banks of the creek, for a distance of about a mile from its mouth.

From Jassini the boundary was demarcated, by pillars erected at the more important places on the line, as far as Laitokitok where cultivation ended. No further demarcation was undertaken until

---

[1] Arrangement between Great Britain and Germany fixing the Boundary at Jassin and in the bend of the Umba River. January–April 1900. Hertslet, iii. 921, and accompanying Atlas Maps, Nos. 26 and 27.

[2] For a description of this interesting procedure, the result of which showed that Jassini lay in German and not British hands, see Hardinge, op. cit., p. 231.

[3] Hertslet, iii. 924. Above, pp. 84–5.

1904 when an Anglo-German commission proceeded to mark the boundary eastward from Lake Victoria to Laitokitok, a distance of approximately 280 miles. In order to minimize the effect of discrepancies in triangulation, it was agreed that when this section of the boundary had been marked as far as a point 20 miles westward from the eastern terminal at Laitokitok, it should then be defined as a straight line joining the point to the terminal.[1] The commission started its work on the eastern shore of Lake Victoria in April 1904. At its western end the boundary had been delimited in 1886 and 1890 as the point of intersection of the eastern side of the lake with the parallel of 1° south latitude. This point lies at Mohuru, a peninsula of such irregular shape that the parallel was found to cut the shore line in no less than seventeen different places. The most westerly of these seventeen intersections, at the extreme tip of the peninsula, was accepted by the commissioners as the terminal point on the lake shore, and from here they marked the boundary eastward to Laitokitok.[2] Demarcation consisted of pillars or piles of stones, placed in such manner that each could be seen from its nearest adjacent neighbour.

Later instructions required the commission to continue its work from Laitokitok to Lake Jipe, following the description contained in Section 1 of the 1893 Anglo-German agreement. Some difficulty was experienced in tracing the old boundary through this sector, since the roads and tracks used to define it in 1893 had disappeared or shifted to new routes as a result of the building of the Uganda Railway.[3]

Mapping of the boundary zone accompanied demarcation, and the commission completed its task at the end of 1905, by which time it had also undertaken sufficient technical work to enable the mathematical computation of the position of boundary points from Zanzibar to the Congo State.[4]

[1] G. E. Smith, 'Report on the Anglo–German Boundary Commission from Victoria Nyanza to Kilimanjaro and Lake Jipe', 1906, Confidential No. 8932, pp. 15–42, F.O. 367/10, p. 25.   [2] Ibid., p. 17.   [3] Ibid., p. 20.
[4] For technical and geographical reports see G. E. Smith, 'From the Victoria Nyanza to Kilimanjaro', Geog. J. 29, 249; L. Ambronn, 'Bericht über die astronomischen und geodätischen Arbeiten, welche zur Festlegung der Grenze Deutsch-Ostafrikas gegenüber dem Kongostaat und Britisch-Ostafrika von seiten der deutschen Kommissare in den Jahren 1902 bis 1905 ausgeführt worden sind', Mitt. 20, 165; Positions, Azimuths, and Length of Sides of the Anglo-German Boundary Commission Triangulation (1902–1906) from Zanzibar to Mount Ruwenzori, The War Office, London, 1907.

West of Lake Victoria another mixed commission had previously demarcated the Anglo–German boundary as far as the meridian of 30° east longitude, at that time the eastern boundary of the Congo State.[1] Britain and Germany signed an agreement in 1906, embodying the recommendations of the two commissions and containing a complete description of the boundary from the Congo State to Lake Jipe.[2] Because of a dispute concerning the location and ownership of Mufumbiro, at the western extremity of the line, this agreement was never ratified, though no disagreement arose with regard to the boundary east of the lake. The Mufumbiro question was settled in 1910 and the draft of a new Anglo-German agreement was prepared in 1914.[3] So far as the Kenya–Tanzania portion is concerned, the description in this agreement is identical in terms to that drawn in 1906. Owing to the outbreak of World War I in August 1914 the new agreement was never signed, but correspondence exchanged in July between the British and German foreign offices indicates that signature was imminent and would almost certainly have taken place had not hostilities commenced between the two states.[4]

The basis of the description east of Lake Victoria, contained in both the 1906 and 1914 agreements, is the work performed by the mixed commission, and there seems never to have been any real doubt that the demarcated line represents the true boundary between Kenya and Tanzania. This view receives support from a letter sent in 1925 to the governments of Kenya and Tanganyika by the Secretary of State for the Colonies, in which he expressed Britain's intention to adopt the 1914 description as correctly defining the boundary between the two countries, and to embody it in a forthcoming Order in Council that awaited the final settlement of the transfer of Jubaland from Kenya to Italy.[5] In his letter, the Secretary of State also raised the question of formal notification to the League of Nations, since adjustment of the boundaries of Tanganyika, a mandated territory, would be possible only with consent of the League Council.[6] He

---

[1] Below, Ch. XX.

[2] Agreement between Great Britain and Germany determining the Boundary between their respective territories in East Africa (East and West of Lake Victoria), Berlin, 18 July 1906. F.O. 367/10.

[3] Agreement Respecting the Boundary Between the British and German Territories in East Africa, From Mount Sabinio to Lake Jipe, 1914. F.O. 372/523.

[4] File 18696, F.O. 372/523.

[5] Letter from L. S. Amery, 23 September 1925. C.O. 533/333, below, Ch. XX, pp. 280–1.

[6] British Mandate for East Africa. Cmd. 1794, Art. 12.

decided, however, that no such formal notification was necessary, as Britain, by adopting the 1914 description, was simply accepting the boundary envisaged by the mandate. The point might also have been made that, for this portion of the line, no specific boundary details are given in the mandate agreement which merely refers to the limits of former German East Africa.[1] The matter was not one of adjustment but of the acceptance of a boundary that both Britain and Germany for many years in practice, though not formally, had regarded as a settled issue.

Unfortunately, the contemplated Order in Council never appeared, and the Jubaland transfer was dealt with separately. Nevertheless, it is submitted that even though no instrument properly defining the boundary has been formally concluded, the validity of the description contained in the 1914 Anglo-German draft agreement has long received the acquiescence of all parties concerned and is no longer open to dispute.

The relevant portion of the 1914 boundary description is drawn eastward across Lake Victoria along the parallel of 1° south latitude, and continues in the following manner:

Article 2. . . . . Thence along that parallel of latitude until it reaches a point 1½ kilom. west of the Mohuru Peninsula. Thence round the southern extremity of the Mohuru Peninsula, at a distance of 1½ kilom. from the coast, until about the middle of Mohuru (Idito) Bay it meets a line drawn from the western extremity of the peninsula south-east to boundary pillar 48 (Kitenden), the position of which is described in article 3.

Article 3. From Mohuru (Idito) Bay the boundary between the British East African Protectorate and the German East African Protectorate shall follow the lines marked out with pillars by a Mixed Commission in 1904–1905, as indicated on Maps 3, 4, and 5 annexed to this Agreement and as described below:—

1. A straight line starting from the point of intersection in Mohuru (Idito) Bay, described in article 2, and passing through boundary pillars 4–47 to boundary pillar 48 (Kitenden);
2. Thence a straight line through boundary pillars 49–53 to boundary pillar 54 (Laitokitok);
3. Thence a line to boundary cross 55 (Kimangeya);
4. Thence a straight line to boundary cross 56 (Useri);
5. Thence a straight line to boundary cross 57 (Lumi);
6. Thence a straight line to boundary pillar 58 on the Eastern rim of the basin of Lake Chala (Dschala);

[1] Ibid., Art. 1.

7. Thence a straight line across the lake to the west shore and on to boundary pillar 59 at the highest point of Chala Hill (Dschala);

8. Thence a straight line to boundary pillar 60 on the highest point of the more northerly of the two hills (Schlobach hills) situated to the south of Lake Chala (Dschala);

9. A straight line to boundary pillar 61 on the more southerly of the two hills;

10. Thence a straight line to boundary pillar 62 on the highest point of Ndui ya Malagogoi;

11. Thence a straight line through boundary pillars 63 and 64 on the Taveta-Moschi route to boundary pillar 65 on the highest point of Latema hill;

12. Thence a straight line to boundary pillar 66 on the highest point of Nadingalera (Lemrika) hill;

13. The meridian of the last named point in a southerly direction to its point of intersection with the thalweg of the River Losoyai;

14. The thalweg of the river down-stream, west of the island of Mokisa to its junction with the River Rufu (Ruwu);

15. The thalweg of the Rufu (Ruwu) up-stream to its exit from Lake Jipé (Djipe);

16. Thence a straight line to the point of intersection of latitude south 3° 32·5′ with the centre line of Lake Jipé (Djipe);

17. Thence the centre line of this lake to boundary pillar 67 at its southern end.

Article 4 of the agreement states that the boundary pillars themselves shall determine the course of the boundary, even in the event of future alteration of their geographical co-ordinates. This provision obviates possible conflict arising from future discovery that a boundary pillar found *in situ* does not satisfy its exact theoretical position.[1] Article 8 annuls Section 2 of the 1893 Anglo-German agreement, describing the boundary sector from Lake Jipe to Laitokitok, and Article 5 requires the removal of old boundary marks whose locations are inconsistent with the present description.

Two interesting points in the new description deserve mention. First, the establishment of the boundary at Mohuru as a line following the shore at a distance of 1½ kilometres, thereby avoiding the awkwardness of the seventeen intersections made by the parallel with the peninsula. Second, the shifting of the boundary from the eastern side of Lake Jipe to the centre of the lake. By the 1886 and 1890 Anglo-German agreements Lake Jipe was placed entirely within German territory, and was a rare example of a lake shore boundary.[2]

---

[1] On this point see above, p. 51.   [2] Below, pp. 201 ff.

The new line produced a more equitable arrangement, and Article 6 of the 1914 agreement provides that the inhabitants on each side of the border shall have equal rights of fishing in the lake.

In April 1902 the Eastern Province of Uganda was detached to form part of Kenya, whose enlarged boundaries, as a result of this transfer, extended into Lake Victoria for the first time.[1] No precise limits were defined in 1902 but the Uganda tripoint in the lake was established by an Order in Council of 1926 which describes it as lying 'in the waters of Lake Victoria on the parallel 1° south latitude, at a point due south of the westernmost point of Pyramid Island'.[2]

A request for alteration of the boundary line which, had it succeeded, would have required League of Nations consent, was put forward in 1924 by European planters in the Kilimanjaro region who sought a frontier rectification that would place their estates within the limits of Kenya. In reply to a question in the House of Commons on 30 June 1924, the Colonial Secretary gave a firm assurance that no such boundary alteration would be made.[3] On the very same day, the matter was also discussed at a meeting of the Permanent Mandates Commission where it was pointed out that any attempt by the British Government to detach the territory concerned would be in contravention of the mandate agreement.[4]

One serious result of the original Anglo-German delimitation is the division of the Masai tribe by the arbitrary boundary. In the words of the Hilton Young commission of 1929: 'The boundary cuts this people in two, with no more concern for their ideas or for the justice or convenience of their administration than the scythe has for a blade of grass.'[5] Even though some slight excuse could be offered for the ignorance of tribal limits displayed by the partitioning powers in 1886, evidence soon became available to show the harmful social effect of this ill-considered boundary. That the problem

[1] Order of the Secretary of State declaring Kisumu and Naivasha Provinces to form part of the British East Africa Protectorate. London, 5 March 1902. Hertslet, i. 385. The East Africa Protectorate became Kenya Colony and Protectorate in 1920. See Kenya (Annexation) Order in Council, 1920, S.R. & O. 1920/2342, and Kenya Protectorate Order in Council, 1920, S.R. & O. 1920/2343.

[2] The Kenya Colony and Protectorate (Boundaries) Order in Council, 1926. S.R. & O. 1926/1733.

[3] 175 H.C. Deb. 5s., 30 June 1924, cols. 931–2.

[4] *Minutes of the Permanent Mandates Commission*, Geneva. 4th Session, 11th Meeting, 30 June 1924, pp. 91–2.

[5] *Report of the Commission on Closer Union of the Dependencies in Eastern and Central Africa*. H.M.S.O., 1929, p. 300.

received scant attention in early years is illustrated by the remarks of Sir Arthur Hardinge, describing his amusement at the reaction of a tribesman during the 1898 demarcation near Laitokitok (Loitokitok) in Masailand:

A Masai warrior came up to one of our parties engaged in erecting a boundary pillar, and proceeded to ask what had brought us there. I replied that the German Governor and I myself had come to let them know—and to leave the pillar as a record of our commands—that the natives living north of it must transact all their business with Mr. Ainsworth, at Machakos, and those south of it with the German Captain Johannes, at Moshi. Our Masai friend informed us that we were labouring under a misapprehension, as the land belonged, not to the Europeans, but to his own tribe; if any dispute on the point existed, it must be settled between Lenana and Sendeyo, the heirs of their great medicine man, M'batian. It was futile to quote European treaties to a primitive savage, so we merely explained that, if any future question affecting his people's rights should arise, it must be referred both to us and to the Germans.[1]

Frontier difficulties persisted after the demarcation of 1904–5, since the Masai refused to recognize the boundary and crossed it at will. Members of this tribe are pastoral nomads, living in an infertile region with only two permanent rivers, the Ruvu and the Ewaso Ngiro. The population on the Kenya side of the border zone increased in 1911 when the Masai living in Laikipia reserve, north of the Uganda railway, agreed to their transfer to the southern reserve, an area stretching along the northern side of the boundary between the rivers Mara and Kikalelwa and already occupied by fellow tribesmen.[2]

Additional demarcation, undertaken in 1925–6 to indicate more clearly the line between the Moshi District of Tanganyika and the Kenya Masai Reserve, consisted of beacons, stone cairns, and trenches dug along certain portions of the line, between the boundary pillars at Sinya Landari (No. 37) and Laitokitok (No. 54).[3] A year later, 1927–8, further demarcation in Masailand was undertaken between pillar No. 24 (35° 15′ E.) and Lake Natron (No. 34). The surveyor's report in 1928 states:

Although, probably owing to the drought, very few Masai were living along the boundary they were constantly seen crossing and recrossing it,

---

[1] Hardinge, op. cit., p. 232.

[2] For details of the 1904 and 1911 Masai agreements, see *Correspondence relating to the Masai*, Cd. 5584 (1911). See also *Ol Le Njogo* v. *A.G.* (1913), 5 E.A.L.R. 70.   [3] Survey Division M.P. 407 (vol. i), Tanzania Govt.

but chiefly proceeding south in search of water and grazing. They disclaimed any knowledge of the boundary's whereabouts and were distinctly hostile to any demarcation at all and gave one no assistance or information.[1]

During the 1920s consideration was given by the Permanent Mandates Commission to the possibility of unifying the Masai people under one administration. Suggestions included the annexation of the entire Masai area to Tanganyika; the attachment of the Tanganyika Masai district to the Kenya administration, without altering its status as part of a mandated territory; and the creation of a special Masai area to be administered under separate mandate.[2] In 1926, however, the British delegate 'doubted whether it was physically and materially practicable to amalgamate the tribe'. He went on to say that no serious problem was involved in the existing situation, and that too much importance should not be attached to 'certain small difficulties on the boundary', since these were analogous to such disputes as might arise on any frontier.[3] Three years later, in 1929, the Permanent Mandates Commission was told that although the Masai boundary had been demarcated its great length made it difficult for government officers to control the trans-frontier movement of cattle. The Masai themselves were said at that time to be satisfied with the boundary.[4]

As Tanganyika and Kenya moved towards independent status after World War II, the Masai problem received some further attention. Petitions to the British Government were made by the Masai people who sought unification and separate independence. In 1960, at a meeting in Kenya, a Masai delegation requested Britain to remain in Masailand after the rest of Kenya became independent.[5] This request, like other proposals, came to nothing, and the boundary dividing the two branches of the Masai remains to this day as originally drawn by the colonial powers.

To complete the boundary history, mention should be made of the demarcation carried out in 1956-7 by the governments of Kenya and Tanganyika, between Lake Jipe and the coast.[6] Between Lake

---

[1] F. Ford, 'Redemarcation, Kenya–Tanganyika Boundary', 14 May 1928. Survey Division M.P. 407 (vol. i), Tanzania Govt.
[2] *Minutes of the Permanent Mandates Commission*, 6th Session, 18th Meeting, 7 July 1925, pp. 121–4.
[3] Ibid., 9th Session, 20th Meeting, 21 June 1926, pp. 135–6.
[4] Ibid., 15th Session, 13th Meeting, 8 July 1929, p. 112.
[5] *The Times*, 12 July 1960.
[6] *Report on Cartographic Activity in Kenya*, United Nations Regional Cartographic Conference for Africa, 1963. E/CN. 14/CART/4, E/CONF. 43/4, p. 3.

Jipe and Jassini, the boundary was marked along the geodesic (the line of shortest distance) connecting the terminal pillars erected by the 1898 and 1904 commissions. From Jassini to the coast the demarcation follows, in effect, the line described in the Anglo-German agreement of 1900, as far as the mouth of the Ngobwe. Some difficulty was experienced in tracing the old stones and baobab trees used in 1900 to define the boundary, but the new demarcation is substantially in accord with the 1900 description to which no formal amendment has been made. From the mouth of the Ngobwe to Ras Jimbo on the coast, the boundary follows the foreshore of the Jimbo Creek. This section, which runs for about a mile, is governed by, and forms the only surviving remnant of, the 1890 boundary description from the coast to Lake Victoria. So far as is known, the precise position of the terminal at Ras Jimbo has not been physically marked.

CHAPTER XII

Tanzania–Burundi and Tanzania–Rwanda

THE northern portion of Tanzania's western boundary forms the eastern limits of Rwanda and Burundi which, until 1960 when they became separate independent states, were a single unit known as Ruanda-Urundi, administered by Belgium. For historical reasons it is appropriate to consider the two boundary sectors together.

From 1890[1] until the end of World War I Ruanda-Urundi was an administrative part of German East Africa. During the war Belgian troops from the Congo assisted in the defeat of the Germans, and by the end of the war Belgian military authority was established throughout Ruanda-Urundi, as well as in other parts of the German colony, such as the Tabora and Kigoma areas. By Article 119 of the Peace Treaty of Versailles, 1919, Germany renounced in favour of the Principal Allied and Associated Powers all her rights over her overseas possessions, including the colony of East Africa. The problem then arose as to the ultimate disposition of these territories.

So far as East Africa is concerned, there is little doubt that Britain wished to take the entire former German colony in full sovereignty. It was with some reluctance that she later agreed to the proposal that she should hold German East Africa, not as her own colony, but under mandate, and she was still unwilling to share the territory with any other power. Belgium, fearing that her military efforts might go unrewarded, vigorously pressed a claim for her share of the territorial spoils, but although she eventually succeeded in gaining the mandate over Ruanda-Urundi, this in fact was not what she actually sought. Belgium's main concern at that time was the Congo mouth where she had only a narrow piece of territory lying between the two Portuguese colonies of Angola to the south and Cabinda to the north. Skilful diplomatic manœuvring between the British and Belgian foreign offices produced a proposal whereby Belgium's war claims in Africa would be satisfied if she received a portion of Angolan territory from Portugal that would permit the construction of a deep water port for

---

[1] The western boundary of Ruanda-Urundi was not settled until 1910. See 103 B.F.S.P. 372; Deutsches Kolonialblatt, vol. 22 (1911), pp. 613–17.

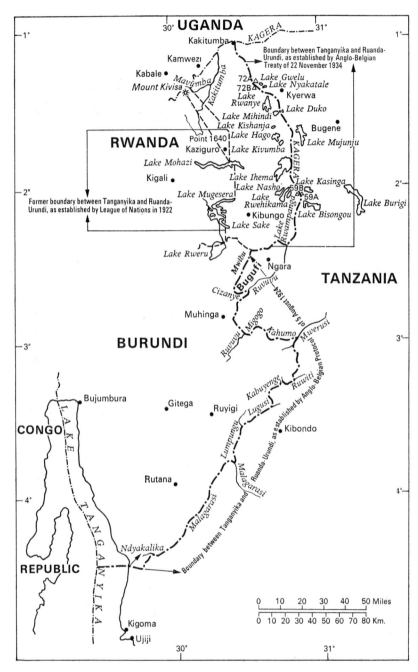

FIG. 6. Tanzania–Rwanda and Tanzania–Burundi Boundary

the Congo. Britain, anxious to keep Belgium out of Ruanda-Urundi, was prepared to persuade Portugal to give Belgium what she wanted and, as compensation, to recommend that Portugal be given part of south-eastern German East Africa, adjoining the Portuguese territory of Mozambique. This proposal very nearly succeeded, though Britain realized that Portugal might not be easily persuaded that the exchange would be in her own interest, and that there might be opposition to the idea of handing over additional native population to the Portuguese. The frustration of the plan came when Belgium, as a condition of acceptance, demanded monetary indemnity from Britain. Britain refused to pay and, almost by accident, Ruanda-Urundi passed into Belgian hands instead.[1]

The Milner–Orts agreement of 30 May 1919 settled the manner in which German East Africa was divided between Britain and Belgium. A few months later, on 7 August, the Supreme Allied Council accepted the Milner–Orts agreement, and the terms of the respective mandates were confirmed by the Council of the League of Nations on 20 July 1922. By the terms of the mandate agreements, the former German East African colony was divided into two parts,[2] lying east and west of a defined boundary, to be administered respectively by Britain and Belgium. This boundary line, which was identical to that contained in the Milner–Orts agreement, is described in the mandate agreements as follows:

From the point where the frontier between the Uganda Protectorate and German East Africa cuts the River Mavumba, a straight line in a south-easterly direction to point 1640, about 15 kilometres south-south-west of Mount Gabiro;

Thence a straight line in a southerly direction to the north shore of Lake Mohazi, where it terminates at the confluence of a river situated about 2½ kilometres west of the confluence of the River Msilala;

If the trace of the railway on the west of the River Kagera between Bugufi and Uganda approaches within 16 kilometres of the line defined above, the boundary will be carried to the west, following a minimum distance of 16 kilometres from the trace, without, however, passing to the west of the straight line joining the terminal point on Lake Mohazi and the top of Mount Kivisa, point 2100, situated on the Uganda-German

---

[1] For details of the negotiations see W. R. Louis, *Ruanda-Urundi 1884–1919*, Clarendon Press, Oxford, 1963, Ch. XXI.

[2] The division was actually into three parts, since the area known as the Kionga Triangle was given to Portugal, though not under mandate. Below, Ch. XV.

East Africa frontier about 5 kilometres south-west of the point where the River Mavumba cuts this frontier;

Thence a line south-eastwards to meet the southern shore of Lake Mohazi;

Thence the watershed between the Taruka and the Mkarange and continuing southwards to the north-eastern end of Lake Mugesera;

Thence the median line of this lake and continuing southwards across Lake Ssake to meet the Kagera;

Thence the course of the Kagera downstream to meet the western boundary of Bugufi;

Thence this boundary to its junction with the eastern boundary of Urundi;

Thence the eastern and southern boundary of Urundi to Lake Tanganyika.[1]

This boundary line is shown on the British 1:1,000,000 map, G.S.G.S. 2932, sheet Ruanda and Urundi. 'Point 1640' and 'point 2100' refer respectively to the ground elevations of 1640 and 2100 metres, as indicated by spot heights on the map. The boundaries of Bugufi and Urundi are as shown in the Deutscher Kolonialatlas (Dietrich-Reimer), scale 1:1,000,000, dated 1906.

Provision is made for the appointment of boundary commissioners to trace and demarcate the boundary line on the ground.[2] Any modification of the terms of the Mandates requires the consent of the League Council.[3]

These two Mandates came into force on 20 July 1922. A few days later, on 28 July, Pastor Anet of the Belgian Protestant Missionary Society to the Congo submitted a note to the Permanent Mandates Commission in which he expressed concern over the partition of the Kingdom of Ruanda, now part of the Belgian Mandate.[4] A similar note was received from Mgr Classe of the Congregation of White Fathers in Ruanda.[5] The delimitation of the boundary in the Mandates had resulted in the severance of the district of Kissaka from the Kingdom of Ruanda and its inclusion in the British Mandated territory of Tanganyika.[6] Both notes emphasize the social, political, and

---

[1] Art. 1 of the British and Belgian Mandates for East Africa, 20 July 1922. The text is given by M. O. Hudson, *International Legislation*, vol. i, pp. 84–99.

[2] Ibid., Art. 2.   [3] Ibid., Art. 12.

[4] *Permanent Mandates Commission. Minutes of the 2nd Session*, 14th Meeting, 9 August 1922, Annex 8, pp. 95–6.

[5] Ibid., Annex 9, pp. 97–100.

[6] The area under the British Mandate became The Tanganyika Territory on 1 February 1920. See *Official Gazette for the Occupied Territory of German East Africa*, vol. i, No. 9, 20 January 1920.

economic harm caused by the imposition of this arbitrary division and they urge the eastward extension of the boundary to the 'natural frontier' of the Kagera River.

During the discussion of these notes by the Permanent Mandates Commission on 9 August 1922, the Chairman referred to the fact that the agreement to separate 'one of the richest and most civilised tracts of the Kingdom of Ruanda' had been due to the desire to 'secure to the British Government uninterrupted railway communication from the north to the south of Africa'.[1] He referred also to the 'deplorable moral effect' that the present arrangement had on the local population and to their strong protests. The Commission agreed that the 'unfortunate results' of the delimitation should be drawn to the attention of the League Council. On 20 September 1922 the President of the Council addressed letters on the matter to the Belgian and the British Governments.

Correspondence between the two governments produced an agreement to alter the boundary between the Mandated Territories so as to follow the Kagera River.[2] The proposed modification was approved by the Council of the League of Nations on 31 August 1923, and Articles 1 of the British and the Belgian Mandates for East Africa were formerly amended to redefine the boundary as follows:

The mid-stream of the Kagera River from the Uganda boundary to the point where the Kagera River meets the western boundary of Bugufi;

Thence this boundary to its junction with the eastern boundary of Urundi;

Thence the eastern and southern boundary of Urundi to Lake Tanganyika.[3]

Demarcation of the new boundary commenced in 1923, and the Commissioners appointed by the British and Belgian Governments signed a Protocol at Kigoma, Tanganyika, on 5 August 1924. The Exchange of Notes between the two governments, accepting the Protocol, was registered with the League Secretariat on 1 September 1926, and contains the detailed description of the demarcated boundary, from Boundary Pillar No. 1 on the eastern shore of Lake Tanganyika, to the junction of the Mwibu and Kagera Rivers. The boundary between the two Mandated Territories in Lake Tanganyika is defined as the 'parallel due west from Boundary Pillar No. 1 to

---

[1] Minutes of the Permanent Mandates Commission, ibid., p. 72.

[2] *Correspondence Regarding the Modification of the Boundary between British Mandated Territory and Belgian Mandated Territory in East Africa.* Cmd. 1974.

[3] Ibid.

the point of intersection with the north and south median line of the Lake' and it was agreed that, notwithstanding this boundary, the customary fishing rights of the inhabitants living on each side should be preserved.[1]

From the junction of the Mwibu and Kagera Rivers to the Uganda boundary the two governments agreed that the midstream[2] of the Kagera should be the boundary between Tanganyika and Ruanda. It was proposed that this line should be provisionally fixed, from a survey of the Kagera to be subsequently undertaken by Belgian officials, and then submitted for final agreement between the governments. The portion of the Kagera forming this section of the boundary extends for 120 miles, and for more than half this distance the river follows a winding and variable course through wide papyrus swamps. By 1930 the exploration of the Ankole-Karagwe tinfield, which extended into both Mandated Territories, indicated that dredging operations might be undertaken in this part of the Kagera valley, and that a more definite boundary than the thalweg of a shifting channel would be required. It was proposed that the line be determined by stone pillars built on islands or promontories in the swamp, at the same time avoiding serious territorial changes by allowing the boundary to follow the general course of the river.[3] Following the completion of this demarcation in 1931, a Treaty was signed by Belgium and Great Britain in 1934 and came into force on 19 May 1938.[4]

For the demarcation of the boundary it was found that, in order to obtain adjacent boundary marks that were both intervisible and planted on firm ground above the level of the marsh, it was necessary to build the pillars some distance inland, thus cutting off pieces of ground that were in some cases of considerable size.[5] To overcome

---

[1] Exchange of Notes Between the Belgian and British Governments, Accepting the Protocol signed at Kigoma, 5 August 1924, Relative to the Tanganyika–Ruanda–Urundi Frontier, Brussels, 17 May 1926. 54 *L.N.T.S.* 239.

[2] The other riparian portions of the boundary are defined by the thalweg. The word midstream may have been deliberately chosen as a less exact provisional description. A caution against the attempted application of precise geographical terms to the Kagera marsh is given by H. P. Rowe, one of the British commissioners. See letter 7577/292, dated 9 October 1928, in Survey Division files, Tanzania Govt., Dar es Salaam.

[3] J. B. Laws, 'A Minor Adjustment in the Boundary Between Tanganyika Territory and Ruanda', *Geog. J.* 80 (1932), 244.

[4] Treaty Between Belgium and Great Britain and Northern Ireland Regarding the Boundary Between Tanganyika and Ruanda-Urundi. Signed at London, 22 November 1934. 190 *L.N.T.S.* 95.   [5] Laws, op. cit., p. 246.

the problem this part of the boundary is described in the Treaty of 1934 as consisting of a series of straight lines formed by adjacent boundary pillars in those places where such lines lie within the marsh or the river channel, and by the shore line between those places where the shore is intersected by the straight lines joining the pillars. Article 2 of the Treaty is as follows:

From the point where the thalweg of the Kagera River is intersected by the straight line joining boundary pillars 59A and 59B, to the point where the straight line joining boundary pillars 72A and 72B intersects the said thalweg, the boundary is determined by the series of straight lines joining adjacent intervisible stone pillars erected either on prominent headlands on the mainland or on islands in the Kagera Valley, wherever such straight lines traverse the river channel or the marsh; but along the stretches other than on islands where these straight lines traverse terra firma, the boundary is determined by the shore of the headlands from the point where the straight line between pillars crosses the shore on departure from the marsh to the point where the same or another straight line crosses the shore again on re-entering the marsh.

In cases where boundary pillars are sited upon islands, the boundary runs by the shortest possible route along the shore of the islands, from the point where a straight line between pillars first cuts the shore on leaving the marsh to the point where the next straight line between pillars last cuts the shore on entering the marsh again. The shore is understood to mean the limit of dry land at extreme low water.[1]

This description, though appearing to be somewhat awkward, has the merit of making the shore line the boundary of the dry land near the pillars, and of placing the islands entirely on one side or the other of the boundary. The straight lines crossing the marsh or river channel do not affect fishing or navigation, to both of which the inhabitants of each bank have free access.[2] The existence of permanent boundary pillars as witness marks, however, enables the owner of a mining concession to establish the boundary as required.

The remainder of this section of the boundary, beyond the limits of the marshy portion described in Article 2 of the Treaty, is defined as the thalweg of the Kagera from its confluence with the Mwibu River to its intersection with the Uganda boundary. The thalweg is

[1] 190 *L.N.T.S.* 95.
[2] Agreement Between the Belgian Government and the Government of the United Kingdom of Great Britain and Northern Ireland Regarding Water Rights on the Boundary Between Tanganyika and Ruanda-Urundi. Signed at London, 22 November 1934. 190 *L.N.T.S.* 103. Arts. 8 and 9.

defined as being the line of minimum level along the river bed but where, owing to rapids or any other cause, the thalweg cannot be determined, the median line of the widest channel shall be the boundary.[1]

At the northern extremity of the boundary, the Uganda tripoint is the confluence of the Kagera and Kakitumba rivers.[2]

It had been intended that a joint Anglo-Belgian triennial inspection of the boundary pillars should take place, but this proposal does not seem to have survived for many years, nor to have resulted in the preservation of the pillars. Even by late 1938 an inspection team reported that pillars were in a bad state of repair. Rainwater collecting in gaps in the pointing caused disintegration of the masonry, and the loosened blocks were then knocked down by goats clambering on to the pillars.[3] Examination of official survey records in Tanzania indicates that there has been no restoration of the boundary during recent years, and that a number of pillars are now missing.

A question concerning the status of Bugufi arose in 1948. It will be recalled that the boundary description contained in the mandate agreements of 1922 follows, in part, the western limit of Bugufi, thereby placing the latter district under British administration. Bugufi is the area lying between the Ruvuvu and Kagera rivers, and contains an area of about 800 square miles. Mwambutsa, the Mwami, or traditional ruler, of Urundi petitioned the Trusteeship Council of the United Nations[4] on 21 July 1948 for the return of Bugufi to Urundi. He claimed that the district of Bugufi was cut off from the remainder of Urundi by the boundary commission in 1923, when he himself was only eleven years old and unable to prevent it.[5] In July of the same year the area was examined by a United Nations Visiting Mission which said in its report:

Geographically the area clearly belongs to Urundi, the natural boundary between Urundi and Tanganyika Territory being the Ruvubu (Ruvuvu) River.

Furthermore, it seems to be generally agreed that the inhabitants of

---

[1] 190 L.N.T.S. 95. [2] See 107 B.F.S.P. 394.

[3] See letter from District Officer, Ngara, dated 9 September 1938. File 292 II, National Archives of Tanzania.

[4] The status of both Tanganyika and Ruanda-Urundi changed from that of League of Nations mandated territories to United Nations trust territories.

[5] Petition from Mwambutsa, the Mwami of Urundi, concerning Ruanda-Urundi and Tanganyika. T/Pet. 2/49, T/Pet. 3/5. A number of counter petitions were later submitted by individual residents of Bugufi.

Bugufi are Barundi. But neither the Belgian nor the British Administration was able to say why this area was included as part of Tanganyika in 1919.[1]

By a resolution dated 25 March 1949 the Trusteeship Council decided to await the result of consultation on the subject between the British and Belgian administrations.[2] The matter was again considered by the Trusteeship Council when, by a further resolution dated 9 February 1950 it decided that since the evidence showed that any alteration of the *status quo* would be contrary to the express wishes of the overwhelming majority of the peoples of Bugufi, no further action by the Council was called for on the petition.[3]

The Rwanda–Burundi–Tanzania tripoint is formed by the intersection of the thalwegs of the Kagera and Mwibu rivers. This is the effect of an ordinance passed by the Belgian administration in 1949.[4] Detailed descriptions of the boundaries of Tanzania with its two neighbours, taken from the Anglo-Belgian agreements of 1926 and 1934, are given below.

[Tanzania–Burundi]

This line corresponds to the following description:

(1) B.P. No. I, situated on the Eastern shore of Lake Tanganyika, at about 13 feet (4 metres) from the water's edge and at the outlet of the Ndyakalika Ravine; thence up the thalweg of this Ravine to B.P. No. II, situated at its head.

(2) The crest of the spur to B.P. No. III, situated on the summit of Lusoro Hill.

(3) The crest of the spur to B.P. No. IV, situated on the summit of Nyangongo Hill.

(4) The crest of the spur to B.P. No. V, situated on the summit of Nganda Hill.

(5) The crest of the spur to B.P. No. VI, situated on the North West end of Mugombe Hill.

(6) A straight line measuring 217 feet (66 metres) in a N.E. direction cutting across the head of the valley of the Nyabitaka River to B.P. No. VII situated at the source of the Sesakuya Stream.

---

[1] *Trusteeship Council Official Records, 4th Session.* Supplement No. 2. T/217/Add. 1. 1 September 1950, p. 101.

[2] *Official Records of the Fourth Session of the Trusteeship Council.* Supplement No. 1. T/328. Resolution 61 (IV).

[3] Ibid., 6th Session, Supplement No. 1. T/635. Resolution 116 (VI).

[4] Ordonnance no. 21/258 du 14 août 1949 fixant l'organisation territoriale du Territoire du Ruanda-Urundi. *Bulletin Administratif du Congo Belge*, 10 September 1949, pp. 1549–68.

(7) Down the thalweg of the Sesakuya Stream to its junction with the Mukelezi River; thence up the thalweg of the Mukelezi River to B.P. No. VIII, situated at its source in Mugombe Hill.

(8) A ridge in an E.S.E. direction to B.P. No. IX, situated at the lowest point of the col separating the River Mutambala to the South and the River Nyamugali to the North.

(9) Down the thalweg of the Nyamugali River to its junction with the Mubarazi River; thence up the thalweg of this latter River to B.P. No. X, situated at the head of its Eastern Source and at the lowest point of the col joining Muharara Hill to the South and Materwa Hill to the North.

(10) Down the thalweg of the Ndihorehi Stream to its junction with the Kiyagira River; thence down the thalweg of this latter River to its junction with the Shuza River; thence up the thalweg of this latter River to the junction of the Nyanvuvu River; thence up the thalweg of this latter River to the junction of the Kasuno Stream (which forms the Northern Branch of the Nyanvuvu River); thence up the thalweg of the Kasuno Stream to B.P. No. XI, situated at its head.

(11) Along the edge of the escarpment forming the pan of the Shuza River Valley in a Northerly direction in straight lines joining B.P. No. XI, XII, XIII, XIV, XV, XVI, XVII, XVIII, XIX, and XX, which last is situated on the Nyamurongozi Col and at the Southernmost Source of the Malagarasi River.

(12) Down the Malagarasi River to the junction of the Lumpungu River; thence up this latter River to the junction of the Mukarasi Stream; thence up the thalweg of this latter Stream to B.P. No. XXI, situated at the source of its Eastern Arm (also known as the Mikungwe).

(13) A straight line in a N.E. direction to B.P. No. XXII, situated on the crest of the Watershed separating the Mukarasi and the Kumbizi (Katungura) Rivers.

(14) A straight line in a N.E. direction to B.P. No. XXIII situated in the Kumbizi (Katungura) Depression.

(15) Down the thalweg of the Kumbizi (Katungura) to its junction with the Lugusi River; up the thalweg of the Lugusi River to the confluence of the Kabuyenge River; up the thalweg of the Kabuyenge River to B.P. No. XXIV, situated at the source of its Western Arm (also known as the Mushagasha).

(16) A straight line to B.P. No. XXV, situated on a prominent rock.

(17) A straight line to B.P. No. XXVI, also situated on a prominent rock.

(18) A straight line to B.P. No. XXVII, situated at the Head of the Mumigomera River.

(19) Down the thalweg of Mumigomera River to its junction with the Lumpungu River; up the Lumpungu River to the confluence of the Lusekera River; up the thalweg of this latter River to B.P. No. XXVIII, situated at its N.E. Source.

(20) A straight line in a N.E. direction to B.P. No. XXIX, situated on the crest of a watershed.

(21) A straight line in a N.E. direction to B.P. No. XXX, situated on the right bank of the Kidobogoro (Akagondo) Stream continuing in this same straight line for a distance of about 120 feet (37 metres) to the thalweg of this latter Stream.

(22) Down the thalweg of the Kidobogoro (Akagondo) Stream to its junction with the Ruwiti River; down the thalweg of the Ruwiti River to the confluence of the Kisuma River; up the thalweg of this latter River to the confluence of the Mwivumba Stream; up the thalweg of the Mwivumba Stream (generally dry) in a N. direction to B.P. No. XXXI, situated at its Source on a narrow col in Lugarama Hill.

(23) Down the thalweg of the Nyakibereko Valley in a N.N.E. direction to its junction with the Kashinga River; down the thalweg of the Kashinga River to its junction with the Mkomero River; up the thalweg of this latter River to B.P. No. XXXII, situated at the head of its N.E. Arm.

(24) A straight line in a N.W. direction to B.P. No. XXXIII, situated on Rwanganiro Col.

(25) A straight line in a N.W. direction and marked by a direction pillar to B.P. No. XXXIV, situated at the head of the Kamiranzovu River.

(26) Down the thalweg of the Kamiranzovu River to its junction with the Nyamuyumbu (Nyabuyumbu) River; up the thalweg of the Nyabuyumbu River to the confluence of the Akayeke Stream; up the thalweg of this latter Stream to B.P. No. XXXV, situated at its head.

(27) A straight line in a N.E. direction to B.P. No. XXXVI, situated in the Ngwa Col.

(28) A straight line in a N.E. direction to B.P. No. XXXVII, situated at the head of the S.E. arm of the Ngwa River.

(29) Down the thalweg of the Ngwa River, subsequently called the Kigenda, to its junction with the Mweruzi River; down the thalweg of this latter River to the confluence of the Kahumo River; up the thalweg of the Kahumo River, following its southern bed, to the confluence of the Mukisuma River; up the thalweg of this latter River to the confluence of the Mukaroba River; up the thalweg of this latter River to the confluence of the Muruhona Stream; up the thalweg of this latter Stream to B.P. No. XXXVIII, situated on a rock at its source.

(30) A straight line in a N.W. direction to B.P. No. XXXIX, situated on a rock on a crest of the Nyamisana Range.

(31) A straight line in a N.W. direction to B.P. No. XL, situated at the head of the Mururama Valley; down the thalweg of this latter Valley to the Mutubiri River; down the thalweg of this latter River subsequently called Nyakondo and Kingoro to its junction with the Luteitavi River; down the thalweg of this latter River subsequently called Magarule, Mkagogo (Migogo) to its junction with the Ruvuvu River; down the thalweg of this latter River to the confluence of the Ichisanye (Chizanye);

M

up the thalweg of this latter River to the confluence of the Murusenye River; up the thalweg of this latter River subsequently taking the names of Nyabitare (Mubitare) to the confluence of the Mukana River; up the thalweg of this latter River to B.P. No. XLI, situated at the head of the Mukina Valley.

(32) A straight line in an E.N.E. direction and marked by a direction pillar to B.P. No. XLII, situated on the Ridge of Ntaretare.

(33) A straight line in a N.N.W. direction to B.P. No. XLIII, situated on the same Ridge.

(34) A straight line in a N.N.E. direction and marked by a direction pillar to B.P. No. XLIV.

(35) A straight line in a N.E. direction to B.P. No. XLV.

(36) A straight line in an E. direction to B.P. No. XLVI, situated on a rocky prominence of Kikomero Hill.

(37) A straight line in a N.E. direction and marked by a direction pillar to B.P. No. XLVII, situated on the S.E. slope of Karambi Hill.

(38) A straight line in a N.E. direction to B.P. No. XLVIII, situated on the Eastern slope of the same Hill.

(39) A straight line in a N.W. direction to B.P. No. XLIX, situated on the same Hill.

(40) A straight line in a N. direction and marked by a direction pillar to B.P. No. L, situated on Lumandali Hill.

(41) A straight line in a N.N.E. direction to B.P. No. LI situated on Lumandali Ridge.

(42) A straight line in a N.N.E. direction and marked by a direction pillar to B.P. No. LII, situated on the same Ridge.

(43) A straight line in a N. Direction to B.P. No. LIII situated on the E. extremity of Kinyami Hill.

(44) A straight line in a N.N.E. direction and marked by a direction pillar to B.P. No. LIV situated in the col joining Kinyami and Bwashishi Hills.

(45) A straight line in a N.E. direction to B.P. No. LV, situated on the S.E. slope of Bwashishi Hill.

(46) A straight line in a N.N.E. direction to B.P. No. LVI, situated on the E. slope of the same Hill.

(47) A straight line in a N.N.E. direction to B.P. No. LVII, situated on the N.E. slope of the same Hill.

(48) A straight line in a N.N.E. direction and marked by a direction pillar to B.P. No. LVIII, situated in the head of the S.W. arm of the Mwibu River.

(49) Down the thalweg of the Mwibu River to its junction with the Kagera River.

[Tanzania–Rwanda]

Article 1.

From the confluence of the Mwibu River with the Kagera River to the inter-section of the straight line joining boundary beacon 59A to boundary beacon 59B with the thalweg of the Kagera River, the boundary follows the thalweg of the Kagera River. (The thalweg shall be understood to be the line of minimum level along the river bed. Where owing to rapids or any other cause it is not possible to determine the position of the thalweg, the median line of the widest channel shall be the boundary.)

Article 2.

From the point where the thalweg of the Kagera River is intersected by the straight line joining boundary pillars 59A and 59B, to the point where the straight line joining boundary pillars 72A and 72B intersects the said thalweg, the boundary is determined by the series of straight lines joining adjacent intervisible stone pillars erected either on prominent headlands on the mainland or on islands in the Kagera Valley, wherever such straight lines traverse the river channel or the marsh; but along the stretches other than on islands where these straight lines traverse terra firma, the boundary is determined by the shore of the headlands from the point where the straight line between pillars crosses the shore on departure from the marsh to the point where the same or another straight line next crosses the shore again on re-entering the marsh.

In cases where boundary pillars are sited upon islands, the boundary runs by the shortest possible route along the shore of the islands, from the point where a straight line between pillars first cuts the shore on leaving the marsh to the point where the next straight line between pillars last cuts the shore on entering the marsh again. The shore is understood to mean the limit of dry land at extreme low water.

Article 3.

The straight lines referred to in the preceding Article are, starting from the point indicated in Article 1:

(a) A straight line towards boundary pillar No. 60 situated on the south-west end of the Island of Zinga;

(b) Thence a straight line towards boundary pillar No. 61 situated on Nyakagasha at the north end of Kagoma;

(c) A straight line towards boundary pillar No. 62 situated on Kalibe at the north-east end of Kanyinya (Kagnigna);

(d) A straight line towards boundary pillar No. 63 situated on the south-west end of the Island of Kyabalelwa (Tschabalelwa);

(e) A straight line towards boundary pillar No. 64 situated on Luterana on the east side of Kageyo (Kageo);

(*f*) A straight line towards boundary pillar No. 65 situated on the west end of Mwoga;

(*g*) A straight line towards boundary pillar No. 66 situated on the west end of Gitega;

(*h*) A straight line towards boundary pillar No. 67 situated on the north-east end of Ndalama (Rurama);

(*i*) A straight line towards boundary pillar No. 68 situated on Magashi at the north-east of Mubari;

(*j*) A straight line towards boundary pillar No. 69 situated on the south point of Gabiro;

(*k*) A straight line towards boundary pillar No. 70 situated on Kito-belaho at the north-east end of Nyakishoz;

(*l*) A straight line to boundary pillar No. 71 situated on Gashoza at the north-east end of Kamakaba;

(*m*) A straight line to the point mentioned in Article 2 where the line joining boundary pillars 72A and 72B, situated respectively on Ryanyawanga and Akanyo at the north end of Kamakaba, intersects the thalweg of the Kagera River.

The boundary line defined above is shown on the map attached to the present Treaty.[1]

Article 4.

From the point referred to in paragraph (*m*) of the preceding Article the boundary line follows the thalweg of the Kagera River to the Uganda frontier.

[1] 190 *L.N.T.S.* 95.

CHAPTER XIII

Tanzania–Congo Republic

THE boundary between Tanzania and the Congo Republic is unique among East African frontiers, since it is formed throughout its entire length by the median line of a lake. At first sight, there may appear to be little that can be said about such a boundary, but it will be appropriate to consider, first, how the line came to be established, and, second, the possible difficulties that arise in interpreting the word median. A further complication is the doubtful location of the Zambia tripoint.

A circular issued in 1885 by the Administrator-General of the Department of Foreign Affairs of the Independent State of the Congo described the eastern limit of the Congo State, in part, as

The median line of Lake Tanganyka;
A straight line drawn from Lake Tanganyka to Lake Moero by 8° 30′ south latitude.[1]

This rather badly worded description stated, in effect, that the boundary ran southward along the median line of Lake Tanganyika from its northern extremity until it reached the point of intersection of the median with the parallel of 8° 30′ south latitude, whence it turned westward along a line connecting the point of intersection with Lake Moero.[2]

The next description that refers to the boundary is contained in the Anglo-German agreement of 1890, where the western limit of the German sphere of influence is defined by 'a line which, from the mouth of the River Kilambo to the 1st parallel of south latitude, is conterminous with the Congo Free State'.[3] This description is misleading since it seems to imply that the Congo State boundary ran

[1] Circular of the Administrator-General of the Department of Foreign Affairs of the Independent State of the Congo, declaring the Neutrality of that State, within its Limits as defined by Treaties. Brussels, 1 August 1885. Hertslet, ii. 552.

[2] The declaration of boundaries contained in the circular was ratified by Germany a few months after its issue. See below, p. 233.

[3] Agreement between the British and German Governments, respecting Africa and Heligoland. Berlin, 1 July 1890. Art. I (3). Hertslet, iii. 899.

along the median of Lake Tanganyika as far as the mouth of the Kalambo River which is at the southern end of the lake, in approximately 8° 36' south latitude, whereas, as has been seen from the 1885 circular, the southern extremity of the Congo State median boundary was said to be 8° 30'. Nevertheless, any possible ambiguity was removed by additional descriptions defining the Congo State's eastern boundaries, of which the next appeared in the agreement made between Britain and King Leopold II of Belgium, establishing the line between the Congo State and the British sphere of influence west of the lake:

> The frontier between the Independent Congo State and the British sphere to the north of the Zambesi shall follow a line running direct from the extremity of Cape Akalunga on Lake Tanganika, situated at the northernmost point of Cameron Bay at about 8° 15' south latitude, to the right bank of the River Luapula, where this river issues from Lake Moëro.[1]

By this description any doubt that the Congo median line boundary extended as far as the mouth of the Kalambo was removed, and confirmation was provided by a further declaration made by the Congo State in 1894, a few months after the signing of the agreement between Britain and King Leopold:

> The median line of Lake Tanganika;
> A line running straight to the extremity of Cape Akalunga, on Lake Tanganika, situated on the northernmost point of Cameron Bay, by about 8° 15' S. lat., to the right bank of the River Luapula, at the point where the river leaves Lake Moëro.[2]

It seems from these various descriptions that the boundary between Zambia and the Congo in Lake Tanganyika is defined by the easterly prolongation of the straight line joining Cape Akalunga and the right bank of the River Luapula (Luvua) at the point where it leaves Lake Mweru (Moero), and that the eastern terminal of this boundary portion, that is to say, the Zambia–Congo–Tanzania tripoint, is formed by the intersection of the prolongation with the median line of Lake Tanganyika. This is probably the correct interpretation and is in accordance with the boundary line as portrayed on maps. Never-

---

[1] Agreement between Great Britain and His Majesty King Leopold II, Sovereign of the Independent State of the Congo, relating to the Spheres of Influence of Great Britain and the Independent State of the Congo in East and Central Africa. Signed at Brussels, 12 May 1894. Art. I (b). Hertslet, ii. 578.

[2] Declaration of the Neutrality of the Congo Free State. Brussels, 28 December 1894. Hertslet, ii. 557, at p. 559.

theless, the line itself remains in doubt, owing to disagreement concerning the exact location of Cape Akalunga. In 1927 a mixed Anglo-Belgian commission, appointed to demarcate the boundary between Northern Rhodesia and the Congo, reported:

> Practically no agreement has been reached in this section. The straight line, defined by treaty, extending from the point where the River Luvua (Luapula) issues from Lake Mweru (on the west) to the Cape Akalunga (on the east) is not possible of demarcation without further agreement. . . . The eastern terminal point has not so far been agreed to. Cape Akalunga cannot be established. It appears that no such name is recognized, and the intention of the treaty is interpreted in different ways by the parties interested.[1]

No subsequent agreement concerning this section of the boundary was reached, and the location of Cape Akalunga is still indeterminate. Possibly the name itself is an error, since it appears that the words *Camp* Akalunga are shown on some of the older maps.[2] A recent map of the Congo indicates that the point where the boundary strikes the western shore of Lake Tanganyika is at Cape Kipimbi (Chipimbi), whereas Zambian maps place this point at Cape Pungu, about 5 miles to the north.[3] The approximate value of 8° 15' south latitude, given for Cape Akalunga in the two 1894 descriptions, lies in between Cape Kipimbi and Cape Pungu. At present, therefore, the exact position of Tanzania's southern tripoint in the lake remains in doubt.

At the northern end of the lake, however, the position is clear, and the Tanzania tripoint is formed by the intersection of the median line with the parallel of latitude of Boundary Pillar No. 1, on the eastern shore, which marks the southern limit of Burundi.[4] There seems little doubt that, if necessary, this northern tripoint could be established without much difficulty.

It will be noted that all the descriptions referred to define the lake boundary in terms of the median. Median is not a term of art and

---

[1] Exchange of Notes Between the Belgian Government and His Majesty's Government in the United Kingdom respecting the Delimitation of the Boundary Between Northern Rhodesia and the Belgian Congo. London, 4 April and 3 May 1927. 140 *L.N.T.S.* 71, at p. 84.

[2] E. H. M. Clifford, Boundary Commissions, *The Royal Engineers Journal*, vol. 51 (1937), at p. 368.

[3] Department of State (Washington), *Tanzania–Zambia Boundary*, International Boundary Study No. 44, p. 2.

[4] 54 *L.N.T.S.* 239, at p. 251.

it can be interpreted in different ways with varying results. Boggs cites three possible definitions:

(*a*) A line being at all points equally distant from each shore;
(*b*) A line following the general lines of the shores and dividing the surface water area as nearly as practicable into two equal parts;
(*c*) A line along the mid-channel dividing the navigable portion of the lake, and being at all points equally distant from the shoal water on each shore.[1]

Boggs describes the first of these definitions by what he calls the 'landsman's or the shore line viewpoint'. He criticizes the method, however, by saying that although it seems reasonable to suppose that the observer would start at one side of the lake and from successive points draw lines to the opposite shore, the line connecting the mid-point of each of these lines cannot be regarded as a true median, since the results obtained by commencing the observations from the opposite shore would produce different results. His criticism of the second definition is that although it may be desirable to create a median line that leaves equal areas of surface water on each side, any number of lines could be drawn that would produce this result, and such a definition is not sufficiently precise. The third definition is held by Boggs to accord more closely with the thalweg than with the true median and, again, he regards it as an unsuitable description of the median.[2]

The solution offered by Boggs himself is that the median should be considered as being 'a line every point of which is equidistant from the nearest points on the shores of the two respective sovereignties', the shore line being specified by a particular water stage, such as the high- or the low-water mark.[3]

It is submitted, however, that instead of resorting to any of the methods referred to or suggested by Boggs, all of which appear to be unnecessarily complex, a series of arbitrary straight lines would, in the case of Lake Tanganyika, be far more suitable. In this way, an arbitrary median would be created, consisting of a series of straight lines connecting the points situated midway between the shores on specified parallels of latitude. Such a boundary was created in Lake Albert, on the Uganda–Congo border, by the Anglo-Belgian agreement of 1915.[4] The actual physical establishment of the change of

[1] Boggs, p. 179.   [2] Ibid., pp. 179–80.
[3] Ibid., p. 184.   [4] Below, p. 247.

direction at any given point on this type of median would not be a difficult technical matter. Determination of the specified parallels of latitude, sufficient for the purpose, could be easily obtained by astronomical observation and the distance between the shores could be found either indirectly by triangulation or by direct measurement with modern electronic surveying instruments.

Perhaps it should be asked what practical purpose would be served by changing the present median boundary, however theoretically vague it may be. While it is true that the existing boundary seems to have caused no particular difficulty in the past there is no reason to suppose that disputes as to its precise location can never arise. Situations might well occur where the exact determination of the location of a vessel is necessary in order to apply the appropriate national customs or fishing regulations.[1] Collisions between vessels, and criminal acts committed on board, are further instances where jurisdictional capacity would be an essential preliminary issue. It is submitted, therefore, that both Tanzania and the Congo Republic could, quite easily and to their common advantage, abandon the present unsatisfactory median line boundary in favour of an exact definition in terms of straight lines.

---

[1] *The Ship Kitty D* v. *His Majesty The King* (1905), 22 T.L.R. 191, concerned the position with respect to the international boundary in Lake Erie of an American fishing vessel, the site of whose nets was marked by a buoy, which was seized by a Canadian cruiser.

CHAPTER XIV

Tanzania–Malawi

EXCEPT for a few miles at its western extremity, the international boundary between Tanzania and Malawi is formed entirely by water features. For about 180 miles, or almost three-quarters of its total length, the line is defined by the eastern and northern shores of Lake Nyasa.[1] This section of the boundary, though appearing at first sight to be legally uncomplicated, presents a territorial problem that finds no modern parallel, nor, as will be shown later, does historical examination of other lacustrine boundaries reveal any useful analogy.

Nyasa is a vast body of water. The third largest lake in Africa, it extends over an area of 11,000 square miles. Some indication of the relative size of this lake is provided by the graphic assertion that it contains a sufficient volume of water to cover the surface of England to a depth of 100 feet.[2]

The modern history of Lake Nyasa can be dated from its discovery by David Livingstone in 1859. In response to his appeal the region soon became an active field for missionary endeavour, beginning with the arrival in 1860 of the Universities' Mission to Central Africa. This was followed by the Livingstonia Free Church Mission which in 1875 brought the first steamer ever to be placed on the lake. A third mission, that of the Church of Scotland, which established a settlement in 1876, found that its main function was being restricted by its efforts to develop local trading and transport facilities, and a commercial company was formed in Scotland in 1878 to relieve the mission of such extraneous tasks. This company was later named The African Lakes Company.[3]

[1] The Malawi Government changed the name of the lake to Lake Malawi in 1965. See Alteration of Place Names Act, No. 2 of 1965. Tanzania does not recognize this alteration and continues to use the name Lake Nyasa. So far as is known, the Portuguese authorities in Mozambique still refer to the lake as Lago Niassa. The name Lake Nyasa is used here for historical reasons only.

[2] F. Debenham, *Report on The Water Resources of the . . . Nyasaland Protectorate . . .*, Colonial Research Publications (No. 2), H.M.S.O., London, 1948, p. 55.

[3] S. S. Murray, *A Handbook of Nyasaland*, Crown Agents, London, 1932. Ch. 13.

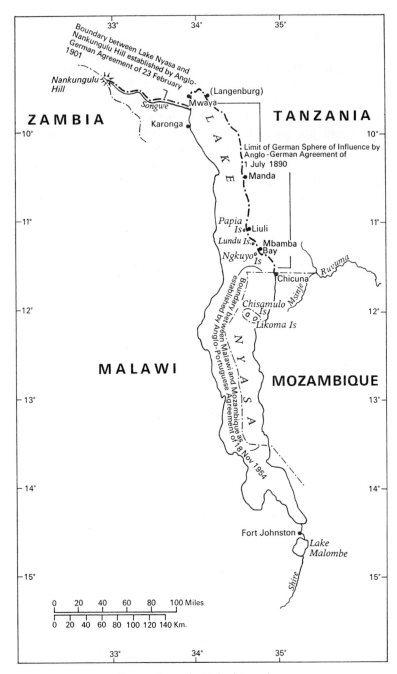

FIG. 7. Tanzania–Malawi Boundary

'The Scramble for Africa', a vivid if hackneyed expression for imperial aspiration and acquisition during the second half of the nineteenth century, remains a particularly apt description of the events in East Central Africa at that time. For here three major colonial powers, Britain, Portugal, and Germany were actively engaged in attempts to thwart each other's territorial ambitions. Portugal had long laid claim to an area in Central Africa that would give her a continuous belt of territory stretching across the continent to provide unbroken connection between her two coastal provinces of Angola and Mozambique. The expansion of British missionary and commercial activity in the Lake Nyasa region revived and stimulated Portugal's hitherto dormant interest, and in 1877 she tried to invoke the provisions of a treaty made with Britain in 1817.[1] By this convention Britain recognized Portuguese possessions in East Africa as consisting of the coastal territory extending from Cape Delgado to Lourenço Marques Bay, and the Portuguese interpretation was that this description included an unlimited amount of hinterland. The British view, on the other hand, was that while they did not dispute Portuguese sovereignty over the coastal area within the limits defined by the treaty, 'with regard to the vast interior of the African continent, respecting which no Treaties exist, they do not admit that the idea of sovereignty can be dissociated from that of *bona fide* occupation and *de facto* jurisdiction of a continuous and non-intermittent kind'.[2] A further statement of the British attitude was made in the House of Lords by the Prime Minister, Lord Salisbury, in July 1888, when he said:

> Now, it is claimed that Portugal had the right to all that zone of territory stretching from the Zambesi to Mozambique on the Indian Ocean, and to Angola on the Atlantic; but the claim could only be made by some extraordinary doctrine of constructive acquisition. I believe it rests upon a decree of Pope Alexander VI, of saintly memory, but how far that can be admitted as an international ground I will not discuss.[3]

Access to the Lake Nyasa basin was not easy. When Livingstone made the famous journey that resulted in his discovery of the lake, he travelled up the Zambezi from its delta in the Portuguese territory

---

[1] Additional Convention between Great Britain and Portugal for the prevention of Slave Trade. 4 *B.F.S.P.* 85, 116.

[2] Morier to Corvo, 14 January 1877, cited by A. J. Hanna, *The Beginnings of Nyasaland and North-Eastern Rhodesia*, Clarendon Press, Oxford, 1956, p. 112.

[3] 328 H.L. Deb. 3s., 6 July 1888, col. 548.

of Mozambique. Finding the Zambezi to be impassable at the Kebra-basa cataract, he returned down the river to its confluence with the River Shire. It was his exploration of the Shire, the only outlet of Lake Nyasa, that led him to the great lake. At that time, and for many years afterwards, the only known navigable entrance to the mouth of the Zambezi for ocean-going ships lay at the Mozambique port of Quelimane, on the River Kwakwa. Even here, however, there was no uninterrupted water communication with the Zambezi, except during floods, and a short overland journey was necessary. Steamers intended for use on Lake Nyasa, such as the *Ilala*, brought by the Livingstonia Mission in 1875, had to be transported in sections.[1] It was this lack of navigability for ocean-going vessels, and the Portuguese control of its entrance, that prevented Lord Salisbury from obtaining a declaration that the Zambezi was an international water-way.[2] Portuguese authorities at first, as a matter of courtesy, allowed free transit at Quelimane to the missionaries and traders. But the growth of the lake missions and the African Lakes Company, and their earnest efforts to suppress the slave trade to which Portugal was at best indifferent, convinced many Portuguese colonists and officials that there was a British plan to take complete possession of the African interior and oust them from an area which traditionally they regarded as their own.[3]

Deteriorating relations between the two countries were aggravated in 1888 by the seizure by Portugal of an African Lakes Company steamer on the Zambezi, and by her restriction on the movement of British supplies at Quelimane. It was now becoming clear that these obstructions were merely the prelude to the assertion of Portuguese sovereignty around Lake Nyasa.[4] Later in the same year Portugal despatched a military expedition to seize the upper course of the Shire and to establish Portuguese rule at the south end of the lake.[5] That the area of potential conflict was not then under the formal sovereignty of either power is illustrated by a statement made in 1889

[1] The *Ilala* was brought by schooner to, and assembled at, the Kongone mouth of the Zambezi which was not at that time a recognized port of entry and was too shallow to admit ocean-going ships. E. Axelson, *Portugal and the Scramble for Africa 1875–1891*, Johannesburg, 1967, pp. 7, 181.

[2] Axelson, op. cit., pp. 180–1, 198, 200–4. See also 2b, *A British Digest of International Law* 176.

[3] Hanna, op. cit., pp. 120–1.

[4] R. Oliver, *Sir Harry Johnston and the Scramble for Africa*, Chatto & Windus, London, 1959, p. 145.

[5] Sir Harry Johnston, *The Story of My Life*, p. 212.

by Sir James Fergusson, Foreign Under-Secretary, in the House of Commons:

Her Majesty's Government have not disputed the right of Portugal to 'control' the navigation of waters within her territories but claim for their vessels the right to navigate the Zambesi so far as it is navigable; nor have they denied the right of Portugal to extend inland the area of her settlement and Government, but claim that British settlements shall not be disturbed by any act of the Portuguese in regions over which they have not hitherto exercised sovereignty or protectorate.[1]

Salisbury, who in the previous year had resisted missionary pressure for the annexation of the Nyasa region,[2] now responded to the Portuguese action by sending H. H. Johnston[3] to Lisbon to see if an agreement could be reached. The resulting proposal involved the abandonment to Portugal of the Shire and part of the western shore of Lake Nyasa, in return for Portuguese recognition of a narrow belt of British influence connecting the Zambezi with the African Lakes Company stations on Lakes Nyasa and Tanganyika.[4]

Johnston regarded this as a satisfactory arrangement, especially as it contributed towards his dream of an all-British 'Cape to Cairo' route. Salisbury disagreed; he knew that any proposal to give up the Shire and the western shore of the lake would be unacceptable to the Scottish missions. He preferred to face Portuguese, rather than Scottish, anger and commenced a skilful manipulation of British public opinion so that his policy might receive the necessary popular support.[5] Public meetings in Edinburgh, Glasgow, and other major cities were followed by a deputation to London, supported by Scottish Peers and Members of Parliament, who presented Salisbury with a petition signed by over eleven thousand church ministers and elders, urging government protection of British interests at Nyasa.[6]

Earlier in the same year, 1889, an event occurred that significantly affected the previous Portuguese domination of the riverine approach to Lake Nyasa. This was the discovery at Chinde of a direct navigable channel from the Indian Ocean to the Zambezi, of sufficient depth to accommodate the draught of ocean-going ships. Johnston's opinion

[1] 335 H.C. Deb. 9 May 1889, col. 1551.
[2] W. P. Livingstone, *Laws of Livingstonia*, Hodder & Stoughton, London, 1921, pp. 244–5.
[3] Later Sir Harry Johnston and the first British Commissioner for Nyasaland.
[4] Johnston, op. cit., p. 216.
[5] Oliver, op. cit., pp. 150–1; Hanna, op. cit., p. 138.
[6] J. W. Jack, *Daybreak in Livingstonia*, Oliphant, Anderson & Ferrier, London, 1901, pp. 300–1.

was that 'in its far-reaching political importance, probably no greater discovery in the history of British Central Africa has been made than that of the navigability of the Chinde River from the Indian Ocean to the main Zambezi'.[1] Access to the Shire no longer depended on Portuguese control at Quelimane, and there remained no reason to deny the Zambezi the status of an international waterway.

Johnston, who had been appointed British Consul at Mozambique, took this new route when he travelled up the Zambezi to meet the Portuguese military party in July 1889. He persuaded the Portuguese to advance no further than the Shire–Ruo confluence, and then proceeded to make treaties with local rulers, an arrangement that had been inspired by the newly formed British South Africa Company of Cecil Rhodes, with the qualified approval of the Foreign Office. During Johnston's absence on his treaty-making expedition, small Portuguese forces twice crossed the Ruo in an attempt to occupy the Shire Highlands. Salisbury now applied pressure to Portugal and threatened to occupy Mozambique Island with a British naval force unless she accepted the Ruo as the limit of Portuguese territory.[2]

Portugal, despite internal political opposition, had no choice but to submit, and the boundary between the respective Portuguese and British spheres of influence was defined by treaty in 1891.[3] By this treaty, Portugal received that portion of the eastern shore of Lake Nyasa lying immediately to the south of the southern boundary of German East Africa, about halfway along the eastern side of the lake, and extending to the limit of the British sphere in 13° 30' south latitude. No part of the lake itself was declared by the treaty to be Portuguese territory.

Germany's interest in the Lake Nyasa region was based less upon her own acquisitive aims than upon her desire to restrict British territorial expansion. In 1886 Germany and Portugal declared the limits of their respective spheres of influence in southern Africa, and by this agreement Germany conditionally recognized the right of Portugal to those 'territories which separate the Portuguese possessions of

[1] Sir Harry Johnston, *British Central Africa*, 2nd edn., Methuen, London, 1898, p. 79.
[2] Salisbury to Queen Victoria, 23 December 1889, cited by Lady Cecil, *Life of Robert Marquis of Salisbury*, Hodder & Stoughton, 1932, vol. iv, pp. 262–3.
[3] Treaty between Her Britannic Majesty and His Majesty the King of Portugal, defining their respective spheres of influence in Africa. Lisbon, 11 June 1891. Hertslet, iii. 1016. For details of the Anglo–Portuguese negotiations see Axelson, op. cit., Ch. 13.

Angola and Mozambique'.[1] Germany thus displayed no ambition to connect her own coastal territories in South-West and East Africa, but was willing to concede the Portuguese claim in order to prevent a British 'all-red route' from Cape to Cairo. By an agreement made with Britain in the same year, the German sphere on the East African coast was also determined, but its western limit was left undefined.[2] This meant that Britain remained free to exploit the vague wording of the hinterland boundary, nor was she of course bound by Germany's recognition of Portuguese claims in the interior. When, in 1888, it was reported that Germany was negotiating with Portugal about Nyasaland, Salisbury warned Berlin that any Portuguese interference in that area might compel the British Government 'to occupy as a material guarantee some one of the possessions of Portugal in the Atlantic Ocean or in India'.[3]

At that time, partly as a result of insufficient capital investment, Germany was finding difficulty in establishing herself on the East African coast. She recognized, however, that the British advance north of the Zambezi into the Nyasa region presented a threat to her own hinterland claims. The new company of Cecil Rhodes was attempting to push northward and, if unchecked, would drive a wedge between the German sphere and the Congo State, in an area which Germany regarded as vital to her economic development in East Africa. The result was a diplomatic clash between Britain and Germany in which two rival principles, the theory of effective occupation and the hinterland doctrine, were brought into play. Britain's attitude to territorial claims was expressed to Portugal two years earlier when, by Lord Salisbury's direction, it was said that a claim in Africa could only be maintained by real occupation.[4]

Hinterland claims, on the other hand, depended on the assertion that the interior of a country belonged to those who held the coast.[5] When Germany pressed this principle on Salisbury he emphasized the difficulty of defining a hinterland, and his only concession was

[1] Declaration between Germany and Portugal respecting the Limits of their respective Possessions and Spheres of Influence in South-West and South-East Africa. Lisbon, 30 December 1886. Hertslet, ii. 703.

[2] Agreement between the British and German Governments, respecting the Sultanate of Zanzibar and the opposite East African Mainland, and their Spheres of Influence. 29 October–1 November 1886. Hertslet, iii. 882.

[3] D. R. Gillard, 'Salisbury's African Policy and the Heligoland Offer of 1890', *English Historical Review*, vol. 75, 1960, p. 636, n. 2.

[4] Above, p. 30.

[5] See also below, p. 267.

that communication between the German sphere and the Congo state should not be cut off. Since this communication could be provided merely by allowing German access to the eastern shore of Lake Tanganyika, without giving Germany control of any land either to the north or the south of that lake, such a concession was more apparent than real. Germany, however, interpreted hinterland as implying the whole territory between her coastal sphere and the Congo State that lay between the parallels of 1° and 11° south latitude. With respect to the Nyasa region, Salisbury's response to the German view was:

As far as the southern portion of this claim was concerned, Her Majesty's Government had a sufficient answer. The country was already occupied by Englishmen; there were English missions and stations of the African Lakes Company upon Lake Nyassa and Lake Tanganyika, and along the Stevenson Road which connects the two, and the rights acquired by these settlements could not be justly set aside by the far vaguer claim which arose from the fact that these regions lay within the same parallels of latitude as those of the German territory more to the east. . . .[1]

Salisbury was prepared later to concede the northern portion of Germany's claim in the area adjoining the Congo State, extending from Lake Tanganyika to the Uganda border. In so doing he abandoned the 'all-red route' a concept for which in any case he was unenthusiastic.[2] As a result of this concession Germany's resistance to the British claims in Nyasa was lowered. Finally, the offer by Britain to cede Heligoland, a barren but strategic island in the North Sea that Germany coveted, led to the signing of an agreement in 1890 whereby, *inter alia*, British control of Nyasa was secured.[3]

It is to the Anglo-German Heligoland Agreement of 1890 that reference must be made for the legal origin of the Lake Nyasa boundary between Tanzania and Malawi. This agreement contains a description of those parts of East Africa which were declared to lie within the respective spheres of influence of the two states. The line

---

[1] Salisbury to Malet, 14 June 1890. F.O.C.P. 6146, F.O. 403/142.
[2] 346 H.L. Deb. 3s., 10 July 1890, col. 1268, where Salisbury referred to '. . . a very curious idea, which has recently become very prevalent in this country, that there is some special advantage in having a stretch of territory extending all the way from Cape Town to the sources of the Nile. . . . I can imagine no more uncomfortable position than the possession of a narrow strip of territory in the very heart of Africa three months' distance from the coast . . .'.
and Heligoland. Berlin, 1 July 1890. Hertslet, iii. 899.
[3] Agreement between the British and German Governments, respecting Africa

dividing the German sphere on the north from the British sphere on the south is described in part as follows:

> To the south by a line which, starting on the coast at the northern limit of the Province of Mozambique, follows the course of the River Rovuma to the point of confluence of the Msinje; thence it runs westward along the parallel of that point till it reaches Lake Nyassa; thence striking northward, it follows the eastern, northern and western shores of the lake to the northern bank of the mouth of the River Songwe; it ascends that river. . . .[1]

By these words, Lake Nyasa was plainly excluded from the German sphere of influence. Neither by subsequent amendment to this description, nor by any other international agreement, has there been anything to suggest that this part of the lake boundary has been altered from its definition in 1890. Since that time, however, considerable confusion has arisen. Claims have been made that the boundary should be drawn, and originally was drawn, not along the Tanzania shore but through the middle of the lake. In support of these arguments, reliance has been placed partly on maps of an official, or a semi-official, nature. Appeals have also been made to common sense, logic, and emotion. It will be shown that confusion concerning this boundary is of long standing and that even during the colonial period genuine ignorance of the true position prevailed for many years, an ignorance which has been fortified by certain erroneous assumptions expressed not only in maps but also in public documents. A legacy of misunderstanding, inherited from previous administrations, results in disagreement over the boundary that now injures Tanzania–Malawi relations. An attempt to trace the source of this confusion and to examine the boundary itself in closer detail must now be made.

It should be noted that the Anglo-German Agreement of 1890 did not establish a precise boundary in East Africa between adjacent territorial sovereigns. Instead it delimited spheres of influence,[2] the limits of which were made subject to rectification by agreement between the two parties, in accordance with local requirements.[3] Boundary commissions were subsequently appointed to demarcate the lines on the ground, but the mixed commission which in 1898 dealt with the Nyasa section of the boundary commenced its work at the mouth of the Songwe and proceeded westward to Lake Tan-

---

[1] Agreement, Berlin, 1 July 1890, Art. I. Hertslet, iii. 899.
[2] For a discussion of spheres of influence see above, Ch. II (b).
[3] Art. VI.

ganyika, without considering the shore boundary of Lake Nyasa.[1] No doubt at the time it seemed obvious that a boundary defined in terms of a lake shore was self-demarcating[2] and required no physical investigation but, as will appear later, the failure to examine more critically this part of the boundary when it was drawn has contributed to the difficulty of the present day.

Why was the boundary of the British sphere with the spheres of both Germany and Portugal taken as the shore of Lake Nyasa, rather than as the median line of the water? Tentative answers can be suggested. First, Britain was determined to control the lake as a means of protecting her missionary and commercial interests, and to eliminate the slave trade. Recommendations that the lake should be entirely British had been made in Parliament.[3] Second, Germany's attention was focused on the Indian Ocean coast; having prevented the danger of the British 'all-red route' and gained the prize of Heligoland, she was less concerned with British ambitions in Nyasa. Third, Germany was given access to, and right of transit upon, Lake Nyasa; the question of sovereignty of the waters was of less importance to her.[4]

It should also be remembered that there was at that time imperfect geographical knowledge of the area in question on the part of the European powers. Despite the great public interest shown in Livingstone and his successors, to most people in Europe the exact location of Lake Nyasa remained something of a mystery for many years. Thus Livingstone himself wrote scathingly of published maps, none of which he could recommend as giving even a tolerable idea of the country. He added: 'One bold constructor of maps has tacked on

[1] *Report by Captain Close, R.E., on the Delimitation of the Nyasa–Tanganyika Boundary in 1898.* Foreign Office, Confidential No. 7115, March 1899. An example of rectification is provided by the alteration of the boundary from 'the northern bank of the mouth of the River Songwe', as described in Art. I of the 1890 Anglo-German agreement, to the thalweg of the river. See Anglo-German agreement of 1901, sec. 2. Hertslet, iii. 925.

[2] Cf. the use of river boundaries, above, p. 76.

[3] 328 H.L. Deb. 3s., 6 July 1888, col. 543.

[4] Art. VIII of the 1890 Anglo-German agreement provides, *inter alia*, for the enjoyment by the two powers of freedom of trade, navigation, and passage of goods in all portions of their respective spheres lying within the free zone defined by the Act of Berlin, 1885. Lake Nyasa, though not a part of the conventional Congo Basin, lay within the eastern zone of the free trade area defined by Art. I (3) of the Berlin Act. See Hertslet, ii. 468. The Anglo-Portuguese treaty of 1891 made no specific provision regarding freedom of navigation in Lake Nyasa. Cf. Art. XI of the unratified Anglo-Portuguese convention of August 1890 (Hertslet, iii. 1006) which granted the right of free navigation to both flags.

200 miles to the north-west end of Lake Nyasa, a feat which no traveller has ever ventured to imitate. Another has placed a river in the same quarter running 3000 or 4000 feet up hill, and named it the "New Zambesi", because I suppose the old Zambesi runs down hill.'[1] Such geographical ignorance was not quickly dispelled, even from the minds of prominent statesmen of the period. Harry Johnston who, on the eve of his departure for Africa in 1889 to take up his appointment as British Consul at Mozambique, was interviewed by Joseph Chamberlain, the Liberal Unionist leader and a future Secretary of State for the Colonies, describes the meeting:

I was shown into his library where I found him looking at some large maps of Africa suspended on a wall of the room. They were all of the 1862–1867 period. He had nothing later showing even an approximate sketch of the great rivers and lakes. Their glazed surface was recalcitrant to pen and ink, and I had with my finger nails to try to indicate the approximate outline and courses of rivers and lakes. I soon gave up as hopeless this attempt to illustrate Central African geography.[2]

It is worth noting that this meeting took place in 1889, only one year before the signing of a treaty which to this day defines the lake boundary.

Diplomatic agreement between Britain and Germany regarding Lake Nyasa still failed to satisfy the missions. On the western side of the lake, the acceptance of the River Songwe as the boundary drew an unsuccessful protest from the Scottish missions which claimed settlements to the north of the river. Even Johnston himself, who, on behalf of the African Lakes Company, had purchased a harbour at the north end of the lake, saw this pass to Germany under the 1890 agreement, and become, under its new name of Langenburg, the German headquarters on Nyasa.[3] On the eastern side, the Universities' Mission to Central Africa, whose work extended all along the shore, had seen the possibility that its settlements might fall under non-

---

[1] Waller, *The Last Journals of David Livingstone*, vol. i, pp. 267–8.

[2] Johnston, *The Story of My Life*, p. 223. See previous note. Although it must be remembered, first, that Livingstone wrote in 1867 and was referring to an even earlier period and, second, that Chamberlain was not at the time directly concerned with the territorial negotiations, there seems little doubt that diplomats possessed geographical knowledge that was frequently scanty and uncertain. Cf. Salisbury's remarks in 1890 concerning the nature of Lake Ngami, above, Ch. VII, p. 97, where he also said of the lake, '. . . our only difficulty being that we do not know where it is. We cannot determine its position within 100 miles, certainly not within 60 miles . . .'.

[3] Johnston, *British Central Africa*, p. 94.

British control. Both before and after the signing of Britain's agreements with Germany and Portugal, Archdeacon W. P. Johnson of this mission made a vigorous plea for the retention of the eastern shore within the British sphere. He complained that the eastern boundary was being drawn in Europe without knowledge of natural divisions or tribal feelings, and insisted that leaving Portugal access to the lake shore would prevent any effective dealing with the slave trade because it would place the harbours used by the slavers in the hands of those who would do least to suppress them. Though he did not doubt Germany's sincerity as an opponent of the slave trade, Archdeacon Johnson advocated the reservation to Britain of a strip of land adjoining the entire eastern side of the lake and extending inland to a depth of ten miles. His proposal was ignored.[1]

Because the origin of the boundary separating Tanzania from Malawi is directly traceable to international agreement, how is it that the position with regard to the lake boundary has not remained free from doubt? The key to this question may lie in an examination of the Orders in Council and other instruments by which the limits of the respective countries were purported to be established.

By Article 1 of The British Central Africa Order in Council, 1902,[2] the limits of the British Central Africa Protectorate are described as comprising '. . . the territories of Africa situate to the west and south of Lake Nyasa, and bounded by North-Eastern Rhodesia, German East Africa, and the Portuguese territories'. The Nyasaland Order in Council, 1907, changed the name of these territories to the Nyasaland Protectorate, the limits of which remained as defined by Article 1 of the 1902 Order.[3]

Since, by her 1890 and 1891 agreements with Germany and Portugal, Britain had placed the whole of Lake Nyasa within her sphere, it would have been more conducive to clarity had the limits of the 1902 Order in Council been described with greater precision. In the absence of other knowledge, it might seem reasonable to interpret Article 1 of the Order as comprising only a land area to the west and south of Lake Nyasa, whereas the lake itself formed almost one-quarter of the total size of the protectorate. Nevertheless, despite the risk of ambiguity, the Order does define Nyasaland as being bounded by German East Africa and, in order to determine the limits of this part

[1] B. H. Barnes, *Johnson of Nyasaland*, U.M.C.A., London, 1933, pp. 88–90.
[2] S.R. & O. 1902/663.
[3] S.R. & O. 1907/541.

of the boundary, the Order in Council of 1902 must be read in conjunction with the Anglo-German agreement of 1890.

That the status of the lake was not always clear to the Nyasaland Government may be seen from the description of provincial and district boundaries, proclaimed by the Governor under the provisions of the 1902 and 1907 Orders in Council, contained in the Laws of Nyasaland, 1933.[1] The districts in the northern part of Nyasaland are described as being bounded on the east by a line midway between the western and the eastern shores of Lake Nyasa. These descriptions may also be found in a handbook, published for the Nyasaland Government in 1932, which contains a map drawn in conformity with the text.[2] It is only in the southern part of Nyasaland, adjoining Mozambique, that the eastern boundaries of the districts are described and shown as coincident with the eastern shore of the lake. By 1946, however, the discrepancy had been noted, for in the Laws of Nyasaland of that year, the boundaries of the northern districts are described as extending to the eastern shore of the lake, and this description has since been maintained in subsequent editions of the Laws.[3]

The nomadic proclivity of the boundary is further illustrated by maps contained in the Nyasaland Annual Reports. For most of the years prior to 1929 the report included no map, and such maps as were published did not show a lake boundary. The annual report for 1929 contains a map showing, for the first time, the boundary passing along the median line of the northern portion of Lake Nyasa. This map was published in each succeeding report, up to and including 1938. No further reports appeared until after World War II, when the annual reports for 1946 and 1947 show a map with no lake boundary. The map in the report for 1948 shows the Tanganyika boundary, for the first time, as the eastern shore of Lake Nyasa, and this has been repeated in all later reports.

The sphere of influence allocated to Germany by the Heligoland Agreement of 1890 was known as German East Africa until the end of World War I. By Article 119 of the Peace Treaty of Versailles, 1919, Germany renounced in favour of the Principal Allied and Associated Powers all her rights over her East African colony.

---

[1] *Laws of Nyasaland*, 1933, vol. ii, pp. 1042-3.
[2] Murray, op. cit.
[3] *Laws of Nyasaland*, 1946. Appendix 1 to the Laws (revised to 31 October 1961). S.I. 1961/1189, sec. 85.

Following the cessation of hostilities, Britain established civil government in the former German possession which, in 1920, became the
Tanganyika Territory.[1] The limits of Tanganyika Territory are
described in the Tanganyika Order in Council of 1920 as being
bounded, in part, by 'the Nyasaland Protectorate'.[2]

In 1922, under Article 22, Part I, of the Treaty of Versailles, the
League of Nations created Mandates for East Africa,[3] whereby the
former German colony was divided into two parts,[4] lying east and
west of a defined boundary, to be administered respectively by Britain
and Belgium. Article 1 of the British Mandate reads: 'The territory
over which a mandate is conferred upon His Britannic Majesty
(hereinafter called the Mandatory) comprises that part of the former
colony of German East Africa situated to the east of the following
line. . . .' Then follows a description of the line dividing the British
and the Belgian mandated territories, henceforth to be known
respectively as Tanganyika Territory and Ruanda-Urundi.[5] Except
for the substitution of the word 'west' for 'east' in the quoted extract,
Article 1 of the Belgian Mandate is identical in terms. Apart from
the establishment of this common line, however, no detailed particulars of territorial boundaries are given in the mandate agreements.
All that one can learn, therefore, from an examination of the Tanganyika Order in Council of 1920 and the League Mandates for East
Africa is that the limits of Tanganyika, when it became a mandated
territory, are the lines enclosing that part of former German East
Africa which lies to the east of the defined Tanganyika/Ruanda–
Urundi boundary, with the exclusion of the Kionga Triangle the
ownership of which had been transferred to Portugal in 1919. If more
specific boundary details are required, they must be sought in the
documents whereby the boundaries were established during the time
of the German administration.

The mandate agreements came into force on 20 July 1922 which

---

[1] *Official Gazette for the Occupied Territory of German East Africa*, vol. i,
No. 9, 20 January 1920.
[2] S.R. & O. 1920/1583. Proclaimed 27 September 1920. Art. 1.
[3] British and Belgian Mandates for East Africa, 20 July 1922. M. O. Hudson,
International Legislation, vol. i, pp. 84–99.
[4] The division was actually into three parts, since the area in the south-eastern
corner of the colony, known as the Kionga Triangle, had been given to Portugal
in 1919 by the Allied Supreme Council, though not under mandate. Below,
Ch. XV.
[5] This line was later changed by an amendment to Art. 1 of both mandates.
See 54 *L.N.T.S.* 239 and 190 *L.N.T.S.* 95.

must therefore be regarded as a critical date for determining the boundaries of Tanganyika. Any alteration of boundaries after the creation of the mandate would be a modification of its terms and could take effect only with the consent of the Council of the League of Nations.[1] It is essential, therefore, to see whether any evidence exists to show that between 1 July 1890 and 20 July 1922, the lake boundary was in fact shifted, either expressly or by implication, from the shore to the median line. What seems quite clear is that there was no written agreement between Britain and Germany regarding an alteration of the boundary as it stood in 1890. It is obvious that if any such agreement existed it could be expected to be found in official or semi-official publications, yet even German sources fail to show that the lake boundary had ever been altered from its 1890 position. Dr. Schnee, the scholarly Governor of German East Africa from 1912 to 1919, lists in his *Deutsches Kolonial Lexikon*, published in 1920,[2] the various protocols and agreements affecting the boundaries of the German colony,[3] and had there been any instrument purporting to shift the shore-line boundary to the median of the lake he would scarcely have failed to include a reference to it. Dr. Meyer, in another authoritative German work, published in 1909, refers to the territorial limits of German East Africa and draws specific attention to the fact that whereas the boundary passes through the middle of Lakes Tanganyika and Kivu, in the case of Lake Nyasa it follows the eastern and northern shore line.[4]

The absence of written agreements would not be conclusive as to the position of the lake boundary if it could be shown that Britain, by her acquiescence, or admission against interest, was precluded in 1922 from denying that the boundary lay along the median line. Evidence on this point appears to be scanty, though a few references, some of admittedly little probative value, may be cited. An article which appeared in *The Navy and Army Illustrated* in 1897, concerning the activities of the British Navy on Lake Nyasa, states that the whole of the lake was included within Nyasaland.[5] A military report on German East Africa, prepared by the British War Office in 1905,

---

[1] Art. 12 of the Mandates. For occasions when this was done, see above, p. 183, n. 5, and 185 *L.N.T.S.* 205.
[2] H. Schnee (ed.), *Deutsches Kolonial Lexikon*, vol. i, Leipzig, 1920.
[3] Ibid., pp. 754–5.
[4] H. Meyer (ed.), *Das deutsche Kolonialreich*, vol. i, Leipzig, 1909, p. 21.
[5] *The Navy and Army Illustrated*, 12 November 1897, cited by P. M. Withers in *The Nyasaland Journal*, vol. 2, January 1949, p. 29.

describes part of the territorial limits in the following words: 'The boundary then approximately follows Lakes Kivu, Tanganyika and Nyasa; rather more than halfway down the latter lake it turns east and joins the Rovuma river, whose course it follows nearly to the sea.'[1] The reason why the boundary is described as 'approximately' following Lakes Kivu and Tanganyika is that in 1905 Germany's western boundary with the Congo State had not then been settled. With regard to Lake Nyasa, however, the report goes on to say: 'Lake Nyasa is about 300 miles long by 15 to 55 miles broad. It is only the northern portion of the lake which touches the German Protectorate.'[2] This statement appears to mean that, in the opinion of the War Office, the northern part of the lake touched, but did not form part of, German East Africa.

In 1916, when Britain and Germany were at war, *A Handbook of German East Africa*, was prepared by the British Admiralty War Staff Intelligence Division.[3] This volume gives comprehensive information of especial value to military and naval authorities and is stated to be 'For Official Use Only'. It touches only lightly upon the history and general geography of the German colony and concentrates, as might be expected, on detailed descriptions of features such as local military forces, defensible towns, resources, supplies, and routes of communication. The international boundaries of German East Africa are referred to in rather general terms, and the following description is given for the Lake Nyasa sector: 'It then follows the middle of Lake Tanganyika to its southern end at Bismarckburg, whence it goes SE. to the northern end of Lake Nyasa. Rather more than half-way down the lake it turns E. and joins the Rovuma river, whose course it follows nearly to the sea.'[4] And, in a later passage: 'Only the northern portion of the lake (Nyasa) abuts on German East Africa.'[5] A comparison between the language used in the handbook to describe this portion of the boundary, with that which appears in the War Office Report of 1905 shows an almost exact repetition of the earlier words. It will be noted that the 1916 description states that Lake Nyasa 'abuts on' German East Africa and, as with the 1905 report which uses the word 'touches', the language employed gives no clear indication that any part of the lake formed part of German territory.

[1] *Military Report on German East Africa*, Prepared by the General Staff, War Office, London, 1905 (confidential pamphlet), p. 2.

[2] Ibid., p. 7.

[3] *A Handbook of German East Africa* (I.D. 1055), London, January 1916.

[4] Ibid., p. 7.   [5] Ibid., p. 285.

Following her occupation of Tanganyika at the end of World War I, and prior to the creation of the mandates, Britain published annual reports on the territory, the first of which covered the period from the conclusion of the armistice to the end of 1920. In this report the western boundary is described as running 'south-east to the northern end of Lake Nyasa. Rather less than half-way down the lake it turns east and joins the Rovuma River whose course it follows to the sea.'[1] Taken by themselves, the words 'rather less than half-way down the lake' could refer either to the median or the eastern shore line, and it will be seen that this part of the description bears a striking similarity to those which appeared in 1905 and 1916. It is submitted that the textual descriptions contained in the three publications of 1905, 1916, and 1920 are ambiguous and cannot in themselves be said to constitute an admission against British interest with regard to the location of the boundary. In other words, they do not affect the plain words of the Anglo-German agreement of 1890. Annual reports by the British administration in Tanganyika for the years 1921 and 1922 contain boundary descriptions written in similarly inconclusive language.

Apart from written descriptions, what evidence can or should be drawn from contemporary maps? Here again, the position is far from clear, since neither German nor British practice displays consistency during the critical period. Maps of German East Africa in Dr. Schnee's *Lexikon* appear to show a median-line boundary for Lake Nyasa,[2] but for the reason already advanced, this is inconsistent with his textual references to boundary agreements. Dr. Meyer's book shows a number of maps of German East Africa, some of which show a median, and some a shore-line, boundary for Lake Nyasa.[3] Those which depict a median line are plainly at variance with Dr. Meyer's own remarks concerning the location of the lake boundary.

An important German map, edited by the Reichs-Kolonialamt, and published by Dietrich Reimer of Berlin in 1918, clearly shows a median-line boundary for Lake Nyasa.[4] Since, however, this is a German map, published at a time when Britain and Germany were at war with each other, its probative value may be very small. Of far more significance are British maps published during the crucial

---

[1] *Report on Tanganyika Territory, covering the period from the conclusion of the Armistice to the end of 1920*, Cmd. 1428 (1921), p. 5.

[2] Schnee, op. cit., facing p. 361.

[3] Meyer, op. cit., pp. 416 ff.

[4] *Mittelafrika in Karten*, 1:2,000,000. Dietrich Reimer, Berlin, 1918.

period. The Admiralty's *Handbook of German East Africa* of 1916, to which previous reference has been made, contains a map at the end of the volume which unquestionably portrays the international boundary in the northern portion of Lake Nyasa as the median line. This map is obviously important since it emanated from an intelligence division which could reasonably be expected to have reliable reference material at its command. Nevertheless, it should be viewed in the light of its surrounding circumstances. First, some attention should be paid to the appearance of the map itself which contains no references to date of publication and name of publisher, nor to the cartographic source from which it was constructed. The absence of these references, the inclusion of which are a normal feature of cartographic practice, suggests that the map is essentially a sketch the prime purpose of which was to illustrate the text of the handbook, not to provide authoritative information concerning international boundaries. Second, it has already been shown that Germany, by the provisions of her 1890 agreement with Britain, was accorded freedom of navigation on Lake Nyasa.[1] The presence on the lake of the *Hermann von Wissmann* and another small German vessel,[2] are noted in the handbook, and it may be that the compilers interpreted the existing, though limited, German activities on the lake as an indication that the international boundary ran along the median line. It is submitted, therefore, that the map affords some, but by no means conclusive, evidence of British admission that their boundary with Germany followed the middle line of Lake Nyasa. As is shown elsewhere, the evidence of maps, in certain circumstances, can have particular significance where ambiguities exist in written texts, as in the *Frontier Land Case*, or where the map has been clearly adopted by a state, as in the *Temple Case*.[3] With respect to Lake Nyasa, however, it is essential to look at British wartime maps in their proper perspective, and it may be stretching the meaning of admission against interest too far to say that they can displace the clear effect of the 1890 Anglo-German agreement. It should also be mentioned that the map contained in the British report for Tanganyika, covering the period from the armistice to the end of 1920, throws no light on the problem, for although it appears to portray an eastern shore line boundary on Lake Nyasa it also shows the eastern shore of Lake

---

[1] Above, p. 179, n. 4, and below, p. 192.
[2] *A Handbook of German East Africa*, p. 286, refers to 'a little steamboat of the Berlin Mission'. [3] Above, Ch. IV.

Tanganyika as the international boundary. This map is obviously of small value as an aid to the interpretation of an ambiguous text in the report.[1] One unofficial, though usually reliable, source that should be noted is *The Times Survey Atlas of the World*, published in 1922. One of the plates[2] in this atlas shows the international boundary in the northern portion of Lake Nyasa as the median line and in the southern (Portuguese) portion as the eastern shore line. This evidence is weakened by another plate in the same atlas which appears to show a median-line boundary for the entire length of the lake.[3]

After the creation of the mandate, Tanganyika authorities, like those in Nyasaland, were uncertain as to the common boundary of their respective countries. The Tanganyika Annual Report to the League of Nations for the year 1924 contains a boundary description, part of which reads: 'Thence it follows the boundary of Rhodesia to the northern end of Lake Nyasa and continues along the centre line of Lake Nyasa to a point due west of the Rovuma River whence the boundary runs east and joins the Rovuma River, whose course it follows to the sea.'[4] This description was repeated in subsequent reports until the year 1935 when it was amended to read 'the eastern shore' instead of 'the centre line' of Lake Nyasa. The amendment appeared without further reference or explanation, and the new description was repeated in all later reports. The accompanying maps in the reports for the years 1924 to 1934 are in conformity with the text and show the boundary to lie in the middle of the lake.

The changes being made by the Tanganyika Government to its boundary description and map were drawn to the attention of the Permanent Mandates Commission in 1934:

M. Orts pointed out a slight inaccuracy in the map of the territory; the frontier line between Tanganyika Territory and Nyasaland, instead of following the eastern shore, should be equidistant from the eastern and western shores of Lake Nyasa.[5]

[1] This map appears at the end of Cmd. 1428 and is entitled 'Tanganyika Territory 1920'. Annual reports for the years 1921, 1922, and 1923, published by the British Government, do not appear to contain a map of the territory, though the copies examined by the author are possibly defective.

[2] *The Times Survey Atlas of the World*, London, 1922, Plate 75, Central Africa—Eastern Section.

[3] Ibid., Plate 70, Central and Southern Africa.

[4] *Report by His Britannic Majesty's Government on the Administration Under Mandate of Tanganyika Territory For the Year 1924*, H.M.S.O., London, 1925, p. 3.

[5] *Permanent Mandates Commission. Minutes of the twenty-fifth session*, Geneva, 1934. Fourteenth Meeting, 7 June 1934, p. 105.

This statement was withdrawn in the following year:

M. Orts observed that the previous year he had pointed out a slight inaccuracy in the map of the Territory; the frontier-line between Tanganyika Territory and Nyasaland, instead of following the eastern shore, should, he had said, be equidistant from the eastern and western shores of Lake Nyasa. This observation was unjustified, because he had since learned that, under the terms of Article 2 [*sic*] of the Treaty of July 1st, 1890, between Great Britain and Germany, the frontier-line did, in effect, follow the eastern bank. He noted, however, that the error he had made had now crept into the report, in which it was said that from the northern end of Lake Nyasa the frontier continues along the centre line of Lake Nyasa to a point due west of the Rovuma River.[1]

The remarks of M. Orts on these two occasions passed without recorded discussion.

By the late 1930s, then, it seemed that the two neighbouring administrations had at last recognized the eastern shore of Lake Nyasa as the boundary, in conformity with the 1890 Anglo-German agreement. In Tanganyika, a government departmental suggestion that the boundary should be altered from the eastern shore to the median line of the lake was made in 1953. The matter was discussed, but eventually dropped because it was felt that the existing boundary presented no real administrative problem.[2]

An exchange of correspondence between the Tanganyika Government and the Government of the Federation of Rhodesia and Nyasaland during the 1950s, concerning the exact definition of the lake boundary, led to a request by the former government to the Secretary of State for the Colonies for his ruling on the matter. During this time the problem received some attention in the Tanganyika Legislative Council.[3] On 15 December 1959 the Minister of Lands and Surveys reported that the opinion of the legal advisers to the Secretary of State 'is that the southern boundary of Tanganyika lies along the Eastern, Northern, and Western shores of Lake Nyasa and that therefore no part of the Lake is within the boundaries of Tanganyika'.[4]

Further discussion took place in the Legislative Council in 1960, when it was argued by some members that the existing boundary restricted

[1] Ibid., twenty-seventh session. Thirteenth Meeting, 10 June 1935, p. 123.
[2] Secretariat File No. 34207, National Archives of Tanzania, Dar es Salaam.
[3] Council Debates, Tanganyika Legislative Council, 34th Session, 26 May 1959, p. 49 and 3 June 1959, pp. 368-71.
[4] Ibid., 35th Session, 15 December 1959, p. 14. By a slip of the tongue the Minister actually said that no part of Lake Tanganyika is within the boundaries of Tanganyika. He corrected his statement in the Legislative Council on 26 April 1960 (Debates, p. 3).

lakeside inhabitants of Tanganyika from enjoying fishing and other advantages of the lake. The following motion was put: 'Be it resolved that this Council request the Tanganyika Government to approach the Nyasaland Government through Her Majesty's Government in the United Kingdom, with a view to securing a more equitable boundary between Tanganyika and Nyasaland.'[1] This motion was debated at some length but was not carried.

Tanganyika became an independent member of the Commonwealth on 9 December 1961, and the Nyasaland boundary continued to engage the attention of Parliament. In reply to a question whether Tanganyika, with respect to the lake boundary, was bound by pre-independence treaties made between Britain and Germany, the Prime Minister, Mr. R. M. Kawawa, replied:

The boundaries of Tanganyika are defined in the Tanganyika Order-in-Council 1920. Excluding Ruanda-Urundi, they follow the boundaries of the territory formerly known as German East Africa. The boundaries of Nyasaland are defined by the British (Central Africa) Order-in-Council, 1902.

No part of Lake Nyasa fell within the boundaries of German East Africa and, accordingly, no part of the Lake is within the boundaries of Tanganyika. By virtue of the Order-in-Council 1902, the whole of the Lake falls within the boundaries of Nyasaland save for the area that forms part of Moçambique.

There is no question of the boundaries of Tanganyika having been altered by any agreement or treaty entered into by the British Government after the assumption of the mandate. The Prime Minister's statement of the 30th November 1961, on the subject of treaty succession has, therefore, no relevance to this issue.

Whatever may be the disadvantages to Tanganyika of the present position, the Tanganyika Government could not contemplate entering into negotiations with the Federal Government or with the British Government for an alteration of the boundaries of Nyasaland. If there are to be negotiations on this question, they must be with the Government of Nyasaland itself and must await the attainment by Nyasaland of full independence.[2]

---

[1] Council Debates, Tanganyika Legislative Council, 36th Session, 12 October 1960, cols. 76–88. The Chief Minister (Mr. Julius K. Nyerere) is reported at cols. 86–7 as saying, '. . . there is now no doubt at all about this boundary. We know that not a drop of the water of Lake Nyasa belong(s) to Tanganyika under the terms of the (1890) agreement, so that in actual fact we would be asking a neighbouring Government, as the Attorney-General said, to change the boundary in favour of Tanganyika.'

[2] Tanganyika Parliamentary Debates, National Assembly, 1st Session, 11 June 1962, col. 264. An unfortunate error occurs on p. 362 of *The Effect of Independence on Treaties* (Stevens, London, 1965) where, owing to the omission of a few words, the Prime Minister is quoted as saying that no part of Lake Nyasa is within the boundaries of Nyasaland.

Nyasaland attained its independence, under the name of Malawi, in July 1964. In April 1964 Tanganyika and Zanzibar formed a union which later in the same year became the United Republic of Tanzania. The drawing of colonial boundaries was an operation in which indigenous inhabitants usually played little or no part.[1] Must boundaries originally established under conditions of enforced tutelage now receive docile acceptance from those who today are able and entitled to determine their own affairs? Can it be argued that pre-independence boundary agreements are *res inter alios acta*, and have no binding effect on neighbouring states unless specifically adopted by them?[2] Experience shows that the vast majority of new African states are in favour of maintaining their inherited boundaries. This attitude arises not from condonation of the manner in which the original colonial partition was undertaken, nor does it imply acceptance of the theory of state succession. Instead, it reflects the practical and common-sense realization that present-day attempts to rearrange African boundaries might encourage territorial fragmentation and prove to be an invitation to disaster. Of particular relevance in this connection is the resolution on boundaries of the Organization of African Unity, passed in July 1964, which was discussed in a previous chapter.[3] It should be noted that both Tanzania and Malawi are, and were at the time when the resolution was passed, member states of the Organization.

Let it be assumed that, despite their inheritance of boundaries created by treaties to which they were not parties, both Tanzania and Malawi, in accordance with the resolution to respect borders existing at the time of their independence, agree that the lake boundary follows the eastern and northern shores of Lake Nyasa, as described in the Anglo-German agreement of 1890. What practical consequences flow from such an assumption? These may involve problems concerning navigation on the lake, fishing rights, the periodic shifting of the shore boundary resulting from changing lake levels, and the ownership of islands.

Owing to the presence of the Murchison cataracts on the River Shire, which are impassable except by portage, Lake Nyasa has no

---

[1] For an argument that local conditions were not always disregarded by the partitioning powers see S. Touval, 'Treaties, Borders, and the Partition of Africa', *Journal of African History*, vol. 7, p. 279.

[2] On this question see above, Ch. II (c).

[3] Organization of African Unity. AHG/Res. 17 (I). For the full text of the resolution see above, p. 22.

uninterrupted water communication with the ocean. Questions of navigation on the lake are therefore likely to be of interest solely to the three bordering states. British vessels continued to dominate Lake Nyasa after the 1890 agreement, Article VIII of which, as has already been stated,[1] granted Germany freedom of navigation on the lake. The first, and only important, German vessel was the *Hermann von Wissmann*, which was placed on Lake Nyasa in 1892 by the German Anti-Slavery Society to aid in suppressing the slave trade.[2] This steamer, which later belonged to the German authorities who used it for commercial purposes, was captured by the Nyasaland administration at the beginning of World War I and subsequently retained by them under the new name *King George*.[3] Since that time no large vessels appear to have been based on the Tanzania shore. Regular lake transport was started in 1931 by Nyasaland Railways which, until 1964, operated steamers that called at Mbamba Bay, Manda, and Mwaya on the Tanzania side of the lake.

No specific provisions relating to fishing are to be found in the 1890 Anglo-German agreement. There cannot be the slightest doubt, however, that the inhabitants of the eastern shore had operated small craft on the lake for fishing and transport from time immemorial. Since they continued to do so after 1890, Britain, who seems never to have disputed the legality of this age-old practice, must be regarded as having acquiesced. Morally, no other construction is possible, for how could Britain, a professed champion of anti-slavery, deny the lake-dwellers this most elementary form of traditional livelihood? Nevertheless, although the unrestricted preservation of traditional fishing rights may have been contemplated in 1890, there is nothing

---

[1] Above, p. 179, n. 4.

[2] Art. I of the Brussels Act, 2 July 1890, to which both Britain and Germany were signatories, declared the establishment of steamboats on inland waters and lakes to be among the most effective means of counteracting the slave trade. See Hertslet, ii. 488. An incident illustrating the amicability of Anglo-German navigational arrangements on Lake Nyasa occurred in 1895 when the Nyasaland administration asked 'the Germans to lend us their fine new steamer' for an expedition against North Nyasa Arabs. The request was granted. Johnston, *The Story of My Life*, p. 299. The 1905 *Military Report on German East Africa*, p. 37, gives a table showing the distribution of German 'small boats' within the colony. None are listed for Lake Nyasa but the report states 'there are also a few Government boats and dhows on the great lakes'. See also S. G. Williams, 'Some Old Steamships of Nyasaland', *The Nyasaland Journal*, vol. 11, No. 1 (1958), pp. 42–56, who gives details of about thirty steam vessels on Lake Nyasa before World War I, of which all except the *Hermann von Wissmann* were British.

[3] Murray, op. cit., p. 405.

to indicate that any attention was paid at that time to the future control of commercial fishing on a more extensive scale. It appears from a discussion in the Tanganyika Legislative Council, in 1960, that the Nyasaland Government claimed the power to regulate the use of motor fishing boats on the lake, and it was partly fear that fishermen living on the Tanzania shore might be restricted in their use of the waters which led to the call for a revised boundary.[1]

User of Lake Nyasa was significantly affected by an agreement made between Britain and Portugal in 1954. In the early 1950s Britain carried out preliminary technical studies relating to the Shire Valley Project, the objects of which include the stabilization of the level of Lake Nyasa and the regulation of outflow to the Shire, the construction of harbours, and the development of hydro-electric power. Portugal offered to contribute one-third of the total cost of both the studies and the subsequent execution of the associated technical projects on the lake, provided Britain would agree to alter the international boundary between Nyasaland and Mozambique. The Portuguese offer was made with the specific condition that the existing boundary on the eastern shore of Lake Nyasa, as defined by the Anglo-Portuguese Treaty of 1891, be moved to the median line of the lake.[2] Britain accepted the Portuguese proposal, and the boundary was changed by an agreement between the two states that came into

---

[1] Council Debates, Tanganyika Legislative Council, 36th Session, 12 October 1960, cols. 76–88. See *Laws of Nyasaland*, Fisheries Ordinance, Cap. 139, and Water Transport Ordinance, Cap. 142.

[2] It is submitted that this is a correct interpretation. Paragraph 2 of the British Note states that Portugal had 'expressed the hope' that Britain 'would be prepared to consider recognizing the frontier of Mozambique and Nyasaland in Lake Nyasa as running along the Median Line of its waters'. Although this language is somewhat equivocal, and could be taken to imply that, in Portugal's view, the boundary already lay along the lake median, the historical evidence suggests that Portugal, in making her request, accepted the lake boundary as running along the eastern shore line, in accordance with the 1891 Anglo-Portuguese Treaty. The British reaction to the Portuguese proposal also supports this interpretation, since, in Paragraph 3 of her Note, Britain agreed to give effect to 'such recognition in an agreement concluded between the two Governments to determine the line of the *new* frontier' and emphasized 'that this undertaking rests on the assumption that the Portuguese Government will, for their part, assume the responsibility' of taking part in the Shire Valley Project. Exchange of Notes Constituting an Agreement Between Her Majesty's Government in the United Kingdom of Great Britain and Northern Ireland and the Portuguese Government Providing for Portuguese Participation in the Shire Valley Project. Lisbon, 21 January 1953. 175 *U.N.T.S.* 13.

effect in 1955.[1] By this agreement the boundary between Nyasaland and Mozambique in Lake Nyasa was drawn 'due west from the point where the frontier of Mozambique and Tanganyika meets the shore of the Lake to the median line of the waters of the same Lake and shall then follow the median line to its point of intersection with the geographical parallel of Beacon 17 . . .'.[2]

From the Tanzanian point of view, the most important part of this agreement is undoubtedly the first sentence of paragraph 3 of Article 1, which reads:

The inhabitants of Nyasaland and the inhabitants of Mozambique shall have the right to use all the waters of Lake Nyasa for fishing and other legitimate purposes, provided that the methods of fishing which may be employed shall be only those which are agreed upon by the Government of Nyasaland and the Government of Mozambique.

It will be noted that this provision applies to 'all the waters' of Lake Nyasa and that Portugal, in addition to Malawi, has the right to operate vessels in the waters adjoining the Tanzania shore, provided only that they are used for fishing and other legitimate purposes.

The Anglo-Portuguese agreement has other interesting features. First, it implies the recognition by Portugal that Britain had the power to transfer to her the sovereignty of a portion of the lake. Second, Britain, though acting on behalf of the Federation of Rhodesia and Nyasaland, did not purport to act on behalf of her trust territory, Tanganyika. Third, the agreement itself has never been declared invalid by the Trusteeship Council of the United Nations as being inconsistent with Britain's duties under the International Trusteeship System, laid down in the Tanganyika Trusteeship Agreement,[3] and in Article 76 of the United Nations Charter. This last point is worth emphasizing since it has been mistakenly argued from time to time that Britain, as a result of her agreement with Portugal, deliberately and improperly shifted the boundary in the northern part of Lake Nyasa from the median line to the eastern shore, thereby depriving Tanzania of her rightful portion of the

---

[1] Agreement Between the Government of the United Kingdom of Great Britain and Northern Ireland (Acting on their Behalf and on Behalf of the Government of the Federation of Rhodesia and Nyasaland) and the Government of Portugal Regarding the Nyasaland–Mozambique Frontier. Signed at Lisbon, on 18 November 1954. 325 *U.N.T.S.* 307.

[2] Ibid., Art. I. See also 450 *U.N.T.S.* 448. Beacon 17 is in approximately 13° 30′ south latitude.

[3] 8 *U.N.T.S.* 91.

lake.[1] As has been shown, however, the boundary line on the Tanzania shore has never been altered since its establishment in 1890.

It was stated earlier that the Anglo-German commission, appointed in 1898 to mark the limits between the British and German spheres in the Nyasa region, made no attempt to demarcate the lake boundary itself. The reason is not far to seek. Water limits, especially those of major drainage features, were at that time popular both with the diplomatists who delimited boundaries and the surveyors who were called upon to trace them on the ground. To diplomatists, the presence of such water features provided valuable geographical material during their negotiations, particularly in areas that were largely unexplored and unmapped. To surveyors, the adoption of water boundaries meant not only that the labour of their field work was reduced but also that the water line itself was more permanent and more easily recognizable than a series of artificial boundary marks.

Article 1 of the Anglo-German Agreement of 1890 describes the lake boundary as following the 'eastern, northern and western shores' of Lake Nyasa. How is the word 'shore' to be interpreted in this connection? In tidal waters, shore is usually said to be the land lying between the lines of high and low water, but how is this to be applied to a non-tidal lake? Does the shore of Lake Nyasa mean the line formed by the edge of the water and, if so, is this line to be determined by the highest or the lowest point ever reached by the water level of the lake, by its position at the time when an actual boundary dispute arises, or by the line of water level as it existed in 1890?

Accurate records of the level of Lake Nyasa were not commenced until 1896 but there is evidence to suggest that, even before that date, the change of water level was a common phenomenon. Since 1896 the lake level has undergone irregular fluctuation over a wide range of heights above mean sea level. For example, the recorded heights for the years 1915 and 1963 show a difference of almost 19 feet.[2] Prior to 1963 the maximum recorded level was in 1937 when rising water forced the abandonment of government offices and a hospital at Mwaya in Tanzania. The former German port of Langenburg,

[1] See, e.g. 'The Troubled Waters of Lake Nyasa', an article in *The Standard*, Dar es Salaam, 3 June 1967.
[2] J. G. Pike and G. T. Rimmington, *Malawi: A Geographical Study*, Oxford University Press, London, 1965, pp. 114–15.

which was forsaken many years before, had also by this time disappeared beneath the surface of the lake.[1]

The periodic rise and fall in the level of the lake means that if the shore is to be regarded as the water's edge the boundary is a continually shifting line. Yet both common sense and doctrine combine to show that no other possibility exists. There is no justification for accepting the shore line as permanently fixed by its position in 1890,[2] or at any other subsequent date. Moreover, unless an arbitrary, immutable line were chosen in a position beyond which the waters of the lake would never retreat, the falling lake level would from time to time uncover a strip of dry land lying between the line and the water's edge. In such an event, access to the lake for fishing and navigation would be possible only by crossing this strip, the ownership of which would continue to vest in the state on the opposite shore.

In municipal law, the solution to problems concerning riparian boundaries is frequently assisted by the technical rules of Roman law, particularly those relating to the acquisition of land *per relictionem* and *per alluvionem*. Dereliction is the process whereby receding water permanently exposes part of its bed, and alluvion denotes the action by which deposits of earth and sedimentary material are washed up to form an addition to the dry land. The appropriate law to be applied in such circumstances by municipal courts, however, is not necessarily relevant to apparently similar questions involving international riparian boundaries. As a modern authority points out, the similarity lies in the underlying natural phenomena, not in the operative rules.[3] Also, the rules of Roman law relating to dereliction and alluvion depend upon a physical process that is both gradual and imperceptible.[4] Imperceptibility in this sense has been held to refer to the rate of progress, not to the visible effect after a lapse of time.[5] If the progress is perceptible the rules are said to be inapplicable.

---

[1] D. F. Clyde, *History of the Medical Services of Tanganyika*, Govt. Press, Dar es Salaam, 1962, p. 16.

[2] Pike and Rimmington, op. cit., p. 114, show a graph giving estimated lake levels prior to 1896.

[3] G. Schwarzenberger, op. cit., vol. i, p. 294.

[4] Inst. II. 1. 20.

[5] *R. v. Yarborough* (1824), 3 B. & C. 91, per Abbott C.J.; affirmed by the House of Lords (1828) 2 Bli. N.S. 147 and *sub nom. Gifford v. Yarborough* (1828), 5 Bing. 163. The rules relating to accretion were held to be inapplicable to lakes in *Trafford v. Thrower* (1929), 45 T.L.R. 502, but the opposite view has been taken in North America; *Kavanaugh v. Rabior* 222 Mich. 68, 192 N.W. 623; *Bruce v. Johnson*, [1954] 1 D.L.R. 571.

Even so, in the case of Lake Nyasa, where the annual change in water level is sometimes as much as 6 feet, perceptibility may be a nice question of degree.

Municipal law, therefore, furnishes uncertain guidance in international riparian boundary questions of this nature, the underlying rules of which appear to rest on the principles of effective occupation and acquiescence. In accordance with these principles it seems to be beyond dispute that the shore of Lake Nyasa must be interpreted as the line formed by the water's edge wherever it happens to be, despite the fact that this line may be subject to periodic positional variation.

A more difficult problem concerns the ownership of islands adjoining the Tanzania shore. The two largest islands in Lake Nyasa are Likoma, which in 1885 became the headquarters of the Universities' Mission to Central Africa, and its near-neighbour, Chisamulo. Both these islands lie in the southern part of the lake and are an undisputed part of Malawi territory.[1] Close to the Tanzania shore are the three islands of Lundu, Papia, and Ngkuyo, the largest of which has an area of only about 70 acres. Lundu lies approximately 1 mile from the shore, while Papia and Ngkuyo are respectively ¼ mile and 1½ miles offshore.[2] The smallness of these three islands suggests that they were probably unknown to the British and German signatories of the 1890 agreement. In any event, as was mentioned earlier, the agreement described spheres of influence, not precise boundaries, and it is not to be supposed that any great attention would have been paid at that time to three insignificant islands, even had they been known to exist.

Since these three islands are not connected to the shore by any natural or artificial causeway and remain permanently surrounded by water, a strict interpretation of the 1890 Anglo-German agreement would mean that they lay outside the German sphere and are not therefore a part of Tanzania. It is submitted, however, that this cannot be the case and that the islands have social and administrative associations with the Tanzania mainland in which the Nyasaland Government had long acquiesced.

At the present time none of the three islands is believed to be populated, though it is understood from local sources that Tanzanian

[1] 325 U.N.T.S. 307, Art. I (2).
[2] Papia was formerly known as New Heligoland, or Mpuulu. Ngkuyo is also known as Nuangwe, or Mbamba, Island.

fishermen sometimes use them as a temporary resting-place, and even cultivate a few crops there. At one time, however, at least two of the islands, Papia and Lundu, were inhabited. A contemporary account says that in 1893 Papia had about 500 inhabitants whose cattle, owing to the scarcity of local vegetation, swam across to the mainland each morning to graze and returned at night.[1] Lundu, on the other hand, appears to have been uninhabited until its establishment as a leper settlement by the German administration. The near-by mainland station of the Universities' Mission to Central Africa was closely associated with medical work among the lepers, and financial aid for this purpose was granted by the Tanganyika Government. In the 1920s the leper population of Lundu was over 100, but partly because the island was difficult to visit in rough weather, and partly because the living conditions there were condemned by the Tanganyika Government as overcrowded and insanitary, the settlement was closed at the end of 1929 and the lepers moved to Mngehe on the mainland.[2]

There is nothing to show that the Nyasaland Government formally asserted ownership of the three islands, either by disputing the right of the German and Tanganyika governments to administer them or by performing acts amounting to effective occupation. The conclusion is that Malawi has always regarded the islands as appurtenant to the Tanzania shore and, through acquiescence, has lost whatever theoretical rights of ownership she may have formerly possessed. An argument that might be raised in support of a claim by Malawi to ownership of the islands is that Nyasaland Railways installed and maintained navigational lights on the adjacent reefs. A recent chart shows that a flashing signal light has been placed at Schloss Rock, south of Liuli, and another at Ngkuyo Reef, north of Ngkuyo Island.[3] Steamers serving the eastern shore of the lake have for many years been operated by Nyasaland Railways, no such facilities being provided by the Tanganyika Government. The mere installation of signal lights, even if performed under the direction of the Nyasaland Government, does not in itself necessarily constitute a sufficient act of sovereignty. Instead, it suggests a routine naviga-

[1] *Central Africa* (U.M.C.A.), vol. 11, 1893, pp. 153–4.
[2] Ibid., vol. 45, 1927, p. 25. A. E. M. Anderson-Morshead, *The History of the Universities' Mission to Central Africa*, 6th edn., U.M.C.A., London, 1955, vol. 2, p. 271.
[3] See chart *Central Africa, Lake Nyasa (Northern Portion), Sheet 13*, Govt. Printer of the Federation of Rhodesia and Nyasaland, 1963.

tional precaution, of too slight a nature to sustain a dubious paper claim to ownership.[1]

The foregoing paragraphs are intended to show what implications might arise should both Tanzania and Malawi agree that their lake boundary follows the eastern and northern shore line. At the present time there is no such agreement. Malawi's attitude is that she owns the entire lake, with the exception of the portion transferred by Britain to Portugal in 1955. Tanzania claims that her lake boundary with Malawi follows the median line.[2]

In any discussion of this disputed lake boundary it should be kept in mind that the issue is symptomatic, and not the cause, of deteriorating political relations between the two states. It is not proposed here to consider at length the reasons for this political estrangement but, put briefly, they can be traced, first, to the asylum granted since 1964 by Tanzania to opponents of the Malawi government and, second, to Tanzania's view that Malawi has an undesirably close association with the Portuguese administration in Mozambique and with the Republic of South Africa.

So far as the boundary itself is concerned, Tanzania's attitude has undergone some alteration. It will be remembered that in 1962, when Tanzania had become an independent state, the Prime Minister stated quite clearly that no part of Lake Nyasa fell within German East Africa and that, in consequence, no part of the lake formed part of Tanganyika.[3] At the same time, he intimated that the problem could

[1] On this point see *The Minquiers and Ecrehos Case*, I.C.J. Rep. 1953, p. 47, at p. 71, where the Court said '[the lighting] and buoying . . . can hardly be considered as sufficient evidence of the intention of that Government to act as sovereign over the islets; nor are those acts of such a character that they can be considered as involving a manifestation of State authority in respect of the islets.' See also *The Twee Gebroeders* (1801) 3 C. Rob. 336, at pp. 348–9: 'Indeed the laying down buoys and beacons is not in its nature to be considered as a necessary indication of territory . . . it may be only, that this is a navigation in which the city of Embden is much interested, and the Dutch comparatively little, and therefore are content to leave the care and expense of it upon their neighbours.'

[2] For a recent statement of Tanzania's attitude concerning the effect of the 1890 Anglo-German agreement on her boundary with Malawi see E. E. Seaton and S. T. M. Maliti, 'Treaties and Succession of States and Governments in Tanzania', a Paper prepared for the African Conference of International Law, Lagos, March 1967. (Typescript), Dag Hammarskjöld Foundation, paras. 32 and 33.

[3] In the following year, on 28 December 1963, Mr. Kawawa, then Vice-President of Tanganyika, said 'the boundary between us is drawn in such a way that the moment a Tanganyikan enters the water of Lake Nyasa he is technically entering another country. If there is a dispute between two fishermen, one from

be taken up with Nyasaland when she attained her independence from Britain. Negotiations with Malawi concerning the lake boundary were commenced but, for the political reasons referred to, they proved abortive and appear to have broken down in 1967. Tanzania's difficulty is that not only has she publicly declared Lake Nyasa to be outside her own territory[1] but that, as a supporter of the O.A.U. boundary resolution passed in 1964, she has undertaken to respect African territorial boundaries as they existed at the time of independence. A possible escape from this dilemma might be for Tanzania to argue that the lake boundary did in fact follow the median line during the German administration and that the Prime Minister's statement of 1962, which was based upon advice received from the British Secretary of State for the Colonies, was in error. This argument has not been pressed in Tanzania with any conviction, though there have been occasional references by politicians to old German maps that show a median-line boundary in the lake. It has already been seen that many of the old maps, even those of a reputedly official nature, are confusing and contradictory, and there is certainly a sufficient variety of them from which a selection could be made to prove almost any point of view to the satisfaction of those who regard a published map as conclusive evidence.[2]

Tanzania's main argument, however, seems to rest not upon documentary evidence concerning the location of the boundary, but on the presumption of international customary law that boundary lakes are divided by the median line. Why, it is asked, were other great African lakes, such as Victoria, Tanganyika, Albert, and Edward, divided, more or less equally, between neighbouring states, while Nyasa alone forms the exception? It is argued that the rules of international customary law say that the waters of boundary lakes shall be shared between the bordering states and that these rules simply reflect fairness and common sense.

the Tanganyika shore and one from the Nyasa shore, then an international incident is created.' *Towards African Unity*, Dar es Salaam, 1963, p. 4. It should be remembered, however, that this statement was made prior to the independence of Nyasaland (Malawi).

[1] In *Tanzania Today*, University Press of Africa, Nairobi, 1968, published for the Ministry of Information and Tourism in Tanzania, it is stated at p. 134: 'In Lake Nyasa, in the area in which Tanzania has a substantial shore-line, all the open waters of the lake fall within the boundaries of Malawi.' The map at the end of this volume, however, shows the boundary of Tanzania as the median line of Lake Nyasa.

[2] For a discussion of map evidence see above, Ch. IV.

International boundaries that follow the shores of lakes are of rare occurrence. A few examples can be found, though their relevance to the Lake Nyasa problem is questionable since, except in one instance, they are of no more than historical interest. Two European lakes that formerly had shore line boundaries are Idro and Garda, both now entirely within the limits of Italy.

In the case of Lake Idro, the boundary between Austria and Italy followed the shore of the lake for about 1,000 metres. Austria, the owner of this part of the shore, had no rights over the water which fronted it. Not only was the boundary between the two states established in such a way that the lake was in Italian territory, but the line itself was declared to be permanently fixed in its position at the date of the boundary agreement, so that even if the lake level subsequently dropped, Austria would have no rights over the exposed bed lying between the boundary line and the water's edge.[1]

Lake Garda formerly lay on the boundary between Austria and Venice, the latter state claiming sovereignty over the lake by ancient tradition. Austria, who occupied part of the shore, disputed this claim but based her argument not on a specific title but on a general submission that boundary lakes should be divided between bordering states in proportion to their frontages. The problem attracted considerable juristic attention in the eighteenth century but the legal question was never settled. Austria refused to acknowledge the Venetian title and her own claim was eventually established as a result of her superior power.[2]

Two African examples have appeared in more recent times. On what is now the Tanzania–Kenya boundary, the line passes through the centre of Lake Jipe, about sixty miles south-east of Mount Kilimanjaro. When the boundary agreement between Britain and Germany was drawn in 1893 the line was described as following the eastern and northern side of Lake Jipe, thereby placing the lake entirely within German East Africa.[3] Following the work of a mixed demarcation commission in 1904–6, a new Anglo-German agreement was prepared which, *inter alia*, shifted the Lake Jipe boundary from the shore line to the centre of the lake.[4]

[1] Adami, op. cit., p. 39.   [2] Ibid., pp. 39–42.

[3] Agreement between Great Britain and Germany respecting Boundaries in East Africa from the mouth of the Umba River to Lake Jipe and Kilimanjaro. Signed at Berlin, 25 July 1893. Hertslet, iii. 911.

[4] Two separate agreements were prepared but neither was ever ratified. The first, signed at Berlin in July 1906, failed to receive ratification owing to a dispute

The second African example of lake-shore boundaries concerns Lakes Chiuta and Chilwa (Shirwa) on the Malawi–Mozambique boundary. By the Anglo-Portuguese treaty of 1891, to which previous reference has been made, the boundary between the British and Portuguese territories was drawn through the southern part of Lake Chiuta to and along its eastern shore, and also along the entire eastern shore of Lake Chilwa. Lake Chilwa, therefore, like Lake Nyasa, was placed entirely within British territory. Both Chiuta and Chilwa are surrounded by level, marshy ground and since their water level varies with the seasons, the exact shore line is difficult to determine. Following the recommendations of a boundary commission, the eastern shore of each lake was replaced as the boundary by a line of boundary pillars following the approximate shore line.[1] Lake Chilwa, which has no outlet, is said to have an area of about 1,000 square miles, but less than half is open water, the remainder being made up of shallow, reed-covered swamp and seasonally inundated grassland. The lake itself has a maximum depth of only about 10 feet and the annual variation in water level sometimes exceeds 7 feet.[2] Although this lake, like Nyasa, is an existing example of a shore-line boundary, its variable size and its artificially fixed eastern limit may mean that, for all practical purposes, it remains an internal, rather than a boundary, lake.[3]

These examples of other lacustrine shore boundaries are interesting but not particularly helpful in dealing with the present problem, and it seems that the Lake Nyasa boundary should be regarded as *sui generis*. It is argued by Tanzania that to deny her a share of the lake is to violate the rules of international customary law. To what extent can these rules assist in finding a solution?

In 1758 Vattel stated the position with respect to lake boundaries: 'If the lake lies between two States it is held to be divided between them by a line through the middle of the lake, so long as there is no

concerning the Mufumbiro section of the boundary. A new draft agreement was prepared in 1914 but it was not signed owing to the outbreak of World War I. The boundary description in this latter draft agreement was subsequently accepted by the Kenya and Tanganyika governments, though not by any formal instrument.

[1] Agreement Between the United Kingdom and Portugal Respecting Boundaries in South-East Africa . . . 6 May 1920. 4 *L.N.T.S.* 93, Annexes 1, 3 and 4.

[2] Pike and Rimmington, op. cit., pp. 117–18.

[3] A new boundary dividing Lake Chiuta was established by the Anglo-Portuguese agreement of 1954, Article 4 of which provides that the fishing and other rights created by Art. I of the agreement with respect to Lake Nyasa shall also apply to Lake Chiuta.

title or fixed and well-known custom to lead to another conclusion.'¹ The proviso to the rule is important since Vattel clearly recognized instances where boundary lakes are not divided. This is shown by his statement regarding alluvion: 'When a lake which forms a boundary of a State belongs entirely to that State, any increase in the extent of the lake goes to the owner of the whole. . . .'² Thus, the cases concerning Lakes Idro and Garda belonged to a class recognized by Vattel as an exception to the general rule. A more modern authority, Hall, makes the following statement:

> In lakes, there being no necessary track of navigation, the line of demarcation is drawn in the middle. When a state occupies the lands upon one side of a river or lake before those on the opposite bank have been appropriated by another power, it can establish property by occupation in the whole of the bordering waters, as its right to occupy is not limited by the rights of any other state; and as it must be supposed to wish to have all the advantages to be derived from sole possession, it is a presumption of law that occupation has taken place.
>
> If, on the other hand, opposite shores have been occupied at the same time, or if priority of occupation can be proved by neither of the riparian states, there is a presumption in favour of equal rights, and a state claiming to hold the entirety of a stream or lake must give evidence of its title, either by producing treaties, or by showing that it has exercised continuous ownership over the waters claimed. Upon whatever grounds property in the entirety of a stream or lake is established, it would seem in all cases to carry with it a right to the opposite bank as accessory to the use of the stream, and perhaps it even gives a right to a sufficient margin for defensive or revenue purposes, when the title is derived from occupation, or from a treaty of which the object is to mark out a political frontier.³

The above passage raises a number of interesting and arguable points, and it is perhaps unfortunate that the author did not support his views by reference to specific cases.

Other writers on international law accept the view that, in the absence of treaties or other evidence, boundary lakes are divided between the bordering states.⁴ In the case of large lakes, having a width of more than six miles, Adami advocates a rule that each of the bordering states extend its sovereignty to a distance of three miles from the shore and hold the central remainder in common with the

---

¹ E. de Vattel, *The Law of Nations*, Translation of the Edition of 1758 by C. G. Fenwick, Oceana, New York, 1964. Book I, para. 274.   ² Ibid., para. 275.
³ Hall, op. cit., para. 38.
⁴ See, e.g. Oppenheim, op. cit., vol. i, para. 199 (2); Fenwick, *International Law*, 2nd edn., p. 277.

other states. An agreement of this nature was made between the European states bordering Lake Constance.[1]

Of the authorities referred to above, only Adami explores specific instances where a departure was made from the general rule that the boundary of a lake situated between two states follows the median line. Even those few more recent writers who have made a special study of international boundaries have tended to overlook the problem presented by Lake Nyasa. Boggs, it is true, in stating that instances of international boundaries along lake shores are not numerous, cites Nyasa as one of his three examples, but he does not pursue the subject.[2] Jones says that a boundary might follow the shore of a lake but that it 'is very likely to be troublesome' because it leaves one state with no control over its water frontage and no right to build wharves or to fill ground in the lake. He develops the topic no further and, apart from Lake Chilwa, makes no reference to particular lake-shore boundaries.[3]

International customary law, as expressed in juristic writing, lends little support to Tanzania's claim. This is far from saying that her claim has no substance. The present shore-line boundary is plainly inequitable, but it is also clear that legal argument alone cannot shift the boundary to the centre of the lake.

Nor should the Tanzania Prime Minister's statement of 1962 and the boundary resolution of 1964 necessarily be regarded as an estoppel. The former arose as the result of inquiry into a problem concerning which there had for many years been honest doubt, and it was expected in 1962 that an amicable adjustment with Malawi could be reached after her independence. The O.A.U. resolution represented, in effect, a modification of a former point of view. Many African political parties, prior to independence, envisaged an eventual rearrangement of colonial boundaries to accord more closely with existing ethnic and cultural divisions.[4] After independence, most African leaders feared that in attempting the adjustment of inherited boundaries, the cure might prove worse than the disease,[5] and the resolution expresses this apprehension. But there is no inherent incon-

---

[1] Adami, op. cit., p. 38.
[2] S. W. Boggs, op. cit., p. 177.
[3] S. B. Jones, op. cit., pp. 134, 141.
[4] See boundary resolution of the All-African Peoples Conference, Accra, 1958, the text of which is given by C. Legum, *Pan Africanism*, pp. 247–50.
[5] *Proceedings of the Summit Conference of Independent African States*, vol. i, Section 2, Addis Ababa, May 1963. (Above, Ch. II (*d*).)

sistency between Tanzania's support for the O.A.U. resolution and her own call for a boundary alteration in Lake Nyasa. The issue is not territorial fragmentation in its usual sense, with an associated problem of minority groups; it is simply a matter of sharing a large body of boundary water.

Adequate machinery exists within the framework of the O.A.U. for the settlement of this boundary dispute.[1] It is in the interests of both Tanzania and Malawi, and of Africa as a whole, that the problem should be resolved before the present poor relations between the two neighbouring states develop into something beyond mere acrimony. A possible solution might be for Tanzania to purchase a share of the lake, as Portugal purchased her share in 1954, by paying to Malawi a sum representing, say, a proportionate part of the cost of the Shire Valley Project. In the light of present political realities, this suggestion might seem to be both naïve and unacceptable to the parties concerned, but it deserves consideration.

A brief mention must also be made of the remainder of the boundary between Tanzania and Malawi, that is to say, the portion not formed by Lake Nyasa. In accordance with the Anglo-German agreement of 1901, this part of the boundary

begins at the mouth of the Songwe River at Lake Nyasa and follows this river upwards to its junction with the Katendo Stream in the Shitete district; it then follows the Katendo upwards to its intersection with longitude 33, east of Greenwich, ascertained by the Commission, which is marked on both sides of the Katendo by a boundary pillar (1); it then runs in a straight line at an azimuth of 230° (from the true north) to the top of Nakungulu (Nkungulu) Hill (2), which is on the waterparting of the geographical Congo Basin. . . .[2]

It will be seen that this section of the boundary is formed mainly by the thalweg[3] of the Songwe and Katendo rivers, and that the only straight line portion is the distance of about three and a half miles between pillars Nos. 1 and 2. So far as is known, no redemarcation of this straight line portion has ever been carried out, but pillar No. 2, which marks the Tanzania–Malawi–Zambia tripoint, was found in 1935 and replaced by a new boundary beacon.[4] It appears, therefore,

[1] Above, pp. 26–7.
[2] Hertslet, iii. 925. Section 1.
[3] By Section 2 of the 1901 agreement, the thalweg of a river or stream forms the boundary line.
[4] For details of the demarcation which led to the replacement of this pillar see below, pp. 224–5.

that this boundary sector could, if necessary, be retraced on the ground without difficulty, for even if pillar No. 1 is now missing, its position can be fixed in accordance with the 1901 agreement which places it at the intersection of the Katendo thalweg with the meridian of 33° east longitude.

CHAPTER XV

Tanzania–Mozambique

A CURSORY glance at the map of Africa shows the boundary dividing Tanzania and Mozambique to be a line of comparative simplicity, since its entire length, except for the westerly thirty miles or so, is formed by the Ruvuma River.[1] Closer examination of the historical and legal origins of this boundary, however, reveals the apparent simplicity to be a deception.

In 1886 a joint commission was established by Britain, France, and Germany to delimit the dominions of the Sultan of Zanzibar, Seyyid Barghash. The southern limit of the Sultan's coastal territories was found by the commission to follow the course of the Minengani River from its mouth for a distance of five sea miles, from which point it continued westward along the parallel of latitude as far as the right bank of the Ruvuma.[2] That the findings of the commission were based on the principle of effective occupation, is indicated by Lord Salisbury's statement in 1887, resisting the subsequent territorial claims made by Portugal, a country which, despite its obvious interest, had been denied representation on the commission: 'Great Britain considers that it has now been admitted in principle by all the parties to the Act of Berlin that a claim of sovereignty in Africa can only be maintained by real occupation of the territory claimed, and that this doctrine has been practically applied in the recent Zanzibar delimitations.[3] Despite the commission's report, however, Germany and Portugal concluded an agreement on 30 December 1886 which provided: 'Art. II. The Boundary line which shall separate the Portuguese from the German Possessions in South-East Africa follows the course of the River Rovuma from its mouth to the point where the

---

[1] In Tanzania, Ruvuma is now the usual spelling but the older form, Rovuma, was used until 1951 when a change was made in the Tanganyika Annual Report.

[2] Procès-Verbal, containing the unanimous opinions of the Delegates of Great Britain, France, and Germany, with reference to the Maritime, Littoral and Continental Possessions of the Sultan of Zanzibar. Zanzibar, 9 June 1886. Hertslet, iii. 874.

[3] *Memorandum by Sir E. Hertslet* . . ., F.O.C.P. 6294, p. 55. F.O. 403/192.

River M'Sinje joins the Rovuma and runs to the westward on the parallel of latitude to the shores of Lake Nyassa.'[1]

The effect of this agreement was that the Germans did not lay claim to the triangular piece of territory between the Ruvuma and

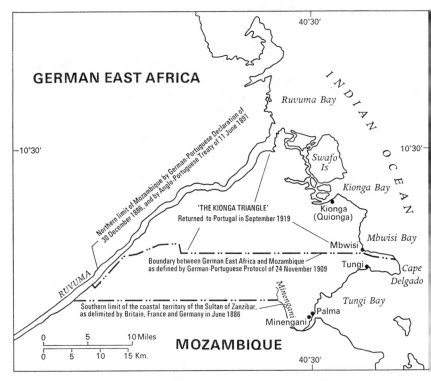

FIG. 8. South-Eastern Part of German East Africa

the Minengani, even though this area lay within the Sultan's dominions as established by the delimitation commission, of which Germany herself was a member.[2] Salisbury's demand for an explanation from Germany produced the following reply:

[1] Declaration between Germany and Portugal respecting the Limits of their respective Possessions and Spheres of Influence in South-West and South-East Africa. Lisbon, 30 December 1886. Hertslet, ii. 703.

[2] On 28 April 1888 the Sultan of Zanzibar granted a concession to the German East African Association over all his mainland territories lying south of the Umba River, but the exact southern limit was not specified in the agreement. Hertslet, ii. 695. Germany received permanent cession of the territories from the Sultan in 1890.

... that the Rovuma constituted the line of separation between the respective spheres of interest of Germany and Portugal; that this in no way prejudiced the recognition of the Sultan's territories south of the Rovuma, as defined in the Anglo-German treaty; that for these reasons the German Government did not propose to intervene in any combinations entered into by the Portuguese Govt., with the Sultan or others, not affecting the sphere of interest of Germany.[1]

In the light of this reply, Salisbury stated on 16 February 1887 that the Ruvuma separated the German and Portuguese spheres of influence, but that the rights of the Sultan were 'in no shape affected'.[2]

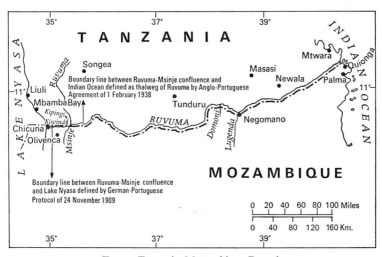

FIG. 9. Tanzania-Mozambique Boundary

Since Germany had no apparent interest south of the Ruvuma, Portugal who, despite the findings of the delimitation commission, claimed territory to the north of the Minengani, now felt free to press her claim against the Sultan. Following diplomatic exchanges in January 1887 Portugal broke off relations with Zanzibar and despatched gunboats to Tungi Bay. In the following month the villages of Tungi and Minengani were bombarded and occupied by the Portuguese, with considerable destruction of property.[3]

[1] Africa No. 53, 10 August 1894. F.O. 179/311. The Anglo-German Treaty referred to is the agreement of October–November 1886 in which the two powers recognized the Minengani River as the southern limit of the Sultan's mainland territories. Hertslet, iii. 882.

[2] Africa No. 53, 10 August 1894. F.O. 179/311.

[3] R. N. Lyne, *Zanzibar in Contemporary Times*, Hurst & Blackett, London, 1905, pp. 137–41.

Ignoring diplomatic protests, Portugal remained in occupation of the disputed area until 1894 when Germany, taking a leaf from the Portuguese book, sent a squadron of five ships to Kionga Bay where they seized possession.[1] It appears that one motive for the German attack was that Kionga offered better harbour facilities than the main mouth of the Ruvuma, and that it was also the only really navigable entrance to the river.[2] The German action was bitterly criticized by Portugal and she pointed out that it had been Germany herself who first proposed the Ruvuma as their common boundary.[3] Moreover, Britain, despite her disapproval of the Portuguese attack on Tungi Bay in 1887, had accepted the Ruvuma as the northern limit of Portuguese territory by the Treaty of Lisbon, 11 June 1891.[4]

The German–Portuguese conflict was finally resolved by an agreement signed in September 1894 which drew the boundary line from Cape Delgado on the coast, westward to the Ruvuma, thus leaving Kionga as German territory but allowing Portugal to retain Tungi Bay.[5] Although Portugal was in effect coerced into making this agreement she had little real complaint, since in 1885 she herself had proposed to the Sultan that Cape Delgado, rather than the Ruvuma, should be accepted as her northern territorial limit.[6] The new boundary line was demarcated by a mixed commission in 1908 and the protocol was ratified on 24 November 1909.[7] Germany's net gain was a piece of territory, containing an area of about 215 square miles, which was subsequently known as the Kionga Triangle and, until the end of World War I, formed part of German East Africa.

Competing claims to ownership of the Kionga Triangle did not affect the remaining portion of the boundary. As established by the

[1] Sir H. MacDonell to the Earl of Kimberley, Africa No. 48, 21 July 1894. F.O. 179/311.
[2] Editor's note to H. B. Thomas, 'The Kionga Triangle', *Tanganyika Notes and Records*, No. 31, 1951, pp. 49–50.
[3] *The Question of Kionga*, a memorandum by L. Thornton, Africa No. 53, 10 August 1894. F.O. 179/311. A detailed and useful account of the events leading to the Kionga dispute.
[4] Treaty between Her Britannic Majesty and His Majesty the King of Portugal, defining their respective Spheres of Influence in Africa. Lisbon, 11 June 1891. Hertslet, iii. 1016.
[5] *Deutsches Kolonialblatt*, vol. 5, 1894, p. 486.
[6] R. Coupland, *The Exploitation of East Africa 1856–1890*, Faber & Faber, London, 1939, pp. 446–7.
[7] *Deutsches Kolonialblatt*, vol. 21, 1910, p. 127. See also ibid., vol. 20, 1909, pp. 56–8, for an account by the German Commissioner, G. Schlobach, containing a map showing the demarcated boundary.

German–Portuguese agreement of 1886,[1] this followed the course of the Ruvuma up to its confluence with the Msinje, and continued westward along the parallel of latitude of the confluence as far as the eastern shore of Lake Nyasa. An early proposal was that the boundary should be the course of the Ruvuma to its source and thence along the parallel of latitude of the source to the lake. The Ruvuma flows south from its source for several miles before turning abruptly east on its long descent to the sea, and had the proposal been adopted there would have been considerable loss of territory to Germany, as well as a reduction in her lake frontage. Owing to uncertainty as to the exact location of the source of the river[2] it was suggested that the parallel should be drawn instead from the confluence of the Ruvuma and the Luchulingo. Portugal then proposed the Msinje, as being higher up the river and well defined.[3] Since the two confluences lie in approximately the same latitude, no appreciable difference in territorial acquisition resulted, and the Msinje was finally selected. The boundary was also described in the Anglo-Portuguese Treaty of Lisbon, 1891.[4]

A mixed commission appointed by Germany and Portugal to demarcate the boundary between the Ruvuma–Msinje confluence and Lake Nyasa completed its work in 1907. Having established the astronomical latitude of the confluence, the two commissioners decided that the boundary should make occasional departures from the parallel in order that it might have the advantage of following natural topographic features. For example, the boundary, on leaving the Ruvuma, proceeds not along the parallel but on the course of the Msinje as far as its tributary, the Kipingi, which it then follows for a few miles. Further to the west, the boundary runs along the road leading to Mtengula for about a mile, and at other points the line has been deflected, either because of difficult terrain or in order to ensure the intervisibility of adjacent boundary marks. Twenty-six stone pillars were erected to define the boundary, only twelve of which lie exactly on the parallel of the confluence. The four boundary protocols were ratified on 24 November 1909.[5] Protocol No. 4 contains a list of geographical co-ordinates of each of the pillars, and

[1] Above, p. 208, n. 1.
[2] The difficulty of establishing a river source is discussed above, pp. 87–9.
[3] Africa No. 53, 10 August 1894. F.O. 179/311.
[4] Above, p. 210, n. 4.
[5] *Deutsches Kolonialblatt*, vol. 21, 1910, pp. 119–26.

reference should also be made to the map showing the results of the demarcation.[1]

Both the German–Portuguese agreement of 1886[2] and the Anglo-Portuguese treaty of 1891[3] refer to the 'course of the River Rovuma', without further qualification, and doubts arose as to which part of the river was intended. Writing in 1909, Meyer says that it was uncertain whether the thalweg or the south bank of the Ruvuma formed the actual boundary.[4] Further problems were caused by the question of title to islands in the river, and a series of border incidents occurred between 1895 and 1912.[5] By an agreement made in 1913 an apportionment was drawn in such a way that Germany acquired the islands in the upper Ruvuma, above its confluence with the Domoni, and Portugal received the islands below the confluence. So far as the Ruvuma itself was concerned, the thalweg was declared to be the boundary. The agreement also contained provisions granting the inhabitants of each bank fishing and certain other rights across the full width of the river.[6]

At the Paris Peace Conference of 1919 Portugal claimed a share of the German colonies, on the grounds that she had participated in the defeat of Germany. Her claims were rejected because it was felt that she already occupied more African territory than her resources could develop.[7] It was agreed, however, that her former claim to the Kionga Triangle should now be admitted and, following a recommendation by the Special Commission on Mandates, the Supreme Council of the Principal Allied and Associated Powers, by its decision of 25 September 1919, recognized Portugal as the 'original and legitimate proprietor of this part of the former German Colony of East Africa, situated south of the Rovuma and known as the Kionga Triangle'.[8]

It is no doubt idle to seek a legal basis for the originality and legitimacy of the Portuguese proprietorship. What, for example, had become of Lord Salisbury's statement in 1887 concerning effective occupation? The plain fact is that the Portuguese demanded terri-

---

[1] *Mitt.* 23 (Map 2), The same volume also contains technical accounts by G. Schlobach, at p. 49, and Prof. L. Ambronn, at p. 54.

[2] Above, p. 208, n. 1.   [3] Above, p. 210, n. 4.

[4] Meyer, op. cit., vol. i, p. 21.

[5] Naval Intelligence, *A Manual of Portuguese East Africa*, H.M.S.O., 1920, p. 526.

[6] *Amtlicher Anzeiger für Deutsch-Ostafrika*, vol. 14, 28 May 1913.

[7] Temperley, op. cit., vol. ii, para. 27.

[8] E. L. Woodward and Rohan Butler (eds.), *Documents on British Foreign Policy 1919–1939*, H.M.S.O., 1947. First Series, vol. i, p. 776.

torial reward and the Kionga Triangle was the most expendable area. The significance of this transaction is that a portion of German East Africa, accepted as such by Portugal and the other interested powers for over twenty years, was severed from the German colony prior to the creation of the British and Belgian mandates.[1] In other words, Portugal received her share in full sovereignty. The shifting of the Portuguese boundary northward to the Ruvuma has been applauded as a 'realistic concession to common sense',[2] but this view seems to be based on the unjustified assumption that a river is always a better international boundary than a mathematical line. But common sense is not necessarily the motivating factor behind political decisions of this kind: Britain had been prepared to offer the Portuguese part of German East Africa extending north from the Ruvuma to the River Mbwemkuru, in an effort to persuade Portugal to transfer to Belgium the Angolan territory she sought at the mouth of the Congo, as an inducement to Belgium to forgo her claim to Ruanda-Urundi which Britain herself coveted.[3]

Does the ultimate disposition of this tiny but contentious piece of territory really matter at the present time? Tanzania might well argue that the Ruvuma, far from being a 'natural' boundary, artificially separates tribal groups, such as the Makonde, living on opposite banks. In April 1967 two people were killed by exploding mines in the Tanzanian village of Kilambo, close to the border. The theory was expressed that the mines may have been laid by Tanzanian members of the Makonde tribe, acting as unwilling collaborators with the Portuguese who had threatened the safety of their relatives on the Mozambique side of the river.[4] This tragic incident followed a similar explosion in November 1966 when four people were reported to have lost their lives.

Following the excision of the Kionga Triangle and its transfer to Portugal, the remainder of German East Africa was divided into the two territories of Tanganyika and Ruanda-Urundi, administered respectively by Britain and Belgium. Tanganyika is described in the Tanganyika Order in Council of 1920[5] as being bounded '. . . on the south by the frontiers of . . . Portuguese East Africa', but no specific boundary details are given. It is important to note that, by the terms

[1] The mandates for East Africa were created in 1922.
[2] H. B. Thomas, 23 *U.J.* 73 (1959).
[3] W. R. Louis, *Ruanda-Urundi, 1884–1919*, pp. 233 ff.
[4] *The Standard*, Dar es Salaam, 14 April 1967.
[5] S.R. & O. 1920/1583.

of Protocol No. 4 of the German-Portuguese agreement of 1909,[1] the demarcated line indicated by the pillars and the topographic features forms the true western portion of the boundary. When the Council of the League of Nations created the British and Belgian mandates for East Africa in 1922, the Preamble included the following words: 'Whereas, in accordance with the treaty of June 11th, 1891, between Her Britannic Majesty and His Majesty the King of Portugal, the River Rovuma is recognized as forming the northern boundary of the Portuguese possessions in East Africa from its mouth up to the confluence of the River Msinje.'[2]

The object of including these words may have been to confirm the decision at the Peace Conference that Portugal was the true owner of the Kionga Triangle and thus to nullify the effect of the German-Portuguese agreement of 1894.[3] Although the treaty of 1891 refers specifically to the parallel of latitude of the Ruvuma–Msinje confluence, it can scarcely have been intended that the German-Portuguese demarcation of 1909, undertaken amicably in an area not the subject of dispute, should be ignored in 1922 and replaced by a theoretical parallel of latitude. The explanation seems to be that little, if any, thought was given to the exact position of boundaries when the mandates were created. This view is borne out by the omission from the mandate agreements of any detailed boundary description for either Tanganyika or Ruanda-Urundi, except with respect to the line which separated the two territories from each other. It is submitted that the line west of the Ruvuma–Msinje confluence which was demarcated jointly by Germany and Portugal and described in their 1909 protocol should still be regarded as the correct definition of this part of the boundary. Examination of records in Tanzania fails to disclose any resurvey of this section since the German occupation, which appears to indicate that the matter is neither contentious nor of pressing concern.

Owing to changes in the position of the river bed, disputes arose in the 1930s concerning sovereignty over islands in the Ruvuma and over certain portions of the bank.[4] In 1938 a boundary agreement was concluded between Britain and Portugal but, despite its title, this does not deal with the entire boundary since it omits the western

---

[1] Above, p. 211, n. 5.
[2] British Mandate for East Africa. Cmd. 1794.　　　[3] Above, p. 210, n. 5.
[4] *Minutes of Permanent Mandates Commission*, Geneva. 31st Session, 3rd Meeting, 1 June 1937, p. 33.

portion between the Ruvuma–Msinje confluence and Lake Nyasa.[1] Failure to confirm the acceptance of the demarcated line of 1909, and thus remove any lingering doubts as to its validity, was therefore a missed opportunity. The 1938 agreement itself is, in substance, an amplification of that concluded between Germany and Portugal in 1913.[2] All the islands situated between the mouth of the Ruvuma and its confluence with the Domoni belong to Portugal, and all the islands above the confluence form part of Tanganyika.[3] The thalweg is declared to be the boundary, but in those cases where the channel between an island and the bank belonging to the other territory is not the thalweg the boundary shall follow this subsidiary channel until it again joins the thalweg. It is provided that the thalweg shall remain the boundary, even when its position is changed by natural alteration of the bed.[4] Freedom of navigation 'in accordance with the treaties and conventions in force' is declared, and the inhabitants of both banks are granted the rights to fish, draw water, and remove saliferous sand over the whole breadth of the river.[5] The agreement came into force on 1 February 1938. A possible difficulty of interpretation lies in deciding what constitutes an island for the purpose of sovereignty. The agreement attempts to overcome this problem by stating 'there shall be considered as islands only those which emerge when the river is in full flood and which contain land vegetation and rock or firm soil and are not shifting sandbanks'.[6]

For the sake of convenience a translation of the relevant part of the German-Portuguese Protocol No. 4, signed on 12 October 1907 and ratified on 24 November 1909, is given hereunder:

In accordance with the decision of Protocol No. 3, the two commissions have set 26 boundary pillars, from the Lake to the confluence of the Msinje and the Rovuma. Boundary Pillar No. 1 was set close to the shore of Lake Nyasa, on the left bank of the Kiwindi (or Tchuindi) stream, and is made of rocks. The upper part is cemented and bears the markings, on the Portuguese side, the letters F.L.G.I.; and on the German side, the letters D.P.G.I. The course of the Kiwindi was taken as a natural boundary up to the point where it leaves the mountains bordering the Lake, at which point a large

---

[1] Exchange of Notes between His Majesty's Government in the United Kingdom and the Portuguese Government constituting an Agreement regarding sovereignty over islands in the River Rovuma and the boundary between Tanganyika Territory and Mozambique. Lisbon, 11 May 1936, and 28 December 1937. 185 *L.N.T.S.* 205.   [2] Above, p. 212, n. 6.
[3] 185 *L.N.T.S.* 205, Art. I (1).   [4] Ibid., Art. I (2).
[5] Ibid., Art. I (4), (5), (6).   [6] Ibid., Art. I (1

live rock forms Boundary Pillar No. 2. This rock bears, on its north and south sides, a cement plaque with the letters D.P.G. II and F.L.G. II, respectively. From this point the boundary goes to Boundary Pillar No. 3, also made of rocks, on the highest point of a prominent ridge of Mount Nahiko. Boundary Pillar No. 4 is on another ridge of Mount Nahiko and lies on the parallel passing through the point of intersection of the confluence of the Rovuma and the Msinje. Boundary Pillars Nos. 5 to 13 inclusive are all on the said parallel. Boundary Pillars Nos. 9 and 10 are on the northern slope of a high bare mountain called Shipirisse by the Portuguese and which is the highest point of the boundary line. Boundary Pillar No. 13 is on the top of Mount Tchuhuro. Leaving this Boundary Pillar the boundary deflects slightly to the north, as far as Boundary Pillar No. 19, making an angle of 1° 43′ 49·9″ with the parallel. Boundary Pillars Nos. 14 to 18 are on the intervening ridges and lie on the line joining Boundary Pillars 13 and 19. Leaving Boundary Pillar No. 19, along a spur of Mount Kilahi or Kipingi (Chilai), the boundary descends to the plain, passing through Boundary Pillar No. 20, as far as Boundary Pillar No. 21, which is also on the parallel of the point of intersection, and very close to the road leading from Mtengula to Rovuma. Leaving this point, the boundary again deflects to the north, following the road, on which Boundary Pillars Nos. 22 and 23 have been placed. From Boundary Pillar No. 23 the boundary is parallel to the parallel of the point of intersection, at a distance of 248 metres from it, and goes as far as the Kipingi (Shipingue), a tributary of the Msinje, where Boundary Pillar No. 24 has been placed. The boundary then follows the course of the Kipingi as far as its confluence with the Msinje, where Boundary Pillar No. 25 has been placed between the courses of the two streams. From this point the boundary follows the course of the Msinje until its confluence with the Rovuma. Boundary Pillar No. 26 is the last boundary pillar. It is situated at the end of a tongue of land close to the left bank of the Msinje and a few metres from the right bank of the Rovuma. It is made of cement and bears the marks: D.P.G. XXVI and F.L.G. XXVI. The departures between the boundary line and the parallel of the point of intersection described above are due to the efforts that have been made to establish so far as possible natural boundaries in territory covered with dense forest, and where the placing of easily visible marks involved necessary compensations. The line between Boundary Pillars Nos. 21 and 24 adjusts the exchanges which have an area of 4,386,815 square metres. In order that the boundary can be easily recognized the line between the pillars has been cleared.

It was decided to include in the Protocol lists showing the latitude, longitude and altitude of each boundary pillar and common triangulation points, showing the mean values of the data.

In addition, each commission attaches to its Protocol a topographic map of the boundary region, giving the location of the boundary pillars and a profile of the terrain. These maps were made by each commission, independently of each other, and a comparison shows that there are only minor differences in topographic detail.

The two commissions having been authorized by their governments to fix a final boundary, the boundary pillars established form the final boundary.[1]

[1] The above translation is taken from the German and French texts given in the *Deutsches Kolonialblatt*, vol. 21 (1910), pp. 124–6. Co-ordinates of the boundary pillars, and their altitudes, are given on p. 126. Reference should also be made to the map mentioned in the protocol, the German copy of which is reproduced in *Mitteilungen aus den deutschen Schutzgebieten*, vol. 23 (1910), as *Karte 2*.

CHAPTER XVI

Tanzania–Zambia

THE international boundary between Tanzania and Zambia has a length of about 210 miles, which includes approximately 40 miles in Lake Tanganyika. Except for this lacustrine portion, the boundary is well marked by pillars and natural features.

The boundary in Lake Tanganyika requires separate treatment and will be considered later. The remaining part of the boundary finds its legal origin in the Anglo-German Agreement of 1890[1] which defined the respective spheres of influence of Britain and Germany in East Africa. By paragraph 2 of Article 1 of this Agreement, the line delimiting the southern portion of the German sphere commences at the northern bank of the mouth of the River Songwe on the western shore of Lake Nyasa. The line then

. . . ascends that river to the point of its intersection by the 33rd degree of east longitude; thence it follows the river to the point where it approaches most nearly the boundary of the geographical Congo Basin defined in the 1st Article of the Act of Berlin as marked in the map attached to the 9th Protocol of the Conference.

From that point it strikes direct to the above-named boundary; and follows it to the point of its intersection by the 32nd degree of east longitude; from which point it strikes direct to the point of confluence of the northern and southern branches of the River Kilambo, and thence follows that river till it enters Lake Tanganyika.

Provision was made in the 1890 Anglo-German Agreement for rectifying, in accordance with local requirements, the boundaries of the two spheres of influence,[2] and in 1898 a mixed commission, led by military surveyors, was appointed to demarcate the line between British and German territory from Lake Nyasa to Lake Tanganyika. The decisions of the commission were embodied in a Protocol dated

---

[1] Agreement between the British and German governments, respecting Africa and Heligoland. Berlin, 1 July 1890. Hertslet, iii. 899.
[2] Ibid., Art. VI.

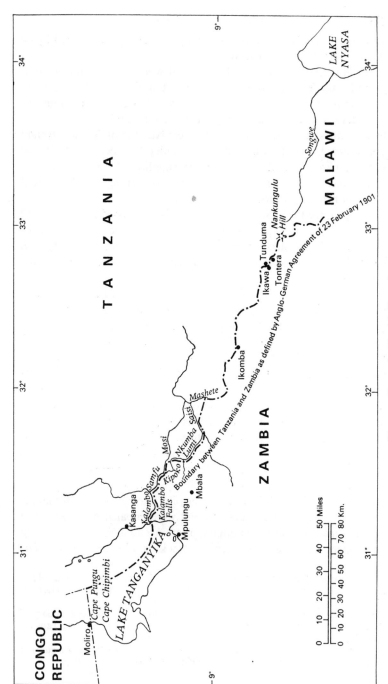

FIG. 10. Tanzania–Zambia Boundary

11 November 1898,[1] and the boundary was finally established by an Anglo-German Agreement of 1901.[2]

An illuminating account of the actual work of the commission is given by the British Commissioner, Captain Close, in his report to the Foreign Office.[3] A detailed list of 156 villages situated along the boundary is arranged according to tribal groups and shows in tabular form Names of Village, Tribe and Chief; Number of Houses; Height above Sea Level; Latitude and Longitude; Number of Cattle and other stock; Availability of water and supplies; Description of road communications. There are also remarks concerning tribal raids and German brutality to local villagers.

The country through which the commission passed had been until then incompletely explored by Europeans and the demarcation of the line itself was accompanied by the surveying and mapping of a strip of territory, 50 miles wide, stretching the entire length of the boundary.

Except for minor alterations made in two places, the Commission established the boundary along the watershed of the Congo Basin, in conformity with the 1890 Agreement. At another point the watershed crossed the Stevenson Road, a track that had been built by the British in 1881, but here the German Commissioner refused to alter the boundary line. The view of Captain Close was that the Germans thereby hoped to secure direct access to the road by keeping part of it within their sphere and, in accordance with his recommendations, about 8 miles of Stevenson Road was shifted southwards, well clear of the watershed, into British territory.

Close's report displays disenchantment with the country, working conditions, and his German colleagues. He complains that nearly every member of the expedition was incapacitated by attacks of fever. Other physical hazards included game pits, into which a British lance-corporal and a German mule fell and were impaled on stakes. The German members of the commission are accused by Close of being unco-operative, and a particular attack is directed against Dr.

[1] Protocol containing the Decisions of the Commissioners appointed to delimit the Nyasa–Tanganyika Boundary. Signed at Ikawa, 11 November 1898. Hertslet, iii. 916.

[2] Agreement between Great Britain and Germany relative to the Boundary of the British and German Spheres of Interest between Lakes Nyasa and Tanganyika. Signed at Berlin, 23 February 1901. Hertslet, iii. 925.

[3] *Report by Captain Close, R.E. on the Delimitation of the Nyasa-Tanganyika Boundary in 1898.* Foreign Office, Confidential No. 7115, March 1899.

Kohlschütter who is described as 'a young astronomer anxious to win a reputation and to get a post in the Geodetic Institute. It was quite immaterial to him whether the commission delimited the frontier or not, but he was very desirous of executing a triangulation which should attract notice'.[1] Further criticism of the Germans include the scale used in their maps, the brutality of their officials in the area, and the theft of supplies by German police. The boundary zone itself is described in the report as being 'as worthless a bit of country as any in Africa', and the indigenous people are referred to in scathing and insulting terms.

Despite the physical difficulties facing the mixed commission and the apparent lack of harmony between the British and the German members, the field work was completed in the short time of four months. This was a remarkable achievement, especially when it is remembered that to demarcate the boundary in accordance with the provisions of the 1890 Anglo-German Agreement involved, *inter alia*, the establishment on the ground of two meridians of longitude, a technical operation requiring, in those pre-radio days, the comparison of a series of time signals exchanged between a telegraph line near Nkata Bay on Lake Nyasa, and the Cape Town observatory, 1,900 miles away.[2]

The line demarcated by the mixed commission forms part of the Tanzania–Malawi, as well as the Tanzania–Zambia, boundary. The Tanzania–Malawi–Zambia tripoint is Boundary Pillar No. 2 at Nakungulu (Nkungulu) Hill, referred to in the Anglo-German Agreement of 1901[3] as being on the waterparting of the geographical Congo Basin. The Tanzania–Zambia portion of the boundary is then described in the Agreement as follows:

Sec. 1. . . . From here the boundary goes along the waterparting past a boundary pillar (3) about 6·5 kilom. from Nakungulu to a boundary pillar

[1] Close, op. cit., p. 33. If this was indeed Dr. Kohlschütter's objective he appears to have been successful. For more mellow comments see Sir Charles Close, 'A Fifty-Years Retrospect', *E.S.R.* 1 (1932), 242, where, at p. 244, we learn that 'it was always pleasant to work with these colleagues of ours'.

[2] For technical and geographical accounts of the survey see (*a*) F. Boileau and L. Wallace, 'The Nyasa–Tanganyika Plateau', *Geog. J.* 13 (1899), 577. (*b*) E. Kohlschütter, 'Bericht über die astronomischen und geodätischen Arbeiten der deutschen Grenzregulierungs-Kommission zwischen dem Nyassa- und Tanganyika-See', *Mitt.* 13, 265. (*c*) Hauptmann Hermann, 'Bericht über Land und Leute längs der deutsch-englischen Grenze zwischen Nyassa und Tanganyika', ibid., p. 344.

[3] Above, p. 220, n. 2.

(4) opposite to the source of the Mpemba Stream; here it leaves the water-parting and follows the Mpemba downstream to a boundary pillar (5) on the left bank about 119 metres north of the village Tontera; from this point it goes in a straight line to the true west to a boundary pillar (6) about 2,560 metres off again on the waterparting; it then follows the water-parting between the Nkana and its affluents on the north and the Karunga and its affluents on the south past the following boundary pillars:

(1) Kumbi Hill (7).
(2) About 3 kilom. north of the English Station Fife (8).
(3) About 400 metres south of the source of the Ntakimba Stream (9).
(4) Between the old and the new Stevenson Road (10).
(5) About 1,700 metres from Nombwe village (11).
(6) About 1,700 metres from Kissitu village (12).

At this boundary pillar the boundary leaves the water-parting and goes in a straight line to a boundary pillar (13) about 1,200 metres north-west of the English Station Ikomba, and thence in a straight line to a boundary pillar (14) in the Suwa (Zuwa) Forest, about 3½ kilom. south of Kariman-sira village, which is again on the waterparting; it then follows the water-parting past the following boundary pillars:

(1) About 700 metres west of Shovere (Chowere) village (15).
(2) Dundundu Hill (16).
(3) About half-way between Mambwe and Mssungo (17).

4, 5, 6. Three boundary pillars in the neighbourhood of the English Station Mambwe, which are marked in the map with the numbers 18, 19, and 20 in red. The last of these boundary pillars is at the same time the point of intersection of the water-parting with longitude 32 east of Green-wich, ascertained by the Commission. The boundary then goes in a straight line to the source of the Massiete Stream and follows this down-stream to its junction with the Masia Stream (21); it runs then in a straight line to a boundary pillar on the left bank of the Ipundu (22) south of the ruins of Ipundu village and then in a straight line to the junction of the Saissi (Saisi) River with the Kassokorwa (Kasokolwa) Stream (23); it follows the Saissi up-stream to its junction with the Rumi (Lumi) Stream, it follows the Rumi upwards to its junction with the Mkumbaw Stream, and follows this up to its source. Hence the boundary goes in a straight line to the middle of the narrow saddle between the sources of the Mosi (Mozi) and Kipoko (Chipoko) Stream, and from there in a straight line to the south-east source of the Safu (Samfu) Stream; this it follows down-stream until it runs into the Kalambo and then the latter down-stream to its mouth in the Tanganyika Lake.

Sec. 2. In all cases where a river or stream forms the boundary, the 'thalweg' of the same shall form the boundary; if, however, no actual 'thalweg' is to be distinguished, it shall be the middle of the bed.

Sec. 3. Any fresh determination of the geographical positions of the

boundary pillars or of other points here mentioned shall make no alteration in the boundary itself.

[Sections 4 and 5 omitted]

It will be seen from the above description that the boundary was
marked mainly by natural features, such as watercourses. Only a few
boundary pillars were erected and most of them were not intervisible.
In 1932 the Government of Northern Rhodesia expressed the desire
for a more detailed demarcation and proposed the substitution of a
series of straight lines for the existing meandering watershed boundary, in order that the northern limits of the British South Africa
Company's property might be more exactly determined.[1]

During the discussion concerning the proposed new demarcation
the Director of Surveys, Tanganyika, referred to the fact that the
existing boundary departed from the watershed between Pillars Nos. 5
and 6. He said:

It is not known why this departure from the watershed was made,
especially as Tontera which by this deviation has been placed in Northern
Rhodesia, is inhabited by the Wanamwanga who are under Chief Mkoma
of Unamwang in the Mbeya District [Tanganyika]. As it is the earnest
desire of these people to continue under this Chief and as by the alteration
of the boundary which is acceptable to both Governments, Tanganyika
will acquire additional territory, there would appear to be no necessity to
refer the question to the Permanent Mandates Commission or to the
Council of the League of Nations.[2]

The line between Pillars 5 and 6 is one of the two instances where the
boundary was made to depart from the watershed during the original
demarcation, and it is referred to in Close's report. He there describes
this deviation as:

. . . a small diversion made to include the village of Tontera in British territory. I obtained the agreement of the German Commissioner to this,
because the village is the nearest village to the Administration station of
Ikawa, and supplies for Ikawa come from Tontera. . . . This diversion has
also the advantage that it gives Ikawa a little more room; the boundary
would otherwise be inconveniently close.[3]

It will be recalled that Article VI of the Anglo-German Agreement
of 1890 provided for boundary rectification in accordance with local

---

[1] Letter from Director of Surveys to Land Officer, Tanganyika, dated 25 October 1932. File DLS 2987.
[2] Letter from Director of Surveys to Chief Secretary, Tanganyika, dated
3 December 1934. File DLS 2987.   [3] *Close Report*, p. 33.

requirements. The mixed demarcation commission appears to have concerned itself more with the technical aspects of the work, and the exchange of equal areas of territory in those places where deviation from the line was considered necessary, than with the social implications of the boundary. Despite the compilation of the detailed list of villages, there is little evidence to suggest that the commission paid very much attention to the fact that the boundary might in some cases separate the members of a tribal group though, in fairness to Close, it must be mentioned that he reports:

> The boundaries between the tribes are not now very definite. Villages of alien tribes are found in many places, and near the administration stations villages of mixed tribes have sprung up. The villages are very small as a rule; a village would ordinarily consist of thirty huts and hold less than 100 men, women, and children.[1]

The reference made by the Tanganyika Director of Surveys to the League of Nations arises from the provisions of the Tanganyika Mandate, 1922.[2] Article 1 sets out the boundaries of Tanganyika, and Article 12 states that the consent of the Council of the League of Nations is required for any modification of the terms of the mandate. The Director seems to err in suggesting that the boundary alteration resulting from the acquisition of additional territory by Tanganyika would not require the permission of the League Council, since this would be a clear modification of the terms. However, the matter did not in fact arise and Tontera, the village in question, remained in Northern Rhodesia.

In 1933 a surveyor of the British South Africa Company commenced a survey of the company's estate in Northern Rhodesia, adjoining the boundary with Tanganyika. He reported that most of the original pillars erected by the Anglo-German demarcation commission in 1898 were now in a bad state of repair, and offered to replace them by concrete beacons. This proposal was accepted and the cost was shared by the two neighbouring governments. All original boundary pillars were incorporated in the new survey, except for a few which were found to be in unsuitable sites, such as ant hills, in which case a new site was chosen as close as possible to the old one. No important departures were made from the line as defined

[1] *Close Report*, p. 25.
[2] British and Belgian Mandates for East Africa, 20 July 1922. Hudson, *International Legislation*, vol. i, p. 84.

by the Anglo-German Agreement of 1901, but the watershed was marked by additional beacons and altogether 39 boundary marks, including the replacements, were placed along the line.[1]

The Tanganyika boundary inspector reported that, despite the new demarcation, most of the adjacent boundary beacons were still not intervisible. Since local inhabitants were often unable to tell on which side of the boundary they were, he recommended the placing of additional beacons, along the original line, to provide intervisibility between adjacent boundary marks. The recommendation was accepted by both Tanganyika and Northern Rhodesia, who agreed to share the cost. This additional work was completed in 1937 and resulted in the establishment of one more boundary beacon and thirty-nine line marks. Each of these new points, together with the thirty-nine beacons placed in 1935, making a total of seventy-nine, was now marked by an iron telegraph pole with a metal target on its top and visible from its nearest neighbour.[2]

A plan showing the 1935 demarcation was signed by government representatives of Tanganyika and Northern Rhodesia.[3] No reference, concerning either this or the 1937 demarcation, appears to have been made to the League of Nations, but it is submitted that since the new survey represents an almost exact retracement of the original boundary, and was accepted by both governments, it should now be regarded as defining the true position of the boundary between Tanzania and Zambia. The 1935 plan contains a written description of the boundary, in conformity with the new demarcation, together with a co-ordinate list of beacons, but no other formal document was apparently drawn up. The legal status of this part of the Tanzania–Zambia boundary, therefore, is that it derives from the Anglo-German Agreement of 1901, as modified by the minor alterations made on the ground in 1935 and 1937, and agreed to by the two neighbouring governments.

The location of the boundary between Tanzania and Zambia in Lake Tanganyika is a matter of some doubt since only the boundary

---

[1] For an account of this work see J. E. S. Bradford, 'A Three-Million-Acre Title Survey', *E.S.R.* 3 (1936), 469.

[2] G. and J. B. Laws, 'Northern Rhodesia–Tanganyika Boundary', Report dated 11 September 1937, in Tanganyika Government File DLS 392. The iron poles were conveniently available for this purpose, owing to the dismantling of the Abercorn–Isoka telegraph line.

[3] Plan showing Final Demarcation of Northern Rhodesia–Tanganyika Territory Boundary, March 1935. Tanganyika Survey Plan TS 100.

terminal points are clearly defined by treaty and, of these, the exact position of the Congo tripoint is still undetermined. The eastern boundary of the Congo Republic is formed in part by the median line of Lake Tanganyika. From the discussion of this boundary in a previous chapter it will be remembered that difficulty in establishing the Congo tripoint stemmed from the problem of interpreting the location of Cape Akalunga, and that two alternative positions are now shown respectively on Congolese and Zambian maps.[1]

The delimitation of the British and German spheres, as established by the 1890 and 1901 agreements referred to previously,[2] describes the boundary on the shore of Lake Tanganyika as the mouth of the River Kalambo. No mention is made in either of these agreements of a boundary in Lake Tanganyika itself, nor has the matter been clarified by any subsequent treaty. It appears to have been assumed, however, that the boundary does in fact extend into the lake and that it follows an approximate median line. Maps of both Tanzania and Zambia show this line as running on a curved course from the Kalambo to the Congo tripoint, and although this is merely geometrical convenience there is no evidence to suggest that it is not acceptable to the two neighbouring states. This part of the boundary, therefore, has a *de facto* origin which appears to have matured into present *de jure* recognition.

What explanation lies behind the absence of a delimited lake boundary between the German and British territories? This question may have been thought to be of little practical importance at the time of the 1890 and 1901 agreements. Lake Tanganyika lay within the limits of the Congo Basin, as defined by Article 1 of the Berlin Act of 1885,[3] and navigation on the lake was declared to be free.[4]

With respect to lake boundaries, the doctrine of international law, in the absence of treaty stipulations, presumes in favour of equal rights and holds that the boundary follows the median line.[5] The problem of interpreting the expression 'median line' was considered earlier and it will be readily seen that the lake boundary between Tanzania and Zambia, as delineated on current maps, does not accord with any of the common definitions of median as presented, for example, by Boggs.[6] Instead, this boundary, as has been stated,

[1] Above, Ch. XIII, p. 167.   [2] Above, pp. 218, 221.
[3] General Act of the Conference of Berlin Hertslet, ii. 468.
[4] Ibid., Art. 2.   [5] Hall, op. cit., para. 38.
[6] Above, Ch. XIII, p. 168.

follows a convenient geometrical line. Although at the present time there is no dispute concerning the lake boundary it would no doubt be preferable to define it more precisely, either by means of a series of straight lines, described by bearing and distance,[1] or by some other form of arbitrary median[2] which followed the existing curved line as closely as possible. This would be a relatively simple procedure and one which would permit the course of the boundary to be physically established should the need ever arise,[3] though the northern terminal will remain indefinite until the position of the Congo tripoint is finally determined.

[1] A. R. Hinks, 'International Boundary Problems', *Geog. J.* 96 (1940), 286, at p. 287.

[2] Above, Ch. VII, pp. 98–9. [3] Above, Ch. XIII, p. 169.

CHAPTER XVII

Uganda–Congo Republic

IN the closing decades of the nineteenth century, when the European imperial powers began to direct their attention towards the partitioning of the East African lake region, the territory which Britain regarded as her own sphere of influence was known loosely as Uganda. Even when the Uganda Protectorate was created in 1902, its limits, for the most part, were vague and unsettled, and it was not until 1926 that the boundary arrangements were completed. While the territorial content of Uganda waxed and waned in accordance with the various boundary agreements the name itself remained a convenient and comprehensive designation for a political unit which by 1926 had lost approximately one-half of its former area, and the boundaries of which had all been adjusted since their original delimitation.[1] Historically the terminology was inexact, since the word Uganda was at first applicable only to the Kingdom of Buganda, itself merely a part of the larger British sphere. It was in Buganda that the Imperial British East Africa Company, incorporated in 1888, established its first commercial foothold west of Lake Victoria. When this company, as a result of its unprofitable operations, decided to evacuate at the end of 1892, the impending political vacuum was filled by the British Government which entered into a provisional relationship with the traditional kingdom. In 1894 Buganda formally became a British protectorate, thus providing the synecdochic nucleus of the territorial agglomeration that makes up the Uganda of the present day.

On Uganda's western frontier the boundary line is determined mainly by well-marked natural features, of which the Mufumbiro volcanoes, the snow-covered peaks of Ruwenzori, and Lakes Albert and Edward in the western rift provide magnificent examples. This situation has not arisen from any careful selection of boundary material during the initial delimitation, but represents instead the culmination of an evolutionary process in which power struggle,

---

[1] The history of Uganda's various boundary changes is shown in an interesting graphical form, with accompanying text, 'Evolution of Uganda's Boundaries', in *Atlas of Uganda*, Govt. Press, Entebbe, 1962.

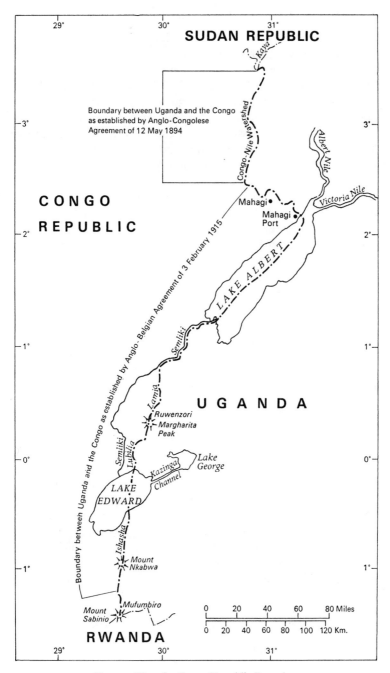

SUDAN REPUBLIC

Boundary between Uganda and the Congo
as established by Anglo-Congolese
Agreement of 12 May 1894

CONGO
REPUBLIC

UGANDA

RWANDA

FIG. 11. Uganda–Congo Republic Boundary

political expediency, commercial exploitation, and administrative convenience have all played their part. Originally the boundary was simply a line on the map, chosen by diplomats to define the eastern limit of the Congo territory sought by King Leopold II of Belgium. This line followed the meridian of 30° east longitude which, in the absence of precise topographical surveys at the time of its selection as a boundary, was an astronomical concept bearing no accurately known relationship to the great land and water features of the area it was intended to divide.[1] It was not until 1910 that the Uganda-Congo boundary was accurately defined.

In 1890 when Britain and Germany agreed to make a clear delimitation of the previously contested East African hinterland, the Congo State was already an established political and geographical entity, with an international personality that had been endowed by the major powers five years earlier. In determining the extent to which their respective spheres might penetrate the hinterland, both Britain and Germany regarded the eastern boundary of the Congo State as the obvious limit. A short account of the emergence of the Congo as an independent state will help to place Uganda's western boundary in its proper historical perspective.

The Congo State came into being as a result of the personal enterprise of King Leopold II, and its subsequent development was shaped largely by his own commercial and political ambitions. European interest in the Congo region was awakened by reports of Stanley's explorations in 1877 and the commercial possibilities of the region were soon appreciated by Leopold who called together a group of financial interests to study trading prospects. This venture, formed in 1878 as the *Comité d'Études du Haut Congo*, was reconstituted the following year when all non-Belgian capital was repaid, and in 1882 it was renamed *Association Internationale du Congo*.[2] The Association had a somewhat misleading title, since it was not in any sense international. Nor was it a national undertaking, enjoying the support of a particular government. Instead it comprised a vehicle for the advancement of Leopold's personal, as distinct from Belgian official, aims. In effect Leopold was the International Association, which depended almost entirely on him for its funds.[3] Legally, however, the

[1] Above, Ch. III, p. 47.
[2] R. Slade, *King Leopold's Congo*, Oxford University Press, London, 1962, pp. 37-8; R. Anstey, *Britain and the Congo in the Nineteenth Century*, Clarendon Press, Oxford, 1962, pp. 79-81.
[3] J. S. Keltie, *The Partition of Africa*, Stanford, London, 1893, p. 210.

Association was an interesting anomaly, since although it was a private commercial undertaking it later acquired the attributes of sovereign power and received international recognition as an independent state.

Leopold's claim to the Congo region faced challenges from France and Portugal which, however, he was able to overcome through the intervention of Britain and Germany. Britain's main concern was to keep France out of an area into which she seemed likely to expand, and the Anglo-Portuguese treaty of 1884[1] that recognized Portuguese sovereignty over two hundred miles of West African coast, including the Congo mouth, was intended by Britain primarily to further her own commercial interests, for if, as was hoped in some quarters, Leopold's organization should become an English company, then Portugal would prove a more tractable coastal neighbour than France.[2] This veiled plan did not succeed, partly because British traders in West Africa resented even nominal Portuguese control of the lower Congo, and partly as a result of opposition from Protestant missionary groups which associated Portugal with the slave trade. British public opinion, coupled with diplomatic protests by France and Germany, forced Britain to abandon the treaty in June 1884 and it was never ratified.[3] Germany, anxious to prevent a British foothold in the Congo, favoured the establishment there of an internationally controlled free trade zone, and she proposed that the European powers hold a conference in Berlin at which the entire Congo question could be discussed.

Meanwhile, Leopold was gaining international support for his proposed creation of an independent Congo State, the first expression of which came in April 1884 when the United States recognized the flag of the International Association as that of 'a friendly government'.[4] The geographical limits of the new state were at that time undetermined and the earliest attempt to define them was made in a convention between Germany and the International Association,

[1] Treaty between Her Majesty and His Majesty the King of Portugal respecting the Rivers Congo and Zambesi, and the Territory on the West Coast of Africa, between 8° and 5° 12′ of South Latitude. Signed at London, 26 February 1884. Hertslet, iii. 1004.

[2] R. Robinson and J. Gallagher, *Africa and the Victorians*, Macmillan, London, 1961, pp. 169–74.

[3] For a detailed discussion of the treaty see Anstey, op. cit., Chs. VI and VII.

[4] Declarations exchanged between the United States of America and the International Association of the Congo. Washington, 22 April 1884. Hertslet, ii. 602.

dated 8 November 1884, only one week before the opening of the Berlin Conference: 'Art. VI. The German Empire is ready on its part to recognize the frontiers of the territory of the Association and of the new State which is to be created, as they are shown in the annexed map.'[1]

The Berlin Conference, attended by the major European powers and the United States, was concluded on the 26 February 1885 by the signing of a treaty[2] which, *inter alia*, defined the geographical limits of the Congo Basin within which all nations should enjoy freedom of trade. By Article 1 of the treaty, this area was described as comprising 'all the regions watered by the Congo and its affluents, including Lake Tanganyika, with its eastern tributaries'.

The International Association of the Congo, which was represented at the Berlin Conference, demonstrated the recognition of its international personality by its immediate accession to the provisions of the treaty,[3] and its proposal to form an independent Congo State was now acceptable to the treaty signatories. Leopold was proclaimed Sovereign of the Congo Independent State, at Boma in July 1885,[4] and in the following month he sent formal notification to the European Powers.[5] Belgian parliamentary approval, constitutionally essential for Leopold's new title, was given reluctantly and subject to the condition that sovereignty over the Congo was personal to Leopold and only for his own lifetime. The Congo and Belgium were declared to be two states absolutely separated from one another.[6]

Notification, on 1 August 1885, of the formation of the Independent State of the Congo, was accompanied by a circular[7] containing both a declaration of neutrality and a description of the limits of the

[1] Convention between the German Empire and the International Association of the Congo. Berlin, 8 November 1884. Hertslet, ii. 572. The map was not published with the convention but its boundary details are described, from the original, by P. Jentgen, *Les Frontières du Congo Belge*, Institut Royal Colonial Belge, Brussels, 1952, p. 37.

[2] General Act of the Conference of Berlin. 26 February 1885. Hertslet, ii. 468.

[3] Accession of the International Association of the Congo to the General Act of the Berlin Conference of 26 February 1885. Hertslet, ii. 550.

[4] Slade, op. cit., p. 43.

[5] Hertslet, ii. 551.

[6] Slade, op. cit., pp. 194–5. The constitutional dichotomy is underlined by, e.g., The Brussels Slave Trade Conference of 1890 where 'His Majesty the King of the Belgians' and 'His Majesty the King-Sovereign of the Independent State of the Congo' were separate participants. See Hertslet, ii. 488.

[7] Circular of the Administrator-General of the Department of Foreign Affairs of the Independent State of the Congo, declaring the Neutrality of that State, within its Limits as defined by Treaties. Brussels, 1 August 1885. Hertslet, ii. 552.

new state which, it should be noted, did not include the entire Congo Basin as defined by Article 1 of the Treaty of Berlin. The circular describes the northern and eastern limits of the Congo State, in part, as follows:

> The 4th parallel of north latitude until it meets the 30th degree of longitude east of Greenwich;
> The 30th degree of longitude east of Greenwich up to 1° 20′ of south latitude;
> A straight line drawn from the intersection of the 30th degree of longitude by the parallel of 1° 20′ of south latitude as far as the northern extremity of Lake Tanganyka;
> The median line of Lake Tanganyka;
> A straight line drawn from Lake Tanganyka to Lake Moero by 8° 30′ south latitude . . .

The location of the boundary sector between Lake Tanganyika and the 30th meridian, as described in the third course of the above extract, differed significantly from that portrayed on maps attached to treaties made by the International Association with Germany in November 1884,[1] and with France in February 1885.[2] On both maps[3] the boundary north of the lake is shown as following a curved, though not identical, line to the west of the straight line now claimed by Leopold. Although this discrepancy was noted at the time by Germany and was later used by her to support her territorial claims, she did not then contest it. The German Foreign Office reported that an examination of the Congo boundaries 'indicated that they on the whole correspond with those arrived at in the previous treaties of the *Association Internationale du Congo* with Germany, France, and Portugal', and the Congo State's declaration, with respect to both its neutrality and its boundaries, was accordingly ratified by Germany on 25 August 1885.[4]

Delimitation of the Congo State's boundaries in 1885 took place before partition of the eastern side of the continent had been completed by the European states. East African territorial claims by Britain and Germany were at first restricted to the coastal regions,

---

[1] Hertslet, ii. 572.   [2] Hertslet, ii. 564.
[3] Friederichsen's Map of Central Africa, 1885, 'taken from the copy annexed to the 9th Protocol of the Berlin Conference of 1884–5', shows the boundaries according to the respective treaties. A copy of this map is given in Hertslet, ii, facing p. 604. Another useful map showing the different boundaries is given in *Petermann's Mitteilungen*, 1911/1, Tafel 46.
[4] Louis, *Ruanda-Urundi 1884–1919*, pp. 5–7.

with an ill-defined hinterland,[1] but the Heligoland Agreement of 1890[2] created interior limits that brought the respective British and German spheres of influence into contiguity with the Congo State. Article 1 of the 1890 agreement gives the boundary details. The western limit of the German sphere is defined by 'a line which, from the mouth of the River Kilambo to the 1st parallel of south latitude, is conterminous with the Congo Free State'[3] and the British sphere is bounded 'To the west by the Congo Free State, and by the western watershed of the basin of the Upper Nile'. The western terminal of the line separating the British sphere in the north from the German sphere in the south is described as the intersection of the '1st parallel of south latitude' with 'the frontier of the Congo Free State', with the proviso that, to the west of Lake Victoria, the line shall if necessary be deflected southward so as to include Mount Mfumbiro within the British sphere:

It is, however, understood that, on the west side of the lake, the (German) sphere does not comprise Mount Mfumbiro; if that mountain shall prove to lie to the south of the selected parallel, the line shall be deflected so as to exclude it, but shall, nevertheless, return so as to terminate at the above-named point.

The object of this proviso was to ensure that Mufumbiro, which Britain claimed on the basis of local treaties said to have been made by Stanley, remained in British hands.[4] Owing to the imperfect geographical knowledge then existing, both Britain and Germany assumed Mufumbiro to lie to the east of the Congo boundary. This subsequently proved to be an incorrect assumption, and one which helped to complicate the eventual boundary settlement.

As a result of the 1890 delimitation, the British and German spheres were each bounded on the west by the Congo State whose easterly limit, between the parallels of 4° north and 1° 20′ south latitude, had been defined by the circular of 1 August 1885 as the 30th meridian. The 30th meridian itself was not identified as the Congo State boundary

[1] Agreement between the British and German Governments, respecting the Sultanate of Zanzibar and the opposite East African Mainland, and their Spheres of Influence. 29 October–1 November 1886. Hertslet, iii. 882.

[2] Agreement between the British and German Governments, respecting Africa and Heligoland. Berlin. 1 July 1890. Hertslet, iii. 899.

[3] This description is misleading since the Congo boundary, though drawn along the median line of Lake Tanganyika, did not extend to the River Kilambo (Kalambo) which is at the southern end of the lake. Above, pp. 165–6.

[4] Below, p. 268.

in the 1890 agreement. This, so far as Britain was concerned, was no doubt intentional since proposals had already been put forward for an adjustment of the boundary between the Congo State and the British sphere of influence.[1] On 24 May 1890, a little more than a month before the completion of the Anglo-German agreement, the so-called Mackinnon Treaty was made between the Congo State and the Imperial British East Africa Company. The company had recently extended its operations into Buganda and was empowered by its charter to enter into certain territorial arrangements, subject to the approval of the British Government.[2] Sir William Mackinnon agreed on behalf of the company that the respective spheres should be drawn along the Semliki River. The treaty recognized the Congo State's rights west of a line drawn from the south-west corner of Lake Albert northward along the Nile as far as Lado.[3] In return, the Congo State agreed that the company should receive a strip, five miles wide, stretching from the southern shore of Lake Edward[4] to the northern tip of Lake Tanganyika. British acquisition of this five-mile strip would have given them a link in the 'all-red route' connecting their territories lying to the north and the south of the German sphere, but strong opposition from Germany dissuaded the British Government from ratifying the Mackinnon Treaty and it did not become operative.[5] Though unratified by Britain, however, it was used by Leopold to justify his expansion into the region lying to the north of the Congo State's self-defined boundaries of 1885. Britain claimed, but did not then effectively control, this northern region and although she formally protested to Leopold she was willing to accommodate him in order to keep the French away from the upper Nile where their presence would be considered a threat to British policy in Egypt.[6]

---

[1] Britain recognized the International Association of the Congo by a declaration signed on 16 December 1884 and ratified on 9 May 1885, but this declaration made no reference to boundaries. See Hertslet, ii. 573.

[2] For text of the company's charter, which was granted on 3 September 1888, see McDermott, op. cit., p. 476.   [3] McDermott, op. cit., pp. 316–19.

[4] The lake was then known as Lake Albert Edward but its name was changed to Lake Edward in 1908 by order of the Uganda Government. See The Uganda Official Gazette, 15 December 1908, p. 283. In fact, this order was extra-territorial in its application since at that time the lake lay to the west of the 1894 treaty boundary and was therefore entirely within the limits of the Congo State.

[5] W. L. Langer, The Diplomacy of Imperialism, Knopf, New York, 2nd edn., 1951, p. 119; Louis, op. cit., pp. 27–8.

[6] Robinson and Gallagher, op. cit., p. 330. Langer, op. cit., p. 125. For a different explanation by the Foreign Office see Hertslet, ii. 582.

By an agreement made between Britain and King Leopold on 12 May 1894[1] the Congo State recognized the British sphere of influence as delimited by Britain and Germany in 1890. The boundary between the British sphere and the Congo State is described in Article 1 of the agreement as follows:

Art. 1 (a). It is agreed that the sphere of influence of the Independent Congo State shall be limited to the north of the German sphere in East Africa by a frontier following the 30th meridian east of Greenwich up to its intersection by the watershed between the Nile and the Congo, and thence following this watershed in a northerly and north-westerly direction.

In return for the Congo State's recognition of this boundary and of British sovereignty over the area to the north, Britain agreed to grant a lease to Leopold of the region between the Nile–Congo watershed and the River Nile, extending as far north as the parallel of 10° north latitude. Article 2 of the agreement describes the extent and terms of the lease:

The territories shall be bounded by a line starting from a point situated on the west shore of Lake Albert, immediately to the south of Mahagi, to the nearest point of the frontier defined in paragraph (a) of the preceding Article. Thence it shall follow the watershed between the Congo and the Nile up to the 25th meridian east of Greenwich, and that meridian up to its intersection by the 10th parallel north, whence it shall run along that parallel directly to a point to be determined to the north of Fashoda. Thence it shall follow the 'thalweg' of the Nile southward to Lake Albert, and the western shore of Lake Albert to the point above indicated south of Mahagi.

This lease shall remain in force during the reign of His Majesty Leopold II, Sovereign of the Independent Congo State.

Nevertheless, at the expiration of His Majesty's reign, it shall remain fully in force as far as concerns all the portion of the territories above mentioned situated to the west of the 30th meridian east of Greenwich, as well as a strip of 25 kilom. in breadth, to be delimited by common consent, stretching from the watershed between the Nile and the Congo up to the western shore of Lake Albert, and including the port of Mahagi.

This extended lease shall be continued so long as the Congo territories as an Independent State or as a Belgian Colony remain under the sovereignty of His Majesty and His Majesty's successors.

---

[1] Agreement between Great Britain and His Majesty King Leopold II, Sovereign of the Independent State of the Congo, relating to the Spheres of Influence of Great Britain and the Independent State of the Congo in East and Central Africa. Signed at Brussels, 12 May 1894. Hertslet, ii. 578.

Two distinct interests were created by this article. In the territory lying to the east of the 30th meridian the lease terminated with the end of Leopold's reign as sovereign of the Congo State, and was therefore personal to him. In the area to the west of the 30th meridian

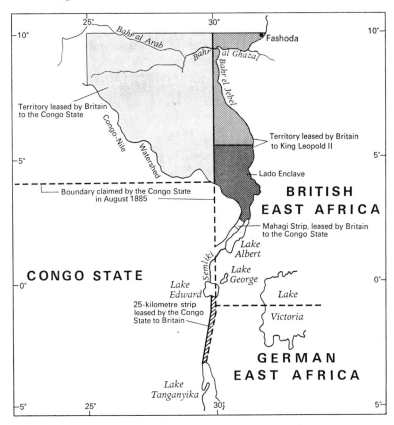

FIG. 12. Sketch to illustrate the Anglo–Congolese Boundary Agreement of 12 May 1894

the lease continued so long as Leopold and his successors reigned over the Congo, either as an independent state or as a Belgian colony, and it therefore contemplated the possible Belgian annexation of the Congo territories. The retention in the eastern portion of a lease over the Mahagi Strip, 25 kilometres wide, ensured that even after the cessation of Leopold's reign, the Congo State would have access to Lake Albert.

Article 3 of the agreement was a surprising inclusion since it had no necessary connection with the other provisions and it revived the old notion of a British 'all-red route' which, in the face of German opposition that remained as firm as ever, had been abandoned by the British Government only four years earlier. The article reads:

The Independent Congo State grants under lease to Great Britain, to be administered when occupied, under the conditions and for a period hereafter determined, a strip of territory 25 kilom. in breadth, extending from the most northerly port on Lake Tanganika, which is included in it, to the most southerly point of Lake Albert Edward.

This lease will have similar duration to that which applies to the territories to the west of the 30th meridian east of Greenwich.

Although the description given in Article 3 does not specifically say so, it appears from the map attached to the agreement[1] that the strip was intended to be contiguous with the Congo State boundary. In other words the eastern limit of the strip was drawn from the northern end of Lake Tanganyika along a straight line to the intersection of the 30th meridian with the parallel of $1° 20'$ south latitude, and thence northward along the meridian to Lake Edward.[2]

The signing of the 1894 agreement, which was really a modified version of the unratified Mackinnon Treaty of 1890, produced immediate reaction from France and Germany. France had recently failed to conclude her own boundary arrangements with the Congo State and she did not recognize the northern limits of the British sphere of influence. Germany was angered at the inclusion of Article 3 and although at first she seemed willing to accept a British strip connecting Lakes Tanganyika and Edward, provided it was kept inside the Congo State and twenty kilometres clear of the German boundary, she later demanded the removal of the offending article, threatening the withdrawal of her recognition of the Congo State's neutrality if this were not done.[3] Combined French and German pressure forced Britain to yield and Article 3 was abrogated in June 1894, having survived for only a month.[4]

---

[1] A copy of this map is given in Hertslet, ii. facing p. 580. See also E. G. Ravenstein, 'The Recent Territorial Arrangements in Africa', *Geog. J.* 4 (1894), 54.

[2] Lake Edward was incorrectly thought at this time to be intersected by the 30th meridian, and therefore partly within each sphere.

[3] Louis, op. cit., pp. 37–8.

[4] Declaration between Great Britain and the Congo Free State, withdrawing Art. 3 of the Agreement of 12 May 1894, respecting the Territory between Lake Tanganyika and Lake Albert Edward. Brussels, 22 June 1894. Hertslet, ii. 584.

French objections to the British agreement with Leopold had still to be met. Under threat of military force, Leopold was compelled[1] to sign an agreement with France in August 1894,[2] in Article 4 of which he undertook to abandon his occupation of the greater part of the territory leased by him from Britain three months earlier:

The Free State binds herself to renounce all occupation, and to exercise in the future no political influence west or north of a line thus determined: Longitude 30° E. of Greenwich (27° 40′ E. of Paris), starting from its intersection of the watershed of the Congo and Nile basins, up to the point where it meets the parallel 5° 30′, and then along that parallel to the Nile.

Of the vast territory contained in the lease, Leopold was confined by his agreement with France to the portion lying east of the 30th meridian and south of the parallel of 5° 30′ north latitude, an area which became known as the Lado Enclave.

Leopold's financial difficulties, which led him to contract Belgian and foreign loans and to consider alienation of Congo territory, produced a proposal for the annexation of the Congo State as a Belgian colony. This proposal, to which Leopold was forced to agree, was abandoned in the face of political opposition in Belgium, and the treaty of cession, signed on 9 January 1895, was withdrawn.[3] Among the documents submitted for the approval of the Belgian Parliament during the annexation discussions was a new declaration of neutrality of the Congo State,[4] containing a description of the boundaries as amended since 1 August 1885 by the various agreements with France, Britain, and Portugal. The relevant part of the description contained in this declaration reads:

The watershed of the Nile and Congo up to its intersection by the meridian 30° E. of Greenwich (27° 40′ Paris);
The extension of this watershed until its second intersection by the aforesaid meridian 30° E. of Greenwich;
The 30th degree of long. E. of Greenwich up to 1° 20′ of S. lat.;
A straight line drawn from the intersection of the 30th degree of E. long. with the parallel 1° 20′ S. lat. to the northern extremity of Lake Tanganika;

---

[1] Langer, op. cit., p. 139; Robinson and Gallagher, op. cit., p. 332.
[2] Boundary Agreement between France and the Congo Free State. 14 August 1894. Hertslet, ii. 569.
[3] Slade, op. cit., pp. 203–5.
[4] Declaration of the Neutrality of the Congo Free State. Brussels, 28 December 1894. Hertslet, ii. 557.

The median line of Lake Tanganika;

A line running straight to the extremity of Cape Akalunga, on Lake Tanganika, situated on the northernmost point of Cameron Bay, by about 8° 15′ S. lat., to the right bank of the River Luapula, at the point where the river leaves Lake Moëro; . . .

France, by her agreement with Leopold in 1894, had frustrated the British plan to establish him as lessee of the upper Nile territory as far north as Fashoda and she now felt free to advance towards the river. After a period of inconclusive diplomatic skirmishing in which France and Britain failed to agree on the extent of the British sphere, a French military expedition was despatched in 1896 to gain a foothold on the Nile. Britain, unwilling in 1894 to support Leopold's claim to his lease, was now prepared to control the Nile by force if necessary, and the crisis came when Marchand, the French commander, was confronted by Kitchener's army at Fashoda in September 1898.[1] Final settlement was reached by an Anglo-French agreement of March 1899,[2] when the British and French spheres north of the Congo State boundary were delimited as lying respectively east and west of the Nile-Congo watershed, thus ending any further French claims to the Nile valley.

Following the removal of French influence from the upper Nile, Leopold attempted a northward expansion, on the basis of his 1894 lease from Britain which he claimed was still valid. He argued that his delayed occupation of the leased area should be permitted to resume now that France had been forced to evacuate, and that his treaty with France in August 1894 by which he purported to relinquish his rights as lessee was, as against Britain, *res inter alios acta*. Years of argument followed, in which the rejection of offers and counter-offers was accompanied by the prospect of military conflict, and it was not until 1906 that a settlement was reached.[3] By an agreement made with Britain in May 1906 Leopold relinquished the greater part of the leasehold interest acquired by him in 1894 and retained only the lease of the Lado Enclave. The lease of the Mahagi Strip, created in 1894 to give the Congo State access to Lake Albert,

[1] For an account of the Fashoda incident and its effects see, e.g., Robinson and Gallagher, op. cit., Ch. XII.

[2] Declaration completing the Convention between Great Britain and France of 14 June 1898 (Spheres of Influence in Central Africa and the Soudan). Signed at London, 21 March 1899. Hertslet, ii. 796.

[3] For details of the negotiations see Langer, op. cit., pp. 571–3; R. O. Collins, 'Anglo-Congolese Negotiations, 1900–1906', Zaïre, 12 (1958), 479, 619.

was continued, under its original conditions, by the 1906 agreement.[1]

The first demarcation of any portion of the Uganda–Congo boundary came in 1902 when a mixed commission was sent to mark that part of the line dividing the British and German spheres which extended westward from Lake Victoria to the Congo State boundary. By the terms of the Anglo-German agreement of 1890, the boundary line in this sector lay along the parallel of 1° south latitude, and its western terminal was the 30th meridian, in accordance with the Congo State's declarations of 1885 and 1894 and the Anglo-Congolese agreement of 1894. The location of the boundary tripoint, therefore, as agreed to by the three neighbouring states, was the intersection of the 30th meridian of east longitude with the parallel of 1° south latitude. When this point was established on the ground by the demarcation commission some interesting facts were revealed. First, the 30th meridian as portrayed on the treaty maps was now found to be in error by having been drawn about 12 miles too far west. To shift the boundary eastward, 12 miles away from the features it had been thought to divide, would result in a considerable loss of territory both for Britain and for Germany. Secondly, Lake Edward, named in 1889 by Stanley after the then Prince of Wales and assumed to lie at least partly within the British sphere, was shown to be completely inside the boundaries of the Congo State.[2] Thirdly, Mufumbiro, British control of which had been specially safeguarded by the clause in Article 1 of the 1890 Anglo-German agreement providing for a southward deflection of the boundary so as to include the mountain within the British sphere, was also found to be a part of the Congo State.[3]

Mufumbiro, however, was only part of a larger territorial issue. Germany had her own claims against the Congo State and was engaged in a struggle for the Lake Kivu area. Although she had accepted the Congo State's boundaries as described in the circular of 1 August 1885, she now argued that this acceptance was subject to prior treaties and that by the convention which she had signed with the International

[1] Agreement between Great Britain and the Independent State of the Congo, modifying the Agreement signed at Brussels, 12 May 1894. Signed at London, 9 May 1906. Hertslet, ii. 584.

[2] C. Delmé-Radcliffe, 'Reports connected with the Work of the British Commission for the Delimitation of the Anglo-German Boundary West of Lake Victoria Nyanza', July 1906. F.O. 2/898, p. 40.

[3] Ibid., pp. 28, 60–1. Below, Ch. XX.

Association in 1884 the map boundary north of Lake Tanganyika followed a curved line lying considerably to the west of the straight line defined by the circular.[1] Germany's legal argument was weak, if not groundless, but she persisted in a claim against the Congo that involved the extension of her western boundary as far as Lake Kivu and the Ruzizi River. Since Leopold proved adamant in his refusal to admit this claim, Germany turned to Britain for negotiation. The Anglo-German Mufumbiro Conference, held at Berlin in April 1909, was inspired partly by German fears that Leopold might offer Mufumbiro to Britain in return for her support over the Kivu dispute, and partly because Britain was enticed by Germany with the promise of access to Lake Kivu. In the following month an understanding was reached between the two states that if Germany succeeded in her Kivu claim she would place all except the southern slopes of Mufumbiro in British hands.[2] The course was now set for Britain and Germany to obtain their respective territorial demands by exerting their combined power. A bizarre incident occurred in 1909 when Britain sent a small military force, known as the Kivu Mission, to seize Mufumbiro and oust the Belgian troops who occupied it.[3] Germany continued her pressure in the Kivu region and although Leopold was prepared to defend his territory by force, the need for negotiation was evident and his death at the end of 1909 paved the way for a diplomatic settlement in the following year.

It is interesting to note that a procedure for the settlement of disputes between Britain and King Leopold in connection with the boundaries of the Congo State was established by Article 8 of their 1906 agreement.[4] This article provided that in the event of the parties failing to reach an understanding concerning the boundaries, the issue would be referred to The Hague Tribunal for its binding decision. The reason why no advantage was ever taken of this provision can be explained partly by the changing constitutional position of the Congo State.[5] For a variety of commercial, political, and ideological

[1] Above, p. 233, n. 3.

[2] Agreement respecting the Boundary between the North-Western portion of German East Africa and Uganda. Signed 19 May 1909. Berlin. A typescript copy of this secret agreement is held in the Library MSS. Files of the Royal Geographical Society, the Map Room of which also has a map (Uganda S/Spec. 2) showing the territorial arrangements.

[3] For a first-hand account of this clumsy episode, see J. M. Coote, 'The Kivu Mission, 1909–1910', U.J. 20 (1956), 105.

[4] Hertslet, ii. 586.

[5] An additional explanation is given by Louis, op. cit., p. 73.

reasons, the Belgian Government's proposal to annex the Congo State in 1895 was the subject of intense controversy and the draft treaty of cession was withdrawn. Outside intervention contributed to an eventual settlement of the question.[1] World opinion, focused on the Congo State by such publications as the Casement Report of 1904 which supported charges of oppression and maladministration by Leopold's officials, led to a renewed call for Belgium to accept responsibility for the area, and annexation finally came in 1908.[2]

In 1909, when the dispute over Mufumbiro approached a crisis, Belgium was still discussing with Britain the effect of annexation upon her succession to treaties, and it was not until 27 June 1913 that Britain formally recognized the transfer of Congo sovereignty.[3] Instead of resorting to Article 8 of the 1906 agreement, to which Germany of course was not a party, it was considered preferable to discuss the competing territorial claims at a meeting between the three states. This led to the convening of a conference at Brussels in February 1910,[4] two months after Leopold's death. One advantage possessed by the delegates to this conference that had not been available to those responsible for the early delimitations, was that accurate topographical information now existed. The Anglo-German demarcation commission of 1902–4, in addition to marking the boundary, mapped a 20-mile strip from Lake Victoria to the 30th meridian.[5] In 1907–8 the Uganda–Congo boundary commission mapped the frontier region from the parallel of 1° south latitude to the southern end of Lake Albert.[6] Despite its title, however, the latter commission did not attempt to demarcate the boundary but confined itself to producing cartographical material from which an exact boundary line could be later determined.[7]

---

[1] Slade, op. cit., p. 207.

[2] For the treaty of cession, dated 28 November 1907, see Hertslet, ii. 548. Annexation took effect from 15 November 1908.

[3] 107 *B.F.S.P.* 351.

[4] Officially entitled, 'Conference respecting Frontiers between Uganda, German East Africa, and the Belgian Congo'.

[5] Delmé-Radcliffe's Report, pp. 28–9.

[6] *Official Report of the British Section of the Uganda–Congo Boundary Commission, 1907–8*, H.M.S.O., London, 1909.

[7] Ibid., p. 4. For technical results of the commission's work see *Positions, Azimuths and Length of Sides of the Uganda–Congo Boundary Commission Triangulation (1907–1908) from 1° South to 2° North Latitude along the 30th Meridian East of Greenwich*, War Office, London, 1909. For geographical and technical accounts given by the senior British commissioner, see R. G. T. Bright, 'The Uganda–Congo Boundary Commission', *Geog. J.* 32 (1908), 488; 'Survey

The Brussels Conference, a most interesting example of diplomatic haggling over territory by colonial powers, need only be briefly summarized. Germany based her arguments partly on the desirability of employing natural features for boundaries instead of straight lines, partly on her insistence that the map attached to her 1884 convention with the International Association, and not the Congo State's declaration of 1885, governed her western boundary, and partly on a fantastic submission that a false treaty map had been malevolently substituted for the original to Germany's detriment. Britain claimed Mufumbiro on the basis of her 1890 agreement with Germany and argued that the Congo State, in accepting the limits of the British sphere in the Anglo-Congolese agreement of 1894, had automatically conceded Britain's rights over the disputed mountains. Belgium countered with the argument that Germany could not undertake to give Britain what she did not own. After three months of tedious diplomatic jousting Britain and Germany obtained most of what they demanded from Belgium.[1] The conference ended in May 1910 with the signing of separate boundary protocols by the three states.[2] Mount Sabinio in the Mufumbiro range was chosen to mark the new boundary tripoint of Uganda, German East Africa, and the Congo State. The 30th meridian, whose precise location had for so many years remained in doubt, was completely abandoned as a boundary and it no longer held legal or political significance.[3]

The Anglo-Belgian protocol of 14 May 1910 delimited Uganda's new western boundary.[4] In the absence of detailed topographical information the southerly portion, about 30 miles in length, from the tripoint at Mount Sabinio to Mount Nkabwa near the parallel of 1° south latitude, was defined as a straight line. The boundary then

and Exploration in the Ruwenzori and Lake Region, Central Africa', *Geog. J.* 34 (1909), 128; 'An Exploration in Central Equatorial Africa', *Journal of the African Society*, 9 (1910), 225.

[1] For accounts of the conference see 'Memorandum by Lieutenant-Colonel C. F. Close on the Agreement signed in Brussels on 14 May 1910, with reference to the Eastern Frontiers of the Congo and the Uganda–German East Africa Frontier', 25 May 1910. F.O. 367/175; Louis, op. cit., Ch. 8; Close, 'A Fifty-Years Retrospect', *E.S.R.* 2 (1933), 130, at pp. 135–7.

[2] For texts of the three protocols see 103 *B.F.S.P.* 372 (German–Belgian); 107 *B.F.S.P.* 348 (Anglo–Belgian); 107 *B.F.S.P.* 394 (Anglo–German).

[3] 'The new frontier, being based on natural features instead of on the 30th Meridian, will enable any future vagaries of that interesting nomad to be regarded with comparative indifference.' *The Times*, London, 26 May 1910.

[4] Agreement between Great Britain and Belgium Settling the Boundary between Uganda and the Congo.—Signed at Brussels, 14 May 1910. 107 *B.F.S.P.* 348.

followed natural features to and across Lake Edward, down the Semliki River to Lake Albert, and across this lake to and along the southern boundary of the Mahagi Strip as far as the Congo–Nile watershed. Northward from this point the watershed remained the boundary, in accordance with the Anglo-Congolese agreement of 1894. By this delimitation Britain acquired most of what she had sought in the Mufumbiro region, as well as the Kigezi district and a share of Lake Edward. Belgium made a territorial gain in the north, for in the section between the 30th meridian and the Mahagi Strip, the boundary, which had followed the watershed under the 1894 agreement, was shifted south-easterly to the Semliki River and the middle of Lake Albert. The reason for this alteration is of interest since it illustrates a situation where the prior selection of a natural feature proved to be an unsuitable boundary. Before this part of the frontier was mapped by the Uganda-Congo Commission of 1907–8, it had been thought that the watershed lay sufficiently far from Lake Albert to give Britain some sizeable territory on the north-western shore. In the course of its survey, however, the commission discovered that the watershed ran very close to the shore and that the 'much vaunted British territory on the west of Lake Albert was apparently reduced to a strip not a mile wide of rough, rocky ground falling sheer into the lake'.[1] Since this left 'only a cliff face to be administered by the British',[2] it was abandoned to Belgium and the line was drawn through the lake instead.

Provision was made in the protocol for the rectification by a mixed commission of the straight line boundary in the southern sector from Mount Sabinio to Mount Nkabwa, in order to make it conform to natural features. Those local inhabitants who wished to cross the new boundary so as to remain under their present administration were given six months to move themselves and their belongings, and the right to harvest their standing crops.

The Anglo-Belgian commission met at Mount Nkabwa in February 1910 to establish the boundary southward to Mount Sabinio and to map the frontier zone.[3] Minor deviations were made from the straight line described in the 1910 protocol and the boundary was demarcated mainly by natural features, though twelve boundary pillars were

[1] E. M. Jack, *On the Congo Frontier*, T. Fisher Unwin, London, 1914, p. 134.
[2] A. R. Hinks, 'Notes on the Technique of Boundary Delimitation', *Geog. J.* 58 (1921), 417, at p. 420.
[3] *Report on the Work of the British Section of the Anglo-German-Belgian Boundary Commission, 1911*, H.M.S.O., London, 1912.

erected. Only three months were required to complete this work, despite the difficult and mountainous nature of the country, and a protocol setting out the new boundary was signed by the commissioners at Busuenda on 4 May 1911.[1]

Perambulation of the boundary from Mount Sabinio to the mouth of the Semliki River in Lake Albert was carried out by British and Belgian political officers, contemporaneously with the work of the mixed commission. A few more pillars, additional to the twelve erected by the commission, were placed along the boundary between Sabinio and Lake Edward.[2] In accordance with its instructions the mixed commission completed its share of the demarcation at Mount Nkabwa, to the north of which the boundary had been delimited by the 1910 protocol in terms of natural topographical features. This northern part of the boundary was visited by two groups of officials, of which one group inspected and demarcated the sector from the north shore of Lake Edward to the source of the Chako River, while the other dealt with the portion from the source of the River Lamia to the mouth of the Semliki.[3] Although one might have thought that the rivers themselves would be readily identifiable as the boundary, the two demarcation groups apparently found it necessary to define their thalwegs by artificial marks, of which the two upper points were placed at the respective sources of the Chako and Lamia rivers.[4] Across the Ruwenzori, for a distance of about 30 miles, the boundary is delimited by a straight line drawn from each of the two river sources and intersecting at the summit of Margharita Peak which, at a height of nearly 17,000 feet above sea level, is the highest altitude in Uganda. Apart from the demarcation undertaken by these mixed parties of British and Belgian officials, their task included the proclamation of territorial transfers resulting from the new delimitation.

It remained to dispose of the Mahagi Strip, created in 1894 to allow the Congo State access to Lake Albert and no longer necessary now that the boundary passed through the lake itself. The intention, expressed in the 1910 Brussels protocol, was that the strip should revert to Britain, and its southern limit, between Lake Albert and the Congo–Nile watershed, therefore formed part of the new boundary. This southern limit was described in the protocol as a straight line extending from a point on the shore of Lake Albert immediately south of Mahagi Port to the nearest point on the watershed. It was later

[1] Thomas and Spencer, op. cit., p. 35.   [2] Ibid., p. 38.
[3] Ibid.   [4] Above, pp. 87–8.

decided that the arbitrary straight line should be replaced by a more realistic boundary, and a mixed commission was sent to the area at the end of 1912. The recommendations of the commission, submitted in May 1913, resulted in the handing over of a portion of the strip, including Mahagi Port, to Belgium.[1] Demarcation of the finally agreed boundary was completed by an Anglo-Belgian party which erected twenty-six boundary pillars and signed a protocol on 24 October 1915.[2]

Delimitation of the boundary across Lake Edward consists of a straight line drawn from the mouth of the River Ishasha on the southern shore to the mouth of the River Lubilia-Chako on the northern shore. In Lake Albert the boundary is drawn as a series of straight lines starting from the mouth of the Semliki River and passing successively through the points situated midway between the lake shores on the parallels of $1° 30'$, $1° 45'$, and $2° 00'$ north latitude, to a point midway between the shores on $2° 07'$ north latitude. From this latter point the boundary runs northward along the meridian for a distance of about 4·5 kilometres and thence westerly in a straight line to Boundary Pillar No. 1, erected on the western shore of the lake by the Mahagi demarcation party in October 1915. The use of artificial straight lines to define the boundaries in Lakes Edward and Albert has resulted in an approximately equal division of the lakes between the two adjoining states without the inconvenient employment of a theoretical median such as exists, for example, in Lake Tanganyika.[3]

A description of the entire boundary line from Mount Sabinio to the Congo–Nile watershed is contained in an Anglo-Belgian agreement signed in February 1915, but not ratified until 20 October 1919.[4] The basis of this description is the Anglo-Belgian protocol of 1910, with the modifications made by the mixed commissions of 1911 and 1913. Surprisingly, however, the boundary description does not refer to the three additional sets of demarcation undertaken by the

[1] 'Anglo-Egyptian Soudan and Belgian-Congo Boundary', a report by Captain A. M. Coode, the British commissioner, contained in a file entitled 'Uganda–Congo Boundary Delimitation Agreements and Correspondence 1910–1915', Catalogue No. 13024, Commonwealth Relations Office Library, Great Smith Street, London.

[2] Thomas and Spencer, op. cit., p. 37.   [3] Above, Ch. XIII.

[4] Agreement between the United Kingdom and Belgium respecting Boundaries in East Africa (Mount Sabinio to the Congo–Nile Watershed), Signed at London, 3 February 1915. (Ratifications exchanged at London, 20 October 1919). U.K. Treaty Series, 1920, No. 2, Cmd. 517.

political officers in 1911, nor does it include any reference to the twenty-six boundary pillars erected during the Mahagi demarcation of October 1915. While it is true that the latter demarcation was completed a few months after the signing of the Anglo-Belgian agreement, the long delay in ratification should have allowed ample time for the preparation of a new agreement incorporating the changes in a final description. Those concerned with tracing the legal history of the Uganda–Congo boundary details must therefore supplement their examination of the 1915 agreement with a tiresome and inconvenient reference to the four protocols describing the further demarcation that had all been completed long before the agreement was ratified.[1]

The description contained in the Anglo-Belgian agreement of 1915 ends at the knoll on the Congo–Nile watershed that forms the western terminal of the Mahagi delimitation, a point which was later marked by Boundary Pillar No. 26. Northward from this point the boundary follows the watershed, for a distance of about 90 miles, as far as the Sudan tripoint. This watershed section, which is the only part of the Uganda–Congo boundary that has survived unaltered from Britain's agreement with King Leopold in 1894,[2] appears never to have been artificially demarcated, though this is perhaps not a practical necessity. A local expert, referring to the watershed in 1937, stated that 'the boundary is mutually well known, for it follows for the most part the crest of a gentle treeless undulation, and the absence of monuments has given rise to no difficulty'.[3]

The Sudan tripoint was established in 1914, upon the transfer to Uganda of the southern part of the Lado Enclave, as the point on the Congo–Nile watershed which is nearest to the source of the Kaia (Kaya) River.[4]

---

[1] See, however, the boundary description given in Schedule 1 to *The Constitution of the Republic of Uganda*, 1967, which does include references to the later demarcation. Below, Appendix A, pp. 293–4.

[2] Above, p. 236.

[3] Thomas and Spencer, op. cit., p. 37.

[4] *The Uganda Official Gazette*, 30 May 1914, p. 255. See below, pp. 262, 294.

CHAPTER XVIII

Uganda–Kenya

THE present Uganda–Kenya boundary results from transfers of territory of which the most recent was made in 1926, but for many years the line was substantially undemarcated and it is still not completely marked. An anomalous situation arose in 1931 when the two neighbouring governments agreed that, for reasons of convenience, a portion of Kenya should be administered as part of Uganda. No formal transfer of territory was involved and the area concerned remained within the legal boundaries of Kenya. This arrangement continued until July 1970.

Unsuccessful proposals by Sir Harry Johnston and others for an East Africa Federation[1] resulted in the transfer on 1 April 1902[2] of the Eastern Province of Uganda to the East Africa Protectorate.[3] This transfer did not define precise boundaries and the line was delimited by a two-man commission which reported in July 1902. Although some effort was made to avoid tribal separation, the governing factor of the delimitation appears to have been the ease with which a particular area could be administered, and in several places the line disregarded tribal limits. North of Mount Elgon there was at that time no effective government administration and an arbitrary, provisional boundary was adopted, which ran from the mountain, by way of the Suam-Turkwell river to Lake Rudolf.[4] As a result of this delimitation, the area actually transferred in 1902 included not only Uganda's Eastern Province but also parts of its Central and Rudolf Provinces. Following the extension of administration, the provisional boundary was adjusted in 1910 by the transfer of additional territory from Uganda.[5]

[1] For historical accounts of the proposals see K. Ingham, 'Uganda's Old Eastern Province: The Transfer to East Africa Protectorate in 1902', *U.J.* 21 (1957), 41, and A. T. Matson, 'Uganda's Old Eastern Province and East Africa's Federal Capital', *U.J.* 22 (1958), 43.　　　　[2] Hertslet, i. 385.
[3] The East Africa Protectorate became the Colony and Protectorate of Kenya in 1920. See S.R. & O. 1920/2342; 1920/2343.
[4] G. Bennett, 'The Eastern Boundary of Uganda in 1902', *U.J.* 23 (1959), 69.
[5] Ibid., p. 71.

Finally, in 1926, the remainder of the Rudolf Province of Uganda was transferred to Kenya by Order in Council,[1] the schedule to which contains the following boundary description:

(1) Boundary From 1° South Latitude, Through Lake Victoria To The Mouth Of The Sio River.

Commencing in the waters of Lake Victoria on the parallel 1° south latitude, at a point due south of the westernmost point of Pyramid Island; thence the boundary follows a straight line due north to that point; thence continuing by a straight line northerly to the most westerly point of Ilemba Island; thence by a straight line, still northerly, to the most westerly point of Kiringiti Island; thence by a straight line, still northerly, to the most westerly point of Mageta Island; thence by a straight line north-westerly to the most southerly point of Sumba Island; thence by the south-western and western shores of that island to its most northerly point; thence by a straight line north-easterly to the centre of the mouth of the Sio River.

(2) Boundary From The Mouth Of The Sio River To The Summit Of Mount Elgon.

Commencing at the centre of the mouth of the Sio River the boundary follows the centre of the course of that river up-stream to its confluence with the Sango River; thence continuing by the centre of the course of the latter river up-stream to its source, marked by a cairn; thence by a straight line to that cairn, and onwards by a straight line north-easterly to a cairn on the abandoned road (now a footpath) from Busia to Mumeri's (Lukoli's); thence by the eastern edge of that road to its intersection with the Alupe River; thence by the centre of the course of that river down-stream to its confluence with the Kame River; thence by the centre of the course of the latter river to its intersection with the eastern boundary of the Mjanji–Busia–Mbale Road, such boundary being 100 feet distant from and parallel to the centre line of the said road; thence by that eastern boundary northerly to its intersection with the River Malawa (or Malaba); thence by the centre of the course of that river (also known as the Lwakaka or Lwagaga River) up-stream to its source; thence by a straight line north-easterly to the highest point of Mount Elgon.

(3) Boundary From The Summit Of Mount Elgon To Mount Zulia, On The Boundary Of The Anglo-Egyptian Sudan.

Commencing at the highest point of Mount Elgon, the boundary follows a straight line north-easterly to the point where the more north-westerly of the two streams forming the River Suam (Swam) or Turkwel emerges from

---

[1] The Kenya Colony and Protectorate (Boundaries) Order in Council, 1926. S.R. & O. 1926/1733.

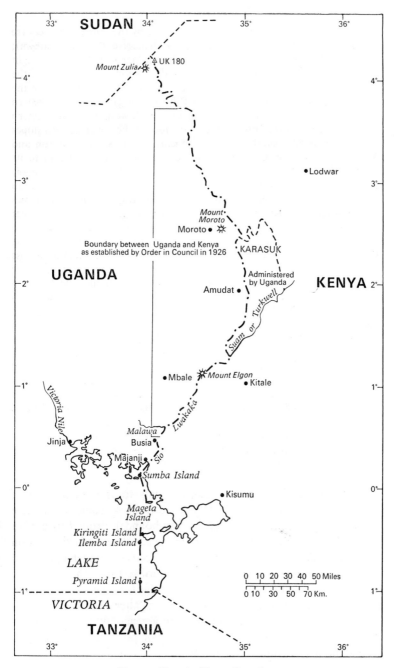

FIG. 13. Uganda–Kenya Boundary

the Crater of Mount Elgon; thence continuing by the centre of the course of that river down-stream to its confluence with the river Bukwa (Kibukwa); thence north-westerly following a line of cairns approximately in a straight line, and at first following a small natural depression, to the source of the Kanyerus River (marked by a large tree); thence following the foot of the eastern portion (Moriting) of Mount Riwa northerly to its north-eastern extremity; thence following a straight line north-westerly to the western extremity of Kassauna Hill; thence by the foot of the north-western slopes of that hill north-easterly to the confluence of the streams Maron and Maragat; thence by the centre of the course of the latter stream to its source; thence by a straight line to the summit of the hill Murogogoi; thence along the highest points of the rocky ridge (forming a continuation of Mount Riwa and known collectively by the Karamojans as Kogipie) known severally as Karenyang, Muruebu, Kogipie (Karamojong) or Sagat (Suk), and Sagat (Karamojong) or Kogipie (Suk) to Sagat Hill; thence in a generally northerly direction by straight lines to Korkurao Hill, to the hillock known as Kokas, to the small hillock known as Lokwamor, across the Kunyao River to Nong'alitaba Hill, across the Kanyangareng River to the hill known as Kauluk, to the hillock Morumeri, to the hillock known as Sumemerr (known to the Suk as Sumaremar) and thence to the western-most of the small hillocks known as Lewi Lewi; thence continuing by a straight line, still northerly to the foot of the western spur of the hill known as Aoruma, and by the foot of that spur to a beacon; thence north-westerly by a straight line to a beacon at the highest point of the ridge known as Kariemakaris; thence northerly by a straight line to the hillock called Lokuka; thence by a straight line to the top of the pass known as Kara-muroi (Suk) or Karithakol (Karamojong); thence down the centre of that pass to the base of the Turkana Escarpment; thence the boundary follows the base of that escarpment in a generally north-westerly direction (following the base of the spurs known as Yelele Hill, Sogwas Hill and Ougume Hill) to Mount Zulia, and the base of that mountain to its intersection with the boundary of the Anglo-Egyptian Sudan.

Thus the Order in Council, 1926, not only transferred the rest of Rudolf Province to Kenya but included in its schedule a complete description of the entire Uganda–Kenya boundary from Tanganyika to the Sudan. No map is referred to in the schedule, and examination of the text shows that its interpretation depends very much upon local knowledge. While, for example, in the third sector of the boundary, an elaborate identification of the rocky ridge forming a continuation of Mount Riwa is provided by a variety of alternative local names, the boundary then proceeds vaguely 'in a generally northerly direction by straight lines'. Other examples of poor definition can be found in the schedule, which nevertheless remains the only legal description of the boundary.[1] Agreement with Kenya regarding the interpretation of the boundary across the crater of Mount Elgon was reached in 1936.[2]

Boundary demarcation was not undertaken for a number of years, and even by 1938 it consisted only of a few beacons near Busia.[3] Demarcation of the boundary from the Sio River to Mount Elgon was subsequently completed. The most recent work appears to have been carried out in 1959–60[4] when 180 pillars were erected along that part of the boundary defined by the base of the Turkana escarpment, that is to say, the final course described in Part 3 of the schedule. The last boundary pillar (UK 180) was in fact deliberately placed about 4 miles to the south of the Sudan tripoint, since the precise location of the Sudanese boundary at this point is still undetermined.

By an agreement made in December 1931, between the Governments of Uganda and Kenya, a mountainous region of Kenya known as Karasuk passed to Ugandan administration. Karasuk has an approximate area of 1,800 square miles and is bounded on its eastern side by a line which follows the Suam-Turkwell River as far as the foot of the Turkana Gorge, and thence along the base of the Turkana Escarpment to Moroto Mountain.[5] Its western limit is the international boundary, as defined in the schedule to the Order in Council of 1926, given above.

The inhabitants of Karasuk are usually referred to as the Suk tribe, although the correct anthropological name, and the one which the tribal members use themselves, is Pokot.[6]

Karasuk formed an administrative part of Upe County in the Karamoja District of Uganda, a district peopled mainly by the Karamojong. Over the years this region has been the scene of violence and raiding, in which the Karamojong have clashed not only with the Suk but also with other tribes, such as the Turkana, living on the Kenya side of the international boundary. The Karamojong and the Suk

[1] See, however, 'The Boundary of Uganda', contained in Schedule 1 to *The Constitution of The Republic of Uganda*, 1967, which gives map references and a detailed description of the 1959–60 demarcation. Below, Appendix A.

[2] Thomas and Spencer, op. cit., p. 39.

[3] Ibid.

[4] 'Report on Cartographic Activity in Kenya, 1950–1963', United Nations Regional Cartographic Conference for Africa, E/CN. 14/CART/4, E/CONF. 43/4, p. 4.

[5] J. Brasnett, 'The Karasuk Problem', *U.J.* 22 (1958), 113.

[6] N. Dyson-Hudson, 'The Karamojong and the Suk', *U.J.* 22 (1958), 173.

have ethnological similarities and both are pastoral people, but they are alien to each other in custom and social organization. A major source of friction is the use of water holes and pasture in Karasuk, and a constant westerly pressure by the Suk has resulted in the Karamojong having been pushed out of what they regarded as their traditional dry-season grazing grounds. The Suk, in turn, appear also to have been subjected to territorial pressure from the Turkana. In such a large and remote area, inhabited by nomadic tribes, the idea of a rigid boundary is completely unknown. Territorial limits are considered to be flexible and are apt to change according to ecological circumstances.[1]

The adoption in 1926 of a new inter-territorial boundary that extended from Mount Riwa to the Turkana Escarpment allowed the Suk more land than they had previously occupied, but during the years 1923–8 drought, aggravated by an invasion of locusts, encouraged them to trespass even beyond the new boundary. In 1928 a proposal was made for the transfer to Kenya of that part of Uganda lying between the legal boundary and the recently constructed road from Kitale to Lodwar. This suggestion was resisted by the Karamojan administration which felt that the Karamojong, who as a result of the 1926 transfer had now lost access to the Turkwell River, could not afford to give up any further grazing area.

A meeting held in December 1931, between the neighbouring Provincial Commissioners of Uganda's Eastern Province and Kenya's Turkana Province, produced the recommendation that the administrative boundary should revert to the Turkwell, that is to say, where the inter-territorial boundary had been prior to 1926. The main reasons for this proposal were to allow the Suk access to grazing and water in Karamoja, to bring the troublesome border area under one administration, to control inter-tribal raiding and to avoid the difficulty that had been found in recognizing and administering the 1926 boundary. It was recommended further that this arrangement should be given a trial period of two or three years, after which the problem could be reconsidered.[2] The administration of Karasuk thus passed to Uganda in August 1932 but no alteration was made to the *de jure* territorial boundary. Even after this new administrative arrangement had been made, the Suk continued their westward pressure, the main

[1] N. Dyson-Hudson, *Karimojong Politics*, Clarendon Press, Oxford, 1966, p. 148.
[2] *Kenya Land Commission Evidence*, Nairobi, 1933, vol. 2, p. 1754.

incentive for which was the need for greater grazing land for their increasingly large numbers of cattle. The present limits of Suk penetration were reached about 1937.

Inter-tribal relations in Karamoja are marked by hostility, and reports of cattle raiding, often involving loss of life, are frequent. Erosion caused by overgrazing, and a substantial increase in Karamojong stock have worsened an already difficult situation. A special committee appointed by the Uganda Government reported in 1961 that the problem facing Karamoja is a virtual breakdown of law and order,[1] and it is evident from recent parliamentary debates that the district still lacks an effective administration.[2] The cause of the disorder is summed up by the 1961 committee as the desire of the inhabitants, whose emotional life is intricately bound up with cows, to acquire cattle by any means and at any cost. The problem does not consist merely of the urge for individual economic gain, but has three underlying social causes. First is the high prestige associated with the possession of a large number of cattle, and the glorification of the homicide connected with their acquisition. Secondly, the fact that a man's social standing is enhanced by his having a number of wives, whose bride price is payable only in cows, is a further incentive to cattle raiding.[3] Thirdly, ancient disputes over grazing grounds and watering-places demand the continuation of hostilities against traditional enemies and the seizure of their cattle.[4]

Cattle raiding and inter-tribal warfare still persist in the Karamoja area, both within the district itself and between neighbouring tribes on each side of the international boundary. Recent statements in the Uganda National Assembly suggested that attempts were being made by the governments of Uganda and Kenya to find a solution to the problem. It seemed likely that some adjustment would have to be

[1] *Report of the Karamoja Security Committee*, Govt. Printer, Entebbe, 1961, para. 10.

[2] For Ministerial assertions to the contrary see Uganda Parliamentary Debates, vol. 66, p. 1328, 9 December 1966, and p. 1364, 12 December 1966. Volumes 66 and 70 of the Debates contain exhaustive discussion concerning the incidence of cattle raiding and inter-tribal warfare affecting Karamoja.

[3] A Ministerial suggestion that the high bride price (between 20 and 100 cows for a wife) could be reduced by local by-law was met with the argument that a previous unsuccessful attempt of this kind had merely resulted in a black market. Uganda Parliamentary Debates, vol. 66, pp. 1369–70.

[4] The conflict is complicated by the fact that the eight tribes in Karamoja have created between themselves and with certain neighbouring tribes in Kenya a 'labyrinth of alliances and enmities'. *Report of the Karamoja Security Committee*, paras. 13 and 14.

made to the *de jure* boundary to make it coincide with the *de facto* limits of Ugandan administration which, as mentioned earlier, were intended in 1932 to be established as a provisional measure only. By an agreement made with Uganda, however, the Kenya Government resumed administration of Karasuk (Karapokot) in July 1970. Both dominant tribes in the area will be permitted, as before, to cross the border to graze and water their cattle.[1] It appears to be recognized by both governments that the legal boundary between Karasuk and Uganda remains as defined by the Order in Council of 1926. At present this boundary sector is not demarcated.

[1] *East African Standard*, 31 July 1970.

CHAPTER XIX

Uganda–Sudan

WHEN Britain and Germany delimited their East African spheres of influence in 1890, the northern boundary of that part of the British sphere now known as Uganda was not precisely determined. At that time the name Uganda connoted only the Kingdom of Buganda, on whose northern and eastern flanks lay her tributaries of Bunyoro and Busoga. North of these traditional kingdoms was a vaguely defined region that formerly had been regarded by Egypt as part of her administrative province of Equatoria.[1] Egypt's claim to this amorphous area, whether of substance or of shadow, ceased to have practical meaning when Mahdist forces captured Khartoum in 1885 and overran the greater part of the Sudan. The remaining vestiges of the Khedive's control in southern Equatoria disappeared in 1889 when the provincial governor, Emin Pasha, was persuaded to evacuate.

Anglo-German rivalry for control of the territory lying west and north of Lake Victoria ended in German acceptance of a British sphere stretching northward from the parallel of 1° south latitude. Exactly how far north this sphere penetrated was not decided, but it appeared from the 1890 agreement to extend as far as the fluid and uncertain limits of the 'confines of Egypt'. Even when Britain and Egypt defeated the Mahdists at Omdurman in 1898 and established a condominium over the Sudan in the following year, the southern boundary with Uganda was still left indeterminate. Two reasons can be suggested for the lack of precision in delimiting this boundary sector. First, both Uganda and the Sudan were then under British control, for while it is true that a condominium existed in the Sudan, there is no doubt as to which state was the senior and dominant partner.[2] Politically, therefore, an exact boundary between the two

[1] Bunyoro was proclaimed an Egyptian province in 1872 by Sir Samuel Baker, but by 1880 it had been given up and the Victoria Nile, at the north-eastern end of Lake Albert, formed the Khedive's southern boundary. See Sir Harold MacMichael, *The Anglo–Egyptian Sudan*, Faber & Faber, London, 1934, pp. 37, 42.

[2] 'Egypt's only practical function in the Sudan turned out to be that of carrying the deficit on its budget.' G. N. Sanderson, *England, Europe and the Upper Nile, 1882–1899*, Edinburgh University Press, 1965, p. 367.

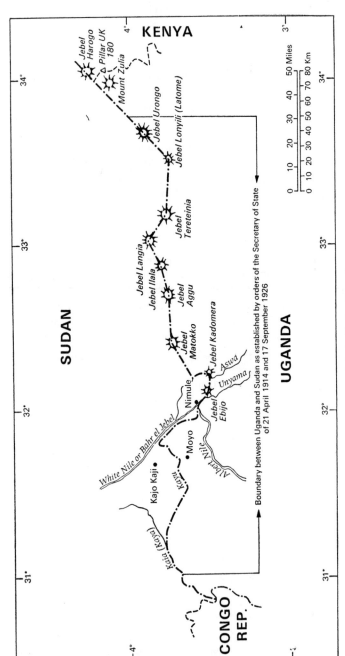

FIG. 14. Uganda–Sudan Boundary

administrative units was of no immediate importance to Britain. Secondly, the border area was hostile and difficult to govern, and its effective control by the British administration did not commence until about 1910. Despite early and inconclusive attempts by Britain to establish the northern limit of her sphere along the parallels of first 10°, and later 5°, north latitude, it was not until 1914 that a clearly defined Uganda–Sudan boundary emerged.

The boundary between the British sphere of influence and the Congo State was delimited by an agreement made between Britain and King Leopold II in May 1894.[1] This agreement also created certain leases, the details of which were given in an earlier chapter.[2] One of these leases was granted by Britain to Leopold, for the duration of his reign as sovereign of the Congo State, over the region lying to the north of Lake Albert between the Nile and the Congo–Nile watershed, and bounded respectively on the west and north by the meridian of 30° east longitude and the parallel of 10° north latitude. It will be recalled that, as a result of French pressure, Leopold was obliged to enter into an agreement with France whereby his enjoyment of this lease was restricted to that portion lying east of the 30th meridian and south of the parallel of 5° 30′ north latitude, and that this area became known as the Lado Enclave.[3] Following the removal of French influence in the upper Nile, fresh negotiations commenced between Britain and Leopold concerning the leased territories. The matter was not settled until 1906 when, by an agreement made with Britain, Leopold relinquished the greater part of the leasehold interest acquired by the Congo State in May 1894 and retained only the lease of the Lado Enclave for the duration of his reign as sovereign of the Congo State. By the terms of this new agreement, the Lado Enclave was required to be handed over to the Sudan Government within six months of the termination of the king's occupation.[4] Leopold died in December 1909, and the Lado Enclave

[1] Agreement between Great Britain and His Majesty King Leopold II, Sovereign of the Independent State of the Congo, relating to the Spheres of Influence of Great Britain and the Independent State of the Congo in East and Central Africa. Signed at Brussels, 12 May 1894. Hertslet, ii. 578.

[2] Above, Ch. XVII.

[3] Boundary Agreement between France and the Congo Free State. 14 August 1894. Hertslet, ii. 569.

[4] Agreement between Great Britain and the Independent State of the Congo, modifying the Agreement signed at Brussels, 12 May 1894. Signed at London, 9 May 1906. Hertslet, ii. 584.

passed in June 1910 to the Anglo-Egyptian authorities who attached it to the Mongalla Province of Sudan.[1]

The transfer of the Lado Enclave from the Congo to Sudan created a wedge of Sudanese territory that penetrated deep into Uganda. The southern part of the Lado Enclave was not only a considerable distance from the nearest administrative station in Sudan, but its rugged physical nature, marked by parallel ridges and ravines, running from east to west, meant that administration from the north was difficult to undertake. On the other hand, the area could be approached more easily from Uganda, by means of the tributaries that flowed eastward from the Enclave to the Nile. Partly for this reason, and owing also to the increasing extension of effective administration in Sudan, it was proposed that the southern part of the Lado Enclave should be transferred to Uganda and that, in return, a portion of northern Uganda should go to Sudan.[2]

Adjustment of the boundary was agreed to in principle by the governments of Uganda and Sudan in 1912, and in the following year a mixed boundary commission was appointed to examine the ground and submit recommendations for the new line. With respect to the area west of the Nile the commissioners were instructed that Uganda should take over that portion of the Lado Enclave lying south of a line running from the Nile–Unyama confluence along the northern boundary of the Lugware tribe to the Kaia River, and thence along that river to the Congo boundary. Delimitation of the proposed boundary along exact tribal limits depended upon detailed local knowledge, yet the commission made no visit to the area. Recognizing that a closer investigation would be necessary before the boundary could be finally established, the commissioners proposed a provisional line, with the recommendation that this should be adjusted later by officials who were more familiar with local conditions.[3] Despite its supposed provisional nature, however, the boundary recommended by the commission was adopted, and its description is given in an Order of the Secretary of State, dated 21 April 1914, which transferred the southern part of the Lado Enclave (West Nile District) to Uganda.

A line beginning at the intersection of the thalweg of the river Bahr-el-Jebel or White Nile with the thalweg of the river Unyama; thence in a

---

[1] Collins, 'The Transfer of the Lado Enclave . . .', p. 193.

[2] C. H. Stigand, *Equatoria: The Lado Enclave*, Constable, London, 1923, p. 4; Collins, 'Sudan–Uganda Boundary Rectification . . .', p. 140.

[3] Collins, ibid., p. 144.

straight line due west to the bottom of the foothills of the escarpment running north-west from Jebel Elengua; thence following the bottom of the foothills of this escarpment in a north-westerly direction, or such a line as shall exclude the riverain people below Nimule, to the westernmost point of the foothills; and thence following a straight line due northwest to the thalweg of the Khor Kayu (Aju); thence following the thalweg of the Khor Kayu (Aju) upwards to its intersection with the thalweg of the Khor Nyaura (Kigura); thence following the thalweg of the Khor Nyaura (Kigura) upwards to its source; thence following the southern boundary of the Kuku tribe to the thalweg of the river Kaia; thence following the thalweg of the river Kaia upwards to its source, in a re-entrant of the Congo–Nile watershed about 9 miles west-north-west of the village Kegui and about 11 miles south of the village Bangali; thence following a straight line to the nearest point on the Congo–Nile watershed. . . .[1]

A number of unsatisfactory features appear in this description. First, the Nyawa (Khor Nyaura) is not a tributary of the Khor Kayo (Kayu), nor does it flow from the source assumed by the commission. Secondly, a description in terms of the 'southern boundary of the Kuku tribe' is meaningless unless it is supplemented by identifiable geographical reference points. Strictly interpreted, this portion of the boundary description is a flexible, uncertain line whose location is susceptible of variation in accordance with tribal movement. Thirdly, it is not clear why Sudan retained the strip between the left bank of the Nile and the foothills of the escarpment. Even Stigand, who had a close knowledge of the southern part of the Lado Enclave and on whose advice the commission's recommendations were, in part, based, can only say that Sudan retained the strip 'so as to have both banks in its possession'.[2]

The passage of time served only to make permanent what had been intended merely as a provisional boundary. Attempts to remove anomalies in the boundary description were made by the Uganda Government in 1930 and 1932 but these were coupled with a request that the boundary along the foot of the escarpment be shifted eastward to the Nile and they proved unsuccessful.[3] The exact location of the mysterious southern boundary of the Kuku tribe was the subject of prolonged discussion between the two neighbouring administrations, and the problem is said to have been settled by compromise in 1936.[4]

[1] Order of the Secretary of State, 21 April 1914. *The Uganda Official Gazette*, 30 May 1914. G.N. No. 241 of 1914, p. 255.
[2] Stigand, op. cit., p. 98.   [3] Collins, op. cit., pp. 144–5.
[4] Thomas and Spencer, op. cit., p. 39.

A recent description of Uganda's boundary with Sudan west of
the Nile, contained in the 1967 Uganda Constitution, indicates certain changes in definition.[1] No reference to the limits of the Kuku
tribe appears in this description and the boundary is partially redefined by straight lines marked by boundary beacons. The riverain
strip on the left bank of the Nile remains part of Sudan. It seems
likely that the amended description given in the Uganda Constitution represents the result of compromise agreements made with the
Sudan administration prior to independence. It must be stressed,
however, that no formal amendment to the description contained in
the 1914 Order has yet been made.

The Uganda–Sudan–Congo tripoint is described as the point on
the Congo–Nile watershed nearest to the source of the Kaia (Kaya)
River. It appears that the exact location of the tripoint has never
been demarcated, but it is stated to lie on the watershed about
0·3 kilometres to the south of the source of the Kaia.[2]

East of the Nile, the 1913 boundary commission was required to
provide recommendations for the delimitation of a line running from
the Nile–Unyama confluence to Sanderson Gulf in Lake Rudolf,
which at that time formed the eastern border of Uganda. That portion of Uganda lying to the north of this line was to be transferred to
Sudan in exchange for the southern part of the Lado Enclave. The
recommendations of the commission in this section, unlike those
relating to the delimitation of the Lado Enclave boundary, were based
on actual visit and investigation, although at the eastern end of the
line, along what is now the Kenya–Sudan boundary, the commission's
work was far from satisfactory and it has produced difficulties which
remain to this day.[3] Working eastward from the Nile, the commissioners examined tribal limits and natural features, in an attempt to
establish a boundary that would not cut across existing tribal divisions. When they reached Madial, further joint investigation was
found to be impossible and the Sudan party proceeded alone as far
as Jebel Mogila.[4]

The territory lying to the north of the line recommended by the
commission was also transferred by the Order of the Secretary of
State that dealt with the transfer to Uganda of the southern part of

[1] *The Constitution of the Republic of Uganda*, 1967. Schedule 1, p. 85. Below,
Appendix A, p. 295.
[2] Below, Appendix A, p. 294.   [3] Above, Ch. X.
[4] Above, pp. 129–31.

the Lado Enclave. The relevant part of the boundary description contained in this Order[1] extends south-westerly from Jebel Mogila:

. . . thence following a straight line in a south-westerly direction to the southernmost point at the bottom of Jebel Harogo; thence following a straight line to the summit of Jebel Latome; thence following a straight line to the northernmost point of the northernmost crest of the long spur running north-west from Jebel Tereteinia; thence following a straight line to the summit of Jebel Tiya; thence following a straight line to the southern summit of Jebel Lanhia; thence following a straight line to the summit of Jebel Ilala; thence following a straight line to the summit of Jebel Aggu; thence following a straight line to the northernmost point of the bottom of Jebel Matokko (Batogo or Atokko); thence following a straight line in a south-westerly direction towards the village Lokai as far as the intersection of this line with the thalweg of the river Assua; thence following the thalweg of the river Assua upwards to its intersection with a straight line from the summit of Jebel Ebijo to the summit of Jebel Kadomera; thence following a straight line to the summit of Jebel Ebijo; thence following a straight line due west to the thalweg of the river Unyama; thence following the thalweg of the river Unyama downwards to its intersection with the thalweg of the Bahr el Jebel.

Although this boundary was delimited with greater care than that in the Lado Enclave it did not escape criticism. Stigand, a former Governor of Mongalla Province of Sudan, wrote in 1923: '. . . the boundary on the east bank (of the Nile) has been delimited by arbitrary straight lines severing villages from their water and cultivation and chiefs from their dependants. As most of the country thus dealt with was perfectly well known, there appears to be no justification in following such ancient methods of delimitation.'[2] In 1914, however, the description was probably considered adequate to define a boundary dividing two territories which, in effect, both fell under British jurisdiction. It should also be remembered that there was no effective administration on either side of the line in the eastern section of the border area until about 1926, so that the need for a more suitable boundary definition can scarcely have been felt before that time. Nevertheless, no excuse can be offered for the continued retention of an unsatisfactory boundary, one practical effect of which was the severance of the Uganda Acholi from their kinsmen in Sudan. A minor rectification of the eastern boundary occurred in 1926 when a portion of Uganda in the Tereteinia area (Chua District) was

---

[1] Above, p. 261, n. 1.   [2] Stigand, op. cit., p. 4.

transferred to Sudan. The reason for this transfer was partly to reunite members of the Lango tribe in Uganda with those in Sudan and also to facilitate the control of sleeping sickness.[1] The area was formally transferred to Sudan by an Order of the Secretary of State, dated 17 September 1926,[2] and consisted of that part of Uganda lying to the north of

A line beginning at the point on the line described in the Order of the Secretary of State dated the 21st of April, 1914, hereinbefore mentioned named in that Order as the southern summit of Jebel Langia:[3] thence following a straight line to the most south-easterly foothills of Jebel Tere-teinia: thence following a straight line in an easterly direction to Jebel Lonyili:[4] thence following a straight line to the point on the line described in the Order of the Secretary of State dated the 21st of April, 1914, hereinbefore mentioned named in that Order as the southernmost point at the bottom of Jebel Harogo.

Earlier in the same year, 1926, the Rudolf Province of Uganda was transferred to Kenya by Order in Council, thereby giving Kenya a common boundary with Sudan.[5] The northern extremity of the new Uganda–Kenya boundary is described in the Order in Council as running from the base of Mount Zulia to its intersection with the boundary of Sudan. Along the most easterly course of the Uganda–Sudan boundary, that is to say, the straight line running north-easterly from Jebel Lonyili (Latome) to Jebel Harogo, demarcation by arti-ficial marks has been undertaken as far eastward as Jebel Urongo. The Uganda–Kenya–Sudan tripoint is said to be a point north of Mount Zulia lying approximately 31·5 miles north-easterly from Jebel Urongo.[6] Joint demarcation of the Uganda–Kenya boundary in 1959–60 also stopped short of the Sudanese boundary, the last pillar being placed about 4 miles south of the theoretical line. The exact location on the ground of this tripoint, therefore, like that on the Congo boundary, still remains uncertain.

[1] MacMichael, op. cit., p. 184 (footnote).
[2] Order of the Secretary of State, 17 September 1926. *The Uganda Official Gazette*, 15 November 1926. G.N. No. 509 of 1926, p. 403.
[3] The 1914 Order, as printed in the *Uganda Gazette*, refers to 'Jebel Lanhia'.
[4] Also known as Jebel Latome, and referred to by that name in the 1914 Order.
[5] The Kenya Colony and Protectorate (Boundaries) Order in Council. S.R. & O. 1926/1733.
[6] *Uganda Constitution*, Schedule 1, p. 86. Below, Appendix A, p. 295.

CHAPTER XX

Uganda–Tanzania and Uganda–Rwanda

UGANDA'S boundaries with her two southern neighbours, Tanzania and Rwanda, coincide with the former Uganda–German East Africa boundary and, for historical reasons, it is convenient to consider them together. Despite their common origin, however, the two boundaries present a marked and interesting contrast. The Uganda–Rwanda section is defined almost entirely by physical features and therefore exhibits the characteristics of a natural boundary. The original selection of these features, however, depended less upon the search for desirable boundary criteria than upon Britain's ability to enforce her political claims in an area to which her title was at best dubious. Had natural boundaries, *per se*, been a governing consideration then the principle should have applied also to the Uganda–Tanzania section but here, as will be shown, a classic example of bad delimitation has resulted in a boundary which is not only anomalous but approaches the absurd.

In 1886 Britain and Germany delimited the boundary between their respective spheres of influence in East Africa by a line extending from the Indian Ocean coast to the eastern shore of Lake Victoria.[1] This line, with later modifications, became the boundary between Kenya and Tanzania and is considered elsewhere,[2] but it provides a convenient starting-point for the present discussion. By this Anglo-German agreement, the western terminal of the boundary between the two spheres is described as 'a point on the eastern side of Lake Victoria Nyanza which is intersected by the 1st degree of south latitude'.

It was agreed by Britain and Germany that each party would respect the other's sphere of influence and refrain from territorial acquisition across the delimited line. German apprehension that the

---

[1] Agreement between the British and German Governments, respecting the Sultanate of Zanzibar and the opposite East African Mainland, and their Spheres of Influence. 29 October–1 November 1886. Hertslet, iii. 882. See above, p. 137, n. 2, regarding German retention until 1890 of Witu and other territories to the north of the delimited line.

[2] Above, Ch. XI.

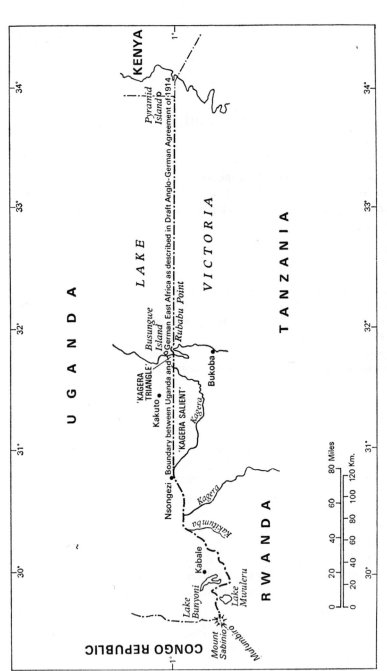

FIG. 15. Uganda–Tanzania and Uganda–Rwanda Boundary

Emin Pasha relief expedition led by Stanley in 1887 might be utilized for the establishment of a British protectorate to the west of the German sphere resulted in a further agreement between the two states in which Britain reassured Germany as to the object of Stanley's expedition and undertook: '. . . to discourage British annexations in the rear of the German sphere, on the understanding that the German Government would equally discourage German annexations in the rear of the British sphere'.[1] The absence in either of these agreements of any provision for the delimitation of the western boundaries of the two spheres subsequently led to competing claims concerning the ill-defined hinterland region between Lakes Victoria and Tanganyika. In support of these claims two rival principles, the hinterland doctrine and the theory of effective occupation, were pressed into service by Germany and Britain respectively.[2] Britain's attitude towards the hinterland doctrine was expressed in 1890 by Lord Salisbury when he said:

> The claims of the German Government are based chiefly on the contention that where one Power occupies the coast, another Power may not, without consent, occupy unclaimed regions in its rear. It would be too much to affirm that this contention is entirely destitute of support from international usage, but its operation cannot be unlimited, while the boundaries within which it should be restricted are very hard to draw. The original contention of the German Government I understand to have been that the whole of the territory between their sphere of influence and the Congo State naturally fell to them as the 'Hinterland' of their own possessions. This would have carried the German boundary along latitude 1° south on the north, and on latitude 11° south on the south, up to the frontier of the Congo State.[3]

The theory of effective occupation, on the other hand, is exemplified by the statement made by the British Government in 1887.[4] In Britain's view, the elements of effective occupation consisted not merely of the prior discovery of a region but also of colonizing factors such as the establishment of commercial stations and missions, and the conclusion of treaties with local tribes.

British commercial pressure for a territorial link between her East

---

[1] Agreement between Great Britain and Germany, respecting the Discouragement of Annexations in Rear of their Spheres of Influence in East Africa. July 1887. Hertslet, iii. 888.
[2] See also, above, Ch. XIV, p. 176.
[3] Salisbury to Malet, 14 June 1890. F.O.C.P. 6146, p. 29. F.O. 403/142.
[4] Above, p. 30.

and Central African possessions was resisted by Germany who strongly opposed the creation of a British wedge that would separate her own East African coastal territory from the Congo State. Support for the British claim rested, in part, on treaties alleged to have been made between Stanley and local rulers in the area lying between Lake Victoria and the northern end of Lake Tanganyika.[1] Such treaties, even though they had not as yet been adopted by the British Government, represented claims to territory which it would be 'scarcely permissible' to transfer to Germany.[2] But even Stanley himself, a leading proponent of British imperial expansion, conceded that he had made no treaties south of 'Mount Mfumbiro',[3] a mountain which, as will be seen later, proved to be a complicating factor in the final boundary settlement.

The effect of the two Anglo-German agreements of 1886 and 1887, together with the absence of local treaties, weakened Britain's claim to the disputed region behind the German sphere. At the same time, Germany, having prevented the creation of the British wedge, was prepared to compromise her own claims in the north and, after a period of negotiation in which the cession by Britain to Germany of Heligoland, a barren but strategic island in the North Sea, was used as a bargaining counter, the hinterland boundary was defined by an agreement made between the two states in 1890. The relevant portion of the boundary enclosing the German sphere of influence in East Africa is described in Article 1 of this agreement as commencing at:

. . . the point on the eastern side of Lake Victoria Nyanza which is intersected by the 1st parallel of south latitude; thence, crossing the lake on that parallel, it follows the parallel to the frontier of the Congo Free State, where it terminates.

Mount Mfumbiro

It is, however, understood that, on the west side of the lake, the sphere does not comprise Mount Mfumbiro; if that mountain shall prove to lie to the south of the selected parallel, the line shall be deflected so as to exclude it, but shall, nevertheless, return so as to terminate at the above-named point.[4]

[1] The genuineness and validity of these treaties is questioned by Sir John Gray, 'Early Treaties in Uganda, 1888–1891', *U.J.* 12 (1948), 25.

[2] W. R. Louis, 'The Anglo-German Hinterland Settlement of 1890 and Uganda', *U.J.* 27 (1963), 71, at p. 72.

[3] Ibid., p. 72. There is no documentary evidence to support Stanley's claim that he acquired treaty rights to Mufumbiro itself.

[4] Agreement between the British and German Governments, respecting Africa and Heligoland. Berlin, 1 July 1890. Hertslet, iii. 899.

By this agreement, therefore, the new western terminal of the boundary between the British and German spheres was the point at which the parallel of 1° south latitude intersected the eastern boundary of the Congo State. The Congo State boundary at this point had been previously defined, in 1885,[1] as the meridian of the 30th degree of longitude east of Greenwich. This meridian was subsequently confirmed as the boundary by an agreement between Britain and King Leopold II in 1894,[2] and by a declaration made by the Congo State later in the same year.[3]

Despite the adoption in 1890 of the parallel of 1° south latitude as the dividing line between the two spheres, a number of German incursions were made into British territory, and in 1900 a German post was established near Kakuto, about 9 miles to the north of the boundary.[4] The need for a physically demarcated line soon became apparent and a mixed Anglo-German boundary commission was appointed in 1902 to survey the section of the boundary from the western side of Lake Victoria to the 30th meridian of longitude. The mixed commission was required to erect boundary pillars along the parallel of 1° south latitude and also to make a topographic survey of a strip of territory, about 10 miles on each side of the parallel, stretching from the western shore of the lake as far as the Congo boundary. In order to establish on the ground the western terminal of the boundary, the commission had to determine the precise location of the 30th meridian. Determination of longitude is essentially a comparison of time differences and before the days of radio a common method of making such comparisons was by an exchange of telegraphic signals. Starting from a point at Mombasa whose latitude and longitude had been previously fixed, the commission attempted to establish telegraphic communication with Entebbe. The British party at Entebbe failed to exchange signals with their German colleagues at Mombasa, owing to unfavourable weather conditions and the poor condition of the western section of the line. The difficulties encountered by the commission in undertaking this work are well illustrated by the remarks of the British Commissioner, Lt.-Col. Delmé-Radcliffe.[5] After

---

[1] Hertslet, ii. 552; above, Ch. XVII, p. 233.
[2] Hertslet, ii. 578; above, Ch. XVII, p. 236.
[3] Hertslet, ii. 557; above, Ch. XVII, p. 239.
[4] Thomas and Spencer, op. cit., p. 12. See also Sir John Gray, 'Anglo-German Relations in Uganda, 1890–1892', *Journal of African History*, 1 (1960), 281.
[5] 'We worked night after night, but it was found impossible to get signals through on the section Port Florence–Entebbe. The line was in every way

completing a satisfactory exchange of signals between Mombasa and Port Florence (Kisumu), the longitude was carried, by means of triangulation, to a point near the mouth of the Kagera River on the western lake shore, and thence to the 30th meridian.

It will be remembered that the Anglo-German agreement of 1890 specifically provided that, if necessary, the boundary along the parallel of 1° south latitude should be deflected southward in order to exclude 'Mount Mfumbiro' from the German sphere. The agreement was drawn up in the light of imperfect geographical knowledge and it was then assumed that the mountain lay to the east of the 30th meridian. The object of this rather curious provision was not, as has sometimes been assumed,[1] to compensate Britain for agreeing to the inclusion of Mount Kilimanjaro within the German sphere. Instead, it represented German acceptance of the British claim to Mufumbiro, based on the treaties said to have been made by Stanley.[2] Subsequent British fears that Mufumbiro might in fact be found to lie to the west of the 30th meridian, and therefore outside the limits of their sphere as defined by the 1890 agreement, were realized when the mixed demarcation commission reached the Congo boundary. Delmé-Radcliffe, the British commissioner, reported that Mufumbiro was now 'shown to lie considerably to the west of the 30th meridian, and therefore cannot be claimed directly as lying within the British sphere'.[3] In other words, Mufumbiro was situated within the limits of the Congo State, as previously recognized by Britain in 1894.[4] Since the German commissioner refused to extend the survey

unsuitable. Originally only a telephone line, it was incompletely insulated. Earth currents continually affected the wire. Every thunderstorm in the neighbourhood, also, and an incessant crackling in the instrument, indicated lightning somewhere on the line. Besides this, white ants destroyed the poles; tall grass grew up over the wires; trees drooped their branches on to it, or the poles took root and enclosed the wire in bushy growths, cattle and wild animals upset the poles when rotten; grass fires damaged both the poles and the wire; finally, an elephant went off with half a mile of the wire round his neck, eventually strangling himself after a terrified flight through Usoga. . . . We therefore had to give up this bit of the line, and we proceeded to make the exchanges over the Mombasa–Port Florence permanent line.' C. Delmé-Radcliffe, 'Surveys and Studies in Uganda', Geog. J. 26 (1905), 481, at p. 492.

[1] See, e.g. Sir Charles Close, 'A Fifty-Years Retrospect', at p. 135.

[2] Memorandum by Sir E. Hertslet, 'Mfumbiro as a quid pro quo for Kilimanjaro', 17 April 1906. F.O. 367/10.

[3] C. Delmé-Radcliffe, 'Reports connected with the Work of the British Commission for the Delimitation of the Anglo-German Boundary West of Lake Victoria Nyanza', July 1906. F.O. 2/989, pp. 60–1.

[4] Hertslet, ii. 578.

beyond the 30th meridian, Delmé-Radcliffe was instructed by the Foreign Office not to go to Mufumbiro,[1] and to leave the problem for decision by the two governments following receipt of the commission's reports.

The mixed commission completed its work in 1904 and erected 42 pillars along the boundary line. Pillar No. 1 marked the western terminal of the boundary at the 30th meridian, and Pillar No. 42 was placed near the northern extremity of Rubabu Point on the western side of Lake Victoria.[2] Completion of the boundary demarcation was followed in 1906 by a protocol, Article 9 of which stated that Germany recognized Britain's right to Mufumbiro.[3] Because of this article the protocol was never ratified. Geographical exploration had shown Mufumbiro to be not a single mountain but a region of volcanic peaks, some still active, and Germany was not prepared to allow the enlargement of Britain's claim to 'Mount Mfumbiro', under the 1890 agreement, so as to include the whole mountain region. A member of the Uganda–Congo demarcation commission who visited the area stated that neither Mufumbiro nor any other single place-name was applied to the range by the inhabitants of the vicinity, though the name Mufumbiro was used to describe the region by people living at a distance.[4] British interest in asserting a claim to these obscure mountains was awakened by memoranda submitted by Delmé-Radcliffe and his assistant commissioners who pointed out that Britain was allowing her 'claims to a valuable upland region to go by default, and that meanwhile the Congo State had occupied the greater part of it'.[5]

Settlement of the Mufumbiro question involved protracted diplomatic negotiations between Britain, Germany, and Belgium.[6] Britain,

[1] 'Extracts from Lt.-Col. C. Delmé-Radcliffe's Typescript Diary Report on the Delimitation of the Anglo-German Boundary, Uganda, 1902–1904', *U.J.* 11 (1947), 9, at p. 28.

[2] For details of the mixed commission's work see Delmé-Radcliffe's Report, above, p. 270, n. 3; and L. Ambronn, *Mitt.*, 20 (1907), 165.

[3] Agreement between Great Britain and Germany determining the Boundary between their respective territories in East Africa (East and West of Lake Victoria), Berlin, 18 July 1906. F.O. 367/10.

[4] E. M. Jack, 'The Mufumbiro Mountains', *Geog. J.* 41 (1913), 532, at pp. 533–4.

[5] Memorandum by Lieutenant-Colonel C. F. Close on the Agreement signed in Brussels on 14 May 1910, with reference to the Eastern Frontiers of the Congo and the Uganda–German East Africa Frontier, 25 May 1910. F.O. 367/175, para. 3.

[6] Belgium annexed the Congo State in November 1908.

under the 1890 agreement, had a claim against Germany to territory which was now found to lie within the Congo. Germany, on the other hand, was making territorial claims against Belgium in the Lake Kivu area of the Congo.[1] Early maps had shown the 30th meridian considerably to the west of its true position, and both Germany and Britain appreciated the territorial advantages to be gained by settling their disputes on the basis of the meridian as it had been assumed to be on the old maps.[2] The outcome of this tangle of territorial disputes was that Britain and Germany, by supporting each other's positions, brought diplomatic pressure against Belgium at a conference held in Brussels in 1910.[3] So far as the British claim against Belgium was concerned, the issues were relatively simple. Britain argued that Mufumbiro was hers by virtue of the 1890 Anglo-German agreement, while Belgium claimed the territory to the west of the 30th meridian under the 1894 agreement between Britain and King Leopold. Belgium's legal position appears to have been strong. Quite apart from the fact that the British claim to Mufumbiro had magnified from a single mountain to a mountain range, and thence to an entire district, Germany in 1890 had no power to dispose of territory which lay outside the boundaries of her own sphere. Legal argument might therefore have rested on the principle *nemo dat quod non habet*. Legal argument, however, proved to be inconclusive and the boundary disputes were settled on the basis of compromise, rather than historical title, nor was the legal identity of Mufumbiro ever determined. By separate agreements made in 1910 between the three states, Mount Sabinio, in the Mufumbiro region, was established as the tripoint marking the Uganda–Congo–German East Africa boundary.[4]

Article 5 of the Anglo-German agreement[5] provides that if any territory lying to the north of the agreed boundary be found to be a political part of the Ruanda district of German East Africa, then

[1] Above, Ch. XVII, pp. 241–2.

[2] See the Agreement respecting the Boundary between the North-Western portion of German East Africa and Uganda. Signed 19 May 1909. Berlin. A typescript copy of this secret agreement is held in the Library MSS. Files of the Royal Geographical Society, the Map Room of which also has a map (Uganda S/Spec. 2), showing the territorial arrangements.

[3] For accounts of this conference see Close's memorandum, above, p. 271, n. 5, Louis, *Ruanda-Urundi 1884–1919*, Ch. 8.

[4] 103 *B.F.S.P.* 372; 107 *B.F.S.P.* 348, 394.

[5] Agreement between Great Britain and Germany Settling the Boundary between Uganda and German East Africa. Signed at Brussels, 14 May 1910, 107 *B.F.S.P.* 394.

such territory should revert to Germany, on the basis of an exchange of equal area to be made by rectification of the eastern sector of the boundary. Provision is also made for the free movement of inhabitants and their personal goods across the new boundary within six months of the completion of the boundary demarcation which is to be undertaken by a mixed commission. This commission was appointed later in the same year, 1910, and demarcation of the Uganda–German East Africa portion of the boundary was commenced in July 1911 by the Anglo-German party working eastward from Mount Sabinio whose highest point, marked by Pillar No. 1, became the new boundary tripoint. In his report, Major Jack, the British commissioner, describes the difficulty experienced by the commission in identifying many of the points referred to in the 1910 Anglo-German agreement:

On the German boundary a number of points had to be identified by their names on the Convention map. The name 'Musongo' was found as that of a small foothill of Muhavura; 'Mulemule' gave some trouble until it was found, by Capt. Fonck, to apply to a cave or hole near Musongo in which the natives buried their dead. The word 'vigaga', which was given as the name of a river which was to form part of the boundary, means 'river'.[1]

Relations between the three sections of the mixed commission are described in Jack's report as being 'most friendly throughout' and the Anglo-German party completed its work at the end of October 1911, with the signing of a protocol at Kamwezi.[2] Article 7 of the 1910 agreement provided for the 'ceremonial transfer of territory' to be undertaken by the two local administrations and this was done in December 1911 when a protocol was signed at the ferry of Nsongezi.[3]

The boundary demarcated by the Anglo-German section of the 1911 commission follows natural physical features. Thirty-eight boundary pillars, together with several additional pillars to indicate direction, were erected along this part of the boundary and the final

[1] E. M. Jack, *Report on the Work of the British Section of the Anglo-German-Belgian Boundary Commission, 1911*, p. 13. For an account by the German Commissioner see G. Schlobach, 'Die Vermarkung der deutsch-englischen Ruanda-Grenzen, 1911', *Deutsches Kolonialblatt*, 23 (1912), 1041.

[2] Protocol between Great Britain and Germany describing the Frontier between the Uganda Protectorate and German East Africa. Signed at Kamwezi, 30 October 1911. 107 *B.F.S.P.* 397.

[3] Thomas and Spencer, op. cit., p. 38.

pillar, No. 38, was placed by the commission at the source of the south-western branch of the River Chizinga. Eastward from this point the boundary is defined by the 1910 agreement and follows the thalwegs of the rivers Chizinga and Kachwamba-Kakitumba to the confluence of the latter river with the Kagera River. It then follows the thalweg of the Kagera to the point where this river makes its second crossing of the parallel of 1° south latitude, and thence runs eastward along the parallel to the shore of Lake Victoria. The point at which the Kagera makes its second crossing of the parallel lies between Pillars Nos. 26 and 27, placed in 1904 by the Anglo-German commission whose demarcation eastward from this point continued to define the boundary.

It remained to embody the description of the Uganda–German East Africa boundary, as demarcated by the commissions of 1902 and 1911, in a new convention between Britain and Germany, since the descriptions contained in the 1890 agreement and in the unratified 1906 agreement no longer represented the true boundary between the two territories. A new agreement was drawn up in London in 1914, describing the Anglo-German boundary from Pillar No. 1 on Mount Sabinio to the southern end of Lake Jipe, about 60 miles south-east of Mount Kilimanjaro.[1] Correspondence concerning the draft of this agreement was proceeding in July 1914 and it appears from letters exchanged at that time between the Foreign Office and the German Ambassador that signature was imminent. Owing to the outbreak of World War I in the following month, however, the agreement was never signed.

In the previous year, 1913, the Secretary of State, acting under the provisions of Article 1 of the Uganda Order in Council of 1902, published the following boundary description,[2] in conformity with the Anglo–German and Anglo–Congolese boundary agreements and protocols of 1910 and 1911:

Anglo–German Boundary

1. The watershed from the highest point of Sabinio over the highest point of Mgahinga to the highest point of Muhavura, marked by Boundary

---

[1] Agreement Respecting the Boundary Between the British and German Territories in East Africa, From Mount Sabinio to Lake Jipe. London, 1914. F.O. 372/523.

[2] *The Uganda Official Gazette*, 30 June 1913, p. 254, G.N. 256 of 1913, and 15 July 1913, p. 286, G.N. 284 of 1913. The boundary is incorrectly described in G.N. 256 and a new description is substituted by G.N. 284.

Pillar No. 1 where the road from north to south of the volcanoes crosses it between Sabinio and Mgahinga.

2. The spur in a north-easterly direction (referred to in the Convention as the Mulemule–Mussongo spur) to the summit of the hill Nyarubebsa, marked by a direction pillar; thence to B.P. No. 2 situated between the hills Nyarubebsa and Mussongo, and on the road leading southwards; thence to the top of Mussongo, marked by a direction pillar; thence along the crest to the summit of the hill called (x) in the Convention, marked by B.P. No. 3.

3. A curved line as shown on the map, marked by B.P. Nos. 4, 5, 6, 7 and 8 to B.P. No. 9, which is on the point called (y) in the Convention; thence a straight line to the top of the hill called (z) in the Convention, marked by B.P. No. 10; thence a straight line to the southern summit of the Vugamba (Wugamba) range, marked by B.P. No. 11.

4. The crest of this range marked as follows: by B.P. No. 12 on the hill Kanyaminenya, by direction pillars to B.P. No. 13 on the most northerly point of the range, by direction pillars to B.P. No. 14, on the hill Mabaremere, by a direction pillar to B.P. No. 15, which is due west (true) of the confluence of the rivers Vigaga (or Kirurumu) and Mugera (Narugwambu); thence a straight line marked by a direction pillar to the confluence of these two rivers, marked by B.P. No. 16.

5. The thalweg of the Kirurumu to its source, marked by B.P. No. 17; thence a straight line to B.P. No. 18, which is situated 4 kilometres north-west of the summit of the hill Gwassa, and is on the point called (b) in the Convention.

6. A straight line to the top of the hill Akasiru, marked by a direction pillar; thence a straight line to the top of the hill Sanja, marked by B.P. No. 19.

7. A straight line to B.P. No. 20 in the valley east of Sanja and on the path[1] running east and west; thence a straight line to the top of the hill Kisivo, marked by B.P. No. 21.

8. The spur of the hill Kisivo in an E.N.E. direction and marked by direction pillars to a conspicuous knoll at its foot, marked by B.P. No. 22; thence to a direction pillar on the edge of the swamp; thence the centre line of the swamp, as shown on the map, to B.P. No. 23, situated at the foot of a prominent spur.

9. The crest of this spur, marked by a direction pillar, to B.P. No. 24 on the summit; thence the crest of the hill, marked by direction pillars, to the top of the hill Kavimbiri, marked by B.P. No. 25.

10. The crest of the hill to B.P. No. 26, thence a straight line, marked by a direction pillar in the valley, to the summit of the conspicuous small hill Nyakara marked by a direction pillar; thence a straight line to the summit of the hill Kitanga, marked by a direction pillar; thence the crest of this hill and the spur leading north and north-east to a conspicuous knoll in the valley, marked by a direction pillar; thence a straight line to a

---

[1] 'Point' is misprinted for 'path' in G.N. 284.

direction pillar on a conspicuous spur of the hill Nebishagara; thence to the crest of this spur to the top of the hill, marked by B.P. No. 27.

11. A line following the crest and a long spur of this hill as shown on the map, and marked by direction pillars, to the top of the hill Magumbizi, marked by B.P. No. 28, thence a line following a very conspicuous water-parting to the top of the hill Kivisa, marked by B.P. No. 29; thence along a spur of this hill to its northern end, marked by a direction pillar; thence a straight line to a direction pillar in the valley, thence a straight line to the southern summit of the hill Ndega, marked by B.P. No. 30; thence a straight line to a conspicuous small hill on the east side of the river Muvumba (Luvumba), marked by a direction pillar; thence a straight line to the top of another conspicuous small hill, marked by B.P. No. 31.

12. A series of straight lines, as shown on the map, following the eastern slopes of the Mashuri range, and marked at each change of direction by a direction pillar, and by B.P. Nos. 32 and 33, both on prominent spurs.

13. A similar series of straight lines, following round the slopes of the valley formed between the Mashuri range and the spur ending in the hill Kitoff (Kitofu), marked by direction pillars and by B.P. Nos. 34 and 35, on prominent spurs; continuing as shown on the map round the slopes of the hill Kitoff marked by direction pillars and by B.P. No. 36, on a prominent spur at the southern end of that hill.

14. A straight line to a direction pillar on a spur on the south-east of Kitoff; thence a straight line to a direction pillar on a spur on the east of Kitoff; thence a straight line to a knoll at the foot of this spur, marked by a direction pillar; and thence a straight line to the saddle between Kitoff and Mavari (Mabare); marked by B.P. No. 37.

15. The thalweg leading north-eastwards, marked by a direction pillar, to the source of the south-western branch of the river Chizinga (Kissinga) marked by B.P. No. 38.

16. From the source of the river Chizinga (Kissinga) the boundary follows the thalweg of the river Chizinga (Kissinga) to its confluence with the river Kachwamba-Kakitumba.

17. From the confluence of the rivers Chizinga (Kissinga) and Kachwamba-Kakitumba the boundary follows the thalweg of the river Kachwamba-Kakitumba to the confluence of the rivers Kachwamba-Kakitumba and Kagera.

18. From the confluence of the rivers Kachwamba-Kakitumba and Kagera the boundary follows the thalweg of the river Kagera as far as the second crossing of the parallel 1° south by the river Kagera between boundary pillars numbered 26 and 27.

19. The boundary then follows the line of boundary pillars already erected along the 1° south as far as the intersection of this line with the western shore of Lake Victoria.

This boundary description corresponds, in all important particulars, with that contained in the draft Anglo-German agreement of

1914. No alterations have been made to this description which, with minor changes of wording that do not affect the substance, is reproduced in the Uganda Constitution of 1967.[1]

By Article 119 of the Peace Treaty of Versailles, 1919, Germany renounced in favour of the Principal Allied and Associated Powers all her rights over her overseas possessions, including the colony of East Africa. In 1922 the League of Nations created Mandates for East Africa whereby the former German colony was divided into two parts, Tanganyika and Ruanda-Urundi, to be administered by Britain and Belgium respectively. Under the provisions of Article 1 in each mandate, the northern limit of Ruanda, which coincided with Uganda's southern boundary, extended from Mount Sabinio in the west to the River Mavumba in the east.[2] The delimitation of the boundary between the two mandated territories resulted in the severance of the district of Kissaka from Ruanda and its inclusion in Tanganyika. Objections concerning this arbitrary division were made to the Permanent Mandates Commission and, following agreement between Britain and Belgium, the boundary between Ruanda and Tanganyika was moved eastward to the Kagera River. This agreement was approved by the League of Nations and Article 1 of each of the two mandates was amended accordingly.[3] The new Ruanda–Tanganyika–Uganda tripoint was defined as the intersection of the Uganda boundary with the 'mid-stream' of the Kagera River.[4] In other words, the confluence of the Kagera and the Kakitumba became the new tripoint.

Examination of the new Uganda-Ruanda boundary was undertaken by a joint Anglo-Belgian commission, and a protocol of verification and identification was signed at Lake Chahafi in March 1925.[5]

From the Ruanda tripoint the Uganda–Tanzania boundary follows the Kagera River only as far as its second crossing of the parallel of 1° south latitude, and eastward from this point the boundary leaves the river and continues along the parallel to Lake Victoria. Two interesting questions arise. First, why was the parallel retained as the

---

[1] *The Constitution of The Republic of Uganda*, 1967. Schedule 1; below, Appendix A.
[2] Mandates for East Africa. M. O. Hudson, *International Legislation*, vol. i, p. 84; above, Ch. XII, p. 153.
[3] Cmd. 1974; above, Ch. XII, p. 155.
[4] 54 *L.N.T.S.* 239, at p. 249. 'Thalweg' later replaced 'mid-stream' in 190 *L.N.T.S.* 95, at p. 98.   [5] Thomas and Spencer, op. cit., p. 38.

boundary, rather than the course of the Kagera to its outlet in the lake, and, secondly, what practical consequences have resulted from this?

During the course of the negotiations between Britain and Germany which led to the hinterland delimitation of 1890, Germany was prepared to concede that Uganda should fall within the British sphere, provided the boundary was drawn along the parallel of 1° south latitude to the Congo State. Writing in January 1890, the Uganda missionary A. M. Mackay points to 'the absurdity of . . . acceding to Germany's wish to draw the boundary-line west of this Lake, along the 1st parallel of S. Lat., as that would cut the kingdom of Buganda into two halves'.[1] Stanley, also, would have preferred[2] to see the boundary shifted from the parallel to the Kagera which he regarded as the natural boundary between Uganda and the kingdoms of Karagwe and Buziba.[3] There is evidence to suggest that Germany would in fact have been willing to accept the Kagera as the boundary, instead of the parallel.[4] Britain, however, did not force the issue and the parallel became the boundary by the 1890 agreement.

In his report to the Foreign Office, following the completion of the Anglo-German demarcation in 1902–4, Delmé-Radcliffe recommended that the parallel of 1° south latitude should be replaced as the boundary by a line following natural features, from Lake Victoria to the Congo State.[5] It is unnecessary to consider his recommendations in the western section of the boundary, since natural features were accepted there as a result of the Anglo-German agreement of 1910 and protocol of 1911. But in the eastern section, that is to say eastward from the point where the Kagera makes its second crossing of the parallel downstream from its confluence with the Kakitumba, no substantial departure was ever made from the artificial boundary created by the adoption of a parallel of latitude.

Delmé-Radcliffe proposed that the boundary should commence at the mouth of the Kagera and follow the course of the river to its confluence with the Kakitumba. The mouth of the Kagera lies about 4 miles north of the parallel; the river then crosses the parallel about 6 miles west of the lake to make a southward loop before returning

---

[1] H. M. Stanley, *In Darkest Africa*, Low, Marston, Searle, and Rivington, London, 1890, vol. ii, p. 392.

[2] Louis, 'The Anglo-German Hinterland Settlement', p. 75.

[3] H. M. Stanley, *Through the Dark Continent*, Sampson Low, London, 1880, p. 138.

[4] Louis, op. cit., p. 74.   [5] Delmé-Radcliffe's Report, pp. 58–61.

to the parallel at 'the second crossing' referred to in the 1910 Anglo-German agreement. The retention of the parallel as the boundary meant that each state owned territory on its far side of the Kagera. The eastern portion, south of the Kagera mouth, was British, and the western portion, between the two points where the river crossed the parallel, formed part of German East Africa. These two portions have been conveniently described as the Kagera Triangle and the Kagera Salient respectively.[1] The Kagera Triangle consists of two parts. First, it includes the northern tip of Rubabu Point, a small piece of barren, rocky promontory lying to the north of Pillar No. 42. Secondly, it contains a larger area, including Busungwe Island and Mizinda Bay. The combined area of these two parts is roughly 15 square miles. The Kagera Salient is a much larger area, containing about 600 square miles, and is described by Delmé-Radcliffe as consisting of 'a pitiless swamp, an expanse of virgin forest, and tsetse-fly-infested, waterless, uninhabited jungle'.

Delmé-Radcliffe proposed that Britain should give the Kagera Triangle to Germany, in exchange for the Kagera Salient. Although Britain would thereby receive a greater territorial area, she would also be parting with Mizinda harbour, described as being the only British harbour on the west side of Lake Victoria,[2] whose value would more than balance the advantage of the territory gained by her. He argued that if such an exchange was made, advantages would accrue to both sides. Administration would be facilitated, since neither government would have to cross the Kagera.[3] Each state would control one bank of the river up to the mouth of the Kakitumba and would thus have full use of the river as a means of communication. Also, the Kagera itself formed a natural obstacle, impossible to cross without boats, and would therefore provide a strong boundary tending to reduce raids and other border incidents.

The substance of these recommendations is a plea for a strong, practical boundary. Less attention is paid to the wishes of local inhabitants. Those living in the Kagera Salient, at that time about 3,000 people, are referred to as 'of no particular value either to the British or the German Administration', although it is conceded that

---

[1] H. B. Thomas, 'The Kagera Triangle and the Kagera Salient', *U.J.* 23 (1959), 73.

[2] Delmé-Radcliffe's Report, p. 40.

[3] Both British and German administrators had previously pleaded unsuccessfully for an alteration of the boundary. See Sir F. Jackson, *Early Days in East Africa*, Arnold, London, 1930, p. 283.

they 'belong by rights to Buddu and Ankole, of which countries the Kagera River was formerly the southern boundary'.[1] The arguments presented by Delmé-Radcliffe did not, however, prevail. The final boundary settlement in 1910 left the eastern section unaltered and it continued to follow the parallel of 1° south latitude. Although the opportunity to alter the boundary to the Kagera might have been taken after World War I, no such attempt was made. At the present time, therefore, the Kagera Salient, traditionally a part of Buganda and Ankole, lies within the boundaries of Tanzania, while in the Kagera Triangle, a small area of Uhaya country is part of Uganda.

As was mentioned earlier, part of the Kagera Triangle consisted of the northern extremity of Rubabu Point, a portion of which lay on the Uganda side of the boundary. The legal title to this small rocky piece of territory remains uncertain and requires examination. The boundary across Lake Victoria was defined by the 1890 Anglo-German agreement as being the parallel of 1° south latitude. The lake boundary was not referred to in the 1910 Anglo-German agreement or in the Secretary of State's Order of 1913, both boundary descriptions terminating at the western side of the lake. Nevertheless, the unsigned Anglo-German agreement of 1914 did describe the lake boundary and, in so doing, made provision whereby Rubabu Point fell entirely within German East Africa. Article 2 of this draft agreement provides:

> Across Lake Victoria the boundary continues to follow latitude south 1°, as shown in Maps 2 and 3 annexed to this Agreement, to a point 1½ kilom. west of the coast of Rubabu (Rubawa) Peninsula, whence it runs parallel to and at a distance of 1½ kilom. from the coast line round the northern extremity of the peninsula until it again meets latitude south 1°. Thence along that parallel of latitude . . .[2]

Since this agreement was never signed, of what legal significance are the terms of its draft? Must the lake boundary continue to be defined by the 1890 Anglo-German agreement which remains the only completed treaty concerning it? Assistance in answering these questions is given by a statement made in 1925 by the Colonial Secretary, Mr. L. S. Amery, when, with respect to the Kenya–Tanganyika boundary between Lake Victoria and Lake Jipe, he said: 'It is proposed to adopt this boundary as laid down in the Draft Agreement as the correct boundary between Kenya and Tanganyika, and to

---

[1] Delmé-Radcliffe's Report, p. 59.   [2] F.O. 372/523.

embody the description in the Boundaries Order-in-Council for Kenya which is waiting for the final definition of the new boundary of Jubaland.'[1] The draft agreement referred to here is that prepared by Britain and Germany in 1914. No Order-in-Council embodying the description was ever made and, in any case, it would have referred only to the Kenya–Tanganyika boundary. Nevertheless, the argument put forward by the Colonial Secretary for using the draft agreement was that its completion had been interrupted by the outbreak of World War I, and it is submitted that the same argument can be justifiably applied to the Lake Victoria boundary. If this view is accepted, the conclusion is that the portion of Rubabu Point lying to the north of the demarcated boundary, together with a contiguous lake zone, $1\frac{1}{2}$ kilometres in width, now fall within the boundaries of Tanzania.

Near the eastern side of the lake, the Uganda–Kenya–Tanzania tripoint lies at the intersection of the parallel of $1°$ south latitude with a line drawn due south from the westernmost point of Pyramid Island.[2]

Despite the most careful precautions observed by a boundary commission when attempting to establish on the ground the precise position of a geographic line such as a parallel of latitude, the possibility remains that the demarcated points, as a result of further investigation and computation, may not fall exactly on the theoretical line. In such cases there is a risk of ambiguity in the final boundary description unless it is clearly specified therein that the line as demarcated defines the true boundary.[3] It appears from recent large-scale maps, published by the governments of Uganda and Tanzania,[4] that the boundary pillars placed by the 1902–4 Anglo-German commission actually lie several hundred feet to the north of the parallel. Despite this discrepancy, however, it is submitted that the pillars themselves, if found *in situ*, define the boundary, rather than the theoretical parallel.[5] Support for this submission is found in the boundary description contained in the 1913 Order, paragraph 19 of which states that the boundary follows 'the line of boundary pillars

---

[1] 23 September 1925. C.O. 533/333.
[2] The Kenya Colony and Protectorate (Boundaries) Order in Council, 1926. S.R. & O. 1926/1733.
[3] Above, Ch. III, pp. 47–53.
[4] See, e.g., Map Series Y732, Sheet 88/111 and Y742, Sheet 3/2.
[5] For a report on the 1958 resurvey of part of the boundary, when several original pillars were found, see Tanganyika Survey Dept. File 887 (Comps).

already erected along the 1° south as far as the intersection of this line with the western shore of Lake Victoria'.[1] Where no demarcation exists, as in that part of the lake boundary extending eastward from the eastern shore of Rubabu Point, the boundary should be taken as coincident with the true parallel.

[1] See also Art. 4 of the Anglo-German draft agreement of 1914 which provides that the boundary pillars themselves shall determine the boundary, even in the event of future alteration of their geographical co-ordinates.

PART FOUR

CONCLUSION

CHAPTER XXI

Summary and Recommendations

PROBABLY the most useful single source of documentary material relating to international boundaries in Africa is *The Map of Africa By Treaty*, to which frequent reference has been made throughout the preceding chapters. This work, compiled by Sir Edward Hertslet, the distinguished librarian of the British Foreign Office, not only reproduces the texts of boundary treaties and other instruments, but also contains copies of correspondence between the various contracting states, together with the editor's own explanatory notes. Despite its unquestionable value, *The Map of Africa By Treaty* has not been revised since the third edition, published in 1909.[1] Since that time, however, nearly all East African international boundaries have undergone some alteration or adjustment. The point is worth remembering, for although the colonial scramble for Africa is usually thought to have been completed soon after the commencement of the present century, many boundary agreements were not finalized until long after that time and indeed some, such as that between Kenya and Sudan, have yet to be completely settled.

The emergence of almost all African countries from non-self-governing status to sovereign independence and their attitude towards the acceptance of colonial frontiers, as expressed in the O.A.U. boundary resolution of 1964, enables a writer of the present day to discuss the legal position of African boundaries with more assurance than would have been possible even as recently as a decade ago, when there was a not unreasonable expectation that Africans, in rejecting colonialism, would also reject one of its most obvious manifestations, the imposition of arbitrary boundaries. For reasons already presented, the independent states of Africa are prepared to accept the principle that inherited boundaries should now be respected, even though there still remain some reservations to this view by certain individual states, such as the Somali Republic and Morocco.[2] East African boundaries, with two exceptions, lie between states that

---

[1] Reprinted by Frank Cass, London, 1967.   [2] Above, Ch. II (*d*).

emerged from foreign tutelage to full independence during the years 1956 to 1964. The first exception is Ethiopia who, even during the heyday of European imperialism, was recognized as a sovereign state not only entitled but sufficiently influential to play an active part in the shaping of her own territorial limits. Secondly, on Tanzania's southern border lies the territory of Mozambique, one of the few countries of Africa whose inhabitants have yet to attain self-government but whose boundary with Tanzania, so far as can be predicted, does not appear likely to give rise to dispute when Mozambique secures its independence from Portugal.[1]

The two main problem areas relating to international boundaries in East Africa are, first, the dispute between Kenya and the Somali Republic and, second, Tanzania's disagreement with Malawi concerning the boundary in Lake Nyasa. Both problems have been discussed in some detail in the relevant chapters and, as has been seen, in neither case are the issues so clear cut as to justify unequivocal assertions with respect to the proper placing of the respective boundary lines, having regard to all the surrounding political and economic circumstances. So far as the Kenya–Somali issue is concerned, the recent improvement in relations between the two neighbouring states, greatly assisted by the mediation of President Kaunda of Zambia, is a source of optimism that an amicable solution will eventually be reached, even though the basic difficulties have yet to be overcome. The Tanzania–Malawi problem is more complex, since it is not merely a boundary dispute but involves other considerations of a mainly political nature and, at the present time, the rift between the two disputants seems to be as wide as ever. One can only hope that a compromise solution, fostered by the O.A.U., will lead to a reconciliation of what at the moment appear to be irreconcilable views.

Two examples of what may be regarded as a form of agency relationship exist on the Uganda–Kenya and the Kenya–Sudan borders. The Karasuk district is recognized by both Uganda and Kenya as lying within the *de jure* limits of Kenya, yet by a consensual

---

[1] The legal status of Mozambique is controversial. Portugal claims that from a legal as well as a *de facto* point of view her European territory and her overseas possessions are under the same organs of sovereignty and that the latter therefore form an integral part of Portugal. (See *Yearbook of the United Nations*, 1956, p. 291.) The General Assembly of the United Nations, however, by its adoption of Resolution 1542 (XV), dated 15 December 1960, specifically declares Mozambique to be a Non-Self-Governing Territory within the meaning of Chapter XI of the United Nations Charter.

arrangement that existed for nearly forty years the area was administered by the Uganda authorities. So long as both Kenya and Uganda fell under British control there may have been no great practical objection to a *de facto* division of administration with respect to Karasuk, but once both countries became independent states it seemed desirable that the legal status of the district should be clarified, either by severing it from Kenya and attaching it to Uganda, or by placing what was originally a provisional administrative arrangement on a more formal footing by the creation of an appropriate international agreement.[1] Somewhat similar considerations apply to the portion of Sudan, forming part of the Ilemi Triangle, which is administered by Kenya. In this case, however, the legal description of the boundary is far from clear, owing partly to ambiguities in the original instrument which established it. Here again, the evidence suggests that Sudan is quite willing to allow Kenya to continue the administration of this difficult area, and it would be in the interests of both states to put the existing arrangement, which is rather vague in its scope and intent, on a clear legal basis.[2]

Subject to the exceptions noted above, the three East African states are fortunate in possessing territorial limits that are remarkably stable and uncontroversial. In every instance, with the exception of the line separating Tanzania from Zambia in Lake Tanganyika,[3] the legal origin of the various boundaries can be traced directly to international agreement. The fact that these boundaries, even though drawn by colonial powers, have in nearly every case been precisely described and demarcated, has made it very much easier for the new states to accept them. This factor distinguishes East African acceptance of the territorial *status quo* at the time of independence from the somewhat artificial doctrine of *uti possidetis* that was sought to be applied in Latin America where colonial boundaries were largely undemarcated and frequently described in ambiguous terms.[4] For the sake of legal tidiness, however, it should be mentioned that a correct description of that portion of the Kenya–Tanzania boundary extending from the eastern side of Lake Victoria to Lake Jipe has never been incorporated in a formally concluded instrument. Although there appears to be no doubt that this boundary, which was demarcated over sixty years ago and a description of which appears in the unsigned

---

[1] Kenya resumed administration of Karasuk in July 1970. Above, Ch. XVIII, p. 256.   [2] Above, Ch. X.
[3] Above, Ch. XVI.   [4] Above, Ch. II (*e*).

Anglo-German draft agreement of 1914,[1] is accepted by both Kenya and Tanzania, its legal status would perhaps be enhanced and clarified by the embodiment of the boundary description in a new agreement between the two states. The same draft agreement of 1914, it will be recalled, described the line between Uganda and Tanzania, and here also there appears to be little doubt that both states recognize it as defining their common boundary. One slight anomaly remains, however, with regard to Rubabu Point, in Lake Victoria, the northern tip of which was reported by the mixed demarcation commission of 1902–4 to lie on the Uganda side of the demarcated boundary. A boundary pillar was in fact placed by the commission on the peninsula. In order to avoid the absurdity of placing an international boundary so as to cut off a minute portion of barren territory the draft agreement made provision for the inclusion of the whole of Rubabu Point, together with a contiguous maritime zone of $1\frac{1}{2}$ kilometres in width, inside German East Africa.[2] For reasons already advanced, the draft agreement, though never signed, should be regarded as representing the true intention of the contracting parties and it is submitted that possible future confusion could be avoided by the drawing of an agreement between the two states that Rubabu Point and its maritime zone lie entirely within the limits of Tanzania.[3]

Lake Tanganyika presents another situation where although there is no present controversy between the bordering states, it is desirable that a more satisfactory boundary line be drawn. The median line of the lake forms the boundary between Tanzania and the Congo Republic and, as has been shown, the interpretation of the word 'median' gives rise to difficulties which could be overcome by re-defining the boundary in terms of arbitrary straight lines.[4] In the southern portion of Lake Tanganyika, the boundary between Tanzania and Zambia has never been adequately described, though cartographical practice, which appears to be acceptable to the adjoining states, shows it as a geometrical curve following the approximate middle line of the lake.[5] Here again a more exact definition, in terms of straight lines, would be appropriate.

Part II of this work describes some of the problems of interpreting certain geographical terms such as crest, watershed, thalweg, and

[1] Above, pp. 145–6.　　　　　　　　　　　　　　[2] Above, pp. 280–1.

[3] See *The Boundaries of Uganda*, Appendix A, below, p. 300, where it appears that Uganda has not taken into account the provisions of the 1914 draft agreement with respect to Rubabu Point.

[4] Above, Chs. VII and XIII.　　　　　　　　　　　[5] Above, p. 226.

source of a river. These expressions are of frequent occurrence in boundary descriptions and it is too often assumed by draftsmen that their meaning is unambiguous. International boundary adjudication, such as the *Temple Case*, *Argentine–Chile Award*, *Honduras–Nicaragua Award*, and the *Chamizal Case*, among others, shows that the meaning of seemingly common geographical terms cannot be taken for granted, and that they should be carefully defined at the time of their inclusion in the original boundary agreements. Although most of the East African boundary agreements appear to contain few difficulties of this nature, there might well be some value in appending to existing descriptions a list of definitions of technical terms which would remove any possible doubt as to their meaning.[1] Such action, if undertaken jointly between neighbouring states, would help to prevent the risk of uncertainty of description and would thereby reduce the likelihood of future dispute. A possible objection to this suggestion is that its attempted implementation might in itself cause the emergence of boundary disagreements which at present do not exist. It is submitted, however, that it is precisely because East African boundary descriptions are fairly well drawn and, in the majority of cases, amicable relations exist between the neighbouring states, that the incorporation of boundary definitions would be a relatively simple matter and one which would contribute towards the strengthening of the legal status of territorial limits in East Africa.

A final point to be observed is that although international boundaries should possess the desirable quality of legal stability, in certain instances it is inappropriate to regard them as serving a purely static function. Situations arise where economic and social circumstances suggest that a boundary be looked at not simply as a line of rigid separation but as an area in which local needs can be satisfied to the fullest possible extent. Thus, in the case of the East African boundary lakes the establishment of a line precisely separating the bordering states is in itself insufficient; what is also required is a system of bilateral or multilateral agreements dealing, *inter alia*, with such matters as fishing, navigation, and water pollution. In Lake Nyasa particularly, the problem of changing lake level is one that should be approached jointly by the three riparian states although, as has been shown, the settlement of the Tanzania–Malawi boundary dispute in the lake is a necessary prelude to any such inter-state co-operation.

[1] See, for example, the definition of thalweg with respect to the Ruvuma River boundary between Tanzania and Mozambique. Above, pp. 81–2.

Similar problems exist with respect to the trans-frontier movement of nomadic peoples for grazing and watering purposes. The outstanding example of this is the Kenya–Somali Republic border, though here again a settlement concerning the actual location of the international boundary must precede the establishment of agreements regulating the freedom of tribal movement across the boundary line. Another situation of this type occurs on the Kenya–Tanzania border, where Masai tribesmen live on opposite sides of the line. Here the location of the boundary is not disputed by the adjoining states and it appears that an opportunity exists to provide for amicable arrangements concerning the traditional trans-frontier movement of this pastoral people, without in any way impairing the territorial integrity of the two neighbouring sovereignties.

APPENDIX A

The Boundaries of Uganda

A R T I C L E 2 (2) of *The Constitution of The Republic of Uganda*, 1967, states: 'The Republic of Uganda shall consist of all those areas which are more particularly delineated in Schedule 1 to this Constitution.'

Schedule 1, with the insertion of the appropriate sub-boundary headings, is reproduced hereunder.

[The Uganda–Congo Republic Boundary]

Commencing at the highest point of Mt. Sabinio; thence in a north-easterly direction to the southern extremity of the Mdagana ridge marked by Boundary Pillar 1; thence along the watershed of Mdagana to its highest point, marked by BP 2; thence in a north-westerly direction in a straight line to the summit of the knoll Chieshire, marked by BP 3; thence in a straight line in a north-easterly direction to the confluence of the Rivers Nyarugando and Nkanka (Kanga); thence following the thalweg of the River Nyarugando to its source; thence in a straight line in a north-westerly direction to the highest point of the hill Giskio, marked by BP 4; thence following the watershed between the hill Giskio and the hill Lubona and its continuation as far as a point, marked by BP 5, about 400 metres north-west of the summit of the hill Lubona; thence along the crest of the spur running in a north-westerly direction to the River Sinda (Lulangala); thence along the crest of the opposite spur, as shown on the map, to the summit of the hill Kirambo, marked by BP 6; thence in a curved line, as shown on the map, along the crest of a spur running from Kirambo in a north-easterly and northerly direction to the northernmost elbow of the River Kaku or Rutshuru; thence in a straight line across this river to the mouth of the stream Kasumo (Sumo); thence along the thalweg of this stream to its source; thence in a straight line to the lowest point, marked by BP 7 of the col north-east of the above-mentioned elbow of the River Kaku or Rutshuru; thence in a straight line to the confluence of the Rivers Kyarakibi and Murungu; thence following the thalweg of the River Murungu downstream to its junction with the thalweg of the River Chonga; thence in a straight line to the summit of a hill (Muko), marked by BP 8, about 700 metres north-north-east of this junction; thence in a straight line in a northerly direction to the summit of the hill Chikomo (Deko South) or Katwakare, marked by BP 9; thence in a straight line to the summit of the hill Deko North; thence in a straight line to the summit of a hill (Nteko) about 3 km north by west of Deko North; thence in a straight line to the point, marked by BP 10, where the Kayonsa road crosses the River Ivi;

thence in a straight line to a point marked by BP 11, about 1 km to the north of BP 10, on a prominent spur of the Nkabwa-Salambo range; thence following the crest of this spur to the summit of the hill Salambo; thence along the watershed of the Nkabwa-Salambo range to the summit of the hill Nkabwa, marked by BP 12.

From the summit of Nkabwa hill, the boundary runs in an easterly direction to the summit of the hill Kyeshero, marked by BP 12A; thence in the same straight line to the point known as Kakoraza, marked by BP 13; thence in the same straight line eastwards to the River Munyaga; thence along the thalweg of this river, downstream, to its junction with the thalweg of the River Ishasha; thence along the thalweg of the River Ishasha, downstream, to its mouth in Lake Edward; thence in a straight line in a northerly direction across Lake Edward to a point marked by BP 1 at the mouth of the River Lubilia-Chako; thence along the thalweg of this river to a point marked by BP 2; thence along the thalweg of this river to a point marked by BP 3; thence along the thalweg of this river to a point marked by BP 4; thence along the thalweg of this river to the point where it separates into the rivers Lubilia and Chako as marked by BP 5; thence along the thalweg of the River Chako to a point marked by BP 6; thence continuing along the thalweg of the River Chako, upstream, to its source at a point marked by BP 7; thence in a straight line to the highest point of the Ruwenzori Range, the summit of Margharita Peak; thence in a straight line to the source of the River Lami, situated about 5·4 km north-west of the Peak Kalengili and about 20 km south-west of the hill-top Karangora; thence along the thalweg of River Lamia, downstream, to its junction with the thalweg of the River Semliki; thence along the thalweg of the River Semliki, downstream, to its mouth in Lake Albert; thence across Lake Albert in a succession of straight lines passing through the points situated mid-way between the shores of the lake on parallels of 01° 31',[1] 01° 45' and 02° 00' north latitude, to a point mid-way between the shores of the lake on the parallel of 02° 07' north latitude.

From this point the boundary runs in a northerly direction along the meridian for a distance of approximately 4·5 km north of the point on the parallel of 02° 07' north latitude; thence in a straight line to a point marked by BP 1 on the shore of Lake Albert and on the prolongation of a straight line from the hill Kagudi (Uduka) to the knoll Marombe on the escarpment overlooking Lake Albert about 1·7 km south-east by east of the hill Kagudi, and is about 100 metres from the lakeshore on the said straight line; thence in a straight line to BP 2 on the hill Marombe, about 2 km from the lakeshore; thence in a straight line to BP 3, on the summit of the hill Kagudi (Uduka); thence in a straight line to BP 4 on the neck of the hill Ngumuda and on a straight line from the hill Kagudi to the summit of the hill Biet (Otal), which is about 1·04 km from the hill Kagudi; thence in a straight line to BP 5 on the hill Biet (Otal), at a distance of 3·04 km from the hill Kagudi; thence in a straight line to BP 6 on the hill Virkidi on a straight line from the hill Kagudi to the hill Biet at a distance of about 4·8 km from Kagudi; thence in a straight line to BP 7 at the intersection of a straight

[1] Anglo-Belgian Treaty of 1915 gives 01° 30'. See above, p. 247.

line from the hill Kagudi to the hill Biet and a straight line from the hill
Milia to the junction of the Rivers Nashiodo and Alala, close to the River
Otal on its left bank and is known as Utal; thence in a northerly direction
along the meridian of BP 7 on a straight line from the hill Milia to the
junction of the Rivers Nashiodo and Alala to BP 8 about 4 km from the
junction of the said rivers on the hill Wellingondo; thence along the meridian to BP 9 on the hill Nyatabu (Niatabu), about 2·48 km from the
junction of the said rivers; thence along the meridian to BP 10 on the hill
Nyatabu II (Niatabu) about 1·2 km from the junction of the said rivers in
one of the villages known as Parombo; thence along the meridian to
BP 11 on the right bank of the river Nashiodo (Achodo) at its junction
with the river Alala; thence along the thalweg of the river upstream to its
source to BP 12 on the summit of the hill Keresi; thence along a curved
line following the watershed of the river Sido basin to BP 13 on the summit
of the hill Aminzi; thence in a straight line to BP 14 on the summit of the
hill Kiti in a straight line from the hill Aminzi to Monda (Omunda) Rock
at a distance of about 2 km from Aminzi; thence in a straight line to BP 15
on the east immediately below the summit of the rock Monda; thence in
a straight line to BP 16 on the right bank of the River Niabola (Nyibola)
about 15 feet above its junction with the rivers Nyarwodo (Narodo) and
Niabola (Nyibola); thence along the thalweg of the river Niabola (Nyibola)
to BP 17 upon the summit of the hill Agu; thence along a curved line
following the watershed of the river Aioda (Ayuda) basin on BP 18 on the
summit of the hill Asina about 3·44 km south-west by south from the hill
Agu; thence along the watershed to BP 19 on the summit of the hill Sisi;
thence along a curved line following the watershed of the river Leda to
BP 20 on the summit of the hill Ajigu; at a distance of about 2·56 km
north-west by west of the hill Sisi; thence along a curved line following the
watershed of the river Leda basin to BP 21, at a point 2·16 km west of
BP 20; thence along a curved line following the watershed to BP 22 on the
knoll Okiyo situated about 4·2 km south-east by east of the summit of the
hill Cho; thence along a curved line to BP 23 on a small group of rocks
(Matijo) upon the watershed between the river Niagak basin and that
tributary which joins the Niagak just below the confluence of the rivers
Niagak and Amoda and is about 2 km south-east by east of the hill Cho;
thence along a curved line to BP 24 on a small knoll on the above described
watershed at a distance of about 200 metres from the confluence of the
rivers Niagak and Amoda; thence in a straight line to BP 25 on the right
bank of the river Amoda (Ammodar), immediately above its confluence
with the river Nyalidha, at a point about 1,600 metres south-west of the
summit of the hill Akar; thence along the thalweg of the river Nyalidha to
BP 26 upon the Nile-Congo watershed about 6·2 km west-south-west of
the summit of the hill Akar and about 5·6 km south-south-east of the hill
Utzi, close to the source of the river Omithameri.

From this point the boundary follows the Nile-Congo watershed in a
northerly direction to a point about 0·3 km south of the source of the river
Kaia (Kaya) the tri-junction of the Uganda/Congo/Sudan International
Boundaries;

[The Uganda–Sudan Boundary]

thence in a straight line to the source of the river Kaia (Kaya); thence along the thalweg of the river Kaia (Kaya), downstream to its confluence with the unnamed river which runs immediately south of Chei and Lodwa rocks, and then runs in a northerly direction; thence in an easterly direction in a straight line to a point on the western summit of the hill Kirwa, marked by a surface beacon; thence in a south-easterly direction in a straight line to the confluence of the rivers Adjika and Khor Nyaura (Nyawa); thence in a north-easterly direction in a straight line to a point on the top of J. Jalei, marked by a surface beacon; thence in an easterly direction to the source of the river Khor Kayo (Kayu), approximately ¾ miles from J. Jalei; thence following the thalweg of the Khor Kayo to a point on the thalweg directly opposite the westernmost point of the foothills of the escarpment running north-west from Jebel Elengua; thence in a straight line to the westernmost point of the foothills; thence following the bottom of the foothills of this escarpment in a south-easterly, or such a line as shall exclude the riverain people below Nimule; thence following due east to the intersection of the thalweg of the river Bahr el Jebel (White Nile) with the thalweg of the river Unyama; thence along the thalweg of the river Unyama, upstream, to a point on the thalweg along the latitude of Jebel Ebijo; thence following due east to the summit of Jebel Ebijo; thence following in the direction of Jebel Kakomera to the thalweg of the river Achwa; thence following the thalweg of the river Achwa, downstream, to the intersection of the thalweg and a straight line towards the village Lokai to the northernmost point of the bottom of Jebel Marokho; thence following the summit of Jebel Agu; thence following the summit of Jebel Ilala (Lomwaka); thence in a straight line in a north-easterly direction to the hill (Jebel) Modole; thence following a straight line in a south-easterly direction to the most south-easterly foothills of Jebel Tereteinia; thence in a straight line in a south-easterly direction to a point on the summit of the hill (Jebel) Lonyili marked by a triangulation mark 9.Y.2; thence on bearing 44° 45′ and for a distance of 58,506 feet approximately to triangulation mark 9.Y.9; thence on bearing 44° 45′ and for a distance of 17,831 feet approximately to a triangulation mark 9.Y.8; thence on bearing 44° 45′ and for a distance of 26,945 feet to a triangulation mark 9.Y.6; thence on bearing 44° 45′ and for a distance of 17,854 feet to a triangulation mark 9.Y.5; thence on bearing 44° 45′ and for a distance of 7,320 feet to a triangulation mark 9.Y.4; thence on bearing 44° 45′ for a distance of 6,420 feet to a triangulation mark 9.Y.3; thence on bearing 44° 45′ and for a distance of 20,306 feet to a triangulation mark 9.Y.1 on the summit of the hill (Jebel) Urungo; thence on bearing 44° 45′ to a point north of Mount Zulia at a distance of 31·5 miles approximately from 9.Y.1 and which is to the tri-junction of the Uganda/Sudan/Kenya International Boundaries.

[The Uganda–Kenya Boundary]

From this point the boundary is defined by a series of Boundary Pillars joined by straight lines as follows; on an approximate bearing of 127° for an approximate distance of 21,500 ft. to Pillar UK 180;
thence on a bearing of 132° 41' for a distance of 4,444 ft. to Pillar UK 179;

bearing	distance	Pillar
151° 51'	14,674 ft.	178;
217° 00'	9,935 ft.	177;
153° 39'	11,091 ft.	176;
116° 35'	6,799 ft.	175;
153° 08'	9,457 ft.	174;
180° 05'	5,313 ft.	173;
193° 47'	3,942 ft.	172;
252° 36'	11,338 ft.	171;
175° 13'	6,533 ft.	170;
108° 18'	7,280 ft.	169;
136° 07'	12,882 ft.	168;
118° 30'	12,368 ft.	167;
184° 26'	1,847 ft.	166;
193° 32'	8,426 ft.	165;
195° 43'	12,045 ft.	164;
208° 42'	606 ft.	163;
225° 39'	1,958 ft.	162;
244° 44'	4,290 ft.	161;
244° 37'	5,256 ft.	160;
186° 44'	7,960 ft.	159;
185° 09'	797 ft.	158;
141° 19'	224 ft.	157;
105° 28'	1,390 ft.	156;
62° 15'	6,590 ft.	155;
79° 18'	6,628 ft.	154;
79° 24'	562 ft.	153;
98° 30'	7,857 ft.	152;
86° 30'	6,719 ft.	151;
19° 35'	2,151 ft.	150;
54° 05'	1,326 ft.	149;
52° 46'	1,387 ft.	148;
84° 15'	7,907 ft.	147;
88° 38'	2,969 ft.	146;
93° 11'	3,880 ft.	145;
162° 13'	10,907 ft.	144;
169° 22'	1,233 ft.	143;
180° 05'	6,988 ft.	142;
276° 03'	4,216 ft.	141;
269° 35'	12,526 ft.	140;
220° 56'	4,826 ft.	139;
213° 23'	4,857 ft.	138;
244° 58'	2,355 ft.	137;
262° 40'	1,631 ft.	136;
176° 51'	2,685 ft.	135;
71° 53'	2,157 ft.	134;
141° 01'	1,898 ft.	133;
73° 20'	2,900 ft.	132;

thence on a bearing of 95° 51′ for a distance of 1,882 ft. to Pillar UK 131;

107° 02′	5,231 ft.	130;
193° 16′	1,233 ft.	129;
164° 54′	3,325 ft.	128;
249° 32′	2,213 ft.	127;
248° 20′	5,751 ft.	126;
257° 52′	1,900 ft.	125;
131° 49′	3,476 ft.	124;
72° 43′	4,611 ft.	123;
81° 33′	1,335 ft.	122;
69° 56′	6,268 ft.	121;
68° 27′	4,067 ft.	120;
68° 08′	2,676 ft.	119;
108° 26′	1,514 ft.	118;
120° 39′	591 ft.	117;
174° 30′	1,137 ft.	116;
177° 54′	1,945 ft.	115;
73° 00′	766 ft.	114;
29° 30′	2,694 ft.	113;
79° 44′	907 ft.	112;
66° 16′	1,937 ft.	111;
79° 55′	2,194 ft.	110;
145° 27′	8,509 ft.	109;
156° 21′	6,769 ft.	108;
135° 26′	8,205 ft.	107;
125° 22′	6,438 ft.	106;
129° 06′	5,399 ft.	105;
187° 04′	4,979 ft.	104;
190° 48′	3,490 ft.	103;
206° 19′	1,348 ft.	102;
90° 43′	989 ft.	101;
19° 19′	13,434 ft.	100;
43° 44′	3,513 ft.	99;
72° 50′	4,525 ft.	98;
77° 44′	6,713 ft.	97;
91° 40′	5,820 ft.	96;
119° 12′	3,050 ft.	95;
137° 48′	9,847 ft.	94;
138° 59′	2,497 ft.	93;
166° 14′	4,695 ft.	92;
208° 52′	5,792 ft.	91;
109° 54′	13,971 ft.	90;
130° 36′	3,998 ft.	89;
189° 05′	11,610 ft.	88;
190° 53′	9,774 ft.	87;
173° 59′	11,720 ft.	86;
185° 18′	3,718 ft.	85;
185° 17′	8,946 ft.	84;
185° 17′	9,408 ft.	83;
214° 56′	3,320 ft.	82;
223° 42′	6,391 ft.	81;
234° 33′	4,606 ft.	80;
264° 01′	9,781 ft.	79;

thence on a bearing of 305° 56′ for a distance of 2,607 ft. to Pillar UK 78B;

254° 05′	658 ft.	78A;
166° 43′	3,498 ft.	78;
135° 44′	7,662 ft.	77;
147° 08′	7,410 ft.	76;
171° 43′	6,334 ft.	75;
212° 11′	6,726 ft.	74;
249° 27′	3,158 ft.	73;
181° 55′	13,506 ft.	72;
170° 05′	2,587 ft.	71;
129° 00′	5,641 ft.	70;
137° 01′	8,709 ft.	69;
165° 27′	13,939 ft.	68;
159° 01′	9,269 ft.	67;
174° 59′	14,818 ft.	66;
179° 35′	5,101 ft.	65;
172° 44′	9,833 ft.	64;
178° 53′	6,324 ft.	63;
148° 52′	3,609 ft.	62;
98° 07′	3,818 ft.	61;
124° 01′	5,022 ft.	60;
122° 27′	284 ft.	59;
147° 13′	4,281 ft.	58;
157° 07′	5,115 ft.	57;
66° 06′	6,710 ft.	56;
107° 46′	9,418 ft.	55;
117° 32′	4,055 ft.	54;
151° 38′	10,044 ft.	53;
131° 09′	6,896 ft.	52;
171° 33′	7,589 ft.	51;
185° 03′	3,500 ft.	50;
181° 55′	6,136 ft.	49;
177° 35′	11,141 ft.	48;
156° 20′	4,169 ft.	47;
142° 05′	3,944 ft.	46;
175° 32′	7,091 ft.	45;
170° 00′	21,063 ft.	44;
112° 40′	13,232 ft.	43;
119° 36′	3,082 ft.	42;
160° 39′	14,972 ft.	41;
105° 33′	5,819 ft.	40;
87° 07′	6,099 ft.	39;
98° 58′	2,741 ft.	38;
32° 32′	6,258 ft.	37;
120° 25′	2,826 ft.	36;
157° 06′	3,252 ft.	35;
113° 29′	3,665 ft.	34;
106° 38′	2,097 ft.	33;
109° 05′	1,927 ft.	32;
119° 28′	2,032 ft.	31;
154° 27′	4,336 ft.	30;
156° 57′	7,396 ft.	29;
74° 05′	4,234 ft.	28;

thence on a bearing of 140° 39′ for a distance of 3,143 ft. to Pillar UK 27;

Bearing	Distance	Pillar
159° 12′	1,522 ft.	26;
159° 02′	1,137 ft.	25;
162° 28′	6,582 ft.	24;
164° 56′	11,085 ft.	23;
173° 19′	6,900 ft.	22;
181° 26′	2,542 ft.	21;
191° 10′	3,580 ft.	20;
190° 36′	12,898 ft.	19;
133° 27′	7,521 ft.	18;
161° 49′	6,006 ft.	17;
162° 32′	4,634 ft.	16;
136° 59′	17,307 ft.	15;
157° 19′	6,478 ft.	14;
145° 56′	9,097 ft.	13;
128° 23′	7,482 ft.	12;
79° 21′	3,788 ft.	11;
6° 50′	6,123 ft.	10;
75° 11′	5,044 ft.	9;
144° 31′	2,289 ft.	8;
169° 05′	14,429 ft.	7;
165° 40′	12,000 ft.	6;
92° 56′	7,352 ft.	5;
160° 24′	1,785 ft.	4;
167° 20′	4,482 ft.	3;
158° 00′	10,395 ft.	2;
86° 07′	2,112 ft.	1;

situated on the east bank of the River Kanamuton at Map Reference YT 1773 (Sheet NA-36-8); thence following a straight line up the centre to the top of the pass known as Karamuroi (Suk) or Karithakol (Karamojong); thence southerly following a straight line to the hillock called Lokula; thence south-easterly following a straight line to a beacon at the highest point of the ridge known as Kariemakaris; thence continuing following a straight line, still southerly, to the foot of the western spur of the hill known as Aoruma, and following the foot of that spur to a beacon; thence in a generally southerly direction following straight lines to the westernmost end of the small hillock known as Lewi Lewi, to the hillock known as Sumemerr (known to the Suk as Sumaremar) to the hillock Morumeri, to the hill known as Kauluk, across the Kanyangareng River to Nongalitaba Hill, across the Kunyao River to the small hillock known as Lokwamor, to the hillock known as Kokas, to Korkurao Hill; thence to Sagat Hill and along the highest points of the rocky ridge (forming a continuation of Mount Riwa and known collectively by the Karamojong as Kogipie) known severally as Sagat (Karamojong) or Kogipie (Suk), Moruebu and Karenyang; thence to the summit of the hill Muregogoi; thence following a straight line to the source of the river Maragat; thence by the centre of the River Maragat to its confluence with the river Maron; thence south-westerly by the foot of the north-western slopes of Kassauria Hill to the western extremity of that hill; thence following a straight line south-easterly to the north-eastern extremity of Mount Riwa; thence following the foot of the eastern portion of Mount Riwa to the source of the Kanyerus River (marked by a large tree); thence south-easterly following a line of cairns, approximately in a straight line to the confluence of the River Bukwa (Kibukwa) with the River Suam (Swam); thence following the thalweg of the River Suam, upstream, to the point where the more north-westerly of the two streams forming the River Suam (Swam) or Turkwell emerges from the crater of Mount Elgon; thence following a straight line south-westerly to the highest point of Mount Elgon (Sudek).

From this point, the boundary continues following a straight line in a north-westerly direction to the Wagagai summit of Mount Elgon; thence following a straight line, south-westerly, to the source of the River Malaba (also known as the Lwakaka or Lwagaga); thence following the thalweg of the River Malaba to its intersection with the eastern side of the Majanji-Busia-Tororo road at Map Reference XR 2765 (Sheet NA-36-15); thence in a south-westerly direction following a line on the east side of and 100 feet distant from and parallel to the centre line of the said road to its intersection with the River Okame at Map Reference XR 2458 (Sheet NA-36-15); thence upstream following the thalweg of the River Okame to its confluence with the River Alupe; thence upstream following the thalweg of the River Alupe to a point at Map Reference XR 2453 (Sheet NA-36-15) marked by a boundary cairn; thence following successively in a south-westerly direction, a number of boundary cairns at distances from each other of 550 feet, 1226 feet, 959 feet, 976 feet, 1007 feet, 580 feet, 1512 feet, 463 feet, 2364 feet (on the northern side of the main Busia-Mumias road) and 1436 feet at the source of the River Sango at Map Reference XR 2251 (Sheet NA-36-15); thence downstream following the thalweg of the River Sango to its confluence with the River Sio; thence following the thalweg of the River Sio to its mouth in Lake Victoria.

From this point, the boundary continues following a straight line south-westerly to the most northerly point of Sumba Island; thence by the western and south-western shores of that island to its most southerly point; thence following a straight line south-easterly to the most westerly point of Mageta Island; thence following a straight line, still southerly, to the most western point of Kiringiti Island; thence following a straight line southerly to the most westerly point of Ilemba Island; thence following a straight line southerly to the westernmost point of Pyramid Island; thence following a straight line due south to a point on latitude 01° 00′ S.

[The Uganda–Tanzania Boundary]

From this point the boundary continues following the 01° 00′ S parallel to the western shore of Lake Victoria; thence following the boundary pillars already erected along the 01° 00′ S as far as the second crossing of this line by the River Kagera, between boundary pillars Nos. 27 and 26; thence following the thalweg of the River Kagera, upstream, to its confluence with the River Kakitumba;

[The Uganda–Rwanda Boundary]

thence following the thalweg of the River Kakitumba, upstream, to its
confluence with the River Chizinga; thence following the River Chizinga,
upstream, to the source of its south-western branch marked by BP 38, and
continuing along the thalweg in a south-westerly direction to BP 37 on
the saddle between the hills Mavari and Kitoff; thence north-westerly in a
straight line to a direction pillar on a knoll at the foot of the easterly spur
of Kitoff; thence in a straight line along the easterly spur of Kitoff to a
direction pillar; thence in a straight line to a direction pillar on the south-
easterly spur of Kitoff; thence in a straight line to BP 36 on the prominent
southerly spur of Kitoff; thence continuing around the slopes of the hill
Kitoff marked by direction pillars to BP 35 and by direction pillars along
the westerly spur of Kitoff and in a series of straight lines to BP 34; thence
continuing to BPs 33 and 32 along the eastern slopes of the Mashuri range
marked at each change of direction by a direction pillar as far as BP 31 on
a conspicuous small hill; thence in a straight line in a south-easterly direction to another conspicuous small hill marked by a direction pillar; thence
in a straight line across the River Muvumba to the southern summit of the
hill Ndega (Mbega) marked by BP 30; thence in a straight line to a direction pillar in the valley between the hills Ndega and Kivisa; thence in a
straight line to a direction pillar on the northern spur of the hill Kivisa;
thence along the spur of this hill to its summit marked by BP 29; thence
continuing along a very conspicuous water parting to the top of the hill
Magumbizi marked by BP 28; thence along a line marked by direction
pillars following the long easterly spur of the hill Nebishagara to its summit marked by BP 27; thence along the crest of the conspicuous western
spur to a direction pillar; thence in a straight line to a direction pillar on
a conspicuous knoll in the valley; thence along the crest of a spur leading
south-west and south to the summit of the hill Kitanga marked by a direction pillar; thence in a straight line to the summit of the conspicuous small
hill Nyakara marked by a direction pillar; thence in a straight line marked
by a direction pillar in the valley to BP 26 on the northern crest of the hill
Kavimbiri; thence along the crest in a southerly direction to the top of
Kavimbiri marked by BP 25; thence along the crest of this hill in a north-
westerly direction, marked by direction pillars to BP 24; thence down the
crest of a prominent spur to BP 23 at its foot, as more particularly delineated on Uganda 1/50,000 sheet 94/3 (Series Y 732). The boundary then
crosses the Kamuganguzi or Murinda swamp and follows the thalweg of
the Kiruruma swamp to a direction pillar at the edge of that swamp and
thence to BP 22 on a conspicuous knoll; thence in a west-south-westerly
direction marked by direction pillars along the spur of the hill Kisivo to
its summit marked by BP 21; thence in a straight line to BP 20 in the valley
east of the hill Sanja; thence in a straight line to the top of the hill Sanja
marked by BP 19; thence in a straight line to the top of the hill Akasiru
marked by a direction pillar; thence in a straight line to BP 18 which is
situated 4 km north-west of the summit of the hill Gwassa; thence in a
straight line to the source of the River Kiruruma marked by BP 17; thence

following the thalweg of the River Kiruruma (Vigaga) downstream to BP 16 at its confluence with the River Mugera (Narugwambu); thence in straight line due west marked by a direction pillar to BP 15; thence along the crest of the Vugamba range by direction pillar to BP 14 on the hill Maberemere; thence by direction pillars to BP 13 on the most northerly point of the range; thence by direction pillars to the hill Kanyaminyenya marked by BP 12; thence continuing along the crest of the Vugamba range to its southern summit marked by BP 11; thence in a straight line to BP 10 on the top of the hill Lugendabare; thence in a straight line to BP 9 on the hill Namujera; thence in a curved line marked by BPs 8, 7, 6, 5 and 4 to the summit of the hill Musonga (East) marked by BP 3 as more particularly delineated on Uganda 1/50,000 sheet 93/4 (Series Y 732). The boundary continues along the crest of this hill in a south-westerly direction marked by a direction pillar to BP 2 situated between the hills Nyarubebsa and Musongo and on the track leading southwards; thence to the summit of the hill Nyarubebsa marked by a direction pillar; thence in a south-westerly direction along the spur referred to as the Mulemule-Musongo spur to the highest point of Muhavura; thence along the watershed from the highest point of Muhavura to the highest point of Mgahinga; thence in a westerly direction to BP 1 on the north-south track running between Mgahinga and Sabinio; thence along the watershed to the highest point of Mount Sabinio the point of commencement.

APPENDIX B

Maritime Boundaries

1. *Proclamation Regarding the Territorial Sea of Tanzania*

THE following is the relevant part of a proclamation by the President of Tanzania, published in the *Tanzania Gazette* as Government Notice No. 137 on 14 April 1967:

Whereas the Law of Nations recognizes that the sovereign power of a state extends to a belt of sea adjacent to its coasts:

And Whereas, in the absence of uniformity in international practice relating to the extent of the territorial waters of states, it is necessary that a declaration be made of the extent of the territorial waters of the United Republic of Tanzania:

Now Therefore, I Julius Kambarage Nyerere, President of the United Republic of Tanzania, do hereby declare and proclaim that, notwithstanding any rule of law or any practice which may hitherto have been observed in relation to the territory of Tanganyika or the territories formerly subject to the sovereignty of the Sultan of Zanzibar or the territorial waters thereof, except as hereinbelow provided, the territorial waters of the United Republic of Tanzania extend across the sea a distance of twelve nautical miles measured from the mean low water line along the coasts and adjacent islands as marked on charts numbers 1 to 4 issued by the Surveys Division of the Ministry of Lands, Settlement and Water Development, Dar es Salaam, on 30th March, 1967 and registered with the Secretary-General of the United Nations:

Provided that in respect of the island of Pemba where the distance between the base line measured on Pemba and the mainland of Kenya is less than twenty-four nautical miles, the territorial waters of the United Republic of Tanzania extend up to the median line every point of which is equidistant from the nearest points on the base-line between Pemba and the mainland of Kenya as marked on the aforesaid charts.

This Proclamation shall be deemed to take effect as from the thirtieth day of March 1967.

2. *Proclamation Regarding the Territorial Sea of Kenya*

The following is the relevant part of a proclamation by the President of Kenya, published in the *Kenya Gazette* as Legal Notice No. 147 on 13 June 1969:

Whereas International Law has always recognized that the sovereignty of a state extends to a belt of sea adjacent to its coast.

And Whereas international practice is not uniform as regards the extent of this sea belt commonly known as the territorial sea of the state, and consequently it is necessary to make a declaration as to the extent of the territorial sea of the Republic of Kenya,

Now Therefore, I, Jomo Kenyatta, President of the Republic of Kenya do hereby declare and proclaim

1. That notwithstanding any rule or practice to the contrary which may have been observed in the past relating to Republic of Kenya or the territorial sea of the Republic of Kenya, the territorial waters of the Republic of Kenya shall extend across the sea to a distance of twelve nautical miles, measured from the appropriate baselines.

2. This declaration shall not extend to the waters lying between the Republic of Kenya and the Republic of Tanzania in the Pemba Channel, where the width of such waters measured from the appropriate baselines is less than twenty-four miles, but the extent of the territorial waters shall be taken as a median line every point of which is equidistant from the nearest points on the baselines from which the breadth of the territorial sea of the two States is measured.

3. In order to safeguard the vital economic interests of the inhabitants of the coastal region and to confirm the practice which has always existed, Ungwana Bay otherwise known as Formosa Bay is declared a historic bay constituting internal waters of the Republic of Kenya.

Signed and Sealed with the Public Seal at Nairobi on 6th day of June one thousand nine hundred and sixty-nine.

3. The Territorial Sea of the Somali Republic

The maritime zone of the Somali Republic adjacent to Kenya is part of the former Italian Somaliland and its limits were defined in the Maritime Code (*Codice marittimo*) which came into effect on 1 April 1959. The Somali Republic, which became an independent state in 1960, has not altered these limits, and the following is the text of Article 1 of the official English translation of the Code, as supplied by the Somali Government:

The sovereignty of the Territory embraces the zone of the sea to the distance of six nautical miles along the continental and insular coasts.

The above distance is measured from the coastline marked by the low tide.

The different provisions which might be established by laws, regulations, or international agreements for definite purposes are hereby excluded.

4. The Territorial Sea and Contiguous Zone of Mozambique

Law No. 2130 of the Government of the Republic of Portugal, passed on 22 August 1966, and published in *Diário do Governo*, Series I,

No. 194, establishes the maritime zone of the Portuguese State. Since Mozambique is regarded by Portugal as an integral part of the Portuguese State the limits of its maritime boundaries are apparently determined by this law.[1] The following are extracts from Law No. 2130, taken from a translation by Helen L. Claggett which appears in *International Legal Materials*, vol. v, pp. 1094–5:

BASIS I

1. The normal base line from which the extent of the territorial sea is measured is defined by the low water mark along the coast, as indicated on the maritime charts officially recognized for this purpose by the Portuguese State.

BASIS III

The Portuguese State exercises in the high seas contiguous to its territorial sea, up to a distance of twelve miles from the base line, the powers accorded by International Law. . . .

BASIS IV

When there exists no agreement to the contrary with a State whose coasts are adjacent to or facing those of the Portuguese State, the delimitation of the territorial sea or contiguous zone shall not go beyond the median line, all points of which are equidistant from the nearest points on the base lines from which the extent of the territorial sea of each of the two States is measured.

BASIS V

1. Without prejudice to historic rights, conventions, and other international agreements, the Portuguese State exercises fishing rights, and exclusive control over fishing activities in the high sea zones adjacent to its territorial sea, up to twelve miles measured from the base line of said sea.
2. Within the zone comprised between the sixth and twelfth miles measured from the base line of its territorial sea, the Portuguese State has authority to regulate fishing and to enforce such regulations, provided there is no discrimination against foreign vessels having a right to fish in this zone.
3. The outer limits of the fishing zones established in this Basis shall be delineated pursuant to the provisions of the preceding Basis (IV).

---

[1] *Political Constitution of the Portuguese Republic*, Arts. 1 and 150.

BIBLIOGRAPHY

ADAMI, V., *National Frontiers in Relation to International Law* (translated by T. T. Behrens), Oxford University Press, London, 1927.

AMBRONN, L., 'Bericht über die astronomischen und geodätischen Arbeiten, welche zur Festlegung der Grenze Deutsch-Ostafrikas gegenüber dem Kongostaat und Britisch-Ostafrika von seiten der deutschen Komissare in den Jahren 1902 bis 1905 ausgeführt worden sind', *Mitt.* 20 (1907), 165.

—— 'Bericht über die astronomischen Bestimmungen der deutsch-portugiesischen Grenzexpedition unter Hauptmann (jetz Major) Schlobach von Prof. Dr. L. Ambronn in Göttingen', *Mitt.* 23 (1910), 54.

ANDERSON-MORSHEAD, A. E. M., *The History of the Universities' Mission to Central Africa*, 6th edn., U.M.C.A., London, 1955.

ANSTEY, R., *Britain and the Congo in the Nineteenth Century*, Clarendon Press, Oxford, 1962.

ARDREY, R., *The Territorial Imperative*, Atheneum, New York, 1966.

AUSTIN, H. H., *With Macdonald in Uganda*, Edward Arnold, London, 1903.

AXELSON, E., *Portugal and the Scramble for Africa 1875–1891*, Witwatersrand University Press, Johannesburg, 1967.

BANCROFT, A. D., 'Modern Techniques applied to a boundary survey in the mountains of Southern Iran', *The Chartered Surveyor*, May 1962.

BARBER, J., 'The Moving Frontier of British Imperialism in Northern Uganda 1898–1919', *U.J.* 29 (1965), 27.

—— *Imperial Frontier*, East African Publishing House, Nairobi, 1968.

BARBOUR, K. M., *The Republic of The Sudan*, University of London Press, 1961.

—— and PROTHERO, R. M., *Essays on African Population*, Routledge & Kegan Paul, London, 1961.

BARNES, B. H., *Johnson of Nyasaland*, U.M.C.A., London, 1933.

BENNETT, G., 'The Eastern Boundary of Uganda in 1902', *U.J.* 23 (1959), 69.

BERBER, F. J., *Rivers in International Law*, Stevens, London, 1959.

BLOOMFIELD, L. M., *The British Honduras–Guatemala Dispute*, Carswell, Toronto, 1953.

BLUM, Y. Z., *Historic Titles in International Law*, Martinus Nijhoff, The Hague, 1965.

BOGGS, S. W., *International Boundaries*, Columbia University Press, New York, 1940.

BOILEAU, F., and WALLACE, L., 'The Nyasa-Tanganyika Plateau', *Geog. J.* 13 (1899), 577.

BOUCHEZ, L. J., 'The Fixing of Boundaries in International Boundary Rivers', 12 *I.C.L.Q.* 789 (1963).

BOULNOIS, P. K., 'On the Western Frontier of the Sudan', *Geog. J.* 63 (1924), 465.

—— 'International Boundary Delimitation', *The Royal Engineers Journal*, vol. 43 (1929), pp. 425–38.

BRADFORD, J. E. S., 'A Three-Million-Acre Title Survey', *E.S.R.* 3 (1936), 469.

BRASNETT, J., 'The Karasuk Problem', *U.J.* 22 (1958), 113.

BRIGHT, R. G. T., 'The Uganda–Congo Boundary Commission', *Geog. J.* 32 (1908), 488.

—— 'Survey and Exploration in the Ruwenzori and Lake Region, Central Africa', *Geog. J.* 34 (1909), 128.

—— 'An Exploration in Central Equatorial Africa', *Journal of the African Society*, vol. 9 (1910), pp. 225–32.

BROWNLIE, I., *Principles of Public International Law*, Clarendon Press, Oxford, 1966.

—— *Basic Documents in International Law*, Clarendon Press, Oxford, 1967.

—— 'A Provisional View of the Dispute Concerning Sovereignty over Lake Malawi/Nyasa', 1 *Eastern Africa Law Review* 258 (1968).

BUTTER, A. E., *Report by Mr. A. E. Butter on the Survey of the Proposed Frontier between British East Africa and Abyssinia.* Africa No. 13 (1904). Cd. 2312.

CARRINGTON, C. E., 'Frontiers in Africa', *International Affairs*, vol. 36 (1960), pp. 424–39.

CASTAGNO, A. A., 'The Somali–Kenyan Controversy: Implications for the Future', *J.M.A.S.* 2 (1964), 165.

CHURCH, R. J. HARRISON, *West Africa*, 3rd edn., Longmans, London, 1961.

CLIFFORD, E. H. M., 'Boundary Commissions', *The Royal Engineers Journal*, vol. 51 (1937), pp. 363–74.

CLOSE, SIR C., 'A Fifty-Years Retrospect', *E.S.R.* 1 (1932), 242; *E.S.R.* 2 (1933), 130.

CLYDE, D. F., *History of the Medical Services of Tanganyika*, Government Press, Dar es Salaam, 1962.

COLLINS, R. O., 'Anglo-Congolese Negotiations, 1900–1906', *Zaïre* 12 (1958), 479, 619.

—— 'The Transfer of the Lado Enclave to the Anglo-Egyptian Sudan, 1910', *Zaïre* 14 (1960), 193.

—— 'Sudan–Uganda Boundary Rectification and the Sudanese Occupation of Madial, 1914', *U.J.* 26 (1962), 140.

COLLINS, R. O., *King Leopold, England, and the Upper Nile, 1899–1909*, Yale University Press, New Haven, 1968.

COOTE, J. M., 'The Kivu Mission, 1909–1910', *U.J.* 20 (1956), 105.

COUPLAND, R., *The Exploitation of East Africa 1856–1890*, Faber & Faber, London, 1939.

CRUTTWELL, C. R. M. F., *A History of Peaceful Change in the Modern World*. Oxford University Press, London, 1937.

CUKWURAH, A. O., *The Settlement of Boundary Disputes in International Law*, Manchester University Press, 1967.

CURZON OF KEDLESTON (LORD), *Frontiers*, The Romanes Lecture, Clarendon Press, Oxford, 1907.

DELMÉ-RADCLIFFE, C., 'Surveys and Studies in Uganda', *Geog. J.* 26 (1905), 481, 616.

—— 'Extracts from Lt.-Col. Delmé-Radcliffe's Typescript Diary Report on the Delimitation of the Anglo-German Boundary, Uganda, 1902–1904', *U.J.* 11 (1947), 9.

DRYSDALE, J., *The Somali Dispute*, Pall Mall Press, London, 1964.

DYSON-HUDSON, N., 'The Karamojong and the Suk', *U.J.* 22 (1958), 173.

—— *Karimojong Politics*, Clarendon Press, Oxford, 1966.

EAST, W. G., and MOODIE, A. E. (eds.), *The Changing World*, Harrap, London, 1956.

ELIOT, SIR C., *The East Africa Protectorate*, Edward Arnold, London, 1905.

EMERSON, R., *Self-Determination Revisited in the Era of Decolonization*, Occasional Papers in International Affairs No. 9, December 1964. Center for International Affairs, Harvard University.

FAWCETT, C. B., *Frontiers*, Clarendon Press, Oxford, 1918.

FISCHER, E., 'On Boundaries', *World Politics*, vol. 1 (1948), pp. 196–222.

FISHER, F. C., 'The Arbitration of the Guatemalan–Honduran Boundary Dispute', 27 *A.J.I.L.* 403 (1933).

GEOGRAPHER, THE, *International Boundary Study*. A pamphlet series prepared by the Department of State, Washington. Particular reference should be made to Nos. 37 (Tanzania–Malawi), 39 (Tanzania–Mozambique), 44 (Tanzania–Zambia), 69 (Tanzania–Rwanda), 70 (Tanzania–Burundi), and 71 (Kenya–Tanzania).

GIFFORD, P. and LOUIS, W. R. (eds.), *Britain and Germany in Africa*, Yale University Press, New Haven, Conn., 1967.

GILLARD, D. R., 'Salisbury's African Policy and the Heligoland Offer of 1890', *English Historical Review*, vol. 75 (1960), pp. 631–53.

GOBLET, Y. M., *Political Geography and the World Map*, George Philip, London, 1956.

GRAY, SIR J., 'Early Treaties in Uganda, 1888–1891', *U.J.* 12 (1948), 25.

—— 'Anglo-German Relations in Uganda 1890–1892', *Journal of African History*, vol. 1 (1960), pp. 281–97.

GREENFIELD, R., *Ethiopia*, Pall Mall Press, London, 1965.

GROTIUS, H., *De Jure Belli ac Pacis, Libri Tres* (translated by F. W. Kelsey), Oceana, 1964.

GWYNN, C. W., 'A Journey in Southern Abyssinia', *Geog. J.* 38 (1911), 113.

—— 'The Frontiers of Abyssinia', *The Journal of the Royal African Society*, vol. 36 (1937), pp. 150–61.

HACKWORTH, G. H., *Digest of International Law*, vol. i, Washington, 1940.

HALL, H. DUNCAN, 'The International Frontier', 42 *A.J.I.L.* 42 (1948).

HALL, W. E., *A Treatise on International Law*, 8th edn. (ed. A. P. Higgins), Clarendon Press, 1924.

HANNA, A. J., *The Beginnings of Nyasaland and North-Eastern Rhodesia*, Clarendon Press, 1956.

HANNA, W. J. (ed.), *Independent Black Africa: The Politics of Freedom*, Rand McNally, Chicago, 1964.

HARDINGE, SIR A., *A Diplomatist in the East*, Jonathan Cape, London, 1928.

HARGREAVES, J. D., 'Towards a History of the Partition of Africa', *The Journal of African History*, vol. 1 (1960), pp. 97–109.

HATCHELL, G. W., 'The Boundary Between Tanganyika and Kenya', *Tanganyika Notes and Records*, No. 43 (1956), p. 41.

HENDERSON, K. D. D., *Sudan Republic*, Ernest Benn, London, 1965.

HERMANN, H., 'Bericht über Land und Leute längs der deutsch-englischen Grenze zwischen Nyassa und Tanganyika', *Mitt.* 13 (1900), 344.

HERTSLET, SIR E., *The Map of Africa By Treaty*, 3rd edn. 3 volumes with portfolio of maps, H.M.S.O., London, 1909.

HILL, N., *Claims to Territory in International Law and Relations*, Oxford University Press, London, 1945.

HINKS, A. R., 'Notes on the Technique of Boundary Delimitation', *Geog. J.* 58 (1921), 417.

—— 'International Boundary Problems', *Geog. J.* 96 (1940), 286.

—— *Maps and Survey*, 5th edn., Cambridge University Press, 1947.

HODGSON, R. D., and STONEMAN, E. A., *The Changing Map of Africa*, Van Nostrand, New York, 1963.

HOLDICH, SIR T. H., 'The Use of Practical Geography Illustrated by Recent Frontier Operations', *Geog. J.* 13 (1899), 465.

—— 'Geographical Problems in Boundary Making', *Geog. J.* 47 (1916), 421.

—— *Political Frontiers and Boundary Making*, Macmillan, London, 1916.

HOLLAND, T. E., *Lectures on International Law*, Sweet and Maxwell, London, 1933.

HUDSON, M. O., *International Legislation*, vol. i, Carnegie Endowment for International Peace, Washington, 1931.

HUDSON, M. O., *World Court Reports*, Carnegie Endowment for International Peace, Washington.

HYDE, C. C., 'Notes on Rivers as boundaries', 6 *A.J.I.L.* 901 (1912).

—— 'Maps as Evidence in International Boundary Disputes', 27 *A.J.I.L.* 311 (1933).

INGHAM, K., 'Uganda's Old Eastern Province: The Transfer to East Africa Protectorate in 1902', *U.J.* 21 (1957), 41.

—— *The Making of Modern Uganda*, George Allen and Unwin, London, 1958.

—— *A History of East Africa*, 3rd edn., Longmans, London, 1965.

International Law Association (auspices), *The Effect of Independence on Treaties*, Stevens, London, 1965.

JACK, E. M., *Report on the Work of the British Section of the Anglo-German-Belgian Boundary Commission, 1911.* H.M.S.O., London, 1912.

—— 'The Mufumbiro Mountains', *Geog. J.* 41 (1913), 532.

—— *On the Congo Frontier*, T. Fisher Unwin, London, 1914.

JACK, J. W., *Daybreak in Livingstonia*, Oliphant, Anderson & Ferrier, London, 1901.

JACKSON, SIR F., *Early Days in East Africa*, Edward Arnold, London, 1930.

JACKSON, H. C., *Behind the Modern Sudan*, Macmillan, London, 1955.

JACKSON, W. A. D., (ed.) *Politics and Geographic Relationships*, Prentice-Hall, New Jersey, 1964.

JENNINGS, R. Y., *The Acquisition of Territory in International Law*, Manchester University Press, 1963.

JENTGEN, P., *Les Frontières du Congo Belge*, Institut Royal Colonial Belge, *Mémoires*, tome xxv, Brussels, 1952.

JOHNSTON, SIR H. H., *The Kilima-Njaro Expedition*, Kegan Paul, Trench, London, 1886.

—— *British Central Africa*, 2nd edn., Methuen, London, 1898.

—— *Liberia*, vol. i, Hutchinson, London, 1906.

—— *The Story of My Life*, Bobbs-Merrill, Indianapolis, 1923.

JOLOWICZ, H. F., *Historical Introduction to the Study of Roman Law*, 2nd edn., Cambridge University Press, 1952.

JONES, S. B., *Boundary-Making*, Carnegie Endowment for International Peace, Columbia University Press, New York, 1945.

KAECKENBEECK, G., *International Rivers*, Oceana, New York, 1962.

KAPIL, R. L., 'On the conflict potential of inherited boundaries in Africa', *World Politics*, vol. 18 (1966), pp. 656–73.

KELTIE, J. S., *The Partition of Africa*, Stanford, London, 1893.

Kenya Land Commission, *Evidence*, Nairobi, 1933.

KIBULYA, H. M., and LANGLANDS, B. W., *The Political Geography of the Uganda–Congo Boundary*, Occasional Paper No. 6, Department of Geography, Makerere University College, Kampala, 1967.

KING, L. N., *Report on the work of the Jubaland Boundary Commission, 1925–1928* (typescript). A copy of this report is held as Catalogue No. DT 436, Commonwealth Relations Office Library, Great Smith Street, London.

—— 'The Work of the Jubaland Boundary Commission', *Geog. J.* 72 (1928), 420.

KOHLSCHÜTTER, E., 'Bericht über die astronomischen und geodätischen Arbeiten der deutschen Grenzregulierungs-Kommission zwischen dem Nyassa- und Tanganyika-See', *Mitt.* 13 (1900), 265.

LAMB, A., *The China-India Border*, Oxford University Press, London, 1964.

LANGER, W., *The Diplomacy of Imperialism*, 2nd edn., A. Knopf, New York, 1960.

LAPRADELLE, P. DE, *La Frontière*, Les Éditions Internationales, Paris, 1928.

LAUTERPACHT, E., 'River Boundaries: Legal Aspects of the Shatt-al-Arab Frontier', 9 *I.C.L.Q.* 208 (1960).

LAWS, J. B., 'A Minor Adjustment in the Boundary between Tanganyika Territory and Ruanda', *Geog. J.* 80 (1932), 244.

LEGUM, C., *Pan Africanism*, Pall Mall Press, London, 1965.

LESTER, A. P., 'State Succession to Treaties in the Commonwealth', 12 *I.C.L.Q.* 475 (1963); 14 *I.C.L.Q.* 262 (1965).

LEWIS, I. M., *Peoples of the Horn of Africa*, International African Institute, London, 1955.

—— *The Modern History of Somaliland*, Weidenfeld and Nicolson, London, 1965.

—— 'Recent Developments in the Somali Dispute', *African Affairs*, vol. 66 (1967), pp. 104–12.

LIVINGSTONE, W. P., *Laws of Livingstonia*, Hodder and Stoughton, London, 1921.

LOUIS, W. R., *Ruanda-Urundi, 1884–1919*, Clarendon Press, Oxford, 1963.

—— 'The Anglo–German Hinterland Settlement of 1890 and Uganda', *U.J.* 27 (1963), 71.

LUGARD, F. D., 'Treaty Making in Africa', *Geog. J.* 1 (1893), 53.

LYNE, R. N., *Zanzibar in Contemporary Times*, Hurst and Blackett, London, 1905.

MACMICHAEL, H., *The Anglo-Egyptian Sudan*, Faber & Faber, London, 1934.

MARCUS, H. G., 'A History of the Negotiations Concerning the Border between Ethiopia and British East Africa, 1897–1914', in *Boston University Papers on Africa*, vol. 2, Boston University Press, 1966.

MATSON, A. T., 'Uganda's Old Eastern Province and East Africa's Federal Capital', *U.J.* 22 (1958), 43.

MAUD, P., 'Exploration in the Southern Borderland of Abyssinia', *Geog. J.* 23 (1904), 552.

BIBLIOGRAPHY 311

MAZRUI, A. A., *Towards a Pax Africana*, Weidenfeld and Nicolson, London, 1967.

MCDERMOTT, P. L., *British East Africa or IBEA*, 2nd edn., Chapman and Hall, London, 1895.

MCMAHON, SIR A. H., 'International Boundaries', *Journal of the Royal Society of Arts*, vol. 84 (1935), pp. 2–16.

MCNAIR (LORD), *The Law of Treaties*, Clarendon Press, Oxford, 1961.

MELAMID, A., 'The Kenya Coastal Strip', *The Geographical Review*, vol. 53 (1963), pp. 457–9.

MEYER, H., *Das Deutsche Kolonialreich*, vol. i, Leipzig, 1909.

MINGHI, J. V., 'Boundary Studies in Political Geography', *Annals of the Association of American Geographers*, vol. 53 (1963), pp. 407–28.

MOODIE, A. E., *Geography Behind Politics*, Hutchinson University Library, London, 1949.

MOORE, J. B., '*Uti Possidetis*: Costa Rica-Panama Arbitration, 1911', in *The Collected Papers of John Bassett Moore*, vol. 3, Yale University Press, 1944.

MOYSE-BARTLETT, H., *The King's African Rifles*, Gale and Polden, Aldershot, 1956.

MUNGER, E. S., 'Boundaries and African Nationalism', *The California Geographer*, vol. 4 (1963), pp. 1–7.

MURRAY, S. S., *A Handbook of Nyasaland*, Crown Agents, London, 1932.

NAVAL INTELLIGENCE, *A Manual of Portuguese East Africa*, London, 1920.

—— *A Handbook of German East Africa*, London, 1916.

O'CONNELL, D. P., 'International Law and Boundary Disputes', *Proceedings of the American Society of International Law* (1960), pp. 77–84.

—— *The Law of State Succession*, Cambridge University Press, 1956.

—— *International Law*, vol. i, Stevens, London, 1965.

—— *State Succession in Municipal Law and International Law*, vol. ii, *International Relations*, Cambridge University Press, 1967.

OLDAKER, A. A., 'Tribal Customary Land Tenure in Tanganyika', *Tanganyika Notes and Records* (1957), pp. 117–44.

OLIVER, R., *Sir Harry Johnston and the Scramble for Africa*, Chatto and Windus, London, 1959.

—— and others (eds.), *History of East Africa*, Clarendon Press, Oxford, vol. i (1963), vol. ii (1965).

OPPENHEIM, L., *International Law*, vol. i, 8th edn. (ed. H. Lauterpacht), Longmans, London, 1955.

Organization of African Unity, *Proceedings of the Summit Conference of Independent African States*, vol. i, Addis Ababa, 1963.

—— *General Record of the First Assembly of Heads of State and Government*, Addis Ababa, 1964.

312 BIBLIOGRAPHY

PEAKE, E. R. L., 'Northern Rhodesia–Belgian Congo Boundary', *Geog. J.* 83 (1934), 263.

PIKE, J. G., and RIMMINGTON, G. T., *Malawi: A Geographical Study*, Oxford University Press, London, 1965.

PRAGER, M., 'Die Inseln im Njassasee', *Deutsche Kolonialzeitung* (1905), pp. 153–4.

PRESCOTT, J. R. V., *The Geography of Frontiers and Boundaries*, Hutchinson University Library, London, 1965.

RAVENSTEIN, E. G., 'The Recent Territorial Arrangements in Africa', *Geog. J.* 4 (1894), 54.

REYNER, A. S., 'The Republic of the Congo: Development of its International Boundaries', *Duquesne Review*, vol. 6 (1961), pp. 88–95.

—— *Current Boundary Problems in Africa*, Duquesne University Press, Pittsburgh, 1964.

ROBERTS, A., 'The Evolution of the Uganda Protectorate', *U.J.* 27 (1963) 95.

ROBINSON, R., and GALLAGHER, J., with DENNY, A., *Africa and the Victorians*, Macmillan, London, 1961.

RÖLING, B. V. A., *International Law in an Expanded World*, Djambatan, Amsterdam, 1960.

RUTHERFORD, G. W., 'Spheres of Influence: An Aspect of Semi-Suzerainty', 20 *A.J.I.L* 300 (1926).

RYDER, C. H. D., 'The Demarcation of the Turco–Persian Boundary in 1913–1914', *Geog. J.* 66 (1925), 227.

SANDERSON, G. N., *England, Europe, and the Upper Nile, 1882–1899*, Edinburgh University Press, 1965.

SCHLOBACH, G., 'Die deutsch-portugiesische Grenzregulierung zwischen dem unteren Rowuma und Kap Delgado', *Deutsches Kolonialblatt*, vol. 20 (1909), pp. 56–8.

—— 'Allgemeiner Bericht über den Verlauf der deutsch-portugiesischen Grenzexpedition zwischen dem Knie des Rowuma-Flusses und dem Ostufer des Njassa', *Mitt.* 23 (1910), 49.

—— 'Die Vermarkung der deutsch-englischen Ruanda-Grenzen, 1911', *Deutsches Kolonialblatt*, vol. 23 (1912), pp. 1041–6.

SCHWARZENBERGER, G., *International Law*, vol. i, Stevens, London, 1957.

—— 'Title to Territory: Response to a Challenge', 51 *A.J.I.L.* 308 (1957).

SEATON, E. E. and MALITI, S. T. M., 'Treaties and Succession of States and Governments in Tanzania', A Paper prepared for the African Conference of International Law, Lagos, March 1967 (typescript), Dag Hammarskjöld Foundation.

SHUKRI, M. A., *The Concept of Self-Determination in the United Nations*, Al Jadidah Press, Damascus, 1965.

SINGH, CHANAN, 'The Republican Constitution of Kenya: Historical Background and Analysis', 14 *I.C.L.Q.* 878 (1965).

SLADE, R., *King Leopold's Congo*, Oxford University Press, London, 1962.

SMITH, C. S., 'The Anglo-German Boundary in East Equatorial Africa. Proceedings of the British Commission, 1892', *Geog. J.* 4 (1894), 424.

SMITH, G. E., 'From the Victoria Nyanza to Kilimanjaro', *Geog. J.* 29 (1907), 249.

—— *Report on the Anglo-German Boundary Commission from Victoria Nyanza to Kilimanjaro and Lake Jipe*, 1906, Confidential No. 8932, F.O. 367/10.

STAMP, L. DUDLEY (ed.), *A Glossary of Geographical Terms*, Longmans, London, 1961.

STANLEY, H. M., *Through the Dark Continent*, Sampson Low, London, 1880.

—— *In Darkest Africa*, Low, Marston, Searle, and Rivington, London, 1890.

STIGAND, C. H., *Equatoria: The Lado Enclave*, Constable, London, 1923.

STUHLMANN, F., 'Bericht über das deutsch-portugiesische Grenzegebiet am Ruvuma', *Mitt.* 10 (1897), 182.

TEMPERLEY, H. W. V. (ed.), *A History of the Peace Conference of Paris*, Henry Frowde, Hodder & Stoughton, London, 1920.

THOMAS, H. B., 'The Kionga Triangle', *Tanganyika Notes and Records*, No. 31 (1951), pp. 47–50.

—— 'The Kagera Triangle and the Kagera Salient', *U.J.* 23 (1959), 73.

—— 'Evolution of Uganda's Boundaries', *Atlas of Uganda*, Govt. Press, Entebbe, 1962.

THOMAS, H. B., and SPENCER, A. E., *A History of Uganda Land and Surveys of the Uganda Land and Survey Department*, and Government Press, Entebbe, 1938.

THRUSTON, A. B., *African Incidents*, John Murray, London, 1900.

TOUVAL, S., *Somali Nationalism*, Harvard University Press, 1963.

—— 'Treaties, Borders, and the Partition of Africa', *The Journal of African History*, vol. 7 (1966), pp. 279–92.

—— 'Africa's Frontiers', *International Affairs*, vol. 42 (1966), pp. 641–54.

—— 'The Organization of African Unity and African Borders', *International Organization*, vol. 21 (1967), pp. 102–27.

TROTTER, J. K., 'The Science of Frontier Delimitation', *Minutes of Proceedings of the Royal Artillery Institution*, vol. 24 (1897), pp. 207–30.

VATTEL, E. DE, *The Law of Nations* (translation of the edition of 1758 by C. G. Fenwick), Oceana, New York, 1964.

VISSCHER, C. DE, *Theory and Reality in Public International Law* (translated by P. E. Corbett), Princeton University Press, New Jersey, 1957.

WALDOCK, C. H. M., 'Disputed Sovereignty in the Falkland Islands Dependencies', 25 *B.Y.I.L.* 311 (1948).

WALLER, H., *The Last Journals of David Livingstone*, vol. i, John Murray, London, 1874.

War Office, *Positions, Azimuths and Length of Sides of the Anglo-German Boundary Commission Triangulation (1902–1906) from Zanzibar to Mount Ruwenzori*, The War Office, London, 1907.

—— *Official Report of the British Section of the Uganda–Congo Boundary Commission, 1907–1908*, H.M.S.O., London, 1909.

—— *Positions, Azimuths and Length of Sides of the Uganda–Congo Boundary Commission Triangulation (1907–1908) from 1° South to 2° North latitude along the 30th Meridian East of Greenwich*, The War Office, London, 1909.

WARD, F. KINGDON, 'Explorations on the Burma–Tibet Frontier', *Geog. J.* 80 (1932), 465.

WEIGERT, H. W., *Principles of Political Geography*, Appleton-Century-Crofts, New York, 1957.

WEISSBERG, G., 'Maps as Evidence in International Boundary Disputes: A Reappraisal', 57 *A.J.I.L.* 781 (1963).

WESTLAKE, J., *International Law*, Part 1, *Peace*, 2nd edn., Cambridge University Press, 1910.

WHITEMAN, M. M., *Digest of International Law*, vol. 3, Washington, 1964.

WIDSTRAND, C. G. (ed.), *African Boundary Problems*, Scandinavian Institute of African Studies, Uppsala, 1969.

WILLIAMS, J. H., *Historical Outline and Analysis of the Work of the Survey Department of Kenya Colony*, Government Printer, Nairobi, 1931.

WINTERBOTHAM, H. ST. J., 'The Demarcation of International Boundaries', in *Empire Conference of Survey Officers, 1928, Report of Proceedings*, Colonial No. 41, H.M.S.O., London, 1929.

WOODWARD, E. L., and BUTLER, ROHAN (eds.), *Documents on British Foreign Policy 1919–1939*, First Series, vol. i, H.M.S.O., London, 1947.

ZARTMAN, I. W., 'The Politics of Boundaries in North and West Africa', *J.M.A.S.* 3 (1965), 155.

—— *International Relations in the New Africa*, Prentice-Hall, New Jersey, 1966.

ZEMANEK, K., 'State Succession After Decolonization', 116 Hague *Recueil* 187 (1965).

INDEX OF CASES CITED

INDEX